Food Equipment Facts

A HANDBOOK

FOR THE

FOOD SERVICE INDUSTRY

FOOD
EQUIPMENT
FACTS

A HANDBOOK
for the
FOOD SERVICE INDUSTRY

CARL SCRIVEN & JAMES STEVENS

175 YEARS OF PUBLISHING

1807 1982

John Wiley & Sons
New York • Chichester • Brisbane • Toronto • Singapore

Library of Congress Cataloging in Publication Data:

Scriven, Carl.
  Food equipment facts.

  Includes index.
  1. Food service—Equipment and supplies.
  I. Stevens, James, 1932-   .II. Title.

TX9912.S37   1982   681'.7664   81-24088
ISBN 0-471-86819-1   AACR2

Printed in the United States of America

10 9 8 7 6 5 4 3 2 1

DJ21588

To our wives

JOYCE SCRIVEN
WINNIE STEVENS

F.E.F. Personal Assistance Service: If you find any item in the book that you would appreciate more information on, send your request with a self-addressed, stamped, legal size envelope enclosed to:

F.E.F.
9 Glenmore Road
Troy, New York 12180

THE AUTHORS

Jim Stevens (V.P. Sales) and Carl Scriven (Designer) together have over 50 years of experience with The Lewis Equipment Co., Inc., of Albany, N.Y.

FOREWORD

An agonizing ritual that must be performed by faculty members prior to each semester is the selection of a textbook for each of their courses. I knew that the selection task for my course in Facility Layout and Design would be extremely easy the first time I leafed through a copy of *Food Equipment Facts.*

When selecting a textbook for students I have three primary requirements:
1. Content and relevance to the subject material.
2. The long-term use of the book as a reference when the student becomes a manager.
3. The price-value ratio.

I am seldom able to find a book like *Food Equipment Facts* that fulfills *all* of my requirements.

Most schools offering either Associate or Baccalaureate degrees in Hotel and Restaurant Administration, require courses in the various aspects of Hospitality Engineering. The objective of these engineering classes is not to make architects out of the students, but to teach them how to become better problem solvers in subject areas such as equipment capabilities, space utilization, storage specifications, dining room appointments, energy saving methods, and sanitation requirements.

A significant step in any problem-solving procedure is to gather the relevant data. In the past, my students have had to search through the endless numbers of manufacturer's equipment catalogs fraught with missing pages and excessive puffery only to discover later on that they had missed some important bit of information, and then they must go back and repeat the process. This succinct book has eliminated a considerable amount of wasted time and has led students to a much better understanding of the course material.

This book is a timesaver because it is comprehensive and contains thousands of useful statistics with helpful hints; also it is written in a reference format, which eliminates unnecessary words.

In the past, I perceived a need for a handbook written especially for food service managers. However, the complex nature of the business almost precludes such a manual because surely many relevant areas would be omitted. To compensate for the lack of such a manual, the successful hospitality manager has at his fingertips many references on the subject of management, law, marketing, sales, energy, labor relations, and cost control. Now, thanks to Jim Stevens and Carl Scriven, two experienced food service equipment specialists, a void has been filled. *Food Equipment Facts* should be within easy reach of every Food Service Manager's desk.

Melvin N. Barrington, Jr.
Chairman, Hotel, Restaurant and
Tourism Administration
University of South Carolina

PREFACE

In writing this book our intention was to produce an indispensable handbook and guide for anyone in the food service industry.

Consultants, architects, designers and engineers will find quick access to volumes of information they need in the many facts, reference charts and brainstorming sections.

Purchasing agents, dietitians, food service managers and restaurateurs will find the production capability charts, lists of options for equipment, portion control charts, helpful hints, and dimensional and power specifications most helpful in selecting equipment and accessories.

Equipment salesmen and manufacturers' representatives will find that they have the equivalent of 500 catalogs and technical reference books right in their pockets.

Any student in any branch of the industry will discover in this book an invaluable collection of information. Teachers also will find it an easy reference source.

It was never our intention to make this book the final authority on anything. Too many very good books have been written about each and every phase of the industry. *Food Equipment Facts* is a handbook and guide only. Space limitations make it impossible to list all available supplies from all manufacturers. Items described in this book were selected as typical, or in some cases as unique. Undoubtedly on the day the book was printed some item was discontinued and a new one introduced. We cannot, therefore, assume responsibility for any misstatements regarding equipment. (Have you ever noticed that the manufacturers themselves always add to equipment brochures the fine-print statement, "Specifications subject to change without notice?")

We have made *Food Equipment Facts* as complete and accurate as we could, but we realize that errors and omissions can always occur. To make the next edition even more valuable we need your input, so let us hear from you. We want to make *F.E.F.* the best little book in the business, and with your help we know we can do it. Thanks.

Carl Scriven
James Stevens

ACKNOWLEDGMENTS

The authors sincerely appreciate the cooperation received from the many manufacturers of food service and related equipment whose prompt responses to our request for additional information were a great aid in compiling this book. We gratefully acknowledge the assistance from our co-workers and the manufacturers reps who gave so freely of their time when and wherever it was needed.

Special thanks to:

MR. J. FRED LEWIS, President
Lewis Equipment Co., Inc., Albany, New York

MISS ELSIE LALONE, Legal Secretary

MISS NANCY OFFENBACKER, Mailing and Distribution

MR. & MRS. FRANK RAFFERTY & FAMILY
(The Best Printers in Upstate N.Y.)

MR. MIKE McALLISTER, Eastern Regional Manager
Microwave Division, SHARP Electronics, Inc.

MR. SAM VENEZIA, District Manager for HOBART
Food Service Dealer Division

MR. RALPH A. MEYER, Representing AVTEC Industries,
AMCO Wire, PENN Refrigeration,
GARLAND Commercial Industries,
AMERICAN BEST COFFEE CO., INC.

MR. RAY MacDONALD, Eastern Regional Manager
WELLS Manufacturing Corp.

and particularly to

DR. JEROME J. VALLEN, Dean of
College of Hotel Administration
University of Nevada, Las Vegas

for his valued friendship and support.

C.S
J.S.

LIST OF CHAPTERS

LIST OF ILLUSTRATIONS

Food Equipment Facts

A HANDBOOK

FOR THE

FOOD SERVICE INDUSTRY

Chapter One

RECEIVING AREAS

Due to space and budget limitations adequate receiving areas are often neglected. However, today's inflationary prices certainly stress the importance of checking weights received. Where adequate space simply cannot be provided, a mobile table with a scale, having the capacity to check the weights of bulk products purchased, may be rolled into position at the receiving door and be used elsewhere the rest of the time.

Some things to remember when planning receiving areas are:
1. Standard dock height is from 36" to 44".
2. If a truck dock is structurally impossible, mobile and built-in hydraulic lift docks are available. (See Fig. 1-2)
3. Minimum door size is 36" x 6'8". Larger doors are recommended where space permits.
4. Provide ample space for all mobile equipment required to efficiently move merchandise received to its proper storage area.
5. Pest control is always a problem at receiving doors. Self-closing doors, double doors and "Fly Chasing Fans" are invaluable.
6. In establishments where bread or roll consumption is high, as in convenience markets, sandwich shops, hospitals, etc. space for the plastic, stacking racks with dollies should be considered. These are usually supplied by the bakery. The plastic trays measure approximately 31" x 22½" x 6" high and will hold 12 loaves of bread, 8 dozen rolls or the equivalent in each. They may be easily stacked 6 to 8 high and rolled directly to the point of use.
7. A small desk, even if wall mounted, is very useful and it is usually an excellent location for the time clock. Even in the best planned restaurants and institutions a hand sink and water fountain are often overlooked. Both are very useful in receiving areas.
8. Receiving areas should be well lighted and weather protected. Clear vinyl strip curtains for weather protection are listed in Chapter 3.

Following are a few facts on receiving areas and equipment to assist you in selecting the proper items.

SPACE REQUIRED FOR RECEIVING AREAS

The following chart shows suggested sizes for receiving areas in varying establishments. It must be kept in mind that exact sizes will vary depending on frequency of deliveries and menu variations.

Most hospitals and many other large in-plant facilities share dock space with other departments. In such cases only efficient transporting equipment need be considered.

Fig. 1-1

RESTAURANTS

Meals Per Day	200/300	300/500	500/1000	1000/1400	1400/1600
Area in Sq. Ft.	50/60	60/90	90/130	130/160	160/190

HOSPITALS · NURSING HOMES · EXTENDED CARE FACILITIES

Number of Beds	Up to 50	50/100	100/200	200/400
Area in Sq. Ft.	50	50/80	80/130	130/175

SCHOOLS

Meals Per Day	200/300	300/500	500/700	700/900	900/1000
Area in Sq. Ft.	30/40	40/60	60/75	75/90	90/100

IN-PLANT CAFETERIAS AND FOOD FACILITIES

Meals Per Day	200/400	400/800	800/1200	1200/1500
Area in Sq. Ft.	75/80	85/115	115/155	155/200

Hydraulic lift docks, mentioned above, are vertically rising platforms that provide a level surface onto which or over which loads can be transferred at any height between ground level and 58" above ground. They are designed to facilitate the loading and unloading of trucks at the dock. They have self-contained power units with controls. Hydraulic plungers lift or lower the platform in a level position employing scissor action supports.

Fig. 1-2

TYPICAL HYDRAULIC LIFT DOCKS

Type	Platform Size	Capacity	Lift Height	Lift Speed	HP	Wheels
Portable	6' x 6'	4,000 lb.	58"	8 FPM	1½	4" Dia.

STATIONARY DOCKS

Class	Platform Size	Capacity	Lift Speed	HP	Lowered Height
Light Duty	6' x 8'	5,000 lbs.	12 FPM	5	10"
Medium Duty	6' x 8' to 8' x 11'	5,000 lbs. to 6,000 lbs.	12 FPM	5	10"
Average Duty	6' x 8' to 8' x 10'	7,000 lbs. to 8,500 lbs.	8 FPM	5	12"

(Continued)

STATIONARY DOCKS (Cont.)					
Class	Platform Size	Capacity	Lift Speed	HP	Lowered Height
Heavy Duty	6' x 8' to 8' x 11'	10,000 lbs.	6 FPM	5	14"
Extra Heavy Duty	6' x 12' to 8' x 12'	18,000 lbs. to 20,000 lbs.	5 FPM	7½	18" to 20"

There are also available Hydraulic Lift Docks designed to be installed flush with the pavement when in a lowered position.

Fig. 1-3

TYPICAL PLATFORM TRUCK SIZES

Platform Size	Wheel Dia.	Maximum Load
18" x 30"	5" to 6"	400 lbs.
24" x 48"	6"	1000 lbs.
24" x 48"	8"	1500 lbs.
27" x 54"	6"	1000 lbs.
27" x 54"	8"	1500 lbs.
30" x 60"	6"	1000 lbs.
30" x 60"	8"	1500 lbs.

STEEL PALLETS

Listed only are some standard sizes and the load limit of common steel pallets. Many other materials and systems are available.

Pallet sizes are 36" x 48", 40" x 48", 42" x 42", 42" x 48" and 48" x 48". All are 4" high with a load limit of 10,000 lbs. They can be reversible or nonreversible and matching shelving and pallet jacks or lifts are available.

HAND TRUCKS

Hand trucks are available in many styles and capacities. The average overall height is 49". Light-duty hand trucks are available with 6", 8" and 10" wheels with a load limit of 400 lbs. Heavy-duty hand trucks usually have 8" or 10" wheels with load limits of 600 lbs., 800 lbs., 900 lbs. and 1400 lbs. depending on model specified.

Tire options are: solid rubber, pressure tires and inflatable pneumatic tires.

3

Fig. 1-4

TYPICAL CAN AND DRUM HAND TRUCKS
Designed to carry from 30 gal. to 55 gal. drums.

Wheel Size	Load Capacity	Inside Ring Dimension
3" x 13/16"	350 lbs.	14¼"
3" x 13/16"	350 lbs.	17"
3" x 13/16"	350 lbs.	19¼"
3" x 1¼"	600 lbs.	19¼"
3" x 13/16"	350 lbs.	21"
3" x 1¼"	600 lbs.	23-5/8"
3" x 1¼" (Heavy Duty)	1000 lbs.	23-5/8"

DRUM OR BARREL CRADLES

These carts are designed to carry 15 gal. to 55 gal. drums in a horizontal position. They are so designed as to tilt easily, to pick up the drums, then tilt back on four casters for transporting the drums. Average dimensions are 32" long x 20" wide x 18" high and are available with two stationary and two swivel casters or with all four swivel. The average load limit is 700 lbs.

RING DOLLIES

Designed for transporting drums or barrels in a vertical position are constructed with four rubber tired or steel, swivel casters approximately 3" in diameter. Typical load capacities are 350 lb., 600 lb., and 1000 lb. sized to fit 30/55 gal. drums.

GRAVITY FEED ROLLER CONVEYORS

Built with either cylindrical rollers or the more popular "skate wheel" rollers. These conveyors with interlocking sections can transport case goods up to 200' or more. Turn sections are designed with approximately 2½' to 3' radius in various lengths to complete turns of from 30° to 60°. These conveyors will support loads from 50 to over 1500 lbs. per linear foot depending on the distance between supports.

For Power Driven Conveyors, see Ware Washing and Sanitation, Chapter 9.

SCALES

Any research into makes, models and styles of scales available will soon reveal that there are nearly as many different scales as there are things to weigh. If your receiving scale problems are com-

4

plex, the authors recommend that you consult your equipment dealer sales representative. Fig. 1-5 provides some general information concerning the most popular scales for receiving areas.

Fig. 1-5

DIAL TYPE COUNTER SCALES

Average Platform Size	Capacity	Graduations
	30 lbs.	1 oz.
	50 lbs.	1 oz.
11" x 14"	50 lbs.	2 oz.
	100 lbs.	2 oz.
	100 lbs.	8 oz.

DIAL TYPE - MOBILE

	75 lbs.	1 oz.
24" x 20"	150 lbs.	2 oz.
	300 lbs.	4 oz.
	300 lbs.	4 oz.
30" x 36"	600 lbs.	½ lb.
	1200 lbs.	1 lb.
	2400 lbs.	2 lbs.

Fig. 1-6

BEAM SCALES

Total Capacities	Graduations	
110 lbs. to 220 lbs.	100 lbs. x 10 lbs.	10 lbs. x 1 oz.
	200 lbs. x 20 lbs.	20 lbs. x 2 oz.

The popular, small beam scales listed above are available in either counter or mobile, floor models. The average platform size for counter models is 13" x 18". Floor model platforms average 18" x 27".

Some standard **DIGITAL SCALES** are available as follows:

Fig. 1-7

Platform Size	Capacity	Graduations
18" x 18"	20 lbs.	.01 lb.
18" x 18"	40 lbs.	.02 lb.
18" x 18"	100 lbs.	.05 lb.
18" x 18"	200 lbs.	.1 lb.
28" x 28"	200 lbs.	.1 lb.
28" x 28"	600 lbs.	.2 lb.

5

Standard options include remote indicator, metric switch, short or tall columns, casters.

NEW L.E.D. SCALES
with digital readout

These L.E.D. (light emitting diode) scales are the latest in electronic weighing devices and are becoming available in many models and sizes. Some typical models are described below.

Fig. 1-8

Maximum Capacity	Space Required	No.	Features
9.99 lbs.	12'' x 12''	1	Readout mounted behind and above unit. Angled up for easy visibility. 6' grounded cord and plug.
9.99 lbs.	12'' x 12''	2	Same as No. 1 but powered by rechargeable batteries for use in remote areas. Charge life 8 hrs. Scale may be used while batteries are being charged.
9.99 lbs.	7½'' x 9''	3	Angled readout built into front of base. 6' grounded cord and plug.
50.00 lbs.	7½'' x 9''	4	Same as No. 3 above.
50.00 lbs.	11'' x 16-3/8''	5	Same as No. 1 above.
9.99 lbs.	7'' x 7''	6	Remote readout module connects to base with 7' cable. Readout module is 7-1/8'' x 5-3/8'' x 2-5/8'' high
75.00 lbs.	11'' x 11''	7	Same as No. 6 above.

All units have automatic tare buttons. All are accurate to nearest one-hundredth of a pound.

Information on other or larger scales not available at this time.

Chapter Two

DRY
STORAGE

Using valuable space properly is like putting money in the bank. The information in this chapter will help you achieve maximum storage capacity for your particular food service operation. Compute your specific needs which depend on variables, such as menu items, number of meals served and frequency of deliveries. Then use the following charts which show standard sizes matched with some product sizes.

AVERAGE SPACE REQUIRED FOR DRY STORAGE
IN VARIOUS ESTABLISHMENTS

Fig. 2-1

SCHOOL LUNCH PROGRAMS					
Meals Served	200	400	600	800	1000
Square Ft. Required	150/250	250/350	350/450	450/550	550/650
HOSPITAL FOOD SERVICE					
No. of Beds	50	10	200	400	
Square Ft. Required	150/225	250/375	400/600	700/900	
EMPLOYEE FEEDING					
Meals Served	400	800	1200	1500	
Square Ft. Required	350/450	550/650	700/850	950/1050	
RESTAURANTS & CLUBS					
Meals Per Day	100-200	200-350	350-500	500-1000	
Square Ft. Required	120/200	200/250	250/400	300/650	

This chart is intended as a guide only as every food service establishment has its own individual requirements.

HELPFUL HINTS

Properly planned dry storage areas should be well ventilated, well lighted, have flexibility in shelving areas and wherever possible have floor drains and a washdown hose. When planning new storage rooms think in terms of rows of shelving with adequate aisles between. For example: a row of wall shelving, an aisle, another row of shelving (single or back to back), another aisle and a row of shelving along the opposite wall. Too often adding 3 or 4 feet to the width of a room accomplishes nothing. Be sure to place doors at aisles. A door in the corner of any room destroys valuable wall space.

TYPICAL SHELVING SIZES

Fig. 2-2

SHELF WIDTH	LENGTHS AVAILABLE
12" or 14"	24" - 30" - 36" - 42" - 48" - 60"
18" - 21" or 24"	24" - 30" - 36" - 42" - 48" - 60" - 72"

The above units are manufactured as flat or louvered metal shelves and open welded wire shelves. The open wire shelving is recommended where ventilation is important.

All are available in aluminum, galvanized, coated galvanized and stainless steel. Stainless steel is of course the ultimate finish for both wet and dry storage and is accepted by U.S.D.A. for direct food contact. Less toxic, is zinc plated shelving coated with non toxic epoxy. This shelving is suitable for wet storage such as walk-in coolers. Uncoated zinc plated shelving should be used for dry storage only. Various manufacturers have different trade names for the plating and coating materials they use. Be sure the material you select is suited to your needs.

The average shelf load limit is 1,000 lbs.

UPRIGHT SUPPORTS FOR SHELVING

Fig. 2-3

Widths	Heights Available
12"	26"
14"	31-32"
18"	36-37"
21"	53½"
24"	64", 75" or 86"

NOTE: Most shelving units are designed so that shelving in straight runs may be supported by common uprights, and may have corner brackets attached to the side of end shelves to make right angle turns without an additional upright. These features cut costs appreciably. See Page 13 - Planning Guide.

SOME AVAILABLE OPTIONAL EXTRAS FOR BASIC SHELVING:

Back Ledges	Label Strips	18 x 26 Pan Holders
Corner Braces	Sloping Shelves	Short Legs for Dunnage
Wheels	Shelf Dividers	Racks, 6"-8" & 10" above
Dollies	Pan Holders	Floor
Wall Mount Supports	Covers	Wine Shelves

8

SPACE SAVING TRACK STYLE SHELVING

Front and rear tracks mounted between two end units allow units in between to glide easily in either direction providing an access aisle where you want it.

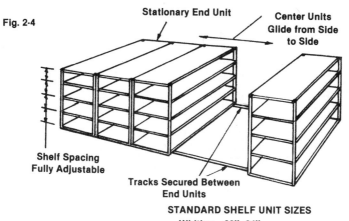

Fig. 2-4

Stationary End Unit

Center Units
Glide from Side
to Side

Shelf Spacing
Fully Adjustable

Tracks Secured Between
End Units

STANDARD SHELF UNIT SIZES
Widths: 20", 24"
Lengths: 36", 42", 48", 54"
Load Rating: 1,500 lbs. Per Unit

Heights are variable to suit your needs. The use of these units can increase storage capacity up to 40% or more depending on the number of units used.

CAN RACKS - MOBILE OR STATIONARY

These new style can holders provide for cans laying on sides to roll forward as needed. Easily loaded from rear; can be loaded from front. Loading from the rear provides automatic stock turnover first in - first out.

TYPICAL SIZES

Wide	Deep	High	Capacity
27"	38"	83"	30 Ctns. No. 10 Cans (180 Cans)
27"	38"	83"	21 Ctns. No. 10 Cans (126 Cans) + 8 Ctns. No. 5 Cans (96 Cans)
27"	38"	83"	28 Ctns. No. 5 Cans (336 Cans)
27"	38"	41"	12 Ctns. No. 10 Cans (72 Cans)

9

This unit available with work top for mounting a can opener with casters so it may be rolled from store room to point of use.

Available also is a "roll forward" type rack which will store 5 cases (30) No. 10 cans and may be fitted to your existing shelving. These units load from the front at top, the cans roll downward and are removed from the bottom. This method of storing makes better use of shelf space and insures inventory turnover.

The unit is approximately 21" wide x 18¼" high x 40" long.

SPECIAL PURPOSE WIRE SHELVING
COMPONENTS AVAILABLE

MOBILE WORK STATIONS
LAUNDRY CARTS - top or side load
UTILITY CARTS
TRAY OR BUS BOX CARTS - with angle ledge glides
FULLY ENCLOSED CARTS - with sliding and locking doors
TRUCK AND VAN INTERIORS - with anchoring clips

Using standard components the above specialty units can be assembled. Various style wheels, brakes and finishes allow you to design your own vehicle.

TYPICAL MOBILE INGREDIENT BINS
FOR DRY STORAGE

Fig. 2-5

SIZES			Capacities			
Width	Depth	Height	Cu. Ft.	Gals.	Lbs. Sugar	Lbs. Flour
12" x 29" x 28"			3.4	26	175	125
21" x 23" x 28"			3.9	34	195	140
15" x 29" x 28"			4.4	34½	220	155
21" x 23" x 23"			5.1	43	260	185
18" x 29" x 28"			5.7	44	285	205

Many sizes and styles of ingredient bins are available in either plastics or metal and can be had with sliding or hinged covers.

The above chart can help you select one with the capacity you require.

Clear plastic, see through covers are available for many models.

PALLETS

Listed only are some standard sizes and the load limit of common steel pallets. Many other materials and systems are available.

Pallet sizes are 36" x 48", 40" x 48", 42" x 42", 40" x 48" and 48" x 48". All are 4" high with a load limit of 10,000 lbs. They can be reversible or nonreversible and matching shelving and pallet jacks or lifts are available.

STANDARD SIZES OF STORAGE ITEMS

The following charts show dimensions and capacities of many items commonly stored. Used in conjunction with the shelving charts these will help you attain maximum use of your dry storage area.

Fig. 2-6

STANDARD CANS				
Number	Dia.	Ht.	Capacity	4 Oz. Portions
2	3½''	5''	18 oz.	4½
2½	4''	5''	26 oz.	6½
3	4¼''	7½''	46 oz.	11½
10	6¼''	7½''	96 oz.	24

Fig. 2-7

APPROX. CAN CARTON SIZES		
Can	Per Carton	Carton Size
#2	24	14'' x 10'' x 9¼''
#2½	24	17'' x 12'' x 10¼''
#3	12	17½'' x 13½'' x 7¾''
#10	6	19'' x 12¾'' x 7¼''

CHINA AND GLASSWARE CARTON SIZES

To aid you in planning storage shelf space Fig. 2-8 shows sizes of the most commonly used china and glassware.

Fig. 2-8

Item	Carton Size
6¼'' Plates	9½'' x 13'' x 6¾'' High
9'' Plates	9½'' x 13½'' x 6¾'' High
Cups	13'' x 16'' x 9½'' High
Saucers	10½'' x 12¾'' x 6¾'' High
Bowls	9½'' x 16'' x 10'' High
Monkey Dishes	9¼'' x 10¼'' x 5½'' High
8 oz. Bulge Glasses	16½'' x 16¾'' x 8½'' High
8 oz. Stemware	19'' x 18½'' x 6¼'' High

11

Shelf width required for some common items:

20" x 20" Dish Racks....................... 21" wide shelf
#10 Cans, 2 deep........................... 14" wide shelf
#10 Cans, 4 deep, staggered............... 24" wide shelf
#2 Cans, 6 deep........................... 21" wide shelf
Gallon jugs, 2 deep....................... 14" wide shelf
18" x 26" Pans, side load................. 21" wide shelf
12" x 20" Pans, end load.................. 21" wide shelf

MISCELLANEOUS ITEMS
Approximate sizes, weights and shelf space required by square feet

REMINDER: To determine square feet when inches are given, multiply length x width and divide by 144.
Example: 21" x 42" shelf = 504 square inches or 3.5 square feet.

Item	Size	Approx. Wt.	Approx. Sq. Ft.
Flour or Sugar Sack	18" x 33" x 11"	100 lbs.	4.0
Shortening Can	16" Dia. x 17"	50 lbs.	1.8
Cooking Oil, 5 gal. can	9½" x 9½" x 13"	40 lbs.	0.7
Case 6 oz. Cans (96)	11¼" x 22½" x 7¼"	37 lbs.	1.7
Case 8 oz. Cans (72)	11" x 16½" x 10"	28 lbs.	1.2
Case #2 Cans (24)	14" x 10" x 9¼"	28 lbs.	1.0
Case #10 Cans (6)	19" x 12¾" x 7¼"	37 lbs.	1.5

SOME COMMON PAPER (DISPOSABLE) ITEMS

Item	Pack	Carton Size	Approx. Sq. Ft.
8 oz. Hot Food - Squat	1,000	10¼" x 16¼" x 29½"	4.2 Flat
10 oz. Hot Food - Squat	1,000	22" x 9" x 39¼"	6. Flat
12 oz. Hot Food - Squat	500	22¼" x 9¼" x 29¾"	4.1 Flat
5 oz. Cold Cups	2,500	13¼" x 13¼" x 15"	1.2 on End
6 oz. Cold Cups	2,500	11¼" x 14¼" x 23½"	1.1 on End
10 oz. Cold Cups	2,500	16½" x 16¼" x 29½"	1.8 on End
6" Plates	1,000	19" x 12" x 6"	1.6 Flat
7" Plates	1,000	22½" x 14½" x 8"	2.2 Flat
8" Plates	1,000	22½" x 16½" x 9"	2.6 Flat
9" Plates	1,000	21" x 19" x 10"	2.8 Flat

See Chapter 15 for more sizes and packs of disposables, page 425.

Time and space limitations prohibit any attempt to catalogue all the items which might end up in your dry storage room. The authors sincerely hope the information provided in this chapter will aid you in planning a new storage area.

At this point however, we would like to quote a friend who asked, "Did you ever have a closet that was big enough?"

HELPFUL HINTS

To eliminate mistakes in re-ordering glassware, take one glass from each pattern and size you use and attach a label or tape to it with your distributor's number or the factory number of the glass and the number of dozens per carton pack. This will eliminate the age old problem of receiving the wrong size or amount of glasses.

SHELVING PLANNING GUIDE

Total Space Avail.	36"	42"	48"	60"	Total Space Avail.	36"	42"	48"	60"
6'0"	2				13'6"	1		2	
6'6"	1	1			14'0"			1	2
7'0"		2			14'6"	3	1		
7'6"		1	1		15'0"				3
8'0"			2		15'6"	1	3		
8'6"		1		1	16'0"		4		
9'0"			1	1	16'6"	1	2		1
9'6"	2	1			17'0"	2			2
10'0"				2	17'6"	1	1		2
10'6"		3			18'0"			2	2
11'0"		2	1		18'6"	1			3
11'6"		1	2		19'0"			1	3
12'0"			3		19'6"	1	4		
12'6"		1	1	1	20'0"				4
13'0"			2	1	20'6"	3			2

— NOTES —

Chapter Three

REFRIGERATED STORAGE

In this chapter we examine "back of the house" refrigeration such as walk-ins and kitchen refrigerators and freezers. The facts shown and information given will aid prospective buyers and students in selecting, by size, refrigeration requirements matched to menu items and frequency of deliveries. Out front, point of service refrigeration including such items as pastry and salad display cases will be covered in Chapter 7 (Serving, Holding and Transporting).

The options and variations available for refrigerators, freezers and walk-in units are numerous. It will pay to study them carefully. The initial costs may have a rapid pay back in energy savings and improved service.

WALK-IN COOLERS AND FREEZERS

With no intent to be facetious the authors of Food Equipment Facts would like to state that in order to absolutely and scientifically size a walk-in cooler or freezer for any given establishment it would be necessary to know the exact menu to be served with any forseeable changes itemized. To know the number and frequencies of deliveries of all items. To have accurate predictions of the ebb and flow of patrons which would necessitate an equally accurate prediction of the future economic status of the community as well as changing weather conditions. If all this information can be assembled and the patrons arrive in the predicted numbers and eat the precise amounts of the specified menu items, your walk-in cooler can be scientifically sized, providing, of course, that the chef doesn't quit or come up with some fancy ideas of his own.

Don't panic dear reader, following are a number of charts and facts to aid you in making at least an intelligent, if not scientific selection of refrigerated equipment. May we remind you of our offer to help you locate full service equipment representatives or consultants covering your area. A stamped, self addressed envelope mailed with your specific request is all that is needed.

WALK-IN COOLER/FREEZER COMPONENTS

Nearly all modular walk-ins have the same general construction and assembly methods as well as the same optional variations. The individual panels which make up the units are usually 4" thick. The main difference is in the height and width of the panels and corner pieces. Some manufacturers use modules of even 1'-0'' divisions. When assembled their coolers could measure 8'-0'' x 12'-0''. Another manufacturer's unit of comparable size might measure 7'-8'' x 11'-6'' or 7'-9'' x 11'-7'' etc. It is important to consider these variations when planning shelving for the walk-ins. Standard heights of common walk-ins average 7'-6'', 8'-6'' and 10'-6''. Modular paneling and interior support systems are available for constructing huge two story refrigerated warehouses. These require a considerable amount of engineering and will not be discussed in this book.

There are available many standard options for walk-in refrigeration units. They are listed below and there careful consideration, coupled with the charts which follow will aid in selecting the proper units for your use.

WALK-IN REFRIGERATOR OPTIONS

Before discussing options and their advantages let us remind you of our statement regarding planning dry storage areas. Plan your rows of shelving with the aisle space you require keeping in mind that simply adding 2 or 3 feet more width to the walk-in box may accomplish nothing more than adding extra cost to the unit.

1. Walk-ins are available for either indoor or outdoor installations. Outdoor units require weather caps for the roof and rain hoods are available for the doors. The compressors may be self-contained and winterized if required. Don't forget the condensate drain line from the blower coils.
2. Indoor units are available in various finishes and with decorator color panels.
3. Walk-in coolers may set directly on an existing concrete or tile floor using screeds available for this purpose, thereby eliminating the step up at the door. This should not be attempted with freezers.
4. To recess the walk-in floor to be level with the outside floor or to carry a tile floor into the walk-in units all manufacturers have detailed drawings of suggested designs to aid your contractor.
5. Where the walk-in floor is to set on an existing floor, interior floor panels with built-in ramps are available for coolers (not to be used in freezers) and outside ramps are available for either. Skid-proof treads are recommended.
6. Reinforced Floors — Diamond tread aluminum, etc. vary by manufacturer. Check with your supplier.
7. Pressure relief vents are available and strongly recommended especially in large freezer units. Warm air will fill the walk-in as the cold air runs out during stocking-up periods. Then when the door is closed the air contracts as it cools building up a partial vacuum inside making it very difficult to open the door. The

16

author remembers well a college installation where the chef used a crowbar to yank open the freezer door and collapsed the roof of the unit. We won't mention who installed the unit.

8. Thermometers, usually built into door panels, are available and called for by health departments in some areas.

9. Audio and visual alarm systems are available for both coolers and freezers.

10. About Doors — Standard door panels which usually contain the thermometer, the vapor proof light and switch and the door heater cables are available with 24", 30" and 34" wide doors hinged to right or left. Self-closing hinges are available. Door pulls are available with cylinder locks or pad lock holes. Inside safety releases are standard. Foot treadle openers may be ordered. Glass view ports with triple thick glass, heated for freezers may be installed. Kick plates and bumper strips may be attached. Track ports above the door opening are available where overhead trolley systems are used.

Reach-in doors, either one above the other or one door at top are available in glass or solid, hinged either side or sliding.

Full height glass display doors with built-in adjustable shelving, vertical fluorescent lighting and heater cables to prevent condensation are available either hinged or sliding. These units may be installed adjacent to each other for the full length of the cooler or freezer.

Sliding doors, either manual or powered are available in various widths for use where hinged doors are impractical or where fork lift trucks are used. They may be right or left sliding or bi-parting.

11. Various options are available for the refrigeration systems. They may be self-contained with the compressor mounted on top of the unit. Saddle mounted with the condensing unit and the blower coils hung over a wall panel or self-contained remote systems have pre-charged snap-on refrigerant lines allowing the compressor to be located in any convenient spot within approximately 20 feet.

12. Plastic air curtains hung at door openings can cut down running time of the compressor and save money for you. These are detailed later in this chapter.

Before we move on let us remind you not to forget about the condensate drain lines from the blower coils. This can be a real headache on a union job. They must be trapped, then run to an indirect waste and a heater tape is required in the freezer. Floor drains are not permissible inside of walk-in boxes. Secondly, be sure of your voltage, phase and horsepower in that they are compatible with your power supply. Last but by no means least, check your warranty.

NOTE: All of the above options for walk-in units may not be available from any single manufacturer.

17

SOME SPECIALIZED WALK-INS

A somewhat specialized walk-in unit is produced with limited options but with some unique features. The most important feature is that the entire refrigeration unit is built into one 2'-0" x 2'-0" corner panel, forming a triangle on the inside. The unit is completely factory sized and assembled and requires only one electrical connection. The panels are in even 1'-0" modules and are only 2½" thick. The metal floor is backed with ¼" plywood. The units are available with or without the floor panels. The sizes available are shown in Fig. 3-1.

Fig. 3-1

OVERALL SIZE W/FLOOR			COMPRESSOR RATING	
Height	Width	Depth	Cooler	Freezer
7'-5½"	6'	8'	¾ HP	1½ HP
7'-5½"	8'	8'	¾ HP	1½ HP
7'-5½"	8'	10'	1 HP	2 HP
7'-5½"	6'	10'	¾ HP	1½ HP
7'-5½"	10'	10'	1 HP	2 HP
7'-5½"	6'	12'	1 HP	2 HP
7'-5½"	8'	12'	1 HP	2 HP

One manufacturer produces sectional wood panel units sheathed with ¾" fir. A unit ideally suited to palletized warehousing has one front panel 14'-8" wide 9'-6" high with two biparting folding aluminum clad doors which open full width. Some typical sizes and capacities are shown in Fig. 3-2. Others available.

Units are well suited to beverage, dairy or general utility storage.

Fig. 3-2

Width	Depth	½ BARREL CAPACITIES			Cases (66)	Refr. Req'd.
		Squat (4 high)	Tall (3 high)	Corded		
14'-8"	16'-6"	312	240	192	1056	2 HP
14'-8"	20'-6"	378	288	240	1320	3 HP
14'-8"	24'-6"	440	336	288	1584	3 HP
14'-8"	28'-6"	568	384	336	1848	3 HP

For those who may be searching this chapter for a beer cooler, the manufacturers of the above mentioned wood clad boxes produce a unique unit where one side is stepped out to form a back bar with top and a drainer plate, the upper portion is fitted with a direct draw, simulated barrel head and glass reach-in doors may be installed on the other side for wine display. Behind the back-bar wall is a full height walk-in cooler. From the inside a row of barrels may be

18

stored under the protruding back-bar and tapped for direct draw. This unit may be constructed to your dimensional requirements.

Working down from large walk-ins to standard reach-in refrigerators and freezers we come to step-in units. These vary in size by manufacturer. One measuring 62" wide x 49" deep x 75½" high plus approximately 18" with compressor top mounted has 79 cu.ft. of storage space. As a cooler it is available with either ⅓ or ½ HP compressor. As a freezer either a ¾ or 1 HP compressor is available. The 1 HP would be required for ice cream storage. Capacities are 60 milk cases or 24 egg cases. As a freezer it will hold 140 frozen food cases measuring 8" x 3" x 13" or 560 gallons of ice cream.

ESTIMATING SPACE REQUIREMENTS

Hundreds of charts, figures and facts have been printed in many different books. Those relating to primary schools, hospitals, nursing homes, military installations and so on, where the variables are kept to a minimum, can be and are often very accurate. For the average independent owner who is almost always faced with limited budgets and space it can be quite a dilemma. One statement which may be very helpful is that in the years that the authors have worked together they have found that in the average restaurant having 100 to 150 seats with normal buying practices and average deliveries a walk-in cooler 7'-8" wide x 11'-6" deep x 7'-6" high with a freezer section approximately 5'-9" deep added to it has proven very satisfactory.

A general rule of thumb for estimating walk-in refrigeration is to allow ½ cubic foot of usable space per meal served. Small walk-ins with only one door and a single aisle can have from 50% to 60% of usable space. Larger walk-ins with multiple aisles and doors can drop to from 35% to 45% usable space.

Use the charts for standard shelving in Chapter 2, consider dunage racks, mobile bins, and rolling angle ledge banquet carts, then use the following information to help in your selection of walk-in units.

REFRIGERATED STORAGE FOR VARIOUS OPERATIONS
(Expressed as Total Square Feet)

Fig. 3-3

In Plant Feeding	Meals Per Day	400	800	1200	1600
	Sq. Ft. Required	75-120	115-135	140-175	170-210
Schools	Meals Per Day	200	400	500	1000
	Sq. Ft. Required	25-35	35-50	50-75	75-100
Central	No. of Beds	50	100	150-200	400
Hospitals	Sq. Ft. Required	40-50	80-100	200	400

RESTAURANT NEEDS BY TOTAL CUBIC FEET

Fig. 3-4

Average 3 Meal/Day	1 to 1½ Usable Cu. Ft. Per Person
Fine Dining - 1 Meal/Day	2 to 5 Usable Cu. Ft. Per Seat

(Note **usable** cu. ft. regarding walk-ins)

EXAMPLE

From the chart above a 150 seat fine dining restaurant using a figure of 3.5 cu.ft./seat could require 525 cu. ft. of refrigeration. This might break down as follows:

Walk-in using approx. inside dimensions of
   7' high unit — 7' x 11' cooler **+** 7' x 5' freezer
   total cu. ft. 784 - 40% usable space................. 313
2 Door Chef's refrigerator............................. 47
1 Door Chef's freezer................................. 17
2 Door undercounter refrigerator...................... 15
Refrigerated open cold pan........................... 10
Sandwich unit....................................... 12
Waitress pantry refrigeration......................... 47
Dessert display refrigerator.......................... 47

TOTAL CUBIC FEET 508

The above chart was compiled as a brainstorming guide only and should not be considered to be an absolute requirement list for any particular operation. It is however typical of any average restaurant, take away the cold pan and add an ice cream cabinet, etc. One thing to note is that with using the comparatively low figure of 40% the usable walk-in storage space is approximately 3/5 of the total refrigeration required.

Another rule of thumb that may help is that on the average 45 lbs. of solid foods will equal 1 cubic foot.

POUNDS OF FOOD PER SHELF
(By width stored 12" high)

12" wide: 45 lbs./ft. — 14" wide: 52 lbs./ft. — 18" wide: 67 lbs./ft. — 21" wide: 79 lbs./ft. — 24" wide: 90 lbs./ft.

PER CENT OF SPACE REQUIRED BY PRODUCT

Meats............... 20/25%   Dairy Products....... 20/25%
Fruit & Vegetables... 30/35%   Salads & Desserts... 10/15%

TYPICAL VOLUME CONSUMED BY GROUP

Meat or Poultry . . . . .010 to .030 Cu. Ft. Per Meal
Dairy Products . . . . .007 to .015 Cu. Ft. Per Meal
Vegetables & Fruit . . . . .020 to .040 Cu. Ft. Per Meal

(Low figure would be 1 meal service as school lunch — High figure
would represent typical full service restaurant.)

The following chart was compiled from one popular manufacturer's catalog. Other manufacturers standard modules will vary only
slightly. Since the combinations of sizes are made nearly infinite
by varying widths and heights of wall, door and corner panels only a
limited typical number are shown and only two heights are given.
Many others are available.

Fig. 3-5 **TYPICAL WALK-IN SIZES SHOWING SQ. FT., CU. FT.
AND REFRIGERATION REQUIREMENTS**

WALK-IN UNIT SIZE	SQ. FT. INTERIOR FLOOR	CUBIC FEET INTERIOR OF WALK-IN		REFRIGERATION REQUIRED	
		7'-6" High	8'-6" High	Cooler Either Hgt.	Freezer Either Hgt.
5'-9" x 4'-9"	20.9	146.3	167.2	½ HP	1 HP
5'-9" 7'8"	35.7	259.9	285.6	½ HP	1 HP
5-9" x 9'7"	45.4	317.8	363.2	¾ HP	1½ HP
5'-9" x 12'-5½"	60.1	420.7	480.8	1 HP	1½ HP
5'-9" x 14'-4½"	70.8	495.6	566.4	1 HP	2 HP
5'-9" x 17'-3"	84.1	588.7	672.8	1½ HP	2 HP
5'-9" x 20'-1½"	98.9	692.3	791.2	1½ HP	2 HP
6'-8½" x 8'-7½"	47.4	331.8	379.2	¾ HP	1½ HP
6'-8½" x 11'-6"	64.2	449.4	513.6	1 HP	1½ HP
6-8½" x 14'-4½"	82.2	575.4	657.6	1½ HP	2 HP
6-8½" x 18'-2½"	105.6	739.2	844.8	1½ HP	2 HP
7'-8" x 7'-8"	49.0	340.2	392.1	¾ HP	1½ HP
7'-8" x 11'-6"	75.6	529.2	604.8	1 HP	2 HP
7'-8" x 18'-2½"	122.5	857.5	980.1	2 HP	2 HP
7'-8" x 20'-1½"	138.8	971.6	1110.4	2 HP	3 HP
8'-7½" x 11'-6"	86.4	604.8	691.2	1½ HP	2 HP
8'-7½" x 16'-3½"	123.2	862.4	985.6	2 HP	2 HP
8'-7½" x 19'-2"	146.4	1024.8	1171.2	2 HP	3 HP
9'-7" x 11'-6"	98.1	686.7	784.8	1½ HP	2 HP

(Continued)

Fig. 3-5 **TYPICAL WALK-IN SIZES SHOWING SQ. FT., CU. FT. AND REFRIGERATION REQUIREMENTS**

WALK-IN UNIT SIZE	SQ. FT. INTERIOR FLOOR	CUBIC FEET INTERIOR OF WALK-IN		REFRIGERATION REQUIRED	
		7'-6" High	8'-6" High	Cooler Either Hgt.	Freezer Either Hgt.
9'-7" x 15'-4"	131.4	919.8	1051.2	2 HP	2 HP
9'-7" x 18'-2½"	157.5	1102.5	1260.2	2 HP	3 HP
10'-6½" x 12'-5½"	117.2	820.4	937.6	1½ HP	2 HP
10'-6½" x 16'-3½"	158.1	1106.7	1264.8	2 HP	3 HP
10'-6½" x 20'-1½"	196.4	1379.8	1671.2	2 HP	3 HP
11'-6" x 13'-5"	140.8	985.6	1126.4	1½ HP	2 HP
11'-6" x 18'-2½"	194.7	1362.9	1557.6	2 HP	3 HP
12'-5½" x 13'-5"	145.2	1016.4	1161.6	1½ HP	2 HP
12'-5½" x 16'-3½"	182.4	1276.8	1459.2	2 HP	3 HP
12'-5½" x 20'-1½"	230.4	1612.8	1843.2	2 HP	3 HP

Use Fig. 3-6 and Fig. 3-7 to help in determining shelf spacing, width and height.

Fig. 3-6

SIZE OF COMMON REFRIGERATOR ITEMS

Item	Package	Approx. Capacity	Height	Width or Dia.	Length
Butter	Box	64 lb.	12"	12"	14"
Cheese	Wheel	20-23 lb.	7½"	13½"	
Eggs	Case	45 lb.	13"	12"	26"
Milk	Can	10 gal.	25"	13½"	
	Case	24½ pt.	10½"	13"	13"
	Case	24½ pt.	7"	13"	19"
Margarine	Box	60 lb.	10"	14"	17½"
Meat, portioned	Tray	40 lb.	3"	18"	26"
Cuts	Box	40 lb.	6"	18"	28"
Cuts	Box	50 lb.	10"	10"	28"
Aples	Box	35-40	10½"	11½"	18"
	Carton	40-45 lb.	12"	12½"	20"
Berries	Crate	36 lb.	11"	11"	22"
Cherries, Grapes	Lug	25-30 lb.	6"	13½"	16"
Citrus	Crate	65-80 lb.	12"	12"	26"
	Carton	40-65 lb.	11"	11½"	17"

22

Fig. 3-7

SIZES AND SPACE REQUIRED FOR SOME FROZEN FOOD ITEMS

Item	BOXES OR CARTONS Capacity	Package Size	No. of Units which can be stored per cu.ft.
Vegetables	2½ lb.	9-5/8" x 5-3/8" x 2½"	13
French Fries	30 lb.	18" x 11½" x 10-1/8"	.83
Fish Sticks	6 lb.	10-1/8" x 8-1/8" x 2¾"	7
Lobster Tails	5 lb.	15" x 7¼" x 3-3/8"	4
Trout	5 lb.	13" x 8¼" x 2¾"	6
Shrimp	5 lb.	11-5/8" x 6¼" x 2¾"	8
Chicken Parts	10 lb.	18¼" x 10¾" x 2¾"	3
Ground Beef	50 lb.	20¾" x 15¾" x5¼"	1
Butter	32 lb.	11" x 11" x 11"	1
Cheese	30 lb.	12" x 12" x 8½"	1.3
Ice Cream Carton	½ gal.	7" x 4¾" x 3½"	15
Ice Cream Round	2½ gal.	9½" Dia. x 10"	1
Fruit	30 lb.	10" Dia. x 13"	1
Fruit	#10 can	6-1/8" Dia. x 7"	10
Fruit	#5 can	4¼" Dia. x 7"	13
Orange Juice	2½ lb.	4-1/8" Dia. x 5½"	19
Concentrated	12 oz.	2¾" Dia. x 5"	49
Concentrated	32 oz.	4" Dia. x 5-5/8"	19

CLEAR HEAVY VINYL, OVERLAPPING DOOR STRIPS

Hung inside of walk-in cooler doors they form an excellent barrier to keep the cold air in. They have many other energy saving applications. Heavier nylon reinforced, double overlapping units are available for outdoor installations such as receiving dock doors. Curtain should be sized 2" over door size on each side and at top wherever possible.

SOME STANDARD SIZES

34"W x 80"H	53"W x 84"H	66"W x 84"H	79"W x 84"H
34"W x 84"H	53"W x 96"H	66"W x 96"H	79"W x 96"H
40"W x 80"H	53"W x 108"H	66"W x 108"H	79"W x 108"H
40"W x 84"H	53"W x 120"H	66"W x 120"H	79"W x 120"H
40"W x 96"H	60"W x 84"H	73"W x 84"H	86"W x 84"H
40"W x 108"H	60"W x 96"H	73"W x 96"H	86"W x 96"H
40"W x 120"H	60"W x 108"H	73"W x 108"H	86"W x 108"H
47"W x 84"H	60"W x 120"H	73"W x 120"H	86"W x 120"H
47"W x 96"H			92"W x 84"H
47"W x 108"H			92"W x 96"H
47"W x 120"H			92"W x 108"H
			92"W x 120"H

23

FORCED AIR CURTAINS

Units blow air downward at the door opening to form a thermal barrier or insect barrier. Available to specifications shown below.

Fig. 3-8

| Door Width | MAXIMUM HEIGHT | | Motor HP |
	Insect Barrier	Thermal Barrier	
2'	4'	6'	$\frac{1}{3}$
3'	8'	11'	$\frac{3}{4}$
4'	8'	11'	1
5'	8'	11'	1½
6'	8'	11'	1½
4'	12'	16'	2
5'	12'	16'	3
6'	12'	16'	3'

RECOMMENDED STORAGE FOR REFRIGERATED FOODS

Fig. 3-9

Food	Maximum Storage Temp. °F	Maximum Storage Period
Dairy Products		
Milk (fluid)	40	3 days
Butter	40	2 weeks in waxed cartons
Cheese (hard)	40	6 months tightly covered
Cheese (soft	40	7 days in tightly covered container
Ice Cream and Ices	10	3 months in original container covered
Eggs	45	7 days
Fish		
Fresh	36	20 days loosely wrapped
Shell Fish	36	5 days in covered container
Fruits		
Peaches, Plums, Berries	50	7 days unwashed
Apples, Pears, Citrus	50-70	2 weeks, original container
Leftovers	36	7 days
Leftovers	36	2 days
Poultry	36	7 days

(Continued)

Meat		
Ground	38	2 days
Fresh Meat Cuts	38	6 days
Liver and variety Meats	38	2 days
Cold Cuts (Sliced)	38	6 days
Cured Bacon	38	1-4 weeks
Ham (tender cured)	38	1-6 weeks
Ham (canned)	38	6 weeks, original container
Dried Beef	38	6 weeks
Vegetables		
Leafy	45	7 days
Potatoes, onions, root vegetables	50-70	7-30 days, dry in ventilated containers

RECOMMENDED STORAGE FOR FROZEN FOODS

Fig. 3-10

Frozen Food	Maximum Storage Period at 0° F
Eggs	6-12 months
Fruit	8-12 months
Vegetables	8-12 months
french-fried potatoes, parfried	2-6 months
Meats	
beef	6-12 months
lamb and veal	6-9 months
pork	3-6 months
sausage and ground meat	1-3 months
cooked meat, not covered with gravy or other sauces	1 month
meat sandwiches	1 month
Poultry	
chickens	6-12 months
turkeys	3-6 months
giblets	3 months
cooked poultry meat	1 month
cooked poultry dishes	3-6 months
Precooked Combination Dishes	2-6 months
Baked Goods	
cakes	
pre-baked	4-9 months
batters	3-4 months
Fruit Pies, baked or unbaked	3-4 months
Pie Shells, baked or unbaked	1.5-2 months
Cookies	6-12 months
Yeast Breads and Rolls	
pre-baked	3-9 months
dough	1-1.5 months

WRAP AROUND HEAT TAPES

Protection to 50⁰ Below Zero
120 Volt

Fig. 3-11

Standard Lengths	Watts
6 ft.	30 Watts
9 ft.	45 Watts
13 ft.	65 Watts
18 ft.	90 Watts
24 ft.	120 Watts
45 ft.	225 Watts
60 ft.	300 Watts
100 ft.	800 Watts

Needed for walk in freezer evaporator drain lines.

SOME STANDARD BLAST FREEZER SIZES

Fig. 3-12

CAPACITIES OF BLAST FREEZERS 10⁰ to 15⁰			
Size	Cu. Ft.	Ice Cream Storage	Frozen Food Storage
8' W x 8' L x 8½' H	318	1400 gals.	270 cases
8' W x 10' L x 8½' H	416	1800 gals.	400 cases
8' W x 12' L x 8½' H	514	2000 gals.	480 cases
8' W x 14' L x 8½' H	612	2500 gals.	570 cases
8' W x 16' L x 8½' H	710	2900 gals.	680 cases
8' W x 20' L x 8½' H	906	3700 gals.	870 cases
8' W x 22' L x 8½' H	1004	4100 gals.	920 cases
8' W x 26' L x 8½' H	1200	4800 gals.	1150 cases
8' W x 28' L x 8½' H	1298	5000 gals.	1300 cases

Ice Cream: Figured in rectangular ½ gallon packages.
Frozen Food Case Size: 12" W x 17" L x 5" H.
All storage capacity for blast freezers allows for working aisles and air
space over stored product.

REMOTE REFRIGERATION

Nearly all refrigeration units may be ordered for remote compress-
or installations. The advantages should be seriously considered.

1. Remoting to a cool, dust-free area will increase the life of the
   compressor.
2. It can increase the cubic capacity of the refrigeration unit, especially in under counter units where space is a premium.
3. It eliminates objectionable running noises.
4. The units may be easily serviced or switched leaving working
   aisles free during a rush period.

5. It could be advantageous to have one local refrigeration company supply all of your units.
6. Systems are available with combined heating and cooling devices built into an enclosed compressor rack that supply controlled temperature at which the compressors operate most efficiently and in turn reduce energy cost and increase compressor life. These units are described in Chapter 14.

REACH-IN REFRIGERATORS AND FREEZERS

Before selecting a refrigerator or for that matter, any piece of equipment, study all of the available options and consider how they may benefit you. Listed below is a check list of options for refrigerators and where applicable, for freezers.

1. Single door units may have full doors or half doors, either glass or solid. Other than the obvious advantage of glass doors for display refrigerators they can save a lot of time in searching for items with the door open where the unit may be used by different operators, waitresses, etc. Half doors lose comparatively little in cubic content and can save in refrigeration loss as opposed to frequent opening of full doors.

   Multiple door refrigerators, in addition to the above may have sliding doors. These are advantageous where aisle space is limited but only one person can use a two door unit at one time.

   Doors may be either right or left hand hinged. Be sure you order the best one to suit your purpose.
2. Refrigerator/freezer combinations are available in many configurations. Single width units may be over-under models with the freezer either above or below the refrigerator. Multiple door boxes are available with thermostatically controlled hot sections having indicator lights and heat adjustment up to 200⁰. These may be ordered in any combination up to 3 sections wide; i.e., refr./freezer, refr./hot, hot/refr./freezer, etc. In order of right to left sequence any arrangement is available.

   Combination refrigerator/freezers may be operated from one compressor or have two, either self contained or remote of course.
3. Pass-through units have doors front and back, particularly suited to through wall service.
4. Roll-in or roll-through units for angle ledge carts. Especially useful for banquet set-up, resorts, etc.
5. Finished backs may be placed on refrigerated units to be installed in open spaces.
6. Refrigerated drawers are very convenient when installed in under-counter or work top refrigerators. Not suited to freezers. A considerable amount of storage space is lost.

7. Fish storage cabinets (handy at broiling stations) have drawers with drain lines which permits icing the stored fillets. Detailed later in this chapter.
8. Check the available interior and exterior finishes your suppliers has to offer, i.e., plastic, stainless steel, aluminum, enamel, decorator color panels, etc.
9. Some units have exterior thermometers as standard, others as optional.
10. Interior lights are not always standard.
11. Newer models have energy saving condensate evaporators and door defoggers which employ internal heat from the condensing coils.
12. Casters are a convenient option to make housekeeping easy.
13. In locations where height may be a problem units are available with the compressor mounted in the bottom using the lower portion of one section leaving approximately a 2/3 sized door in that section. The average overall height of these is 74".

UPRIGHT REACH-IN UNITS

Fig. 3-13

TYPICAL SIZES BY FULL DOORS						
Doors	Cu. Ft.	Height	Width	Depth	High Temp.	Low Temp.
1	22	78"-83"	28"	32"	¼ HP	½ HP
2	50	78"-83"	56"	32"	⅓ HP	¾ HP
3	70-80	78"-83"	84"	32"	½ HP	1 HP
4	100	78"	113"	32½"	¾ HP	(2) ¾ HP

(Sizes are average only. Vary by manufacturer.)

HELPFUL HINTS

A three or four door refrigerator is a very large piece of equipment which will stubbornly resist making a sharp turn in a narrow hallway, will often balk at passing through a normal door opening and can hardly ever be forced to ascend average stairways. Be sure the one you order will enter gracefully.

PAN SLIDES

Pan slide refrigerator storage systems are an option worthy of special attention. Details and dimensions vary by manufacturer. Some have pan slide cages which rest on standard shelving. Others are designed to hold either 18" x 26" pans or 12" x 20" or both when fitted with the proper angle slides.

Below is a check list for sizing pans and portions:
1. Determine plate, bowl or glass size.
2. How many fit on an 18" x 26" pan.
3. Measure height of product on pan to determine spacing.
4. Total the number of portions required.
5. Check the number of trays, by centers to door openings from charts below.
6. Be sure to use the wider angle glides when using 12" x 20" or other pans or trays.

TYPICAL PAN HOLDING CAPACITIES PER DOOR OPENING
(Using 18" x 26" pans 1" deep)

Fig. 3-14

Slide Centers	Half Doors	Full Doors
1"	27 Pans	57 pans
1½"	18 Pans	36 Pans
2"	13 Pans	28 Pans
2¼"	12 Pans	24 Pans
3"	9 Pans	19 Pans
4"	7 Pans	14 Pans
5"	5 Pans	11 Pans
6"	4 Pans	9 Pans

TYPICAL PAN HOLDING CAPACITIES PER DOOR OPENING
Fig. 3-15
(Using 12" x 20" pans)

Pan Size	Slide Centers	Half Door	Full Door
12" x 20" x 2½"	3"	14 pans	32 Pans
12" x 20" x 4"	5"	10 Pans	20 Pans
12" x 20" x 6"	7"	8 Pans	14 Pans

1/2 - 1/3 - 1/4 and 1/6 pans can also be adapted to pan slide use.

AUXILIARY AIR COOLER
For Walk-in Boxes

Unit is 16" H x 48" L x 6" D. Bolts to interior wall of walk-in cooler with intake and exhaust ducts to outside atmosphere. In winter months whenever temperature drops below the thermostatic setting, the intake fan pulls the cold air in. A separate exhaust fan returns it to the ATMOSPHERE. Saves wear and running cost of compressors during cold weather months. Kit packaged, easy to install. Roof styles available, normal maximum run is 15 running feet from outside area.

TYPICAL CAPACITIES OF FOOD ITEMS ON 18" x 26" PANS

Fig. 3-16

Item	Size	Portions Per Pan	Slide Centers	No. of Pans Per 100 Portions
Milk	½ Pt.	40	4"	2½
Cole Slaw	Fruit Dish	21	3"	5
Salad	6" Bowl	11	3"	9
Pie	6-3/8" Plate	11	2"	9
Fruit Cup	Sherbet	40	4"	2½
Fruit Juice	5 oz. Glass	84	4"	1¼
Cream	1 oz. Cup	125	2"	1
Cantaloupe	7-3/8 Plate	8	3"	12½

FISH STORAGE REFRIGERATORS

These cabinets are available in single or double tiers. Each tier contains 4 drawers. The units are 26" deep x 83" high. The single unit is 28" wide. The double 52-1/8" wide. Remote models approximately 71" high. Total drawer capacity 4.5 cu. ft. for the single unit and 9.0 cu. ft. for the double. Compressors ¼ HP for the 4 drawer and ⅓ HP for the 8 drawer unit. Options are limited — dimensions vary by manufacturer. Units require an indirect waste line.

WORK TOP UNITS

These units, averaging 34½" high including legs, and are designed to fit under existing work tables. The tops being sheathed with metal in the same manner as the sides. They may also be ordered as complete units with tops of your choice in stainless steel, plastic or wood with or without back or end splashes. Standard options such as pan slides, right or left door swing, various finishes, remote refrigeration, casters, etc. may be included. All refrigeration units vary considerably in design and size; i.e., some manufacturers use as little as 12" of width for compressors while others occupy up to 24". These variances are most important when you are comparing bid prices and particularly when the unit must fit in a tight space. Figure 3-17 shows three popular sizes of self-contained units to assist in selection of one to fill your requirements.

Fig. 3-17

WORK TOP UNITS

Doors	Cu. Ft.	Width	Depth	Refr HP	Freezer HP
1	8.4	50"	33"	1/5	1/3
2	18.3	77¼"	33"	1/4	1/3
3	28.2	105"	33"	1/3	1/2

FULL SIZE SANDWICH UNITS

The units described here are those that will accept full size pans (12" x 20") as these are most practical for in-kitchen work. Other, more common units with smaller pan capacities are covered in Chapter 7, Holding and Serving. Again, variations and options must be considered.

Fig. 3-18

SANDWICH UNITS

Doors	Cu. Ft.	12" x 20" Pans	H.P.	Width	Depth	Height To Top
1	10	3	1/4	46"	32-5/8"	34"
2	14	4	1/4	60"	32-5/8"	34"
3	18	5	1/4	74"	32-5/8"	34"

These units may have telescoping removable covers and cutting boards. The 12" x 20" openings may be fitted with adapters to hold round inserts for salad dressings. They will of course also accept any standard combinations of pans. See Chapter 8 for capacities.

PIZZA MAKE-UP TABLES

These also vary in dimension and design by manufacturer. The size of the compressor housing is usually the greatest variance. This will effect the cubic content. The units average 39" in overall height x 32" deep. Some have condiment shelves at the rear with the pans being inserted into cut-outs in the shelf and not refrigerated. The more desirable units have the pan insert elevated at the rear of the working top and the pans are refrigerated. Check with your supplier regarding the style, number and size of the pans.

Pizza tables are available with marble, plastic composition, stainless steel or wood tops. Three typical sizes are listed below to aid in your selection.

Fig. 3-19

PIZZA TABLES

Doors	Tray Capacity Self Contd.	Remote	Box Capacity Per Door	Width	H.P.
1	10	20	8	48"	1/4
2	20	40	8 Each	72"	1/4
3	30	60	8 Each	96"	1/3

NOTE: The above would apply to units having a wide compressor housing where remoting would add a full door.

NOTE: Pizza tables using boxes are normally called dough retarders using boxes of either wood, aluminum, plastic or stainless steel. 18" x 26" x 2½" is standard size and normally hold 12 dough balls per box.

COLD PAN UNITS

These refrigerated tables are ideally suited to pantry and salad preparation areas. Although they are available with open shelving underneath they are usually more desirable with refrigerated bases. Some options to consider are:

1. Sliding, insulated removable covers
2. Overshelves
3. Plate shelves on waitress' side
4. Tray slide on waitress' side
5. Pan adapter panels
6. Back and end splashes
7. Remote compressor

Fig. 3-20

TYPICAL COLD PAN REFRIGERATORS

Width	Height	Depth	HP	Pan Depth
36"	34"	24" or 30"	1/4	8"
36"	34"	24" or 30"	1/4	8"
48"	34"	24" or 30"	1/4	8"
60"	34"	24" or 30"	1/4	8"
72"	34"	24" or 30"	1/3	8"

Pan dimensions approx. 4" less than overall size of unit.

GLASS DOOR REFRIGERATION UNITS

For our friends who may be interested in typical display units for a Deli or Convenience Food Market, Fig. 3-21 lists sizes and capacities available.

Fig. 3-21

GLASS DOOR DISPLAY UNITS

Doors	Width	Cu. Ft.	No. of Shelves	Total Sq.Ft. of Shelving	½ Gal. Milk Capacity	½ Gal. Ice Cream Cpy.
3	98"	78	15	78	720	792
4	128"	103	20	104	960	1056
5	159"	128	25	130	1200	1320

All units are 37½" deep 78½" high. Contact your dealer for more detailed specifications.

Fig. 3-22

ICE CREAM CABINETS

Width	Depth	H.P.	CAPACITIES		
			3 Gal. Cans	2½ Gal. Cans	½ Gal. Packages
32"	21"	1/5	4	5	63
56"	21"	1/5	10	13 to 15	136
30½"	30½"	1/5	9	10 to 12	116
43"	30½"	1/4	16	19 to 21	173
54"	30½"	1/4	21	25 to 30	234
66"	30½"	1/3	29	33 to 40	298
89-1/8"	30½"	1/2	40	47 to 56	430

NOTE: A dipper well must be used for bulk scooping.

COMPACT TACO & MEXICAN FOOD STATION

Specifications: 70" wide, 32" deep, 69" overall height, 37" to working surface, 115 volt, 30 amp unit conduit connection. Completely self contained refrigeration and heating well.

Features: 18.7 refrigerated storage. Refrigerated condiment rail with covers. Taco opening with rail holds 15 tacos. Stainless overshelf with heated enclosure. Stainless enclosed paper shelf. Thermostatically controlled hot well with cover.

Options: Tray file for 18" x 26" pans. Pan files for 12" x 20" pans. Stainless steel back.

SPECIALTY UPRIGHT UNITS

The units described below are unique and some may be used in conjunction with other equipment in systems. Our purpose is to alert you to their existence and to again offer our assistance if you are in need of more information concerning any item.

33

1. TRIPLE TEMPERATURE CABINETS. Convertible from 0^0 freezer to 28^0 chiller to 40^0 refrigerator.

2. RAPID COOL REFRIGERATOR. Convected air cools 104^0 degree foods rapidly through the danger zone for bacterial growth to 40^0. May be used as standard 38^0 refrigerator.

3. RAPID DEFROST. Alternating heated and refrigerated forced air bring food rapidly through defrosting. May also be used as a conventional refrigerator.

4. RAPID FREEZER. Two styles, one using air blast the other, nitrogen spray, can bring food temperature down to -100^0 depending on style used. Either converts to -5^0 freezer.

5. A single door unit is available for use where traffic is heavy and the door would normally be opened and closed frequently, i.e. waitress' stations. The door to this refrigerator may be lifted off at rush hours. A curtain of air blows across the opening keeping the cold air in and the hot air out.

6. DOUGH RETARDERS. High humidity refrigeration systems, usually feature oversize coils, to produce maximum temperataure conditions that retard the rising of doughs. Sizes for most applications are the same as standard reach ins and under counter refrigerators.

THE LITTLE FELLOWS

Let it not be said that we overlooked the little office refrigerator so necessary during conferences with visiting V.I.P.'s, in the event that one should feel the need for a refreshing glass of cool spring water.

There is available a wood grained vinyl finished model measuring only 23" wide x 34½" x 23" deep in which an unbelievable amount of mixers, snacks, juices, condiments, ice cubes and a selection of tall, thin, brown bottles may be stored. Ice cubes in the full width freezer drawer, the remainder on the two shelves below it or in the door rack. The cubic content is 6.5 and the little rascal even has a door frame to accept ¼" paneling to match your office decor. A visiting clergyman or your mother-in-law might not even notice it's there.

For those who for some unimaginable reason may require more ice, a cuber is available for the unit which will produce approximately 550 cubes per day with a storage bucket to hold 312 more. This only leaves 2.1 cu. ft. of storage space in the refrigerator, but what the heck — the good stuff is in another cabinet anyhow.

If you have noticed a trend toward longer conferences around the holiday season, a matching ice machine measuring only 14" x 14" x 24" high, that will produce another 550 cubes per day and store up to 300 more is available.

COUNTER TOP FREEZER

A new style counter top ice cream freezer is available that will hold up to 200 novelty items. Portable, this freezer features lift up or lift off lid. Size: 21" wide, 32" deep, 17" high.

F.E.F. HUMOR

Quite a few years ago beer systems using recirculating ice water to chill the beer lines were new and also relatively expensive as compared to ice cooling or air shaft installations. Our firm did quite a bit of promotion for the system it carried. Being both new and expensive didn't make them easy to sell and any lead was promptly pursued.

A reply card from a mailing came in one morning with a request for information on the new beer system. Our top salesman was sent out on the lead. To everyone's joy and surprise, he came back a few hours later with a bonafide order for a complete system.

We were a lot more surprised when we discovered that he had gone to the wrong address.

HELPFUL HINTS

Nearly everyone understands that compressors for refrigeration units are sized by Horsepower ranging anywhere from 1/5 HP or smaller, all the way up to 3 HP or larger. They usually have a reasonably accurate conception of the capabilities of a 1/4 HP, a 1 HP, etc. but, just exactly why air-conditioning units are rated by tons is generally a complete mystery to them.

It may surprise you to know that the American Refrigeration Institute did it for your protection.

The facts are: 1 HP = 9,000 B.T.U.'s — 1 ton = 12,000 B.T.U.'s. It would follow then that a 1-1/3 HP unit would operate a 1 ton air conditioner. This is not necessarily true — a 1 ton air conditioning unit must (now by law) be capable of removing 12,000 B.T.U.'s from a room. A 1-1/3 HP compressor may be incapable of doing that.

HELPFUL HINTS

When using a refrigerator to defrost, allow 1½ hours per pound of product.

Since walk-in refrigeration units and ice machines both require indirect wastes, expensive plumbing costs may be eliminated by planning the location of the ice machine where one floor drain will service both units.

A 20 cu. ft. upright freezer will hold 1400 7 oz. portions in pouch packages.

Chapter Four

PREPARATION EQUIPMENT

In this chapter we cover the "Fun Machines". You will find production data from Burger Forming through Shrimp Peeling and Deveining Machines and on into common sizes of Butcher Blocks, Sinks and Work Tables.

As with all food service equipment a variety of sizes, options, finishes, voltages, etc. are available. This chapter will be most helpful in selecting the proper equipment for your production requirements.

If any of the equipment listed is unfamiliar to you, we repeat our offer to personally assist. Send a self addressed, stamped envelope with your questions and we will help you in locating items to meet your specific requirements.

Additional, point of service, preparation equipment, such as juice and coffee machines, will be found in Chapter 7.

BLENDERS

Common container sizes of blenders range from 24 oz. - 44 oz. - 64 oz. (½ gal.) to 128 oz. (1 gal.) The containers are available in glass, lexan or stainless steel.

Motors may be 115 V. or 220. Motor sizes and blades vary by manufacturer.

BURGER FORMING MACHINES
(Hand Operated)

Hand powered automatic pattie forming machines with 10 lb. or 15 lb. hopper capacities are available. Some adjustment capabilities are shown below:

For the Average Restaurant or Drive-In				For Hotels or Restaurants Serving Thicker Patties			
No. Patties per Pound	Ozs.	Thickness	Diam. of Pattie	No. Patties per Pound	Ozs.	Thickness	Diam. of Pattie
5	3.20	5/16"	4-3/4"	4	4.00	5/8"	3-5/8"
6	2.67	5/16"	4-5/16"	5	3.20	5/8"	3-1/4"
7	2.29	5/16"	4"	6	2.67	5/8"	3-1/16"
8	2.00	5/16"	3-3/4"	7	2.29	5/8"	3"
9	1.78	5/16"	3-9/16"	8	2.00	5/8"	2-11/16"
10	1.60	5/16"	3-11/32"				

For schools, where help is limited to female operators, a machine is available which requires less strength to operate.

POPULAR SCHOOL PATTIE VARIATIONS

No. Patties per Pound	Ozs.	Thickness	Diam. of Pattie
6	2.67	5/16″	4-5/16″
7	2.29	5/16″	4″
8	2.00	5/16″	3-3/4″
9	1.78	5/16″	3-9/16″
10	1.60	5/16″	3-11/32″

(Other variations with ¼″ thicknesses also available.)

The average production of hand operated pattie machines is from 20 to 40 patties per minute.

To preserve the natural juices and attain smooth operation the meat should be 40⁰ F. or above.

Other styles and sizes of machines available.

BURGER OR MEATBALL MACHINES
(Electric)

Designed to produce patties or meatballs, by using plates with various diameter holes and adjusting thickness setting patties of 2″-2½″ or 3″ diameter, numbering from 2 to 12 per pound may be produced at rates of from 1200 to 1500 per hour. An optional automatic patty remover can increase production up to approximately 3000 patties per hour.

By using plates with hole diameters of 1″ - 1¼″ - 1½″ or 1¾″, meatballs may be produced in the same manner as patties in quantities from 3000 up to approximately 9000 per hour using the automatic remover.

The machine described has a 20 lb. capacity hopper — ⅓ HP, 115/230 volt, single phase motor and is 17″ wide x 22″ long x 26″ high.

It is also available with a revolving hopper and stationary propeller where minimum product agitation is desirable.

Other electric machines are available, some up to 1½ HP where very high production is required. Ask your equipment salesman or write F.E.F.

BREADING MACHINES
(3 Popular sizes listed below — others available)

1. Hand operated, drum type approximately 15″ x 18″ can bread up to 20 lb. of chicken in 1 minute.

2. Using same drum with motorized base (115 V plug-in) approximately 15" x 24½" can bread up to 480 lbs. of chicken per hour.

3. Semi-automatic machine, 14" x 20¼" x 20½" high — operator feeds breading and product into chute at one end. Auger pushes and turns food through breading discharging it into pan at other end. (115 V. plug-in) Capacity approximately 280 lbs. of chicken per hour.

Although the above machines are rated by pounds of chicken per hour, they are equally suited for onion rings, fish, etc.

CREPE MACHINE

Size: 14" long, 8" wide, 9" high
Capacity: 4 crepes per minute
115 volt — uses heated roller controlled by thermostat.
Automatic crepe stacker available.

BREADER/SIFTER

A new manual breading/sifting work station is available. Sifting is accomplished by shaking the stainless steel screen which is removable for discarding dough balls.
Size 58" wide x 28½ deep x 52" high w/back shelf. Available without side shelves where space is limited.
Capacity 25 lbs. flour mix and 10 lbs. raw product.

DOUGHNUT SUGARING MACHINE

One model approximately 60" long, 24" wide and 36" high thoroughly coats approximately 350 dozen doughnuts per hour with any type sugar. Equipped with infeed hopper, bin to catch excess sugar at discharge end, one catch basket and knocker. Machine equipped with one drum. Extra drum is optional and may be stored under machine on brackets bolted to base. Legs are adjustable. Powered by single phase, 115V 1/3 H.P. gear head motor. Optional 220 volt, 3 phase motor available. Drums are fabricated from stainless steel and aluminum.
Optional Infeed Conveyor: Three foot long, bolts to feed end of sugar machine. Doughnuts are fed into machine on wire conveyor belt, powered by a separate gear head motor, 115 volt only.
A smaller doughnut sugaring machine, measuring only 40" in length, is available. Infeed conveyor will not operate with the smaller unit.

MANUAL DOUGHNUT GLAZER

This unit available as counter model or with mobile stand. Dip tank holds about 5 gallons of sugar glaze. Tank drain is in center front of unit. In operaton: 6 stainless steel rods are inserted into vertically spaced sockets in the back of the unit (3 each side). Doughnuts are strung on twelve rods, supplied with the unit, after dipping these rods, with doughnuts, are hung bridged across the rods extending out from the back for draining. The unit is fabricated from 16 ga. S/S, enclosed three sides and has a convenient work shelf on top.

AUTOMATIC MOBILE COOKIE DROPPER

Capable of producing a wide variety of cookies at the rate of up to 1200 dozen per hour. The machine measures 66" x 32" x 56" high. Has built-in shelf for die storage.

Features are:
- All parts in contact with dough and under the product zone are rustless:
    Stainless steel hopper
    Stainless steel table top - 22" x 65"
    Stainless steel pan guide and feed roll shafts
    Aluminum alloy feed rolls, feed chute, die holder, and dies
    Aluminum alloy cutter fingers
- Above parts easily removable without the use of tools for washing after use
- 30 quart capacity is standard - larger sizes available
- Compact fully enclosed geared in head motor unit with reduction gears running in oil bath and with direct linkage drive
- Drive gears operate feed rolls and pan belts through silent automatic clutches.
- Pans ride on two adjustable V belts
- Feed rolls are striated for positive dough feed
- Variable speed - 35-70 strokes per minute
- Adjustment knob for cookie thickness
- Adjustment knob for cookie spacing
- ½ HP, 1 phase, 115 volt, or 3 phase, 220 volt, complete with three wire 8 ft. cord with molded three prong grounding plug and adapter
- Mounted on 5" diameter ball bearing rubber tired (or plastic) casters - two swivel and two fixed
- Stainless steel - adjustable for 17" to 19" pans
- Dozens of rustless aluminum dies available. See separate die sheet

CUTTER MIXERS (VERTICAL)

Table top model 20" wide x 14" deep x 24" high. Standard accessories: shaft with narrow knives for all cutting operations, i.e. hamburg, hot dogs, bologna, vegetables, salads, cole slaw, cake batters, cheese and some salad dressings. Also yeast dough where fine textures are required. A knead/mix shaft is provided for mixing yeast dough where higher volume is desired.

Standard motor: 1 HP - 220 V. - Single phase, 10 amp.

Available: 2 HP - 220 V. - Three phase, 7 amp motor.

TYPICAL APPLICATIONS

PRODUCT	Lbs. Per Load	Time
Cookie Dough	8 lbs.	2-3 Min.
Fruit Filling	15 lbs.	1 Min.
Icing/Frosting	15 lbs.	1 Min.
Bread Crumbs	3 lbs.	1 Min.
Cole Slaw	9 lbs.	½ Min.
Mashed Potatoes (instant)	8 lbs.	½ Min.

CUTTER/MIXERS (VERTICAL)

Tilt forward type floor models — both 30 qt. and 45 qt. machines have same 23-3/8" wide x 22¼" deep base. Overall space required approximately 40" in width x 51" front to back in tilt position with cover open and 63" clear height. Both the 30 and the 45 qt. machines have 5 HP motors. Motors have dual voltage configuration - 200/60/3 or 230/460/60/3. Note 3 phase only available. Be sure to check your voltage and phase when ordering. The 200 or 230 V motor requires 30 amp service. The 460 V a 20 amp service.

Typical capacities for these are shown below.

Fig. 4-1

SOME TYPICAL PRODUCTION CAPACITIES			
Item	30 Qt. Unit	45 Qt. Unit	Time
Pizza Dough	12 to 24 lbs.	18 to 36 lbs.	2 to 3 Min.
Meat Loaf	12 to 25 lbs.	20 to 40 lbs.	1 to 2 Min.
Cole Slaw	10 to 20 lbs.	20 to 35 lbs.	30 to 45 Seconds
Mayonnaise	10 to 20 qts.	16 to 32 qts.	2 to 3 Min.
Tossed Salad	4 to 8 heads	6 to 10 heads	5 Seconds

NOTE: These machines are extremely versatile. The items listed in Fig. 4-1 represent only a few that may be processed.

41

Other vertical cutter/mixers are available with bowl sizes up to 120 qt. Motor speeds vary by manufacturer and some machines have two speed motors rated at 1500 and 3000 R.P.M.

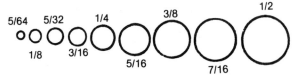

HELPFUL HINTS

A floor sink or floor drain at the point of discharge when the bowl is tilted to empty it and a wash-down hose are very handy and time saving for clean ups.

MEAT CHOPPERS OR GRINDERS

Many sizes and styles are available. Listed below is the typical production capability of various HP choppers to aid you in selecting the proper machine for your requirements.

The machines are table top models and require a space approximately 18" deep by 36" wide.

Machine Horsepower	Pounds of Meat Per Minute
1/4	5
1/2	8
1	16
2	35-40
3	35-40

NOTE: These figures are based on using plates with 1/8" dia. holes. Capacities increase substantially when using plates with larger holes.

Illustrated below are hole sizes of plates available, shown full size for handy reference.

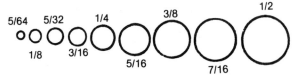

AUTOMATIC MEAT MARINATOR

A mobile, electric plug-in unit occupying approximately 24" x 36" of floor space with a revolving, liquid-tight drum has the capacity of marinating up to 24 head of chicken or 20 lbs. of meat in one 15 minute cycle. The undershelf holds a large capacity drain tray.

BUFFALO CUTTER/CHOPPER (Spinning Bowl Type)

The spinning bowl type food cutter has been a favorite for years. Usually considered a table-top machine, some are available with a pedestal base. Models are available with 1/3 HP motors and also with or without power drive hubs for other attachments. The machines require a space approximately 33" wide x 24" deep.

Fig. 4-2	SOME APPROXIMATE PRODUCTION FIGURES FOR SPINNING BOWL FOOD CUTTERS		
Item		Volume	Time
Bread Crumbs		5 lbs.	2 Min.
Cabbage		6 heads	1 Min.
Potatoes for Hash Browns		8 lbs.	1 Min.
Parsley		4 lbs.	1 Min.
Celery		6 lbs.	1 Min.
Onions		5 lbs.	1 Min.

FOOD CUTTERS (Continuous Feed)

NOTE: In general terms, Food Cutters differ from food processors in that they have a continuous feed only and the cut, grated or chopped food empties into any container of your choice. Food processors have bowls in which the food may be processed with various blades and attachments. Some processors have continuous feed attachments.

One might think of the smaller food processors as "souped-up" blendors having the advantage of larger cutting blades and the versatility of various attachments. The mid-size processors might be called little vertical cutter mixers, while the larger ones, up to 9 HP, actually are vertical cutter mixers equalling and even surpassing them in production capabilities.

HAND POWERED FOOD CUTTERS

These units clamp to table edge and allow food preparation at fairs and other locations without power requirements.

SOME TYPICAL FOOD CUTTER PRODUCTION GUIDES
(Continuous Feed)

Since cheese is considered to be the most difficult product to process some machines are rated as follows:

1/3 HP Motor — 200 lbs. cheese/hr.
1/2 HP Motor — 400 lbs. cheese/hr.
3/4 HP Motor — 600 lbs. cheese/hr.
1 HP Motor — 800 lbs. cheese/hr.

43

SOME OTHER APPROXIMATE PROCESSING CAPACITIES

Fig. 4-3

Food Item	1/2 HP	1 HP
Carrots - shredded	200	300 lbs. per hr.
Lettuce - chunks	400	700 lbs. per hr.
Lettuce - shredded	450	600 lbs. per hr.
Celery	600	600 lbs. per hr.
Cabbage - fine	400	500 lbs. per hr.
Cabbage - shredded	300	300 lbs. per hr.
Potatoes - hash brown	500	800 lbs. per hr.
Onions - chopped	350	350 lbs. per hr.
Bread Crumbs - fresh	150	200 lbs. per hr.

DOUGH DIVIDER - ROUNDER

Floor model machine is approximately 33" wide x 24" deep.
Motor 115 V., 1/2 HP — available in 18, 36 and 48 part dividing heads.
Production capabilities from 500 dozen up to over 1300 dozen rolls
per hour depending on size and dough mix.

FOOD CUTTER DISCS

Available discs for most food cutters are as follows: slicing, cubing, julienne, grating, shredding, french fry, shaving and crinkle cut.
Sizes to match any menu need.

Fig. 4-4

TABLE OF WEIGHTS

18-PART Divides & Rounds 18 Pcs. Range of sizes: 2 - 6 oz.		36-PART Divides & Rounds 36 Pcs. Range of sizes: ¾ - 2½ oz.		48-PART Divides & Rounds 48 Pcs. Range of sizes: ½ - 1¾ oz.	
Weight Each Roll	Weight Whole Dough	Weight Each Roll	Weight Whole Dough	Weight Each Roll	Weight Whole Dough
2 oz.......... 2 lbs. 4 oz.		3/4 oz........ 1 lb. 11 oz.		1/2 oz.......... 1 lb. 8 oz.	
2-1/2 oz....... 2 lbs. 13 oz.		1-1/3 oz...... 3 lbs. 0 oz.		3/4 oz........ 2 lbs. 4 oz.	
3 oz.......... 3 lbs. 6 oz.		1-1/2 oz....... 3 lbs. 6 oz.		1 oz.......... 3 lbs. 0 oz.	
3-1/2 oz....... 3 lbs. 15 oz.		1-2/3 oz...... 3 lbs. 12 oz.		1-1/4 oz....... 3 lbs. 12 oz.	
4 oz.......... 4 lbs. 8 oz.		1-5/6 oz...... 4 lbs. 2 oz.		1-1/2 oz....... 4 lbs. 8 oz.	
4-1/2 oz....... 5 lbs. 1 oz.		2 oz.......... 4 lbs. 8 oz.		1-3/4 oz....... 5 lbs. 4 oz.	
5 oz.......... 5 lbs. 10 oz.		2-1/6 oz....... 4 lb. 14 oz.			
5-1/2 oz....... 6 lbs. 3 oz.		2-1/3 oz...... 5 lbs. 4 oz.			
6 oz.......... 6 lbs. 12 oz.		2-2/2 oz...... 5 lbs. 10 oz.			

FRENCH FRY MACHINE

Dispenses cut and ready to fry portions at the rate of 400 portions per hour using dehydrated potato mix and water.

Machine is adjustable from 1 to 7 servings per cycle. It is a counter top machine 12¾" wide x 25" deep x 27" high — 115 V plug-in unit. Other comparable machines available.

MIXERS

Figure 4-5 shows mixer rating by amount of food which may be processed in relation to bowl size.

Fig. 4-5

Product	BOWL CAPACITY IN QUARTS							
	5	10	12	20	30	60	80	140
Mashed Potatoes	3 lbs.	8 lbs.	10 lbs.	15 lbs.	23 lbs.	40 lbs.	60 lbs.	100 lbs.
Mayonnaise (Qts. of Oil)	1½ qts.	3 qts.	4½ qts.	10 qts.	12 qts.	18 qts.	30 qts.	50 qts.
Pancake Batter	2 qts.	4 qts.	5 qts.	8 qts.	12 qts.	24 qts.	32 qts.	—
Layer Cake	3 lbs.	10 lbs.	12 lbs.	20 lbs.	30 lbs.	60 lbs.	90 lbs.	165 lbs.
Sugar Cookies	8 dz.	16 dz.	20 dz.	35 dz.	50 dz.	100 dz.	125 dz.	225 dz.
Dough (Light)	4 lbs.	11 lbs.	13 lbs.	25 lbs.	45 lbs.	80 lbs.	170 lbs.	210 lbs.
Dough (Heavy)	—	—	—	15 lbs.	30 lbs.	60 lbs.	140 lbs.	175 lbs.
Pie Dough	3 lbs.	9 lbs.	11 lbs.	18 lbs.	27 lbs.	50 lbs.	75 lbs.	125 lbs.
Pizza Dough	—	—	—	—	—	40 lbs.	85 lbs.	130 lbs.
Eggs & Sugar for Sponge Cake	2 lbs.	4 lbs.	5 lbs.	8 lbs.	12 lbs.	24 lbs.	40 lbs.	75 lbs.
Icing	2 lbs.	6 lbs.	7 lbs.	12 lbs.	18 lbs.	36 lbs.	65 lbs.	100 lbs.

NOTE: The above chart is subject to slight changes due to variations in different manufacturers models. It should be considered as maximum production.

MIXER CAPACITY CHART FOR PIZZA DOUGHS

Product	20 Qt. (lbs.)	30 Qt. (lbs.)	60 Qt. (lbs.)	1½ HP 80 Qt. (lbs.)	2 HP 80 Qt. (lbs.)	140 Qt. (lbs.)
Dough, Thin Pizza (40% AR)	9*	14*	40*	55*	85*	135*
Dough, Medium Pizza (50% AR)	10*	20*	70*	90*	155*	190*
Dough, Thick Pizza	20*	40*	70#	90#	155#	190#

The % AR (% Absorption Ratio) = Water weight divided by flour weight.
*1st Speed   #2nd Speed

Fig. 4-6

APPROXIMATE MIXER DIMENSIONS

Bowl Capacity	Width	Depth	Height	Style
5 Qt.	10½"	15"	17"	Counter Model
10 qt.	14"	16"	26"	Counter Model
12 qt.	15½"	19"	27"	Counter Model
20 Qt.	15½"	21"	30"	Counter Model
20 Qt.	21"	21½"	41"	Floor Model
30 Qt.	21"	24"	45"	Floor Model
60 Qt.	27½"	39"	56"	Floor Model
80 Qt.	27½"	41½"	56"	Floor Model
140 Qt.	29½"	45½"	71½"	Floor Model

MIXER HORSEPOWER AND HUB ATTACHMENT SIZES

Fig. 4-7

Quarts	HP	Hub Size
5	1/6	#10
10	1/4	#10
12	1/4	#12
20	1/3	#12
30	1/2	#12
60	1	#22
80	1½ or 2	#22
140	5	#22

COMMON ADAPT DOWN BOWL ATTACHMENTS
(In Quart Sizes)

FROM	TO
10	3
20	12
30	20
60	30-40
80	30-40-60
140	30-40-60-80-100

COMMON ATTACHMENTS FOR MIXERS
SLICER SHREDDER AND GRATER W/PLATES
SPEED DRIVE - Increases hub speed approximately 3 times.

Dicer	Bowl Splash Cover
Meat Chopper	Bowl Extension Ring
Tray Holder	Bowl Truck and Adapters
Oil Dropper	Soup Strainers and Jackets

All mixers of course have available a wide selection of dough hooks, dough knives and whips.

For small mixers up to 20 qt., stands are available with shelves under for attachments and a tool pole at the rear corner. Locking casters optional.

For establishments requiring only the vegetable slicer or the dicer or for those who wish a separate station where slicing, grating, dicing, cutting or shredding may be done without tying up the power source of other machines, two power drive units are available.

One operates at 700 R.P.M. AND IS SUITED TO THE VEGETABLE SLICER ATTACHMENT ONLY.

The other runs at 350 R.P.M. and accommodates either the slicer or dicer attachments.

Each has 115 V - ½ HP motor and is approximately 10" wide x 20" deep x 17" high.

HAND MIXER - COMMERCIAL

This hand held mixer features a 110 volt variable speed drive assembly. The attachments are 16" in length and available as beaters, cutter, blenders and non cutting - blending for mixing only. The unit comes with a wall bracket for storage. The unit may be used for mashing potatoes, whipping cream, batters or dressings and for stirring of stews and soups.

47

PASTA MACHINES

A small pasta machine capable of producing 27 to 35 lbs. per hour is approximately 15" wide x 30" deep x 47" high. By changing dies it will produce typical "Bologna" pasta, sfoglia, noodles and spaghetti of different diameters. A ravioli machine is available as an attachment. The motor is 120 Volt 1½ HP.

LARGER PASTA MACHINES AVAILABLE

Fig. 4-8

| No. | OVERALL SIZE | | | Production Lbs. Per Hour | Voltage | Motor HP | Mixer HP |
	Width	Depth	Height				
1	25"	42"	55"	55 to 65	120/60/1	1.5	1
2	79'	39½"	79"	130 to 155	240/60/1	3	1
3	63"	54"	83'	220 to 265	240/60/1	5.5	1.5
4	98½"	54"	79"	220 to 305	240/60/1	(two) 3	1.5
5	122"	54"	83"	440 to 485	240/60/1	(two) 5.5	1.5

NOTE: Number 3 and 5 are custom.

Number 4 and 5 have two extrusion assemblies, can produce two different types of pasta at the same time.

PEELERS

Available vegetable peelers are listed below. The 1/3 HP model may be ordered as a counter model for use on a sink drainboard or with optional mobile or enclosed base with peel trap. All require electric, water and drain.

Fig. 4-9

| Item | PEELER HORSEPOWER | | |
	1/3 HP	3/4 HP	1 HP
Potatoes Peel Time	15-20 lbs. 1-3 Min.	30-33 lbs. 1-3 Min.	50-60 lbs. 1-3 Min.
Carrots Peel Time	6-12 lbs. 1-3 Min.	15-25 lbs. 1-3 Min.	Not Recommended
Beets Peel Time	10-15 lbs. 1 Min. Maximum	15-25 lbs. 1 Min. Maximum	Not Recommended

The 3/4 HP model is available with an optional base for use with a disposer unit.

PIE FORMING MACHINE

A typical 115 V - 1/4 HP counter unit - 24" wide x 19" deep x 28" high forms up to 700 (1" to 12") plain, crimped or spyder pie crust shells per hour. Other style machines will produce up to 350 top and 350 bottom shells per hour. Specialty styles available for making tarts, shells, and other snack food specialties.

PIE DOUGH ROLLERS

A typical 115 V - 1/4 HP counter pie dough roller 26" wide x 30" deep x 14" high having a 7" upper roller and 14" finishing roller with thickness adjustments is available as a counter top unit or with mobile base.
Many other styles and sizes are available

- combination pie dough roller and pastry sheeters for pie crusts, coffee cakes, buns, sweet rolls, danish, etc.

- triple-duty units for pie crusts, pastry sheeting and bread molding

- all available with various conveyor lengths and motor sizes.

PIZZA CRUST ROLLERS

The three machines listed below are available with right or left hand feed and thickness adjustment. Floor stand optional.

Fig. 4-10

HP	Pizza Dia.	Machine Size	Top Roller	Finish Roller
1/3	9"-11" or 13"	29" x 33" x 14" high	7"	14"
1/3	10"-12" or 14"	32" x 33" x 14" high	7"	17"
1/2	12"-14" or 16"	36" x 33" x 14" high	7"	21"

MEAT SAWS
Fig. 4-11

TYPICAL SPECIFICATIONS

HP	Blade	Cutting Clearance	Movable Table	Travel	Approx. Floor Space Req'd.
1	5/8" x 98"	13-5/16" x 10-7/8" wide	15" x 20"	18"	32" x 45" deep
2 or 3	5/8" x 112"	15-1/4" x 13-1/4" wide	15" x 19"	22"	35" x 45" deep
2 or 3	5/8" x 128"	18-1/8" x 15-11/16" wide	17½" x 24"	24"	40" x 52" deep

NOTE: 1 or 2 HP motors available 115 V to 460 V - 1 or 3 phase.
3 HP high speed motor 3 phase only.

49

SLICERS

Slicers range in sizes as shown in Fig. 4-12 and specifications vary by manufacturer. One important factor to consider when purchasing is whether the slicer is gear or belt driven.

Fig. 4-12

Feed Style	Knife Diameter	Cut Thickness
Flat - Hand	9" to 10"	0" to ¾'
Angle - Hand	8" to 12"	0" to 1¾"
Angle - Automatic	10" to 12"	0" to 1¾"

STANDARD SLICER KNIVES

Slicer knives are available in diameters of 8"-9"-10"-11"-11½"-11¾" or 12".
Available optional slicer attachments:

> Multiple carriage fences to hold tomatoes, etc.
> Tubular chutes for celery, etc.
> Stackers
> Spiked holders
> Heat lamps for hot roast beef, etc.

ELECTRONIC, DIGITAL AUTOMATIC PORTION CONTROL FOR SLICERS

Ideal for sandwich and deli shops, units adapt to most automatic and manual slicers and offer a remote portion control and digital read-out to 1/10th of an ounce.

Weighing unit rests on slicer receiving bed. Remote read-out and control unit automatically shuts off slicer when preselected portion weight is reached.

Available as single push button unit that can be simply re-set to any desired weight or as a unit having 4 push-button settings to meet varied portion control requirements.

OPTIONAL FEATURES: Resetable digital portion counter or non-resetable portion counter which provides a locked-in running count of total portions.

The following chart shows what small overweight errors can cost in lost profits.

Fig. 4-14

Amount Over	Period of Time	WEIGHINGS PER DAY					
		at $2.39 per lb.		at $2.99 per lb.		at $3.69 per lb.	
		100	300	100	300	100	300
1/4 oz.	Week	26.11	78.33	32.60	98.07	40.35	121.04
Over-	Month	109.66	328.98	137.30	411.90	169.47	508.41
Weight	Year	1315.92	3947.75	1647.60	4942.80	2033.64	6100.92

AUTOMATIC SLICER, CONVEYOR, STACKER

Fully automated table top slicing machine. (Stationary or mobile base available.)

Size 23" wide, 20" deep, 20" high — extended carriage and conveyor increase width to approximately 90".

Ideal for Deli or Supermarket installations. Unit is capable of producing a continuous supply of freshly cut food, either shingled (fanned out) or stacked from single pieces up to 5½" x 8-7/8" or from any combination of various items which will fit in the feed tray at one time.

Slice thickness adjustable from approx. 1/64" to 5/16". Unit has a 'last slice' attachment. Standard carriage allows slicing approximately 7¼" without reclamping — long carriage allows for slicing up to 12" without reclamping.

When the desired and preselected number of slices (up to 12 at a time) or a stack up to approx. 3¼" high has been reached the machine switches itself off automatically.

Use of the automatic conveyor belt and receiving tray in conjunction with the control panel provides many options ideally suited to large volume operations, particularly when associated with vacuum packaging.

Use F.E.F. Personal Assistance Service for further information.

HELPFUL HINTS

It is often desirable to have your slicer mobile. Stands with dropdown side shelves and angle ledge pan slides underneath are available.

TENDERIZERS

Typical size: 12" x 20" x 20" high - motor ½ HP - 115V plug-in.
Knife styles: Cutting - tenderizing or cubing only
Cutter-knitter - frozen foods
Variable feed openings. Star knives for scoring meat available.

51

A very versatile piece of equipment — can be used for tenderizing a variety of steaks from beef, pork, veal, lamb or turkey and also to knit in suet, onions, cheese, parlsey or pork fat if desired.

SHRIMP PEELING AND DEVEINING MACHINES

These high production machines, used extensively by commercial shrimp processers, are also ideally suited for restaurants having high volume shrimp consumption. Depending on labor costs and size of shrimp used, the machines usually become economically justified when peeling over 500 pounds per week. The savings then make it profitable even though the machine is idle most of the time. Other advantages are that large quantities can be peeled on short notice for unexpected demands and the quality of the shrimp is improved as a result of less handling.

Two machines, each being 38¾" wide x 27" deep x 37" high, with 1/3 HP motors, 115 or 230 V single phase are available. The machines require water lines and should be operated above a floor drain.

The difference in the two units is that one peels and deveins the shrimp completely and can be set to split the shrimp open for butterfly style serving. The unit will process 4,300 shrimp per hour. This machine can also split the shell, remove the sand vein and leave the shell on for cooked in shell shrimp.

The second model leaves the tail shell on. The style shrimp it can produce are peeled and deveined round, butterfly or western style, all with tail on. This unit processes 3,800 shrimp per hour. The following chart shows production in pounds per hour by shrimp size.

PRODUCTION RATE BY POUNDS PER HOUR
(For 4,300/Hr. Machine)

Shrimp Count	Pounds Per Hr.
10/15	275-300
16/20	210-275
21/25	170-210
26/30	140-170
31/35	120-140
36/42	100-120
43/50	85-100
51/60	70-85
61/70	60-70
71/90	49-60

An operator platform accessory for the machine provides easy mobility so that the machine may be moved to storage space when not in use.

SOME INTERESTING SHRIMP FACTS

Number of Shrimp (Shell on) Per Lb.	Trade Name
Under 10	Extra Colossal
10-15	Colossal
16-20	Extra Jumbo
21-25	Jumbo
26-30	Extra Large
31-35	Large
36-42	Medium Large
43-50	Medium
51-60	Small
61-70	Extra Small
Over 70	Tiny

Raw in-shell shrimp lose 25% weight in peeling.
Raw cleaned, peeled and deveined shrimp lose 25% in cooking.
A skilled worker can hand peel and devein approximately 1 lb. of medium shrimp in 12 minutes.

MOBILE VEGETABLE DRAINERS

Fig. 4-13

Size	Capacity (Lettuce)	
20 Gallon	1 Carton Heads	1¼ Cartons Prepared
32 Gallon	1½ Carton Heads	2 Cartons Prepared

These units have an inter-liner with a perforated bottom. Washed items drip dry into the water reservoir. The spigot permits draining into a floor drain or receptacle. Excellent for thawing meat or poultry. Mobility eliminates double handling. Washed lettuce may be rolled into walk-in cooler. Defrosted foods may be rolled to point of use.

VEGETABLE WASHER-DRIER

A new mobile, 115 volt plug-in vegetable washer and spin-drier with a 20 gallon inner liner can dry up to one case of lettuce per minute. Removable polyethylene liner permits chilling lettuce in same container. Approximate overall dimensions are 18" diameter x 31" high.

VEGETABLE SINKS (Free Standing)

In this chapter we will discuss only vegetable sinks, free standing and drop-ins. If, as in many cases, the sink is to serve both as a

53

pot and vegetable sink we suggest referring to Chapter 9 (Ware-washing) where the many variables in sink construction are illus-trated and described in detail. Garbage disposers can be very useful in vegetable sinks. These also are detailed in Chapter 9.

The most popular size for commercial sink compartments is 24" x 24" x 14" deep. The backsplash is usually 2" thick and the rolled edge on the ends and front usually measure 1½". Using these stand-ards a single compartment would measure 27" side to side x 27½" front to back.

Let's stop right here and clear up a lot of confusion about stand-ard dimensioning practices. Normally as you face a piece of equip-ment the width or length (depending on the proportions) is the dis-tance from side to side — the depth is from front to back and the height, from top to bottom; i.e., a standard electric range is consid-ered 36" wide, 38" deep and 36" high. A standard restaurant range would measure 5'-0" wide x 32" deep x 36" high.

Sinks, especially die stamped drop-ins, are the confusing excep-tions since the depth of a sink is quite naturally considered the ver-tical dimension of the part that holds the water. The distance from front to back becomes the width and side to side becomes the length, even though it may be shorter than the width.

Shelving is another less confusing exception.

Now back to sinks — the less expensive method of constructing 2 or 3 compartment sinks is with a single thickness of metal divid-ing the compartments (these may be N.S.F. approved). To figure the overall length of one of this construction add 3" to the sum of the length of the number of compartments; i.e., the overall length of a 24" x 24" three compartment sink would be 3 times 24" (72") plus 3" for the rolled edges (75").

The preferred method of construction is to have each compart-ment with fully coved inside corners. These are usually constructed with a 1" space between each compartment. Don't forget that 1" when figuring overall lengths. See Page 300-301 for illustration.

SOME POPULAR SINK COMPARTMENTS

Length (Side to Side)		Width (Front to Back)
18"	x	18"
18"	x	21"
18"	x	24"
24"	x	21"
24"	x	24"
30"	x	21"
30"	x	24"
30"	x	30"
36"	x	24"
36"	x	30"

Standard depths — 14" & 16". Others are available.

As mentioned, dimensions and details vary with each manufacturer. Use our charts to guide you but check your suppliers' dimensions if you have a tight fit.

DRAINBOARDS

Once again refer to Chapter 9 for details of construction. Here it will suffice to say that drainboards to fit any width sink are made in standard lengths of 18", 24", 30" and 36". They may be in integral part of the sink or removable. Any drainboard exceeding 36" should have its own support legs at the end.

HELPFUL HINTS

There are many options for standard sinks and those for custom sinks are almost limitless. As with any equipment, when you are shopping for prices be certain of the options and quality you want and that all bids incorporate these items.

Some options to standard sinks are:

14 or 16 gauge metal
430 or 302 stainless steel
Interconnected waste lines
Lever handle or basket wastes
Sink heaters for sanitizing
Stand pipes
Inter-connected overflows
Number of faucets
Soap Holders
Pylon style base

Sink covers
Strainer baskets
Type of gussets
Painted, S.S. clad or S.S.
   tubular legs
White metal, stainless or
   flanged feet
Leg crossbracing
Overshelves

With just a few words of caution we will end the chapter on vegetable sinks and hope you found it more informative than boring.

For sanitation purposes and ease of cleaning, sinks should be set 3" from or sealed to the wall. Shut-off valves are recommended for the water lines. Water and drain lines brought out from the wall make clean-up much easier. Be **sure** drain lines are low enough, especially if you are installing a disposer. Where possible be sure a switch mounting bracket be provided for disposers. Be sure you have enough faucets and consider fast flow faucets for large sinks. Much time can be wasted waiting for sinks to fill. Lastly, consider high end splashes when sinks are in corners or next to high items like refrigerators.

FISH SINKS

Standard fish cleaning sinks are available as follows:

48" or 60" long with 1 sink at left, cutting board and scrap chute right.

72" long with 1 sink centered cutting board and scrap chute each end.

72" long with 2 sinks centered cutting board and scrap chute each end.

96" long with either 2 or 3 sinks, centered cutting board and scrap chute each end.

120" long with three sinks, centered cutting board and scrap chute each end.

120" long with 1 sink each end, 2 cutting boards and scrap chutes centered.

All units 24" wide, sinks 8" deep, faucets 8" centers with hose spray included, wastes 1½" basket type, ¾" thick poly-vance cutting boards — back and endsplash 12" high. Optional: knife guard, knife sterilizer, overhead package shelf.

DROP-IN SINKS

Drop-in stainless steel sinks are available in so many sizes and styles and these vary by manufacturer, that for the purposes of this book, we shall list generalities only.

> Maximum overall width approximately 22"
> Maximum overall length approximately 63"
> Sink depth average 6" to 10"
> Faucet & spray attachments variable
> 18 or 20 gauge 302 stainless steel
> Bowls die stamped for disposers
> Sound deadening coating available

The available styles are: single compartment, single compartment with drainboard, two compartment with equal or different sized compartments, three equal sized or two large compartments with one smaller compartment in center and corner models.

HAND SINKS · STANDARD SIZES

BOWL SIZES

L x W x D	Overall
20" x 16" x 8"	25" x 23"
14" x 10" x 5"	17" x 15"

Wall mounts or pedestal style. Options: Gooseneck faucets, soap dispensers, foot valves, wall mount kits.

56

BUTCHER BLOCKS

Butcher blocks usually measure 34" to the top surface and are available in the following sizes:

12" Thick Blocks:	18" x 18", 18" x 24", 24" x 24", 24" x 30" and 30" x 30"
14" Thick Blocks:	18" x 24", 20" x 20", 24" x 24", 24" x 30" and 30" x 30"
16" Thick Blocks:	18" x 24", 24" x 214", 24" x 30", 24" x 36", 30" x 30", 30" x 36", 30" x 40" and 30" x 60"

BAKER'S TABLES

Baker's tables are available with 1½", 2" or 3" thick maple tops or stainless steel tops. End and backsplashes are usually 1¾" or 3" high.

STANDARD SIZES AVAILABLE

Width		**Length**
24"-30" or 36"	x	48"-60"-72"-84"-96" or 120"

OPTIONS (Single or in Combination)

Plastic composition tops	Tool Drawers
Open bases	Enclosed tier drawers
Undershelves	Portable cutting boards
Tilting Bins	Overshelves
Mobile bins	Overshelves w/spice bins

MOLDED PLASTIC INGREDIENT BINS

These units made from white USDA approved material with all coved corners are available in sizes and options as shown below.
Fig. 4-15

SIZE	CAPACITY				EQUIPMENT
	Cu.Ft.	Gal.	Sugar	Flour	
12"x29"x28¾" h.	3.4	26	175 lbs.	125 lbs.	Removable body - sliding lid - hinged lid - all or two swivel casters.
21½"x23½"x23" h.	3.9	34	195 lbs.	140 lbs.	Sliding or hinged lid - all swivel casters
15"x29"x28-3/8" h.	4.4	34½	220 lbs.	155 lbs.	Sliding or hinged lid - 2 fixed 2 swivel casters
21½"x23½"x28-3/8" h.	5.1	43	260 lbs.	185 lbs.	Sliding or hinged lid - all swivel casters
18"x29"x28-3/8" h.	5.7	44	285 lbs.	205 lbs.	Sliding or hinged lid - 2 fixed 2 swivel casters

STAINLESS STEEL INGREDIENT BINS

Available with all cove corner body on base with full perimeter bumper and swivel casters.

Fig. 4-16

Capacity	Size
100 lb.	12¾'' x 22'' x 29'' high
150 lb.	17½'' x 22'' x 29'' high
200 lb.	20'' x 22'' x 29'' high
250 lb.	23'' x 25'' x 29'' high

OPTIONS: Full sliding, hinged in center or half sliding covers.

STANDARD WORK TABLES

What may be considered standard work tables and optional components (variable by manufacturers) is listed below.
All are 34'' high to working surface.

Standard Widths		Standard Lengths
18'' - 24'' or 30''	x	3'-4'-5'-6'-7' or 8'

Stainless steel tops are usually 14 gauge with roll-down edges and bullnose corners.
Maple top tables are usually 1¾'' or 3'' thick. Either S/S or maple tables may have back and, or end splashes in varying heights from 1½'' to 12''.
Tool drawers are available with either S/S, galv. or plastic bowls in 15'' x 20'' x 5'' or 20'' x 20'' x 5'' sizes. They may be open type construction with channel slides or be semi-enclosed or totally enclosed with roller bearing glides. Locks may also be provided.

AVAILABLE OPTIONS FOR STANDARD WORK TABLES

Sinks
Lazy Susan pot racks
Pan slide cabinets
  (for 18'' x 26'' pans) - may be
  mounted on table top
  or bottom shelf
Enclosed drawer tiers

Extra angle iron, channel or hot
  channel bracing under top
Painted, S/S clad or S/S Tubular
  legs
White metal or S/S feet
Locking casters
Drip troughs for coffee urns

MOBILE PREPARATION TABLE
For Hamburg, Specialty Sandwich or Pizza Assembly

Units are 31½" H x 28¼" W and either 52" or 72" long. 14 ga. stainless steel heated top has crumb chute and drawer. 52" unit holds seven 1/6 size ice chilled pans and three 5" round pans. 72" unit holds eight 1/6 size and two 5" round pans. An optional 3 tier bun rack adds 19" to length. Units are 115 V - 52" model is 135 W. 72" model is 250 W.

Companion mobile unit to hold front return conveyor broiler and toaster is available.

POT RACKS

Common pot racks, either table mounted or ceiling hung, usually have one perimeter bar with a center bar approximately 1 ft. lower. Wall mounted pot racks are available with single bars or with 2 bars, one extending out from the wall above the other. Standard lengths are 48"-60"-72"-84" and 96". Double pot hooks hang over the bars and may be spaced as required.

A single pole merry-go-round pot rack with a round utensil shelf is available for mounting on existing work tables.

The recommended height to the top bar of a pot rack is 7'-6" above the floor.

STANDARD STAINLESS STEEL OVERHEAD SHELVES

Standard widths of shelves are 10"-12"-18" or 24". Standard lengths are 48"-60"-72"-84"-96" or 108". Standard metal gauges used are 18 - 16 or 14.

Naturally the wider and longer the shelf the heavier the metal should be.

The shelving may be ordered for either single or double table mounting. Standard spacing for shelving is 18" from the table top to the first shelf with 12" between shelves.

Standard wall hung shelves are available in the same gauges and sizes as above.

HELPFUL HINTS

Always give careful consideration to the weight of items you intend to place on shelving making certain that the supports are properly spaced. Extra bracing under the shelves may be required. If you intend to have electrical equipment on or under the shelves, such as heat lamps, the wiring may often be run up inside of the support tubing.

The authors cannot over emphasize the importance of making certain that there is ample support in a wall before ordering any wall hung unit.

SPECIALIZED PREPARATION EQUIPMENT

OLD FASHIONED ICE CREAM FREEZERS

These commercial, power driven machines have an appealing 'old fashioned' look and they produce 100% natural ice cream the same way Great Grandma used to with the use of rock salt and ice.

Features: Produces natural ice cream without injecting air or adding chemicals. Melts slowly and will not harden. Makes a batch in approximately 20 minutes. Quick change over. Produces ice cream, sherbet or slush desserts.

SOME AVAILABLE SIZES

Capacity	Dimensions	Motor
20 Qt.	36" x 21" x 39"	3/4 HP - 120/240 - 1 Ph.
15 Qt.	34" x 21" x 39"	3/4 HP - 120/240 - 1 Ph.
10 Qt.	14" x 27" x 22"	1/4 HP - 120V
8 Qt.	14" x 27" x 21"	1/4 HP - 120V
6 Qt.	12" x 12" x 12"	1/12 HP - 120V

TABLE TOP CROISSANT ROLLER

Measuring only 15" H x 15" W x 35" Long can produce from 700 to 1200 croissants per hour from pre-cut dough. Adjustable pressure control allows for more or less curls. Either front or rear discharge as desired. Electrical specifications: 1/2 HP, 115V or 220V, single phase, 2 amps. For high volume establishment machines with up to 3500 and 7000 croissants per hour are available.

Chapter 5

COOKING
EQUIPMENT

The heavyweights of the food service system, a complete list of all cooking equipment giving pertinent data as to power requirements, capacities, preheat times and a host of other facts, all by category from broilers to steamers and on into all the fun food machines.

Do a little brainstorming and you'll be able to match your menu items properly. While keeping with our policy of foregoing brand names of manufacturers, our offer to assist is listed in the front of FEF.

NOTE: Watch your options. Most of the cooking equipment listed will have available numerous options. Review them before final selection, verify your power and venting requirements and breeze through the energy chapter for applicable data.

AVERAGE B.T.U. RATINGS FOR COOKING EQUIPMENT
(The low to high rating will depend on final selection.)

		B.T.U.
BROILERS	Counter or Back Shelf Salamander	30,000-45,000
	Upright Radiant or Infrared	50,000-100,000
	Double Oven and under or side by side style Radiant or Infrared	160,000-280,000
BROILER	Char Style	70,000-96,000
FRYERS	Small	27,000-48,000
	Medium	60,000-170,000
	Large	80,000-212,000
FRYERS	Pressure	57,000-90,000
FRY PANS	Tilt	80,000-105,000
GRILLES		24,000-240,000
RANGES Heavy Duty	Top Burners	17,000-20,000
	Ovens - Range	30,000-35,000
	Total Average Range	92,000-195,000
RANGES	Restaurant Style - 60" Model 6 burners, 24" grill, 2 ovens	190,000
STEAMERS	Kettles	100,000

(Continued)

AVERAGE B.T.U. RATINGS FOR COOKING EQUIPMENT (Cont.)
(The low to high rating will depend on final selection.)

		B.T.U.
STEAMERS	Compartment	40,000-225,000
OVENS	Convection, Counter	35,000 Average
	Full Size	75,000-115,000
	Deck Ovens, per deck	30,000-240,000
	Pizza, per deck	50,000-140,000

NOTE: Sizes of these pieces of equipment and their capacities will be found further ahead in this chapter.

TYPICAL PREHEAT TIMES — GAS EQUIPMENT

Broilers - Radiant	15-20 min.
Infrared	1 min.
Branding Grills	20-30 min.
Char Broilers	20 min.
Grills	20-30 min.
Fryers	10-12 min.
Fry Pan Tilt	5- 7 min.
Hot Top Range	20-30 min.
Ovens - Convection 350⁰	10-15 min.
Ovens - Deck	30-60 min.
Ovens - Range	15-30 min.
Steamer - Compartment	5-15 min.
Steam Kettle	10-20 min.

Steamers and kettles will vary with type of heat generation.

TYPICAL KW RATINGS FOR ELECTRIC COOKING EQUIPMENT
(Sizes and production will be discussed further on in this chapter.)

ITEM		K.W.
BROILERS	Counter	12
	Upright	12 to 32
	Char Type, 2 ft.	8
	Char Type, 3 ft.	12
FRYERS	Small	4.5 to 5.5
	Medium	12
	Large	22

(Continued)

TYPICAL KW RATINGS FOR ELECTRIC COOKING EQUIPMENT (Cont.)

(Sizes and production will be discussed further on in this chapter.)

ITEM		K.W.
FRYERS, PRESSURE		
	Counter Style	6
	Floor Style	11
GRILLS		6 to 32
TILT FRY PAN		7.5 to 21
STEAM KETTLE 5 Gal. to 100 Gal.		6 to 18
COMPARTMENT STEAMER		24 to 48
PIZZA OVENS	Counter	1.8 to 3.5
	Deck - One	7.5
	Two	14
	Three	21
CONVECTION OVENS		
	Counter	5.6
	Full Size Per Section	11
DECK OVENS		7 to 11 per deck
RANGES	Top Burners	11 to 16
	Ovens Below	6

TYPICAL PREHEAT TIMES FOR ELECTRIC COOKING EQUIPMENT

BROILERS	15-20 min.
FRYERS	Average 6 min.
GRILLS - to 325°	5-8 min.
TILT FRY PAN	10 min.
*STEAM KETTLE	10-15 min.
*COMPARTMENT STEAMER	10-15 min.

*Will vary on boiler - pressure and KW load.

OVENS
Range	20 min.
Deck	40 min. average deck
.Convection	9-10 min.

RANGES
Hot Top	50 min.
French Top	30 min.
Open Burners	5 min.

BROILERS — Styles Available

COUNTER MODELS:
- Gas Infra Red
- Gas Ceramic Fired
- Electric - Element Style
- Gas Broiler/Grill Combinations
- Quartz Electric/Grill Combination
- Rotary Style Electric Continuous Run
- Rotary Style - Cradle or Rotating Type
- Over and Under Type Fired Gas & Electric
- Char Electric & Gas
- Branding Char Flavored, called grill or broiler (See Grills)
- Quartz only

FLOOR MODELS
- Gas Infra Red
- Gas Ceramic Fired
- Electric Element Style
- Over and Under Fired
- Rotisseries
- Mobile Broilers - outside use

BRAINSTORMING BROILERS

UPRIGHT BATTERY STYLE, GAS
1) Infra red or ceramic fired?
   (Is oven above heated by excess broiler heat into ceramics - A free oven for finishing and holding product?)
2) Oven below?
3) Adequate grease drawer?
4) Does grid adjust easily?

COUNTER BROILERS, GAS
1) If griddle top, are enough BTU's available to broil efficiently?
2) Is grid adjustable by tension or glides only?
3) If ceramics, are they easily replaced? Separate zone controls? Or does one control heat entire broiler?
4) Do grids have pull out safety stops?
5) Is broiler flue adequate to remove smoke and odors?

ELECTRIC
Optional combinations:
1) Counter style
2) Single section on base oven or convection oven
3) Finishing oven above
4) 2 Sections on base or oven
5) Electrical base for controls
6) Separate controls for all functions
7) Easy adjust grid
8) Ease of cleaning

64

BRAINSTORMING CHAR BROILERS — Electric and Gas

1) Is there separate zone heat control?
2) If gas, is there a finishing grid under main section for casseroles, cheese melting?
3) If gas, will you save on insurance and venting costs with radiant shield style burners over char rock style?
4) Is side and back splash available for safety and clean up?
5) Provision for a work shelf or landing area in front of broiler?
6) Is grid adjustable or tilt design?

NOTE: When grid size and production is listed please allow for size of your particular product for more exact ratings. We find square inch conversion most helpful.

TYPICAL GAS BROILERS
(Rated as sq. ft. usable area for product and approximate BTU's)

Style	Square Feet Area	Approx. BTU
Upright Range Battery	3.3-5	70,000-100,000
Counter Grill/Broiler	2.3-3.3	35,000-45,000
Back Shelf Broiler	1.5-2.8	30,000-45,000
Char Broilers	1.2-2.7	40,000-50,000

UPRIGHT BROILERS, GAS
(Typical Sizes and Load)

OVERALL SIZE: 34" to 36" long, 35" to 42" deep, 60" to 74" high
GRID SIZE: 26" x 26" or 26" x 33" deep

Food Item	Approx. Per Load
T-Bone Steak	12
Sirloin Steak	18
4" Hamburg	42
Lobster	2-6
Lamb Chops	60

65

TYPICAL SIZES ELECTRIC BROILERS

DESCRIPTION	W″	D″	H″	KW
1 Section Counter	36	34-3/8	34	12
1 Section on 1-pan oven	36	38-1/4	64	18
1 Section on convection oven	36	38-1/4	64	18.8
1 Section on cabinet base	36	38	64	12
2 Sections on 1-pan oven	36	38-1/4	78	30
2 Sections on convection oven	36	38-1/4	78	30.8
2 Sections on cabinet base	36	38	78	24

UPRIGHT ELECTRIC BROILERS
(Typical Size and Load - 1 Section Production)

OVERALL SIZE: 36″ x 36″ x 67″ high
GRID SIZE: 25″ wide x 22½″ deep

Item	Product Weight	Production Per Hour
Strip Steak	¾ lb.	124 hr.
Chicken Halves	1 lb.	36 hr.
Lobster Tails	¾ lb.	236 hr.

NOTE: Using square inch of grid and square inch of product divide for actual load.

Above grid $\quad 25$
$$\frac{22}{50}$$
$$\frac{50}{550 \text{ Sq. Inches}}$$

Strip Steak 3″ x 8″ = 24 sq. inches

$$24 \overline{\smash{)}550} = \text{Approx. 22 per load}$$

22
48
70

BROILED FOODS DONENESS GUIDE

Description	Product Is
Rare	Wide, deep red center
Medium Rare	Deep red center
Medium	Deep pink center
Medium Well	Light pink center
Well Done	Brown center

66

COMPARATIVE TIME CHART FOR GAS BROILERS

Food Item	Char Broil	Radiant Broil	Infra Red
1'' Thick Steak	8-9 min.	8-9 min.	4 min.
1½'' Thick Steak	12-14 min.	13-15 min.	6½ min.
2'' Thick Steak (med. rare)	16-20 min.	18-20 min.	8-9 min.
¼ lb. Burger	4 min.	4 min.	2 min.
½'' Thick Burger	5 min.	5 min.	3 min.
¾'' Thick Burger (med. rare)	7 min.	8 min.	4 min.
¾'' Chop (well)	7-8 min.	6-7 min.	3-4 min.

ELECTRIC BROILING GUIDE

MEAT	THICKNESS (Inches)	Total Time, Minutes (One-half time on each side)		
		RARE	MEDIUM	WELL DONE
BEEF				
Rib Steak	1	6-8	8-10	10-12
Club Steak	1	6-8	8-10	10-12
Porterhouse	1	6-8	8-10	10-12
Porterhouse	1½	8-10	11-13	14-16
Porterhouse	2	10-12	13-15	16-18
Sirloin	1	6-8	8-10	10-12
Sirloin	1½	8-10	11-13	14-16
Sirloin	2	10-12	13-15	16-18
Ground Beef Patties	¾	3-4	4-6	6-8
Tenderloin	1	6-8	8-10	10-12
LAMB				
Rib or Loin Chops (1 rib)	¾	—	8-10	10-12
Double Rib	1½	—	11-13	14-16
Lamb Shoulder Chops	¾	—	8-10	10-12
Lamb Shoulder Chops	1½	—	11-13	14-16
Lamb Patties	¾	—	4-6	6-8
HAM AND SAUSAGE				
Ham Slices	½	—	—	6-8
Ham Slices	¹¼	—	—	8-10
Ham Slices	1	—	—	10-12
Sausage Links (12/lb.)	—	—	—	4-5
BROILING CHICKENS				
Halves (1½ lb.)	—	—	—	18-22

QUARTZ BROILER AND GRILL COMBINATION
(Counter Style)

SIZE: 48" wide, 30" deep - 24 KW, 220V, 1 or 3 phase.

A 24" hood above grill slides to desired location over cooking surface. The cooking surface on this unit is both grill and grooved grill. The hood has quartz heaters that provide infrared heat above the food.

These combination quartz broilers are available in many widths and top configurations. The operator may choose solid grill tops, grooved grill tops and combinations. The quartz top may be left in the upright position for grilling only.

QUARTZ BROILER AND GRILL COMBINATION

SUGGESTED COOKING CHART
(This time and temperature chart is suggested as a guide only.)

Grill Temp	Product		Broiler Time
350°	**HAMBURGER**		
	2 patties per lb., 10 per load		3 min.
	4 patties per lb., 16 per load		1½ min.
	6 patties per lb., 20 per load		1 min.
	8 patties per lb., 20 per load		40 sec.
350°	**STEAKS**		
	½" to ¾" thick, medium		3 min.
	¾" to 1¼" thick, medium		4½ min.
350°	**LAMB CHOPS**		
	1" thick		3½ min.
350°	**PORK CHOPS**		
	¾" thick		3½ min.
350°	**LIVER**		
	3/8" thick breaded and oiled both sides		2 min.
350°	**SALMON**		
	Steak or Filet ¾" thick		3½ min.
350°	**LOBSTER**		
	Meat out of shell broil shell at same time to color		2 min.
350°	**HALIBUT**		
	¾" thick		3½ min.
350°	**SOLE**	(Oil both sides - place	1½ **min.**
350°	**SNAPPER**	on grill turn once -	1½ **min.**
350°	**RAZOR CLAMS**	serve.)	1½ **min.**
350°	**GRILL SANDWICHES**		
	Cheese Plain	(Butter bread - place	
	with Crab	butter side on grill	
	with Ham, etc.	open faced. Serve	
	Reuben	closed.)	1½ min.
350°	**BACON**		
	Turn halfway through cooking cycle		2 min.

68

DUPLEX BROILERS - GRILL COMBINATION
(Floor Model)

Available electric or gas. Typical size:

31¼" wide, 25" deep, 42" high

Electric - 12 KW   Gas Model - 80,000 BTU

Heat is applied to both sides of meats simultaneously by two separate sets of stainless steel burners. One is under the broiling griddle which is thermostatically controlled, the other set is above the broiling griddle and is a radiant type producing a penetrating heat. It's also equipped with a gas pressure regulator.

SAMPLE COOKING CHART

Item	Portion	Doneness	Time
Steak	1" thick	Med.	4 min.
Lamb Chops	1" thick	Well	7 min.
Pork Chops	1" thick	Well	7 min.
Fish	1" thick	Well	6 min.
Hamburg	6 to lb.	Well	1 min.
Lobster	1 lb.	Well	4 min.
Chicken	2⅓ lbs. cut up	Well	15 min.

TYPICAL BROILER - GRIDDLE
(Counter Model)
(Production Gas 90,000 BTU - Sliding Broiler Grill)

OVERALL SIZE: 42" wide, 22" deep
GRILL SIZE: 40" wide, 19½" deep
BROILER SIZE: 38" wide, 18" deep
GRILL SECTION HOLDS: 30 average hamburgers, 3 lbs. bacon, 16 average pancakes

BROILER SECTION

Product	Amount Load	Time for Broiling
Club Steak	6 to 7	Rare 3 min.
Club Steak	6 to 7	Med. 4 min.
T-Bone Steak	10	Med. 5 min.
Chops	18-22	3-4 min.
Hamburgs	18-22	2-3 min.
Chicken	6 halves	15 min. to done
Rolls, toasted	18	30 sec.
Bacon	2 lbs.	2 min.

69

CHAR STYLE BROILING CHART AND TIMING GUIDE

Item	Thick	Minutes Each Side		
		Rare	Med.	Well
Porterhouse	1"	6	8	10
T-Bone - Club	1½"	9	10	13
Sirloin	2"	12	16	—
Hamburg	½"	2	4	6
CHICKEN		Done		
Broiling Chicken	¾ lb.	9 min.		
Ready ½ chickens	1 lb.	11 min.		
	1½ lb.	14 min.		
PORK				
Chops	1"	15-20 min.		
Spare Ribs		20-30 min.		

ELECTRIC CHAR BROIL LOAD & PRODUCTION GUIDE

Grid Size	Product	Per Load	Per Hr.
15 x 22	Hamburg	24	340
	Strip Steak	9	80
16 x 20	Hamburg	24	380
	Strip Steak	12	90
20 x 32	Hamburg	48	760
	Strip Steak	24	180
	(Medium doneness)		
	Hamburg 2½ oz.		
	N.Y. Strip 8 x 3 x ½"		

CONVEYOR BROILER
(Single Track, Electric, Counter Top)

46" x 18" or 20" x 23" high

HAMBURG PRODUCTION PER HOUR

Item	Pattie Size	10 KW	14 KW
Fresh Burger	8 to lb.	750	1000
Fresh Burger	4 to lb.	450	720
Frozen Burger	8 to lb.	575	750
Frozen Burger	4 to lb.	325	540

ROTISSERIE STYLE ELECTRIC BROILER

SIZE: 24" wide, 21" deep, 21" high. Rated at 3.2 KW, 208/220 — 250 hamburgs per hour.

NOTE: Check local codes. This rotisserie style cooker may not need venting.

BROILER, ELECTRIC
CONVEYOR - TWO TRACKS
208 or 230V, 1 or 3 phase, 9.9 KW

COUNTER TOP STYLE
SIZE: 42" to 60" x 20" x 22" high
TUNNEL STYLE: Dual controls allow the operator to choose speed for each track.
PRODUCTS: Hamburgs, buns, hot dogs, sausage patties and sandwich steaks.

Approximate Hamburger Production

Patty Size	Food Temp.	Thickness	Per Hr. Production
10 to lb.	40°F	3/16	675
4 to lb.	40°F	5/16	240
10 to lb.	0°F	3/16	300
4 to lb.	0°F	5/16	125

Food temperature end of cook cycle 150°.

MOBILE BROILERS FOR OUTSIDE USE
(on Trailer Style Wheels)

Styles available include L.P. gas, charcoal or wood fired.
FACTS:
102" long x 48" wide x 33" high
Broiler Grates: 2 - 32½ x 26¼ S/S
Griddles: 2 - 32½ x 26¼ cast
LP Gas Tanks: 2 - 20 lb. capacity each
BTU's: 74,000
Automatic pilot light, thermostat and shut off valve.
Trailer has standard 1-7/8" hitch, lights and plate brackets
A 6'-6" serving table slides out to form work/serve area. Covers cook area when not in use.

MOBILE BROILER ACCESSORIES

Corn Cooker
Cast 17" Fry Pans
French Fryer
Rotisserie, roasting and baking compartments

This unique mobile broiler is gaining acceptance for many operators in outside catering, poolside, parades, conventions, amusement parks, flea markets and related outside food operations.

MISCELLANEOUS BROILERS

RANGE BACKSHELF STYLE (Salamander): 32"-36" wide, 17"-22" deep. Grid size: 230-525 sq. inches. BUT's: 30,000-40,000

RESTAURANT RANGE BROILER: Under grill of range. Fired by ceramics from grill burner. Size (typical): 24" wide.
Limited use as heat is also directed to grill area above. Excellent for holding, cheese melting and limited broiling.

CRADLE STYLE DISPLAY MODEL
Countertop unit: 21" high, 24" wide, 20½" deep, 208/240V, 1 or 3 phase, 3.2 KW, enclosed unit with glass door. Cradles rotate ferris wheel style. Production approximately 250 hamburgs/hour. Check local codes. Unit may not require venting.

CRADLE STYLE DISPLAY MODEL
(with warmer space over)

Countertop unit 27" high, 24" wide, 20½" deep, 120V - 1.6 KW, available with cradles for hot dogs or chickens. Enclosed unit with glass door.
Hot dog cradles hold 48 at a time and cooks up to 300 per hour.
Chicken cradles hold 8 chickens; cooking time 2 hours.
There are many other styles and sizes of these small display units available. Ask your equipment rep.

DISPLAY STYLE ROTISSERIE BROILERS

These are large commercial style units, typical "Big City" display units with glass doors for barbecue specialty houses or supermarkets. Some are available as counter models. Holding warmer ovens available as bases for counter models or as separate units. Chain driven spits hold 5 or 6 chickens each. Units are also ideally suited to turkeys, roast, spare ribs and other similar items.

TYPICAL SIZES AND CAPACITIES

Type		Capacity Chickens	Height	Width	Depth
Gas	3—Spit	15	42"	36"	22"
Electric	3—Spit	15	41"	36"	22"
Gas	5—Spit	25	56"	36"	22"
Electric	5—Spit	25	56"	36"	22"
Gas	7—Spit	35	72"	36"	22"
Electric	7—Spit	35	72"	36"	22"
Gas	12—Spit	60	67"	36"	34"
Electric	12—Spit	60	67"	36"	34"
Gas	14—Spit	70	72"	36"	34"
Gas	5—Spit	25	72"	36"	24"
Electric	5—Spit	25	72"	36"	24"
Electric	8—Spit	32	69"	30"	30"

NOTE: Space required at right side for spit removal door swings out approx. 14".

Warmer voltage 115 — all rotisserie units 208 or 240 KW and B.T.U. rates vary by size of units.

DRAWER STYLE BROILER

This is a back bar counter style unit. Available in one or two drawer sizes. Bun or roll warmer drawers above broiler drawer. Units can have covered pan inserts in tops, single or split pans for chili, sauces or holding. Suitable for hamburgs, steaks, etc. Drip pans under broiler cavity. Single drawer units 110/220 Volt — 2 drawer units 208 - 220/240 Volt. Both units 18½" deep x 16½" high. Single 21" wide - double unit 33½" wide, thermostat control, cord and plug supplied.

Check local codes — may not require venting. Able to produce six one quarter pound hamburgers per drawer, 3½ to 4 minutes from a refrigerated state.

FRYER FACTS - ELECTRIC AND GAS

STYLES AVAILABLE:
1) Conventional gas and electric counter and floor models
2) Computerized Fryers
3) Pressure Fryers
4) Conveyor high production types
5) Specialty Fryers - donut, high BTU chicken and fish models
6) Fryers are now available lwith built in automatic filter systems. Also available are fryers with automatic temperature controls, (no thermostats)
7) Air Pressure - new style fryer uses no oil. Further information not available at this time.

FRYER FACTS - BRAINSTORMING

1) Mobile
2) Automatic lifts
3) Computer timers
4) Computer controls
5) Fat melt cycle
6) Test alert system
7) Quick disconnects
8) Drop in
9) Counter
10) Free standing
11) Full or half baskets
12) Ease of cleaning
13) Ease of draining
14) Ease of filtering
15) Dual pots in same housing
16) Simmer cover - gives O pressure frying
17) Apron drain, attaches to side of fryer
18) Spreader - separates 2 fryers or fryer from other equipment
19) Crumb tray
20) Element style if electric

FAT FILTERS

Some french fry units are available with built-in filtering systems. The filtering system may be contained within the fryer or added to the side. The filtering may be continual or in cycles.

Separate, mobile fat filters are available in sizes from approximately 50 lb. to 250 lb. capacities. Each manufacturer offers certain desirable features such as, filter papers or powders, purification cartridges, fat melting capacities, reversible pumps, etc.

Typical Fat Filtering Units

Drum Dia.	Fat Capacity	
	Pounds	Gallson
17"	60	8
17"	120	16½
20"	150	20
20"	250	33-1/3

Above models rated as 5.5 Amp., 110 V., 1/4 H.P.

Manual filters using cotton fiber or reusable, washable filters are normally sufficient for small counter fryers.

Potential savings from proper handling and filtering can be significant. Take a few minutes to read the following "FAT FACTS".

FRYER FAT DECOMPOSITION
(Approximate Temperature Breakdown)

Product	Breakdown Temp.
Corn & Cottonseed Oil	430° - 475°
Hydrogenated Oils	430° - 475°
Lard	385° - 430°
Butter	405°
Olive Oil	333° - 347°

SMOKING TEMPERATURES OF VARIOUS FATS

Hydrogenated	440° - 460°	Lard	340° - 350°
Standard Vegetable	420° - 440°	Olive Oil	300° - 315°
Cottonseed Oil	410° - 430°	Bacon Fat	290° - 300°
Corn Oil	400° - 430°	Beef Suet	235° - 245°
Chicken Fat	400° - 430°		

74

FAT FACTS

Fresh frying fat requires a certain amount of breaking-in or degredation to make it a suitable cooking medium. This process commences when it is first brought up to frying temperature but unfortunately cannot be stopped when the fat reaches the point where it yields fine foods lightly colored and flavored and have a crisp exterior but still remain moist inside. Fat breakdown is caused by heat, air and chemicals from the foods cooked in it.

Fat will change its chemical properties even without the introduction of food due to being heated in the atmosphere. The physical properties of the fat change which lowers its surface tension and increases its viscosity. This changes the heat transfer and soaking properties of the fat.

Antioxidants and antifoamers cannot stop the gradual degradation process, but the useful life of the fat can be maximally extended when —

1. Frequent and effective filtering is employed for partical removal.
2. "Oil cleaning" or treatment is carried out for soluble contaminants.
3. When high volumes of foods are produced in relatively low volumes of fat. This carries away much of the "old fat". When replacement fat is one third of the total fat in the fryer, the quality life cycle can be materially extended.

Soap is an enemy of frying fat. Pioneers produced their own soap by cooking an alkaline product with fat. Soap is produced in the frying fat when the alkaline food juices combine with the free fatty acids in the frying fat. Test chemicals, to show soap content and oil cleaning chemicals and effective filtration systems are available which can restore those properties that exist in an ideal frying fat.

Polymerized or "plasticized" fats show up as gummy deposits on fryer walls. These should be removed by polishing the walls and heating elements in electric fryers with polishing pads. The oil cleaning chemical mentioned above is effective in removing and preventing build-up of plasticized and carbon deposits.

Since the usable fat life span will never be the same in two different kitchens it is wise to carefully establish your own and mark it on a calendar. Simply discarding fat once a week can be an expensive waste.

If you find that your fat can be used for 10 days, the difference between discarding fat once per week and every 10 days would amount to 15.5 loads. If you have two 40 lb. fryers you would be unnecessarily discarding $(15.5 \times 2 \times 40) = 1,240$ lbs. of fat per year.

In summation, to get top mileage from your fat:

1) Use a quality hydrogenated vegetable oil.
2) Check your fat level - if low replenish immediately.
3) Avoid excessive stirring or agitation to prevent air from being whipped into the fat.

4) Check and adjust thermostats often to prevent detrimental over-heating.
5) If two fry kettles are in operation, use one for french fries only, the other for all other food. Take fat from the fries kettle to replenish the other. Add fresh fat to the fries kettle only. This will prolong the life cycle of the fat in each kettle maximally.
6) Choose the proper kettle for your volume of frying and your menu.
7) Never add salt to foods during frying or above the fat.
8) Use a good oil care chemical and filter frequently.
9) Always set thermostat to "standby" 200ºF during slack periods. This preserves fat and saves power costs too.

FRYING TEMPERATURES - SELECTED FOODS

Product	Temp ºF	Time
Chicken, raw to done	325	2½ lbs. - 9-11 min.
Chicken, pre-cooked - breaded	350	3-4 min.
Yeast Donuts	375	1-1½ min.
Frozen Shrimp	350	3 min.
Frozen Fish Fillets	350	4 min.
Fresh Scallops	350	4 min.
Breaded Veal Cutlets	350	4 min.
Breaded Onion Rings	350	3 min.

FRENCH FRIES - Temp 350º

Size	Desired Condition	Fry Time
1/4 cut	Raw to Done	5 min.
1/4 cut	Blanched	2½ min.
1/4 cut	Brown	2½ min.
3/8 cut	Raw to done	6 min.
3/8 cut	Blanched	3 min.
3/8 cut	Brown	3 min.

GAS FRYER FACTS
(Sample production by BTU's)

COUNTER STYLE

Width	Depth	BTU's	Lbs. Fat Capacity	Lbs. French Fries Raw to Done/Hr.
12½"	23"	55,000	18	30
15½"	25½"	109,000	38	55

(Continued)

GAS FRYER FACTS
(Sample production by BTU's)

FLOOR MODELS

Width	Depth	BTU's	Lbs. Fat Capacity	Lbs. French Fries Raw to Done/Hr.
12½"	21½"	55,300	18	35
12½"	25"	66,000	18	55
15½"	28-1'/8"	110,000	38	92
15½"	28-1/8"	130,000	38	110
20"	19-1/8"	135,000	68	120
20"	29-1/8"	165,000	68	135
27½"	34-1/8"	130,000	100	120
27½"	34-1/8"	165,000	100	140
28½"	38"	212,000	130	175
35-3/8"	38"	260,000	195	210

GAS FRYER - Typical Fryer Production in Pounds

FRY KETTLE SIZE

	10"x11"	14"x14"	14"x14"	18"x18"	20"x20"	24"x24"
Gas Consumption, BTU/hr.	66,000	130,000	125,000	165,000	165,000	212,000
Potatoes Blanched	93	170	350	230	225	390
Potatoes Blanched to Finish	93	170	350	230	225	390
Precooked Chicken	75	130		160	170	325
Chicken Raw to Done	40	60	100	120	140	220
Shrimp, Fish, Croquettes	55	100	135	155	165	285
Fritters, Cutlets, etc.	57	110	80	155	165	285
Fat Capacity in lbs.	18	38	42	68	100	130

TYPICAL GAS FRYER TEMPERATURES
(Standard Input versus High Input in Degrees F.)

Food Item	Standard	High Input
French Fries - Blanch	325/370	275/325
French Fries - Brown	350/400	325/350
Fish Fillets	350/375	325/335
Clam Fries	330/390	330/350
Chicken	325/370	320/335
Seafood - Average	330/390	315/350

The fast recovery of high B.T.U. input fryers allows lower frying temperatures. The burner running time is less and preheating is faster. Gas fryers are available with standing pilots or spark ignition. Several states have legislation to outlaw standing pilots. Check your state requirements.

TYPICAL ELECTRIC FRYERS
(Sizes and Production)

OIL CAPACITY (LBS.)	FRENCH FRIES/HR.		KW	PREHEAT TO 350F (MINUTES)	WATTS TO HOLD 350F	OVERALL BODY DIMENSIONS		
						W	D	H (LESS LEGS)
15	27 lbs. raw-to-done		5.5	6	485	17-31/32	20	12-5/16
15	27 lbs. raw-to-done		5.5	6	485	17-31/32	22-1/2	12-5/16
28	2-oz. blanched servings	600	12	6	770	21-1/2	25-5/32	13-3/8
28		600	12	6	770	25-1/2	25-5/32	13-3/8
28		600	12	6	770	20	38	35
28		600	12	6	770	20	38	35
28		600	12	6	770	20	38	22-1/2
28		600	12	6	770	20	38	22-1/2
28		600	12	6	770	20	38	35
30	56 lbs. raw-to-done		11.4	9.5	770	24-4/5	23-1/2	14-5/16
50	50 lbs. frozen fish filets		11	7*	836	15-5/8	28	34-1/2
50	100 lbs. blanched-to-done		16.5	5*	836	15-5/8	28	34-1/2
60	90 lbs. fried chicken		18	10	1300	24	38	35
60	90 lbs. fried chicken		18	10	1300	24	38	22-1/2

MOBILE FRYER BASKET BACKS

For high production stations these units are available in sizes to hold 24, 32 or 48 14" split baskets or 32 18" split baskets. Units have removable crumb tray at base. Average height 58"; widths from 22" to 44" depending on capacity.

SPECIALTY FRYER - ROUND FRY POT

Table top or drop in style round immersion basket, features automatic lift, holds 24 lbs. fat. 4.5 KW electric, 15" wide, 23¾" deep, 29¾" high.

TYPICAL PRODUCTION

Food Item	Food Weight	Temp.	Time
Breaded Chicken	6 lbs.	350°	8 min.
Onion Rings	1¼ lbs.	375°	1½ min.
Frozen Fish Fillets	5 - 4 oz. portions	375°	5 min.
Frozen Shrimp	2½ lbs.	350°	3 min.

DONUT FRYERS · TYPICAL PRODUCTION

ELECTRIC

| Size | | | Fat Capacity | DONUTS | |
Width	Depth	KW	lbs.	Per Load	Per Hour
13"	13"	1.8	11	12	16 dz.
15"	16"	2.4	16	18	25 dz.
20"	20"	5.5	30	24	50 dz.
21"	22"	8	50	36	65 dz.
25"	26"	11	85	60	100 dz.

LARGER GAS DONUT FRYERS

Fat Capacity	BTU	Dz. Donuts Per Hr.
105/120	120,000	60
105/165	150,000	130
195	180,000	160

Also available are automated style fryers with built-in dropping and turning systems for donuts.

LOW PRESSURE FRYER

Top cover operates on 3/4 pound pressure rather than normal 13 pounds high pressure. This unit features automatic lift, front work or landing tray - capacity 1 lb. to 15 lbs. Frying time is same. Immersion basket is round. Power requirements not available at this time.

TYPICAL COOKING TIMES LOW PRESSURE FRYER

Food Product	Time	Food Product	Time
Clams - Scallops	3 min.	Wedge French Fries	7 min.
Onion Rings	5 min.	Pork Chops	8 min.
Bacon - Franks	6 min.	Fish - Frozen	7 min.
Liver	6 min.	Chicken	12½ min.

PRESSURE FRYERS · 13 lb. Pressure

TYPICAL PRODUCTION CAPACITIES
All Temperatures 300°-325°

RAW TO DONE

Food Item	Time	Food Item	Time
Chicken - 1½ lb. halves	8 min.	Oysters	2 min.
Chicken - 2 lb. halves	9 min.	Fish Fillets - 4 oz.	3½ min.
Chicken - 2 lb. whole	12 min.	Shrimp - Jumbo	4 min.
Crabs	3 min.	Spare Ribs	5 min.
Scallops	1½ min.	Gas or Electric models available.	

AUTOMATED FRYING FOR CONVENTIONAL FRYERS

Basically we will unravel in easy to read style the new generation of techniques applied to deep fat frying. The styles are as follows:
1) Factory built fryers with time devices
2) Factory built fryers with computer devices
3) Timers and computers from electronic manufacturers that adapt readily to all style fryers.

The range of timers, controls and options are numerous. We are listing what appears to be emerging as the most popular of these new sophisticated systems.

SOLID STATE FRYERS

Electric solid state fryers, with and without computer controls. Separate timing devices and remote style fryer computer controls. An honest attempt to take the mystery out of advance frying procedures. These facts, along with your manufacturer specification sheet, should be most helpful to your selection. Regular control fryers are covered in previous text.
  A. Solid state control fryers - no computer
    1) Units have food overload warning
    2) Automatic melting of fat cycle
    3) Energy overload protection
    4) Power off - for protection if fire extinguishing system should go off
    5) Precise temperature control by use of probe in fat well
  B. Solid state computer styles have above features plus the following:
    1) Monitor - constantly scans time and temperature to adjust variances
    2) Programmable frying times, signal product doneness
    3) As with regular fryers, styles available with automatic basket lifts
    4) Power test switch

REMOTE TIMERS

Remote timers and computers purchased separately and available for gas or electric fryers.

STYLES
    1) 1 solid state timer factory set for your cooking time. Buzzer and/or light signals end of cook cycle
    2) Solid state timer with twist dials from 3 seconds to 15 minutes. Buzzer and/or lights signal cycle completion
    3) Solid state timer up to 99 minutes - numbers count down to 0. Buzzer at end of cycle

4) Solid state timer with 3 separate preset times - factory set. When using same fryer for many selections (Sample, clam fry, french fry or onion rings.)
5) Solid state timer touch control. One model controls 2 products or 2 batches of 1 product at same time. Shows steady light during cooking - flash lighting at cycle completion. Another model, same as above can control 4 products or 4 batches of 1 product at same time. Tone available for either model.

THE FRYER COMPUTER - REMOTE

Basically the fryer computer monitors the following variables and computes exact frying times.

- Fat temperature
- Quantity of product
- Recovery rate
- Shortening condition
- Product temperature and water content
- Fryer efficiency and capacity

Test results have shown at least 10% more yield using computer technology. Over and undercooked frys, chicken and fish are eliminated and fat life is also extended.

Features:
- Tone alarms
- Light signals
- Crisp controls
- Test switches for fryer and computer
- Programmable by operator changing time chips
- Holding timer
- Probe test switch
- Switch to manual timer in case of computer failure

The basic difference between solid state timer units and computer units is that timers do not have probes. Computerized control units have probes to monitor all necessary functions of the fryer.

If you are interested in purchasing a computer control unit, the following is a sample information sheet which must be completed.

Fryer Manufacturer _____

Fryer model _____

Is the fryer gas or electric _____

      What is the voltage of the fryer _____

Number of baskets in each fry pot _____

Does the fryer have automatic basket lifts _____

      If yes, what is the voltage of the lift's _____

Number of products cooked in the fryer _____

Determine location of computer - freestanding or built into a hood.

      If mounted on wall or hood, determine length of probe cable necessary

      to reach the back wall of fry pot _____ .(ft.) If probe is to

      be built into the fry pot, does the fryer have a factory installed fitting. ____

Do you require a "Holding Timer" _____

Do you require an electronic temperature control with an automatic melt cycle _____

What is the temperature setting on your fryer _____

What are the approximate cooking times for each of your products.

APPROXIMATE COOKING TIMES FOR EACH OF YOUR PRODUCTS	
PRODUCT	COOKING TIME
1	
2	
3	
4	
5	
6	

GRILLS · GRIDDLES

Defined, a grill would have top and bottom heat. This style has been used for grilled cheese sandwiches for years. Griddles were defined as bottom heat only. For this section we will consider both the same and move on to the facts.

Even though the term sandwich grill seems to stick with us, the author tends to think in terms of the cooking appliance as being the griddle and what is accomplished with it as grilling. No one ever orders a "griddled cheese sandwich".

WHEN YOUR ELECTRIC GRIDDLE IS NEW . . .

1) Use the manufacturer's operating manual that came with your griddle. Write for a new manual if yours is missing. Study the manual, then file it in a safe place for ready reference.

2) Check the nameplate on the griddle to satisfy yourself that the voltage and current characteristics match your electrical service. If in doubt, consult your local electric utility company.
3) Have your griddle installed and connected by a competent electrical contractor. Call your electric utility company if you need help.
4) Clean off the rust preventive compound applied by factory. Use a cloth dampened with a grease solvent. Wipe with a clean, damp cloth. Dry thoroughly.
5) After thorough cleaning, the grid plate must be seasoned. Preheat to 400°F. Apply a light film of unsalted cooking oil. Alow to stand for two minutes, then wipe clean. Repeat this process. Thoroughly wipe off excess oil. Your new griddle is now ready for use.

CORRECT OPERATING CARE ELECTRIC GRIDDLES

Turn dial to required temperature (reached when signal light goes out).

With machines having more than one control dial, make sure you know exactly how much of the cooking surface each control serves. Some models also feature separate perimiter control. (Consult the manufacturer's manual or your local electric utility company.)

Load and cook according to recipe. Unless the food product contains fat (e.g. bacon), the grid surface must be grease-filmed before each cooking operation.

Turn foods halfway through cooking time unless otherwise specified in recipe.

Griddle-grills, with independently controlled upper grid, cook both sides at once. (One manufacturer recommends that the upper grid should be approximately 50°F. higher than lower grid temperature to obtain desired browning and doneness.)

After each cooking load, scrape excess food and fat particles off the grid surface with a flexible spatula or wire brush.

During traffic lulls reduce temperature to "idle" (around 200°F.).

At the end of each day's operation, thoroughly clean grid, reseason and turn all temperature controls to OFF.

GRIDDLE PLATES AND SURFACES

CAST GRIDDLE PLATES

These are very porous and do not expand and contract as much as others. Frozen foods will tend to stick. The cast plates require constant cleaning.

HIGHLY POLISHED STEEL PLATES

Food sticking is greatly reduced but the shiny surface, with little adherence causes product shrinkage.

COLD-ROLLED STEEL PLATES

These have excellent heat transfer qualities. The .006 finish allows good product adherence, reducing shrinkage and they are easily cleaned.

CHROME FINISH PLATES

This newer style plate, available either grooved or flat, requires no "seasoning". They have excellent heat transfer quality and the mirror finish is easily cleaned with a blade or scraper, cold water and a dry chemical powder.

HELPFUL HINTS

Grease drains and drawers vary greatly by manufacturer. Rear drains are more troublesome than front or side style drain troughs. With rear drains the grease pan or drawer is often not pushed fully back creating an impossible to clean mess in the base of the unit.

Careless operators often forget to empty the grease drawers. A small hole drilled in the front of the drawer, just below the point of overflow, will prevent the grease from running all over under the unit and also alert the operator to the fact that the drawer needs emptying. If he still doesn't see it, the hot grease will drop on his foot. That'll wake him up.

Another advantage of front or side drain troughs is that the backsplash provides a very handy place to push the product against for turning or scooping up.

Griddles constructed with the griddle plate inserted into a full bottom supporting pan will be less efficient and the temperature control inaccurate.

Be sure the griddle you select has recovery capability for the volume of food you intend to serve with it. Grill area is not the only thing to consider. Investigate the heating pattern in either gas or electric griddles. Zoned control gives better product control. The ability to dial your heat choice gives more flexibility.

GRIDDLE STYLES

1) Standard grill, gas or electric
2) Free standing or range top
3) Counter style
4) Drop in counter style
5) Top heat plate combined with regular grill
6) Grooved grill - branding and marking
7) Grill with quartz hinged top above, as discussed under broilers
8) Energy saving grills
9) Grill above - broiler below

OPTIONS TO CONSIDER:
  1) Separate zone heat
  2) Splash guards back and sides
  3) Cutting boards in front
  4) Adequate drainage front or rear
  5) Signal lights if electric
  6) Thermostats or dial position heat control

SOLID STATE TIMERS

Remote solid state timers are available for either griddle or oven control. They may regulate 2 to 4 products. Dual cycle controls turning of products as hamburgers, steak or baked items. 1 light for turn - 2 for done. Tone alert available.

TYPICAL COUNTER GRILLS
POWER REQUIRED AND PRODUCTIONS

Eectric

Usable Grill Size	Elec. KW	3½ oz. Hamburgs Per Load	Per Hr.
18" x 24"	8	32	480
18" x 36"	12	48	720
18" x 36"	16	65	975
18" x 48"	21	86	1300
18" x 72"	32	120	2400

TYPICAL ELECTRIC GRIDDLE CAPACITIES

Nominal Griddle Dimensions		Grid Surface Area (Sq. In.)	(Min.)	Preheat Time to 350°F 3-1/2 In.)	Hourly Capacity		
Depth (In.)	Width (In.)				Hamburgers (2-1/2 oz., (4-1/2 In.)	Pancakes	Fried Eggs
18	24	400	8	7.5	480 +	'260-320	450 +
	36	610	12		720 +	384-480	675 +
	48	834	16		945 +	450 +	900 +
24	24	533	10.8	7.7	630 +	450-550	600
	36	813	16.2		975 +	450 +	900 +
	48	1110	21.6		1300 +	600 +	1200 +
	72	1667	32.4		2400 +	900 +	1800 +

ELECTRIC GRIDDLE CAPACITIES
(By Griddle Size and Square Inches)

Griddle Size 15" x 18" - 266 Square Inches

Food Product	Per Load	Per Hour
Hamburger	20	300
Eggs	19	320
Pancakes	12	216

Griddle Size 15" x 30" - 445 Square Inches

Hamburger	32	480
Eggs	32	550
Pancakes	28	500

Griddle Size 18" x 24" - 429 Square Inches

Hamburger	30	'510
Eggs	28	560
Pancakes	25	375

Griddle Size 18" x 36" - 645 Square Inches

Hamburger	45	765
Eggs	42	840
Pancakes	38	570

GAS GRIDDLES - TYPICAL SIZES AND BTU'S

Usable Grill Area	B.T.U.'S
18" x 24"	45,000
18" x 36"	65,000
18" x 48"	105,000
24" x 36"	90,000
24" x 48"	138,000

HIGH HEAT TRANSFER GRIDDLES
3/4" PLATE TYPICAL B.T.U.'S OR KW

Overall Size	Griddle Size	B.T.U.'S	KW
27" x 30"	24" x 30"	80,000	7.2
30" x 30"	27" x 30"	80,000	7.2
36" x 30"	33" x 30"	80,000	10.8
42" x 30"	39" x 30"	120,000	14.4
48" x 30"	45" x 30"	160,000	14.4
60" x 30"	57" x 30"	200,000	18.0
71" x 30"	69" x 30"	240,000	21.6

Available 24" x 36" deep also.

ELECTRIC TEPPANYAKI GRIDDLES
For Oriental Steakhouse Restaurants

Complete unit is 58" x 96" x 29½" high. Seats eight comfortably. Cooking plate is 24" x 60" with two elements, thermostats, lights and switches. 208-240 Volt. Available without table.

MINI COUNTER GRIDDLE - HEAT ABOVE AND BELOW

SIZE: Varies by manufacturer. Solid plate top hinges and lays down on top of food. Also available with ribbed or groove plate.

Food Product	Per Load	Minutes to Cook 115V	220V
3/4" Steak	4	3	2
Grilled Sandwich	6	1½	1
Hot Dogs	12	3	2
Sausage Links	18	3	2
French Toast	6	1¼	1
1/2" Swordfish	4-6	6	4
3/8" Ham Steak	4-6	3	2
3 oz. Hamburg	6	1½	1

HIGH SPEED, PORTABLE GRIDDLE

Specifications: 7¼" high, 21½" wide, 14¾" deep, 115 V or 230 A.C., 1725 Watts, plug-in unit, weight 22 lbs. Cooking surface 11" x 21" heavy cast aluminum. Elements, infra-red, radiant type.

Features: Automatic thermostatic temp. control from 150° to 400°F, fast recovery, wide drain lip with grease drawer.

Application: Food demonstrations, rathskellers, terraces, luncheonettes and as stand-by units for restaurants, hotels.

HOT OIL GRIDDLE TOP

Converts your fryer to a griddle by pumping the hot oil through sealed heat transfer passages between the griddle top and base. Ideal for times extra griddle area is required such as at breakfast. Operates with any fryer with well dimensions less than 31½" x 20". Single or double well models may be used.

Overall Size: 31½" x 22" x 8" high with pump pick-up and return pipes extending approx. 7" below griddle. Pump motor and switch mount on rear right corner. Motor is 115V, 2 amp. with 6' cord and plug.

Operation: Pre-heat fryer. Place unit on fryer with base resting on edges and pump lines extending minimum of ½" below oil surface. Set fryer thermostat approx. 30° above desired griddle temperature. Plug in griddle and switch pump motor on. Turn off, remove, drain, and store unit when finished. Weight: 60 lbs.

TYPICAL COOKING TIMES AND TEMPS
FOR CHAR - RIBBED - GROOVED GRILLS

Food Product	Temp.	Minutes to Cook
Bacon	350°	6 min.
Link Sausage	350°	4 min.
Ham Slice	375°	3-4 min.
Hamburger	350°	4 min.
Hot Dogs	375°	2-5 min.
Club Steak	400°	5 min.

SUGGESTED TEMPERATURES FOR SELECTED FOOD ITEMS

Food Item	Grill Temp.	Minutes to Cook
Hamburgers	350°	3-4 min.
Hot Dogs	375°	3-4 min.
Eggs	300°	2-3 min.
Fried Potatoes	350°	3-4 min.
Onion Slices	350°	4 min.
Bacon	350°	5 min.
Cheese Sandwich	375°	3-4 min.
French Toast	350°	2-3 min.
Club Steak 1''	400°	5 min.

OVENS

And the man said, "I need an oven," and my response was, "Yes sir, did you want a cafe, restaurant or heavy duty range oven? Or a regular bake or roast oven? or a convection oven or, a pizza oven, microwave oven, or perhaps a revolving, reel, or rotary oven?" And on and on. Menu matching becomes the absolute necessity in oven selection. After studying the menu and looking at total production needed, a proper selection can be made. As we go thru the section on ovens, you will see the necessity of studying the power requrements and options.

BRAINSTORMING OVENS

- Power requirements
- Venting requirements
- Provisions needed for steam injection for critical baking
- Ease of cleaning
- Working heights adequate
- Will you have the capacity of adding more ovens if necessary?
- What is the preheat time of oven?
- Are legs included?

CONVECTION OVEN FACTS

Convection ovens force heated air, via fans located on the rear oven wall, over and around the food racks. This provides even more cooking speed, better heat efficiency, and a better product - cooked more evenly and thoroughly. Oven temperature settings can be reduced from 25% to 75%. These ovens also accept heavier work loads for greater business volume.

A new snorkel-type gas convection oven combines the basic advantages of convection ovens with the direct-firing principle of regular ovens. The heat is never wasted, but is recaptured and cycled back through the oven — at fuel savings of up to 40 percent.

A pilotless gas convection oven saves operators 25% in fuel costs. Its doors may be opened during any cooking cycle for "putting in" or "taking out."

CONVECTION OVENS - GAS OR ELECTRIC STYLES AVAILABLE

1) Standard 11 pan capacity oven
2) Extra deep ovens for bulk feeding racks
3) Docking ovens for truck style cooking
4) 1/2 size counter convection ovens
5) 36" stacking convection ovens (or counter)
6) Mobile ovens
7) Under range convection ovens
8) Caterer's convection ovens
9) Drive in oven - entire trucks enter oven

AVAILABLE OPTIONS:
1) Solid doors in lieu of glass
2) Continuous clean ovens
3) Wheels
4) Cook and hold (see energy savers)
5) Pan racks under shelves
6) Fan controls separate
7) Electronic pilots (gas)
8) Doors can be french style or conventional
9) Drop down or full hinged doors
10) Timers, mechanical or electric
12) Power on indicator lights
13) Dual power for energy savings
    Frozen food - more power, refrigerated foods - less power

SOLID STATE OVENS

These ovens will cook by normal convection method, move into stored heat cooking and then to automatic holding. They may be also used for holding only. Typical controls on these 11 KW electric ovens include:

1) On/off switch for oven and blower
2) On/off switch for oven lights
3) Normal and cook and hold switch
4) Cook thermostat 150° - 450°
5) Hold thermostat 125° - 175°
6) Quartz timer 1 min. to 29 ¾ hrs.
7) Start and clear buttons for timer
8) LED display shows on or hold mode - dot for element in use light. Remaining cooking time, oven condition is shows as Done — Automatic — Hold and Prob, which indicates probe malfunction.

SOME AVAILABLE SIZES
(Standard Convection Ovens)

Power Requirements: Electric or gas range of KW from 5.5 to 37 KW. Average full size oven — 11 KW. Gas BTU's from 40,000 to 120,000. Fan motors from 1/2 to 2 HP at 1750 R.P.M.

Pan Sizings: See charts for total loads and temperatures. Full size ovens accommodate one 18" x 26" per shelf, or two 12" x 20" pans or six 9" pie pans per shelf. Please see index for product and serving ratings for these pans.

SELECTION GUIDES CONVECTION OVENS

Meals Served

50 to 100	1 - 1/2 size convection oven
100 to 400	1 - Full convection oven
400 to 750	1 - Double convection oven
750 up	1 - Double convection oven plus 1 single convection oven

From 750 meals up, consideration should be given to mobile roll in or drive in style ovens.

PAN CAPACITIES 18" x 26" PANS
(As rated for full size convection oven)

Food Item	Per Pan	Number of Shelves	Total Oven Load
Rolls	5 dz. - 1¼ oz.	4	240 rolls
Sheet Cake	70 cut	6	420 pieces
Cookies	1½ - #24 scoop	6	144
Hamburgs	24 - 3 oz.	11	264
Baked Lobster	20 lbs.	4	64¼ lbs.
Baked Potatoes	40-80	4-6	160-360

See next chart for more production figures.

90

FULL SIZE CONVECTION OVEN PRODUCTION

Food	Number Shelves	Total Pans	Approx. No. Servings Per Oven Load	Approx. No. Servings Per Hour*
BREADS				
Loaf	4	32	512-1 oz.	1024 - 1 oz.
Dinner Rolls	4	4	240 - 1¼ oz.	960 - 1¼ oz.
Hamburger Rolls	4	4	144 - 1½ oz.	576 - 1½ oz.
Sweet Rolls	4	4	144 - 1½ oz.	576 - 1½ oz.
DESSERTS				
Cake	6	6	420	1260
Cake	6	6	480	1440
Cookies	6	6	144	720
Custard or Pudding	6	12	480	960
Pies - Deep				
Dish Fruit	6	12	480	960
Fruit	6	36	216	432
MEATS			**Meat only**	**Meat only**
Bottom Round	4	4	800 - 2 oz.	— —
Chicken Parts	6	12	300 - 2 oz.	900 - 2 oz.
Deep Dish Meat pie	6	12	500 - 2 oz.	1000 - 2 oz.
Hamburgers	11	11	264 - 2 oz.	1500 - 2 oz.
Meatballs	6	12	450 - 2 oz.	900 - 1 oz.
Prime Ribs	2	2	275 - 8 oz.	— —
Sausages	6	6	250 - 2 oz.	500 - 2 oz.
Sirloin Strips	4	8	600 - 3 oz.	— —
Steaks -				
Strip pre-scored	6	6	120 - 6 oz.	350 - 6 oz.
Steamship Round	2	2	500 - 2 oz.	— —
Turkey (off carcass)	6	12	800 - 2 oz.	— —
Turkey (on carcass)	2	4	325 - 2 oz.	— —
SEAFOOD				
Baked Stuffed				
Lobster	4	4	64 - 1¼ lb.	125 - 1½ lb.
Haddock Fillets	6	6	240 - 4 oz.	725 - 4 oz.
Halibut Steak	6	6	175 - 4 oz.	525 - 4 oz.
MISCELLANEOUS				
Baked Macaroni				
and Cheese	6	12	275 - 6 oz.	550 - 2 oz.
Grilled Cheese				
Sandwich	6	6	144 - 2 oz. cheese	556 - 2 oz. cheese
Idaho Potatoes	4-6	4-6	160-360	160-360
Pizza	6	6	70 - 2 oz.	200 - 2 oz.

*Proper loading and unloading time has been allowed when figuring amount of food cooked per hour.

91

CONVECTION OVENS · TYPICAL SIZES

Style	Power	Wide	Deep	High	Holds
Counter	Electric	30½"	27½"	25"	11-14" x 20" pans
Counter	Electric	23-5/8"	23-5/8"	22"	9 pies
Floor	Gas/Electric	38¼"	38-5/16"	66"	11-18" x 26" pans
Floor	Electric	36"	44"	66"	Bulk Food Foil Containers
Compact	Electric	36"	35"	22"	6-18" x 26" pans

While the capacities listed above may be a bit baffling, bear in mind you will be matching your menu needs to the equipment available and if you cross check these guides throughout the book your selection will be easier. In capacities above maximums are listed. (See specific products in other charts.)

TIME AND TEMPERATURE GUIDE
FULL SIZE CONVECTION OVENS

Food	Temp. Setting	Time Setting	No. of Racks*
Frozen fruit pies	350F	45-50 min.	5 racks (20 pies)
Fresh apple pies	350-375F	25-30 min.	5 racks
Sheet cake (5 lbs./pan)	335F	18 min.	5 racks
Beef pot pies	400F	30-35 min.	5 racks
Turkey pot pies	400F	10 min.	5 racks
Toasted cheese sandwiches	400F	10 min.	5 racks
Fish sticks	335F	16-18 min.	11 racks
Chicken back or wing	350F	35 min.	5 racks
Chicken (quarter)	350F	30 min.	5 racks
Lamb chops	400F	6 min.	5 racks
Sugar cookies	300F	15 min.	5 racks
Baked potatoes	400F	50 min.	5 racks
Hamburgers (3½ oz. patties)	400F	10 min.	11 racks
Pizza (7" frozen - preheat pans)	435F	11 min.	6 racks
Halibut (frozen 5 oz.)	350F	30 min.	5 racks
Chicken breasts	350F	33 min.	5 racks
Macaroni and cheese	350F	30 min.	5 racks
Meat loaf	325F	40 min.	5 racks

*Where the number of racks is 5, insert the first rack on the bottom position and place the others on every other rung.

OPERATING HINTS

Position the racks according to the cooking load to be prepared.
- On models with an independent blower switch, snap on the power switch with the doors open. If the blower starts, depress the blower switch so that it only operates when the doors are closed.
- On all other models, close the doors before snapping on the power switch.
- Set the thermostat dial to the required temperature. The signal light will go on.

- You can now preheat the oven in 10 to 15 minutes to reach temperatures from 300-400°F.
- If so equipped, preheat with the load control set at high.
- The oven should not be loaded for baking until the signal light has flashed off and on at least twice.
- To preheat for baking, set the temperature 50°F. higher than required to compensate for heat loss when opening the doors for loading. Adjust to the correct temperature after loading. Then set load control dial (if so equipped) to the correct setting for the product and load to be cooked (see manufacturer's manual).
- Always load quickly to conserve heat, centering the pans on the racks. With light bake products, it is advisable to position pans as far as possible from the blower mechanism to reduce spattering.
- Care should be taken to avoid spillage of batter or liquids while loading.
- Cooking action starts as soon as you close the doors. Set the timer.
- The timer does not control the oven function, so check for doneness as soon as the bell or buzzer sounds.
- Avoid unnecessary door opening during cooking; it disrupts the temperature pattern. Observe cooking progress through the door windows. Use interior oven lights only when necessary.
- You can roast beef, lamb, poultry and ham in a convection oven at 225-324°F; fresh pork at 325-350°F. When roasting, place a pan of water at the bottom of the oven. This supplies humidity to reduce shrinkage.
- Load and unload rapidly to conserve heat.
- Unloading is easier if the racks are pulled forward.

MORE CONVECTION OVEN MENU ITEMS
(By Time, Shelves, Portions and Portions Per Hr.)

	Cooking Time	Number of Shelves	Size Portion	Number Portions per Hour
MEAT, FISH, POULTRY				
Bottom of Round	2-3 hrs*	3	3 oz	425*
Baked Breast of Chicken	45 min	5	5 oz	150
Hamburgers	5-6 min	5	3 oz	950
Meatballs	20-25 min	5	4½ oz	600
Fish Sticks	8-10 min	5	3 oz	800
BAKED GOODS				
Hamburg Rolls	12 min	3	1½ oz	35 doz
Loaf Bread	25 min	3	1 oz	48 lvs.
Brownies	30-40 min	5	2½ oz	45 doz
Custard	25-30 min	5	5 oz	800
Cookies	12-15 min	5	1 oz	600
MISCELLANEOUS				
Oven Browned Cheese Sand.	10-12 min	3	1 each	250
Pizza	15-18 min	3	1 piece	225

COOK AND HOLD CONVECTION OVENS

Typical gas style: 110,000 B.T.U. standard single section.
SIZE: Exterior 40" wide, 36¾" deep, 61¾" high.
    Interior 29" wide, 21½" deep, 20" high.
Available as a deeper oven from most manufacturers for wire basket school lunch systems, or other specific needs.
Features: Oven temperatures are maintained at preset cook temperature setting until timer is satisfied. Fan operates continuously. Meat temperatures rise until nearly done, then the burner turns off and the fan continues to circulate stored heat. When hold temperature is reached, burner and fan cycle only to maintain heat until serving. The lowered energy costs and shrinkage reduction on most meats are very advantageous.

ELECTRIC MOBILE ROAST AND HOLD OVEN CABINETS

Typical size overall: 27" wide, 37¾" deep, 48¼" high and 27" wide, 37¾" deep, 77" high. Each unit rated at 8.5 KW.
Mobile roast and hold ovens use 18" x 26" pans or with universal ledges adapt to standard 12" x 20" pan systems. Large unit will hold maximum of 12 - 18" x 26" pans or 24 - 12" x 20" pans. Smaller oven holds 6 - 18" x 26" pans or 12 - 12" x 20" pans. Another style is available for use with wood slugs for hickory smoking of meats. Options available include vent hood, humidity control with water float system, outer drip troughs and various pan grids. Energy and meat shrinkage advantages, plus point of service positioning are really pluses for these type ovens.

LOW TEMP. ROASTING COOKING GUIDE

Item	No. of Pieces	Estimated Roasting Time	Oven Temp. Degrees F.
Inside top round of beef, split	12-15	5½-6 hrs.	200-210
Steamship round of beef	3	11½-12 hrs.	200-210
#109 beef rib, (fat cap and bone)	14-18	*6-6½ hrs.	200-210
#109 beef rib, (fat cap, no bone)	14-18	4-4½ hrs.	200-210

*Time includes 1 hr. minimum holding at 140°.
NOTES: Internal temperature of meat at start of roasting; 35-45°F. Suggested times are estimated with a moderate load. All meat items on step wire grids (18" x 26" for roasting and to allow air circulation all around pieces of meat. Always sterilize internal meat thermometer before using. Internal temperature of meat for rate is 130°F. This may vary with customers' tastes. Suggested minimum holding temperature for above items is 140°F.

OTHER CAPABILITIES

Item	No. of Pieces	Estimated Roasting Time	Oven Temp. Degrees F.
Leg of Lamb, boned and tied	85-100	4-4½ hrs.	235-250
Lamb shoulder, boned and tied	125-150	3-3½ hrs.	225-235
Canadian backs (boneless pork loin)	30-32	2½-3½ hrs.	235-250
Fresh ham, boned, rolled and tied	30-35	4-4½ hrs.	235-250
Fresh pork shoulder, boned, rolled and tied	50-65	3-3½ hrs.	235-250
*Spare ribs (brush with BBQ sauce)	200-220	2 hrs.	235-250
Chicken halves	168	2 hrs.	255-270
Chicken quarters	320-340	1½-2 hrs.	255-270
Duck halves	120-140	2-2½ hrs.	235-250
Frozen Fish Fillets	500	1-1¼ hrs.	225-250
10" x 12" Retort Pouches (at room temperature)	30	1¼ hrs.	225 - 250
Pre-cooked frozen entrees		2-3 hrs.	225-250

HALF SIZE CONVECTION OVEN

COOKING GUIDE

	Cooking Time	Number of Shelves	Number Size Portion	Portions per Hour
MEAT, FISH, POULTRY				
Baked Stuffed Lobster	10-15 min.	2	1½ #	20
Chicken Breasts	40-50 min.	3	8 oz.	30-35
Cornish Hens	45-60 min.	2	8-10 oz.	24
Meatballs	30-45 min.	3	1½ oz.	100
Roast Sirloin	1-2 hrs.*	1-3	4 oz.	60-150*
BAKED GOODS				
Danish Pastry	12-15 min.	3	1½ oz.	15 doz.
Puff Pastry	25 min.	2	4 oz.	32
Mini Loaves	12-15 min.	2	7 oz.	6 doz.
Pies - Frozen	1 hr.	3	8" pies	9 pies
Pies - Meringue	5-7 min.	2	10" pies	25 pies
MISCELLANEOUS				
Pizza	10-12 min.	3	2 oz.	175
Grilled Cheese Sandwich	8-11 min.	3	1 each	180

*60-150 portions in 1-2 hrs. depending on size of roast(s).

COUNTER ELECTRIC CONVECTION OVEN - GRID STYLE

Overall size: 24" wide, 25" deep, 29" high, using 6.5 KW. Unit will hold 6 1/2 size steam table pans, 1¼" deep or 8 - 1/3 pans 2½" deep or 4 - 2/3 size pans 2½" deep or you may roast directly on grid. For school lunch system 6½" x 5" pre pack meals the capacity per load is 24.

TYPICAL CAPACITY AND COOKING TIME
Capacity and Cooking Time — Single Oven

Dishes	Cooking time in in min.	Pieces on pan	No. of pans	Charges per hour	Output per hour
Hamburgers	15	8	6	4	192 pieces
Cutlets or Chops	12	6	6	5	180 pieces
Liver	6	6	6	12	360 pieces
Sausages, large	9	6	6	6	216 pieces
Steaks	8	6	6	7	252 pieces
Fish Fillets	12	6 6	6	5	
Whole Chlicken (approx. 2½ lb.)	40	3	3	1½-2	18 pieces
Pork Roast	60	1	3	1	15 kg (33 lbs.)
Beef Roast	30	1	3	2	30 kg (66 lbs.)
Bread Rolls	17	12	3	3	108 pieces
Danish Pastries	10	10	6	6	360 pieces

MULTI RACK OVENS OR DRIVE IN CONVECTION OVENS
(Entire truck enters chambers · gas or electric · 2 or 4 rack sizes)

TYPICAL SIZES

Width	Depth	Height	Racks	Heater Location
34"	4'-10"	6'-6"	2	Rear
34"	7'-9"	7'-9"	4	Rear
34"	7'-9"	7'-9"	4	Top

TYPICAL PRODUCTION
(18" x 26" Pans · 4 Rack Oven)

	Cookies	Sheet Cakes	Pies
Per Load	1728	36	216
Rack Centers	3½"	7"	7"
Bake Time	12 min.	30 min.	35 min.
Bake Temp.	375°	375°	375°
Total Per Hr.	6,900	60-70	324

Rack is defined as mobile style 18" x 26" pan carrier constructed for this purpose and not regular tray truck style.

APPROXIMATE BAKE TIMES AND TEMPS · MULTI RACK OVENS

Product	Temp.	Time Minutes
Pizza	600°	5-8 min.
Pie	375/400°	35-50 min.
Cookies	375/400°	12 min.
Rolls	400/425°	20-30 min.
Baked Apple	300/325°	60-70 min.

Power requirements: Electric ovens, 170 KW; gas ovens, 800,000 BTU. Self-cleaning models require 1,000,000 BTU or 170 KW. Units require cold water connection and generate their own steam if required for baking.

HIGH PRODUCTION CONVECTION OVENS

Roll in dolly ovens, electric. Overall sizes: 61" wide, 31½" deep, 63" high. Available in 4 models:
1) Dual speed fan - dual power 27 and 51 KW
2) High speed fan - high heat 51 KW
3) Low speed fan - low heat 27 KW
4) Any of above models adapted for school lunch wire basket systems.

The roll in rack has a removable solid shelf plate which divides the oven into 2 separate cooking compartments and allows to temperature cooking if desired. Some available options to this system include solid state controls, steam injection and vent hood exhaust with motor control. Numerous shelf and grid assemblies available to match cooking requirements.

TYPICAL COOKING GUIDE FOR HIGH PRODUCTION OVENS

Sheet Pans or Racks per Oven Load	ITEM	Pounds/Pieces per Oven Load		Approximate Cooking Time Minutes
4-5	Boneless Beef Rib	280	20	130 - 150
4 - 5	Top Round of Beef	200	10	150 - 165
5 - 6	Top Round Split	240	24	105 - 120
6	Bottom Round Beef	360	18	150 - 165
9 - 18	London Broil, 1"	432	216	10
8	Sirloin Strip Roast	320	32	35 - 45
6	Meat Loaf, 10½"x5½"x4"	300	50	75 - 90
9	Legs of Lamb, boned	288	72	75 - 90
9 - 18	Baked Pork Chops	135	432	20 - 25
9	Baked Chicken Halves	243	162	25 - 30
9	Baked Chicken Quarters	216	288	25 - 30
9	Barbecue Chicken Half	243	162	20 - 25
9 - 18	Sirloin Steaks	202	324	8 - 10
9 - 18	Delmonico Steaks	162	324	8 - 10
9 - 18	Salisbury Steak	169	450	18 - 22
9 - 18	Hamburgers	165	756	5 - 6
9 - 18	Fish Fillet, fresh	304	540	16 - 20

(Continued)

TYPICAL COOKING GUIDE FOR HIGH PRODUCTION OVENS (Cont.)

Sheet Pans or Racks per Oven Load	ITEM	Pounds/Pieces per Oven Load		Approximate Cooking Time Minutes
9	Fresh Fruit Pies	189	54	25 - 35
9 - 18	Cookies, varied	54	864	4 - 6
9 - 18	Sheet Cakes	108	18	25 - 35
9	*Baked Idahos	202	324	35 - 40
9	Frozen Pre-plates	34	54	25 - 30
6	Bread Dressing	120	24	25 - 35
18	Toast/English Muffins	—	432	4 - 5
*From Room Temp.				

FROZEN FOOD PRODUCTS

Sheet Pans per Oven Load	ITEM	Pounds/Pieces per Oven Load		Approximate Cooking Time Minutes	Capacity (Items per pan or grid)
9	Frozen Fruit Pies, 9"x1½", on grid	189	54	45 - 50	6
9 5"x1-9/32"	Individual Pot Pies, 79	180	25	20	
9 4¾"x1-5/8"	Casseroles, Covered, 112	180	45	20	
9	Dinners, Individual - Covered on grids 9"x8½"x1"	31	54	20	6
Baskets per Oven Load 40	School Lunch - Type A, 5"x6½" (10 pans per basket)	350	400	20	400 meals per load
Pans per Oven Load	(All on 12"x20" Stem Table Pans)				
18	Vegetables - Covered	256	18	35 - 45	
18	Potatoes au Gratin - Covered	256	18	45	
18	Beef and Gravy Covered	256	18	45	
18	Spaghetti & Meat Balls Covered	256	18	40	
18	Shrimp Creole - Covered	256	18	40	

OVEN TEMPERATURES

Slow	250-300ºF.	Moderately Hot	400ºF
Slow-Moderate	325º	Hot	425-450ºF.
Moderate	350-375ºF.	Very Hot	475-500ºF.

GAS DECK OVENS - FACTS AND TYPICAL SIZES

Inside Deck Size	Overall Size	BTU's Per Deck
33'' x 22'' x 7'' sections	51'' x 30''	20,000
33'' x 22'' x 2-7'' sections	51'' x 30''	27,000
33'' x 22'' x 12'' sections	51'' x 30''	22,000
33'' x 22'' x 16½'' sections	51 x 30''	27,000
42'' x 32'' x 7'' sections	60'' x 40''	37,000
42'' x 32'' x 2-7'' sections	60'' x 40''	50,000
42'' x 32'' x 12'' sections	60'' x 40''	38,000
42'' x 32'' x 16½'' sections	60'' x 40''	50,000

Using above sizes some possible combinations may be as follows:

Sections	Compartments	Sections	Compartments
1*	1 - 7'' high	1	1 - 12'' high
2	2 - 7'' high	2	2 - 12'' high
3	3 - 7'' high	2	1 - 7'' plus 1 - 12'' high
1	1 - 16¼'' high	3	2 - 7'' plus 1 - 12'' high
2	2 - 16¼'' high	1*	2 - 7'' high
2	1 - 12'' plus 1 - 16¼'' high	2*	4 - 7'' high
2*	2 - 7'' plus 1 - 16¼'' high	2*	2 - 7' plus 1 - 12'' high
2	1 - 7'' plus 1 - 16¼'' high	2*	3 - 7'' high

*These ovens have single burner compartment for 2 decks — all others have burner section for each compartment.

NOTE: Legs available in many heights to accommodate specific requirements.

DECK OVEN PAN CAPACITIES

	DECK SIZE			
Pan Size	33'' x 22''	42'' x 33''	37'' x 54''	56'' x 54''
19-¾'' x 1-7/8''	3	5	7	12
20'' x 11-1/8''	2	5	7	11
23'' x 12-5/8''	1	3	6	8
24-1/16'' x 14-1/16''	1	3	4	7
21-5/8'' x 18½''	1	2	4	6
21-13/16'' x 19-13/16	1	2	2	4
22-1/8'' x 20-1/8''	1	2	2	4
16'' x 20''	2	4	5	8
18'' x 24''	1	2	4	6
18'' x 26''	1	2	4	6
20-7/8'' x 17-3/8''	1	2	4	6

Range ovens normally hold full size 18'' x 26'' pans or smaller pans - 2 per oven.

DECK OVEN
(Suggested requirements by meals served)
12" x 20" Pan Capacity

Meals	Pan Decks Required
250	6
500	10
750	16

HELPFUL HINTS

Deck ovens for baking have a cavity height of approximately 8''. Roasting and general purpose ovens have a cavity height of 11'' to 16''.

When considering a new oven check to see if your present pans will work well in it.

For a completely new system consider a pan flow system from storage to oven and on to serving.

CONVENTIONAL GAS OVEN TIME AND TEMPERATURE
(Guide Only)

Meats	Temperature	Time
BEEF: Ribs	325°	Rare — 16 min./lb.
		Med. — 20 min./lb.
		Well-done — 25 min./lb.
Rolled, Boneless	325°	Add 10 min./lb. to above times
Hip or Rump, Boneless	325°	30 min./lb.
VEAL: Bone-in cuts	325°	25 min./lb.
Boned cuts	325°	30 min./lb.
LAMB: Leg or shoulder	325°	35 min./lb.
Shoulder, Boned	325°	40 min./lb.
PORK: Fresh		
Bone-in cuts	350°	30-40 min./lb.
Boned cuts	350°	40-50 min./lb.
Spareribs	350°	1½ hrs./batch
PORK: Smoked	325°	16-20 min./lb.
Sliced Ham (2'' thick)	325°	1½ hrs.
Picnic Hams	325°	35 min./lb.
Hams	325°	25-30 min./lb.
Bacon	350°	Depends on degree of doneness
Sausages, links, patties	350°	30 min./lb.
Frankfurters	325°	8-10 min./lb.
Meat Loaf, Ham or Beef	325°	1½ hrs.
Roast Beef Hash	350°	30-45 min./lb.
Meat Pies, deep dish	450°	12-15 min./lb.
POULTRY		
Springs	350°	15 min./lb.
Chickens, 2-3 lbs.	350°	35 min./lb.
Chickens, over 5 lbs.	325°	20-25 min./lb.
Chicken Pies	450°	15-25 min.
Turkeys, 10-16 lbs.	325°	18-20 min./lb.
Turkeys, 25 lbs.	325°	15-18 min./lb.
Turkeys, 30-35 lbs.	325°	20-25 min./lb.
Ducks		Same as Chickens
Geese		Same as Turkeys

Weights are for unstuffed birds. Stuffed, add 15 min./lb.

(Continued)

CONVENTIONAL GAS OVEN TIME AND TEMPERATURE (Cont.)
(Guide Only)

Meats	Temperature	Time
FISH		
Fish, whole	350°	15 min./lb.
Fish Fillets	350°	15-20 min./lb.
Shrimp Fondue	350°	45-60 min./lb.
Lobster	400°	Appr. 20 min./lb.
Oysters, Casino	350°	15 min.
Oysters, Devilled	350°	15 min.
Oysters, Rockefeller	450°	10 min.
Salmon Loaf	350°	45-90 min./lb.

Vegetables	Temperature	Time
BAKED		
Bananas	350°	15-20 min./lb.
Beets	350°	45-60 min./lb.
Boston Beans	250°	8 hrs.
Lima Beans	350°	Approx. 2 hrs.
Carrots	400°	Until tender
Egg Plant	350°	Until tender
Macaroni	350°	15-25 min./lb.
Mushrooms	350°	Until brown
Stuffed Peppers	350°	25 min./lb.
Potatoes	400°	75-90 min.
Spinach Loaf	325°	25 min./lb.
Tomatoes	350°	15-20 min./lb.

CHEESE		
Cheese Fondue	350°	40 min./lb.
Cheese Loaf	325°	40 min./lb.
Toasted Cheese	350°	15 min./lb.
Cheese Souffle	300°	20 min./lb.
Au gratin dishes	450°	Until browned

BAKED GOODS		
Breads: Bread, white, yeast	375-425°	30-45 min.
Raisin	400°	40 min.
Breads, rich	400°	30-45 min.
Breads, Vienna	400°	35-50 min.
Breads, rye	375°	45-90 min.
Melba toast	450-500°	Until done
Rolls:Rolls, standard white	375-400°	20-45 min.
Rolls, Parker House	400-425°	15-20 min.
Clover-leaf	400-425°	15-20 min.
Rolls, sweet dough mix	350-375°	20-40 min.
Biscuits	375-400°	15-25 min.
Danish pastry	375-400°	20-35 min.
Pies: Fresh Fruit	375-400°	50-60 min.
Pies, precooked filling	475°	20-35 min.
Pie shells	400-450°	15 min.
Pies, custard	325-450°	Depending upon filling

(Continued)

CONVENTIONAL GAS OVEN TIME AND TEMPERATURE (Cont.)
(Guide Only)

	Temperature	Time
BAKED GOODS		
Cakes: Cookies	400-475°	8-15 min.
Cheesecake, standard	350°	40 min.
Cheesecake, French	Not over 300°	1½ hrs.
Devil's Food	360-375°	20-25 min.
Fruit	300°	1½ hrs., up
White layers	350-375°	20-35 min.
Yellow layers	375°	15-25 min.
Streisel	400°	25-30 min.
DESSERTS AND PUDDINGS		
Baked Apples	400°	Approx. 1 hr.
Brown Betty	325°	45-60 min.
Fruit Pudding	375°	1 hr.
Indian Pudding	325°	3 hrs.
Miscl. Fruits	400-450°	Variable
Rice Pudding	350°	Variable

SAMPLE CAPACITIES OF DECK OVENS
(By size and product)

ELECTRIC OVENS

Deck Size: 42" wide x 32" deep

Product	Pan	No. Pans Per Deck	Produces Per Hr.
Dinner Rolls	18" x 26"	2	16-20 dz.
Layer Cake	8" Diam.	20	60
Macaroni	12" x 20"	4	960 - 4 oz. servings
Potatoes	Size varies		60-140

52" x 37" Deck

Dinner Rolls	18" x 26"	4	54 dz.
Layer Cake	8" Diam.	24	72
Macaroni	12" x 20"	6	1440 - 4 oz. servings
Potatoes	Varies		86 - 200

52" x 56" Deck

Dinner Rolls	18" x 26"	6	48 - 60 dz.
Layer Cake	8" Diam.	42	126
Macaroni	10		
Macaroni	12" x 20"	10	2400 - 4 oz. servings
Potatoes	Varies		130 - 305

102

TOP AND BOTTOM COOKING

Top and bottom cooking is the principle employed in electric bake ovens. Heating units are located within the baking compartment to assure utilization of all heat for thermal efficiency. And since electric ovens require no openings for the entrance of outside air to remove products of combustion, all oven sides can be uniformly insulated. Escape of heat during the baking process is reduced to minimum.

True radiant heat from the upper unit assures perfect quality control of the product top. Balanced convected heat from the lower unit assures perfect quality control of the product bottom.

Each heating unit has an area equal to approximately that of the deck and is arranged for 3-heat (low, medium, high) operation and is thermostatically controlled. This basic arrangement provides uniform heat in all size electric ovens . . . one, two and three deck.

Big advantages: less meat shrinkage and precise heat control.

HELPFUL HINTS

Allow at least 2" clearance for air circulation around pans in convection, roast or bake ovens.

CONVENTIONAL ELECTRIC TIME AND TEMPERATURE GUIDE

Product	Temperature	Top Switch	Bottom Switch	Time Minutes
Two Crust Pies	400-425	Med.	High	40-60
Open Face Pie	400-425	Med.	High	35-50
*Pumpkin Pie	375-400	Med.	Med.	35-50
*Custard Pie	375-400	Med.	Med.	35-50
Meringue Pie (browned)	425-450	High	Off	5-6
Parker House Rolls	400-425	Med.	Med.	20-30
Danish Rolls	375-400	Med.	Med.	20-30
Sweet Rolls	375-400	Med.	Med.	20-30
Tea Biscuits	375-400	Med.	Med.	20-25
Corn Bread	400-425	Med.	Med.	25-35
Layer Cake	350-375	Med.	Med.	20-30
Angel Cake	300-325	Med.	Med.	40-50
Puddings	325-375	Med.	Med.	35-60
Pizza (pre-prepared)	500	High	High	5
Pizza (fresh)	500	High	High	15

*Used when crust and filling are baked as a unit. When crust is pre-baked and filling only is to be baked, most bakers use a temperature of approximately 300-350°F.

103

MEAT ROASTING GUIDE

SWITCH SETTINGS: For best results, set both oven switches on HIGH, with the temperature control at the indicated setting. Measured top heat provides excellent coloring and a caramelized finish to meats, but where a browned appearance is not desired (as in roasting fowl), the upper oven switch should be set to MEDIUM, LOW, or OFF.

Fully Thawed Type of Meat	Temperature Setting	Internal Meat Temp. Deg. F.	Minutes Per Lb.
Beef			
Standing Rib	300⁰	Rare 125⁰	13
7 Rib 20-25 lbs.		Med. 140⁰	15
		Well 150⁰	17
Rolled Rib	250⁰	Well 150⁰	25
7 Rib 16-18 lbs.			
Rump or Chuck 18-23 lbs.	300⁰	140-170⁰	20-30
Lamb			
Leg 7-8 lbs.	300⁰	180⁰	30-35
Shoulder	300⁰	180⁰	40-45
Pork			
Ham Leg 15 lbs.	350⁰	185⁰	30-35
Ham Boned 15 lbs.	350⁰	185⁰	30-35
Boston Butt	350⁰	185⁰	45-50
Cured Ham 20 lbs.	300⁰	160⁰	15-18
Veal			
Leg 25 lbs.	300⁰	170⁰	18-20
Shoulder 15 lbs.	300⁰	170⁰	25
Shoulder Rolled 10 lbs.	300⁰	170⁰	35-40
Poultry			
Chicken, Dressed 4-6 lbs.	250-300⁰	190⁰	35-40
Duck, Dressed 5-8 lbs.	300⁰	190⁰	25-30
Turkey, Dressed 14-19 lbs.	300⁰	190⁰	20-25

NOTE: The above data is of a general nature. Many factors such as size of bone, thickness of meat, temperature at time of roasting, etc. affect cooking time.

REVOLVING TRAY OR REEL OVENS
(Trays Revolve Ferris Wheel Style)

TYPICAL SIZES AND CAPACITIES

Tray Size	Wide	High	Deep	18"x26" Bun Pans	12"x20" Steam Table Pans	CAPACITIES Loaves 1 lb. †	1½ lb. ‡	9" Pies
6—22"x56"	7'10"	6'10"	7'3"	12	24	120	96	72
4—26"x56"	7'10"	6'10"	7'3"	12	20	80	64	68
5—26"x56"	7'10"	6'10"	7'3"	15	25	100	80	85

(Continued)

TYPICAL SIZES AND CAPACITIES (Cont.)

Tray Size	Wide	High	Deep	18"x26" Bun Pans	12"x20" Steam Table Pans	CAPACITIES Loaves 1 lb. †	CAPACITIES Loaves 1½ lb. ‡	9" Pies
6—22"x74"	9'4"	6'10"	7'3"	12	36	168	120	90
4'-16"x74"	9'4"	6'10"	7'3"	16	28	112	96	84
5—26"x74"	9'4"	6'10"	7'3"	20	35	140	120	105
6—22"x94"	11'0"	6'10"	7'3"	18	42	218	168	120
4—26"x94"	11'0"	6'10"	7'3"	20	36	144	128	116
5—26"x94"	11'0"	6'10"	7'3"	25	45	180	160	145
5—26"x94"	11'0"	6'10"	7'3"	25	45	180	160	145
6—22"x112"	12'6"	6'10"	7'3"	24	54	264	192	144
4—26"x112"	12'6"	6'10"	7'3"	24	40	176	160	140
5—26"x112"	12'6"	6'10"	7'3"	30	50	220	200	175
6—22"x148"	15'6"	6'10"	7'3"	30	72	336	288	198
4—26"x148"	15'6"	6'10"	7'3"	32	56	224	192	188
5—26"x148"	15'6"	6'10"	7'3"	40	70	280	240	235
8—26"x74"	10'2"	10'5½"	10'8"	32	56	224	192	168
8—26"x94"	11'10"	10'5½"	10'8"	40	72	288	256	232
8—26"x112"	13'4"	10'5½"	10'8"	48	80	352	320	280
8—26"x130"	14'10"	10'5½"	10'8"	56	96	384	352	304
8—26"x148"	16'4"	10'5½"	10'8"	64	112	448	384	376

These large ovens range from 30 KW to 170 KW in electric models and from 120,000 BTU to 1,000,000 BTU in gas models.

Rotary ovens similar to those above are available, the difference being that the trays revolve on a vertical axis - merry-go-round style.

TYPICAL STEAM HORSE POWER REQUIRED FOR STEAM INJECTION USED IN BAKING

Some products require steam for part of the bake to enhance appearance and quality. These include hearth breads, hard rolls, split-top and some plain-top pan breads.

Low pressure steam (5-7 lbs. p.s.i.) is injected into the oven chamber through interior piping before loading the product, and maintained for five to 10 minutes after loading. After the dough has set, the steam has little effect.

STEAM REQUIREMENTS BY BOILER
(Horsepower Needed and Oven Type)

| EQUIPMENT | CAPACITY | BOILER HORSEPOWER | |
		Electric Oven	Gas Oven
Flat or Brick Ovens:			
Single Deck	8/12 Bun Pans	½	1
Single Deck	18/24 Bun Pans	1	1½
Single Deck	32 Bun Pans	2	3
Single Deck	42 Bun Pans	3	4
Double Deck	6/8 Bun Pans	½	1
Double Deck	12/18 Bun Pans	1	1½
Double Deck	24 Bun Pans	2	3
Double Deck	36 Bun Pans	3	4
Rotary Ovens:			
Single Deck	8 Bun Pans	1	1½
Single Deck	18 Bun Pans	1½	2
Single Deck	24 Bun Pans	2	3
Single Deck	36 Bun Pans	4	5
Double Deck	8 Bun Pans	1	2
Double Deck	12 Bun Pans	2	3
Double Deck	18 Bun Pans	3	4
Double Deck	24 Bun Pans	4	5
Revolving Ovens:			
Single Rack	12/18 Bun Pans	1½	2
Single Rack	18/24 Bun Pans	2	3
Double Rack	24/36 Bun Pans	3	4
Double Rack	36/48 Bun Pans	5	6
Proof Boxes:			
	250 Cu. Ft.	½	—
	450 Cu. Ft.	1	—
	1000 Cu. Ft.	2	—
	2600 Cu. Ft.	4	—

MICROWAVE OVENS

Another book in itself, many articles, books, and demonstrations have brought the commercial microwave to most everyone's attention. After much discussion with manufacturers, reps, and users, FEF has reduced this section to factful, useful, and hopefully easy reading. While we have covered the main points quite thoroughly FEF has two final thoughts on microwaves: 1) Read your user's manual carefully and 2) If you are planning a new operation involving microwave cooking, you may find an in-house demonstration using your specific menu items to be advantageous before final selection.

User's manuals will discuss care and cleaning procedures, utensils to be used in the oven, and specific applications. FEF will touch on food positioning, desirable design features and sample cooking guides for ovens by wattage. Wattage in microwave ovens is discussed in terms of output power.

HOW TO POSITION FOOD ON THE PLATE
FOR MICROWAVE HEATING

Several factors should be kept in mind when selecting utensils to be used for microwave heating.
1. A plate with a narrow rim of about 1/2-inch is recommended. This keeps the food all at the same level for more even, uniform heating.
2. Casseroles and sauced items should be heated in straight sided containers.
3. Containers should be chosen to be large enough to contain foods as they expand with heating. Milk products are especially subject to boil-overs.
4. Plastic, foam and paper plates should not be used when heating high fat or sugar foods such as barbecue as the heat from the fat and sugar may distort the plate.
5. Most foods heat better if they are covered. Covering retains the heat that has been created, reduces dehydration and helps keep the oven clean. There should be an opening for steam to escape from the food. Covers should also be non-metallic to allow for proper heating.
When placing foods on plate for microwave heating remember:
1. Sandwiches should be heated uncovered to prevent sogginess.
2. Sandwiches should be heated on a paper towel or napkin to absorb moisture.
3. Larger pieces of food should be placed around the outside edge of the container for best heating of casseroles or plates.
4. The center of the casserole should be slightly depressed for even heating.
5. The meat and vegetables in a caserole should be coated with sauce to reheat more easily.
6. Casseroles with crusts are the only ones that should be heated uncovered. Covering will help to speed heating of other types of casseroles.
7. Sliced meats should be at least 1/2-inch thick for best heating results. Turning the meat product over once during the heating process will yield more uniform heating.
8. The microwave oven is quite useful in reducing broiling times for steaks and chops. Partially prepare the meat in microwave oven, then broil for a shorter period of time.

9. Small uniform sized vegetables like peas, diced carrots and corn heat easily in the microwave oven. A butter sauce will speed the process.
10. Larger bulkier vegetables like brussel sprouts, small whole carrots and parsnips are slightly more difficult to heat in the microwave oven. They should be placed with the bulkier pieces towards the edges.
11. Pastries, pies and yeast cakes should be heated uncovered to prevent sogginess.
12. When plating an entire meal, place hard to heat food at the perimeter of the plate and easier to heat foods near the center.
13. Place thin slices of meat toward the center of the plate. Thicker slices should be placed towards the outside edge of the plate. Place vegetables and starches on the plate according to their degree of difficulty in heating.

REMINDERS:
1. Do not operate the oven empty. Either food or water should always be in the oven during operation to absorb microwave energy.
2. Limit use of metal to those specific examples given in this book. Generally, metal should not be used in the microwave oven during operation.
3. Do not cook eggs in the shell. Pressure will build up inside the shell and it will explode. Do not reheat cooked eggs unless they are scrambled or chopped. Puncture the yolk before cooking eggs.
4. Do not heat oil or fat for deep fat frying.
5. Pierce the "skin" of potatoes, whole squash, apples or any fruit or vegetable which has a skin covering before cooking.

MICROWAVE OVEN SIZES

The most popular sizes of microwave ovens are those having output power of 650 watts, 1000 watts or 1400 watts. Other outputs available.

650 WATT MICROWAVE
Outside dimensious 22" wide, 17¼", 16" high.
Inside dimensions 13¾" wide, 13¼" deep, 8½" high
Power 115-120 volts - 15 amp circuit

DESIRABLE DESIGN FEATURES:
The 650 watt microwave oven is ideal for low volume installations such as snack bars, waitress stations, bars and grills.

IT FEATURES: 9 computer controlled pushbuttons, easily re-programmed and customized to your needs. It has 32 time settings from 6 seconds to 4 minutes.

INSTANT ON: No delay or waiting time for start-up.

COMPLETION SIGNAL: Alerts operator.

CONCEALED ON-OFF SWITCH: Prevents unauthorized use.

SEE-THROUGH DOOR:

INTERCHANGEABLE STICKER LABELS: For varying or custom-izing menus.

REMOVABLE FILTER: No tools necessary.

3 YEAR WARRANTY on magnetron tube.

25 MINUTE DIAL TIMER: In place of push buttons for longer heat-ing times and larger volume use. Signal bell rings when fin-ished. Cooking indicator light on panel.

VARIABLE POWER: Adjustable from 10 to 100% power.

HEATING AND COOKING TIME GUIDE
(For 650 Watt Oven)

Quantity	Item	Approximate Heating Time
Pastries, Rolls and Baked Goods		
1	Biscuit	10 sec.
2	Buns	10 sec.
1	Danish Pastry	20 sec.
2	Dinner Rolls	10 sec.
1	Doughnut	20 sec.
1	Muffin (small)	10 sec.
1	Pie	60 sec.
1	Sweet Roll	20 sec.
Breakfast Items		
7 oz.	French Toast & Bacon	40 sec.
7 oz.	French Toast & Sausage	40 sec.
7 oz.	Pancakes & Bacon	40 sec.
7 oz.	Pancakes & Sausage	40 sec.
5 oz.	Scrambled Eggs & Bacon	30 sec.
5 oz.	Scrambled Eggs & Bacon	30 sec.
5 oz.	Scrambled Eggs & Sausage	40 sec.
4 strips	Bacon	60 sec.
4 links	Sausage	60 sec.
Sandwiches		
4 oz.	Bacon & Tomato	40 sec.
4½ oz.	Beef Barbecue	40 sec.
4½ oz.	Burger	60 sec.
4½ oz.	Cheeseburger	60 sec.
4½ oz.	Corned Beef	60 sec.

(Continued)

109

HEATING AND COOKING TIME GUIDE (Cont.)
(For 650 Watt Oven)

Quantity	Item	Approximate Heating Time
3 oz.	Frankfurter	40 sec.
5 oz.	Jumbo Frankfurter	60 sec.
3½ oz.	Grilled Cheese	10 sec.
3½ oz.	Ham Sandwich	40 sec.
4 oz.	Ham & Cheese	40 sec.
5 oz.	Italian Sausage	80 sec.
4½ oz.	Pastrami	60 sec.
3½ oz.	Roast Beef	40 sec.
5½ oz.	Submarine/Hoagie	60 sec.
5 oz.	Chili Burger	60 sec.
5 oz.	Chili Dog	40 sec.
5 oz.	Sloppy Joe	60 oz.

Casseroles

Quantity	Item	Approximate Heating Time
7 oz.	Baked Beans	120 sec.
7 oz.	Beef Burgundy	120 sec.
7 oz.	Beef Goulash	120 sec.
7 oz.	Beef Stew	120 sec.
7 oz.	Beef Slices w/gravy	120 sec.
7 oz.	Cabbage Rolls	120 sec.
7 oz.	Chicken Fricassee	120 sec.
7 oz.	Chicken a la King	180 sec.
7 oz.	Chili Con Carne	180 sec.
7 oz.	Creamed Chicken	120 sec.
7 oz.	Lasagna	120 sec.
7 oz.	Meat Loaf	180 sec.
7 oz.	Macaroni (beef sauce)	120 sec.
7 oz.	Macaroni (cheese sauce)	120 sec.
8 oz.	Stuffed Peppers	180 sec.
7 oz.	Pot Pie	180 sec.
7 oz.	Ravioli	180 sec.
7 oz.	Shrimp Creole	180 sec.
7 oz.	Shrimp Newburg	180 sec.
8 oz.	Short Ribs of Beef	180 sec.
7 oz.	Spaghetti	120 sec.
7 oz.	Stew, Chicken	120 sec.
7 oz.	Tuna Casserole	120 sec.
7½ oz.	Turkey Slices	180 sec.
4 oz.	Asparagus	60 sec.
4 oz.	Beans, green	60 sec.
4 oz.	Broccoli	60 sec.
4 oz.	Carrot slices	60 sec.
4 oz.	Cauliflower	40 sec.
4 oz.	Corn niblets	40 sec.
4 oz.	Mushrooms	40 sec.
4 oz.	Peas	40 sec.
4 oz.	Potatoes au gratin	60 sec.
7 oz.	Potatoes pre-baked	60 sec.

(Continued)

HEATING AND COOKING TIME GUIDE (Cont.)
(For 650 Watt Oven)

Quantity	Item	Approximate Heating Time
Defrosting		
8 oz.	Club Steak	40 on 40 off 40 on
14 oz.	Cornish Game Hen	120 on 120 off 120 on
8 oz.	Halibut Steak	40 on 40 off 40 on
8 oz.	Lamb Chops	40 on 40 off 40 on
6 oz.	Lobster Tail	40 on 40 off 40 on
8 oz.	Pork Chops	60 on 60 off 40 on
8 oz.	Salmon Steak	40 on 40 off 40 on
8 oz.	Shrimp	40 on 40 off 40 on
12 oz.	Strip Steak	40 on 40 off 40 on
10 oz.	Vegetable in pouch	60 on 60 off 40 on
Primary Cooking		
2 slices	Bacon	120 sec.
1 ear	Corn on the cob	120 sec.
5 oz.	Scrambled Eggs	120 sec.
6 oz.	Lobster Tail	180 sec.
6 oz.	Small Potato	4 min.
8 oz.	Trout	180 sec.

1000 WATT MICROWAVE
Outside dimensions 22" wide, 24¼" deep, 16" high
Inside dimensions 13¾" wide, 13¼" deep, 8½" high
Power 115-120 volts - 20 amp circuit

DESIRABLE DESIGN FEATURES:
The 1000 watt unit is recommended for moderate volume installations such as coffee shops, restaurants, diners, fast food operations and convenience stores.

IT FEATURES: 9 Computer controlled pushbuttons, easily reprogrammed and customized according to needs. Thirty-two (32) time settings from 6 seconds - 4 minutes.

10 MINUTE DIAL TIMER

TWO MAGNETRONS WITH DUAL CIRCUITRY: For greater durability and more uniform heating.

INSTANT-ON: No delay or waiting time for start up.

AUTOMATIC EDGE-CONTROL: Pulsates at 15 second on/off intervals. Eliminates overheating and crusting of edges.

COMPLETION SIGNAL: Beeps when finished.

CONCEALED ON-OFF SWITCH: Prevents unauthorized use.

ANTI-THEFT DEVICE: Provides for bolting.

SEE-THROUGH DOOR

MAGNETRON FAILURE INDICATOR LIGHT: Green light appears next to first position button.

INTERCHANGEABLE STICKER LABELS: For varying and customizing menus.

REMOVABLE FILTER: No tools necessary.
3 YEAR WARRANTY ON MAGNETRON TUBES.

Above unit is available without dial timer and automatic edge-control.

In place of pushbuttons the same 1000 watt unit is also available with:

COMPUTERIZED*TOUCH CONTROL WITH DIGITAL DISPLAY: Timer allows for settings up to 9 minutes 99 seconds for maximum flexibility and customizing. Programmed by memory key. Electrostatic safety shield prevents unauthorized use.

1000 WATT MICROWAVE
COOKING AND HEATING GUIDE

See the beginning of this section for microwave helpful hints. The following charts will guide you on time for a 1000 watt output oven. Higher wattage units will decrease cooking and heating times. Experimenting with your specific menu needs will be the final determining factor in selection. Almost as important as power output is proper positioning of foods and simple procedures as described in the hint section will produce better results.

1000 WATT MICROWAVE PRODUCTION CHARTS

Quantity	Item	Approximate Heating Time
Appetizers		
6 oz.	Barbecued Ribs	70-80 sec.
4 oz.	Chicken Livers	40-50 sec.
5-6 oz.	Chicken Wings	60-70 sec.
4 medium	Clams, stuffed	60-70 sec.
4 oz.	Dates wrapped in Bacon	30-40 sec.
6 medium	Escargots	50-60 sec.
4-5 oz.	Meatballs in Sauce	40-50 sec.
3-4 oz.	Stuffed Mushrooms	30-40 sec.
3-4 oz.	Olives wrapped in Bacon	30-40 sec.
Breakfast Items		
4 strips	Bacon	40-50 sec.
5-6 oz.	French Toast & Sausage	30-40 sec.
4 oz.	Hash Brown Potatoes	40-50 sec.
6 oz.	Omelet (filled)	50-60 sec.
4 oz.	Omelet (plain)	40-50 sec.
4 oz.	Pancakes	30-40 sec.
6-7 oz.	Pancakes and Bacon	40-50 sec.
6-7 oz.	Pancakes and Sausage	40-50 sec.
4 links	Sausage	30-40 sec.
3 oz.	Scrambled Eggs	30-40 sec.
6 oz.	Scrambled Eggs	50-60 sec.
5 oz.	Scrambled Eggs and Bacon	40-50 sec.
5 oz.	Scrambled Eggs & Sausage	40-50 sec.

(Continued)

112

1000 WATT MICROWAVE PRODUCTION CHARTS (Cont.)

Quantity	Item	Approximate Heating Time
Casseroles/Main Dishes		
7 oz.	Baked Beans	70-80 sec.
7 oz.	Beef Burgundy	80-90 sec.
7 oz.	Beef Goulash	70-80 sec.
7 oz.	Beef Slices with Gravy	70-80 sec.
7 oz.	Beef Stew	80-90 sec.
7 oz.	Cabbage Rolls	80-90 sec.
7 oz.	Chicken a la King	60-70 sec.
7 oz.	Chicken Fricassee	70-80 sec.
7 oz.	Chili Con Carne	70-80 sec.
7 oz.	Creamed Chicken	70-80 sec.
7 oz.	Lasagna	80-90 sec.
7 oz.	Macaroni (beef sauce)	60-70 sec.
7 oz.	Macaroni (cheese sauce)	70-80 sec.
7 oz.	Meat Loaf	80-90 sec.
7 oz.	Pot Pie	80-90 sec.
7 oz.	Ravioli	80-90 sec.
8 oz.	Short Ribs of Beef	80-90 sec.
7 oz.	Shrimp Creole	60-70 sec.
7 oz.	Shrimp or Seafood Newburg	60-70 sec.
7 oz.	Spaghetti	60-70 sec.
7 oz.	Stew, Chicken	80-90 sec.
8 oz.	Stuffed Peppers	80-90 sec.
7 oz.	Tuna Casserole	80-90 sec.
7 oz.	Turkey Slices with Gravy	70-80 sec.
Pastries, Rolls and Baked Goods		
1 slice	Apple Pie with Cheese	20-30 sec.
2	Biscuits	10 sec.
1	Bun	6 sec.
1 slice	Coffee Cake	10 sec.
1	Danish Pastry	10 sec.
1	Dinner Roll	6 sec.
2	Dinner Rolls	10 sec.
1	Doughnut	6 sec.
2	Doughnuts	10 sec.
1 slice	Fruit Pie	20 sec.
1	Muffin	6 sec.
2	Muffins	10 sec.
1	Sweet Roll	10 sec.
Cooked Sandwiches		
4½ oz.	Grilled Cheese with Tomato	20-30 sec.
4 oz.	Ham Sandwich	20-30 sec.
4-5 oz.	Ham and Cheese	20-30 sec.
5 oz.	Italian Sausage	30-40 sec.
4-5 oz.	Pastrami	20-30 sec.
6 oz.	Reuben	30 sec.
4 oz.	Roast Beef	20-30 sec.
4 oz.	Sloppy Joe	20-30 se.c
4-5 oz.	Submarine/Hoagie	20-30 sec.

(Continued)

1000 WATT MICROWAVE PRODUCTION CHARTS (Cont.)

Quantity	Item	Approximate Heating Time
4-5 oz.	Bacon and Tomato	20-30 sec.
4-5 oz.	Beef Barbecue	20-30 sec.
4-5 oz.	Burger	20-30 sec.
4-5 oz.	Cheeseburger	20-30 sec.
5 oz.	Chili Burger	30-40 sec.
4 oz.	Chili Dog	20-30 sec.
4-5 oz.	Corned Beef	20-30 sec.
3 oz.	Frankfurter/Hot Dog	20 sec.
5 oz.	Frankfurter, Jumbo	20-30 sec.
3½ oz.	Grilled Cheese	20-30 sec.

DEFROSTING MEATS

8 oz.	Club Steak	90-120 sec.
8 oz.	Lamb Chops	90-120 sec.
5-6 oz.	Minute Steak	60-75 sec.
8 oz.	Pork Chops	90-120 sec.
6-8 oz.	Rib Eye Steak	90-100 sec.

Poultry

4-5 oz.	Chicken Breast, boneless	60-70 sec.
16-18 oz.	Chicken, halved	3½-4 min.
12-14 oz.	Cornish Game Hen	2½-3 min.

Seafood

12-14 oz.	Crab Legs	2½-3 min.
5-6 oz.	Fillet of Sole	70-80 sec.
5-6 oz.	Halibut Steak	70-80 sec.
6-8 oz.	Lobster Tail	80-90 sec.
6-8 oz.	Salmon Steak	80-90 sec.
6 oz.	Scallops	80-90 sec.
8 oz.	Shrimp	90-120 sec.
12-14 oz.	Stuffed Flounder	2½-3 min.
6-8 oz.	Trout	80-90 sec.

Vegetables

4 oz.	Asparagus	30-40 sec.
1 medium	Artichoke	40-50 sec.
4 oz.	Beans, green	30-40 sec.
4 oz.	Beans, lima	30-40 sec.
4 oz.	Beans, wax	30-40 sec.
4 oz.	Beets	40-50 sec.
4 oz.	Broccoli	30-40 sec.
4 oz.	Brussels Sprouts	40-50 sec.
4 oz.	Carrot Slices	40-50 sec.
4 oz.	Carrots, whole baby	50-60 sec.
4 oz.	Cauliflower	40-50 sec.
4 oz.	Corn Niblets	30-40 sec.
4 oz.	Mixed Vegetables	40-50 sec.
4 oz.	Mushrooms	20-30 sec.
4 oz.	Peas, green	20-30 sec.
4 oz.	Potatoes au gratin	40-50 sec.

(Continued)

114

1000 WATT MICROWAVE PRODUCTION CHARTS (Cont.)

Quantity	Item	Approximate Heating Time
4 oz.	Potatoes, mashed	50-60 sec.
4 oz.	Potatoes, prebaked	40-50 sec.
4 oz.	Spinach	30-40 sec.

Primary Cooking

2 strips	Bacon	80-90 sec.
6-8 strips	Bacon	3-3½ min.
1 medium	Baked Potato	3-4 min.
2 medium	Baked Potatoes	6-7 min.
3 medium	Baked Potatoes	10-11 min.
1 ear	Corn on the Cob	2-3 min.
2 ears	Corn on the Cob	5-6 min.
4 ears	Corn on the Cob	8-9 min.
5-6 oz.	Fish Fillet	1½-2 min.
6-8 oz.	Lobster Tail	2-2½ min.
2 eggs	**Scrambled Eggs**	**50-60 sec.**
6-8 oz.	**Trout**	**2-3 min.**

1400 WATT MICROWAVE
    Outside dimensions 22-1/16" wide, 23-5/8" deep, 16 high
    Inside dimensions 13¾" wide, 13½" deep, 7-9/16" high
    Power 208/230 volts, 15 amp circuit

DESIRABLE DESIGN FEATURES:
    The 1400 watt unit is recommended for high volume installations such as hospitals, restaurants, institutions and nursing homes.
        IT FEATURES: 9 computer controlled pushbuttons easily reprogrammed and customized according to needs. Thirty-two (32) time settings from 6 seconds - 4 minutes.
    10 MINUTE DIAL TIMER
    TWO MAGNETRONS WITH DUAL CIRCUITRY: For greater durability and more uniform heating.
    INSTANT-ON: No delay or waiting time for start up.
    AUTOMATIC EDGE-CONTROL: Pulsates at 15 second on/off intervals. Eliminates overheating and crusting of edges.
    COMPLETION SIGNAL: Beeps when finished.
    CONCEALED ON-OFF SWITCH: Prevents unauthorized use.
    ANTI-THEFT DEVICE: Provides for bolting.
    SEE-THROUGH DOOR
    MAGNETRON FAILURE INDICATOR LIGHT: Green light appears next to first position button.
    INTERCHANGEABLE STICKER LABELS: For varying and customizing menus.
    REMOVABLE FILTER: No tools necessary.
    3 YEAR WARRANTY ON MAGNETRON TUBES

Above unit is available without dial timer and automatic edge-control.

In place of pushbuttons the same 1400 watt unit is available with:
COMPUTERIZED TOUCH CONTROL WITH DIGITAL DISPLAY: Timer allows for settings up to 9 minutes 99 seconds for maximum flexibility and customizing. Programmed by memory key. Electrostatic safety shield prevents unauthorized use.

PIZZA OVENS

STYLES AVAILABLE:
1) Conventional gas and electric
2) Counter or free standing
3) No door - open pizza oven
4) Conveyor ovens - countertop
5) Conveyor ovens - floor and stacking type
6) Open door forced convection oven with rotating shelves

BRAINSTORMING PIZZA OVEN OPTIONS:
1) Steel deck
2) Bricks
3) Composition hearth
4) Maximum temp. available
5) Pan sizes versus capacities
6) Venting requirements

COUNTERTOP PIZZA OVEN
(Electric - 550° to 700° Maximum)

Overall Oven Size					
Wide	Deep	High	Max. Pizza	Per Load	KW
18''	15''	10''	12'' Dia.	1	1,600 (115V.)
23''	19''	10''	16'' Dia.	1	1,700 (115V.)
22''	22''	18''	17'' Dia.	2	1,700 (115V.)
26''	26''	18''	21'' Dia.	2	3,500 (220V.)
32''	26½''	25''	21'' Dia.	4	7,000 (220V.)

550° Temp. = Five Minute Pizza

COUNTERTOP PIZZA OVEN
(No Door Style)

Open front of oven has two heat reflectors which can be raised, lowered or removed. Infra red heaters top and bottom are capable of maintaining 650° oven temperature. Voltages available: 208, single phase, 8.5 KW, 230, single phase, 10.6 KW or 240, single phase, 11.5 KW.

Overall size: 72" wide, 26" deep, 20½" high, including 7" high legs. Ovens may be stacked 3 units high.

Temperature control from 300° to 650°F.

OPEN DOOR PIZZA OVEN
(Rotating Shelves - Forced Convected Air)

Oven features three openings. Unit is 6'-0" wide, 5'-2" deep, 7'-9" high with a built-in exhaust fan and hood. Available in choice of baked enamel color.

Pizzas Per Opening, Size and Total Load

Pizza Size	Per Opening	Total Load
9"	18	54
10"	14	42
12"	6	18
21"	3	9

Available Gas: 290,000 B.T.U.'s or 220V, 440V, 3 phase. Three 48" shelves rotate at 3 R.P.M.

TYPICAL PRODUCTION OF GAS PIZZA OVEN
(By Style Pizza)

Assumes 48" x 36" Deck Size, 124,000 B.T.U.'s

Pan Sizes	Per Load
10"	12
12"	9
15"	6

Per Hour Production

Pizza Style	Pan Diameter		
	10"	12"	15"
Pan Style	78	58	40
Hearth Style	130	98	65
Sicilian	18" x 26" pan, 12 per hour		

PIZZA OVENS - CAPACITIES BY DECK SIZE

Deck Size		16" Pizza
Width	Depth	Per Deck
36" x 26"		3
26" x 36"		4
45" x 36"		4
54" x 36"		6
60" x 36"		Up to 6-18"

117

CONVEYOR PIZZA OVENS · FLOOR MODELS

Stackable decks, production per deck by tunnel length. Variable speed drive.

Pizza Style	Time	Temp.	Production Per Hr. By Tunnel Length 74"	50"	38"
5" - 12 per pan	5.5 min.	700°	372	246	130
7" Pizza	5.5 min.	700°	232	154	64
13" Thick Pizza	7 min.	650°	52	34	—
13" Thin Pizza	9 min.	675°	40	26	—
9" Deep Pizza	14 min.	575/650°	70	46	17
10" Pizza Shells	5 min.	675°	147	98	44

Also used for other breads and sandwiches.

STACKABLE, ELECTRIC CONVEYOR OVENS

FULL SIZE: Overall, each deck - 120" long, 52" wide, 11" high. Cooking tunnel 74" long, 22" wide. Power requirements -14 to 17 KW, 208/230 Volts.

MEDIUM SIZE: Overall, each deck - 96" long, 52" wide, 11" high. Cooking tunnel 50" long, 22" wide. Power requirements - 9.3 to 11.4 KW, 208/230 Volts.

COMPACT SIZE: Overall, each deck - 69" long, 30" wide, 11" high. Cooking tunnel 38" long, 12½" wide. Power requirements - 6 to 7.3 KW, 208/230 Volts.

Infra red heaters above and below the product have separate controls. Adjustable from 200° to 850°F. Combined with adjustable conveyor speed, the units are adaptable to any menu requirements.

The sizes and specifications given are typical for many ovens being produced by various manufacturers. Options for these units include power boosters, hoods, peak load timers, return conveyors and a variety of bases for floor or counter installation. As stated the units are stackable up to 4 decks high.

Other ovens are also available with forced convection heat or forced heat jet nozzles. Gas fired models also available.

Typical Hourly Production · Per Deck

Item	Time	Temp.	Tunnel Length 38"	50"	74"
Seafood - 6" x 9" pan Shrimp, Scallops	5 Min.	850°	84	195	296
Meatballs - 9" pan	10 Min.	675°	25	65	98
12 oz. Steak or 4 oz. Lobster	7 Min.	850°	50	93	140
8 oz. Pork or 8 oz. Chicken	16 Min.	650°	36	92	138
2 oz. Rolls. - 12 to 1/2 size bun pan	12 Min.	500°	108	216	336
Subs/Reubens	4 Min.	650°	62	164	246

118

SMOKE STYLE ROAST OVEN
(Cooks and Holds - Uses Hardwood Chips)

Size: Overall 28" wide, 29" deep, 60" high. Inside: 25" wide, 25" deep, 44" high, 3 KW plus 15V timer motor, slow cook capacities. Gas models also available.

Food Item	Capacity Per Load	Cook Temp.	Cook Time Hrs.
Roast Beef	200 lbs.	200°	8
1/2 Chickens	120	200°	3½
Whole Chickens	60	200°	3½
1" Fish Fillets	75-100	175°	3¾
1" Steak	75-100	200°	1¾
Hamburg, 4½ diam.	250	200°	1¾
Pre-cooked Sausage	200 lbs.	175°	1½
Stuffed Duck	50	180°	4

This all purpose oven roasts, holds, bakes or smokes.

INFRA RED/HICKORY SMOKER COMBINATION COOKER
(Skillet Style)

TYPICAL SIZES AND POWER REQUIREMENTS

	Small	Large	Product Capacity
Width	55"	69"	Small 150 lbs.
Front to Back	37"	49"	
Body Height	19"	34"	Large 300 lbs.
Overall Height	19"	34"	

Power: Small unit 5-6 KW, large unit 10-11 KW.

This unit cooks from top and bottom and has a separate wood smoking unit — smokes while it cooks. Venting only if desired.

COUNTER TOP COOKER-SMOKER

Overall size: 28½" wide, 29¼" deep, 24" high plus legs. Power: 120 V - 1.7 KW, 14 Amp.

Cooks and smokes 80 lbs. of meat per load. Uses safe, easy liquid smoke. Completely automatic, simply set controls and switch to on. Provides efficient cooking with little shrinkage.

TYPICAL PRODUCTION OF INFRA RED/SMOKED COOKERS

NOTE: Can be used with or without smoker on.

SMALL SIZE

Food Product	Amt. Lbs.	Cook Time
12-14 Lb. Shoulder	12	6 hrs.
14-16 Lb. Hams	10	8 hrs.
3 Ribs	15	1½ hrs.
1/2 Barbeque Chicken	40	1½ hrs.
9" Pies	10	25 min.
Steaks	25	10 min.

LARGE SIZE

12-15 Lb. Shoulder	25 portions	6 hrs.
6-8 Lb. Butts	40 portions	4 hrs.
Roast Beef	300	5 hrs.
Barbeque Ribs	35	1½ hrs.
5 Lb. Meat Loaf	60	1½ hrs.
Baked Potatoes	200 ea.	1 hr.
Steaks/Chops	60 ea.	12 hrs.

BARBEQUE PRESSURE COOKER

Size: 22" wide, 27" deep, 30" high. Uses hickory shavings and water or flavorings - 4.25 KW.

Food Capacity	Cooking Time Cold Start	Total Production 12 Hours
45 Lbs. Ribs	1 hr., 30 min.	400 lbs.
18½ Chickens	50 min.	250 lbs.
45 Lbs. Beef	2 hrs., 15 min.	270 lbs.

Venting not required.

RANGES

STYLES AVAILABLE:
1) Small compact electric and gas
2) Restaurant weight and size
3) Heavy duty series
4) Taco range
5) Chinese range
6) Compact cooking centers
7) Stock pot range

BRAINSTORMING:
1) Modular on stand
2) Oven below - regular or convection
3) Broiler above
4) Singe or double back shelves - back guards
5) Continuous clean ovens
6) Choice of tops
7) Finish - standard or stainless steel. Special finish as stainless steel can be front, ends, back or any combination
8) Open or door style base
9) Legs
10) Low roast control on ovens
11) Quick disconnects
12) Spreader plates between ranges
13) Add-a-range sections
14) Wheels for mobility
15) Caution: Gas fired ranges require adequate ventilation for full burner combustion.

RANGES - GAS COMPACT

Size: 30" wide, 31¼" deep, 4 burners on top, 1 oven below. Oven size: 26¼" x 22" x 12½" high.

RESTAURANT RANGES

Size: 36" wide x 30½" deep, 1 oven below.

RESTAURANT SERIES GAS RANGE
(1 or 2 Ovens below)

Size: 60" wide x 30" deep w/2 ovens or one oven and storage cabinet below.

SOME AVAILABLE COMBINATIONS FOR COOKING TOPS

Total Burners	Hot Tops Sections	Griddles
2	2	24"
2	—	36"
—	3	24"
4	—	36"
4	1	24"
4	2	12"
—	1	48"
2	—	48"

Available with or without broiler under griddle — usually 24" or backshelf broiler.

Also available with a variety of cook tops are gas ranges: 23" - 34" - 46" - 57" - 68" left to right, one for nearlly every menu and space problem that you may have.

TYPICAL BTU'S - RESTAURANT STYLE RANGES

TOP	BTU'S
Open Burners	14,000 Ea.
12" Hot Tops	18,000 Ea.
Ovens	35,000 Ea.
24" Grill and Broiler	43,000
36" Grill and Broiler	61,000
12" Grill	18,000
24" Grill	36,000
36" Grill	54,000
48" Grill	72,000
60" Grill	90,000

121

GAS COMPACT COOK CENTER
(78" wide x 32" deep)

Includes:	BTU'S	
Infra Red Broiler	32,000	
Deep Fryer	90,000	
2 Ovens	25,000	Ea.
10 Burners	17-20,000	Per Burner

OR

3' Grill Plus 4 Burners	3' Grill 48,000

OR

2' Grill Plus 6 Burners	2' Grill 64,000

GAS HEAVY DUTY RANGES
(34" wide x 35" or 42" deep - with or without ovens)

AVAILABLE TOP STYLES

STYLE	BTU'S	
Open Burner	20,000	Ea.
Fry Top Grill 34"	43,000	
Even Heat Top (2)	45,000	
Graduated Top (center heat)	80,000	

Oven BTU's: 32,000 to 50,000.

OPTIONAL TOPS FOR 36" WIDE RANGE

- 6 Burners
- 4 Burners 12" grill
- 4 Burners 12" hot top
- 2 Burners 24" grill
- 2 Burners 24" hot top

- 2 Burners 12" grill plus 12" hot top
- All grill
- All hot top
- Broiler above

Oven size inside: 26¼" wide x 22" deep x 13½" high.

ELECTRIC RANGES

COMPACT RANGE:
    Size: 30" wide, 30" deep, 36 high
    Tops: 4 electric elements or 4 french hot plates
    Oven size: 19" wide, 21" deep, 11" high

MEDIUM DUTY RANGE:
    Size: 48" wide, 36" deep, 36" high
    Tops: all grill or grill plus 2 burners or all hot top, oven below. Is 26½" wide, 29" deep, 12½" high. 18" wide add-a-units available. These medium duty ranges are also available in 60" width with double ovens under.

ELECTRIC RANGES · STANDARD SIZES
(Rated by KW and Tops)

Size: 36" wide, 38" deep, 36" high.

TOTAL KW LOAD FOR COMPLETE UNITS

Top Units	With Regular Oven	With Convection Oven	Modular On Stand No Oven
3 12 x 24 Hot Tops	23 KW		
2 12 x 24 Hot Tops Plus 2 - 9" French Tops	20 KW	22 KW	14 KW
1 24 x 24 Grill Plus 2 - 9" French Tops	22 KW	25 KW	14 KW
2 12 x 24 Hot Plates Plus 2 Open Element Burners	20 KW	22 KW	14 KW
1 36" x 24" Grill	22 KW	23 KW	16 KW
6 9" French Plates	18 KW	29 KW	12 KW

COMPUTERIZED ELECTRIC RANGE
(100% Solid State Circuitry)

This full sized commercial range with oven, griddle and hot plates is provided with an on-off switch a complete, touch control panel. Signal lights show which heat zones are turned on. Number pads set temperature and time control. Digital read-out shows time and temperatures selected. Oven controls allow setting of oven and probe temperatures, direction and intensity of heat from elements and a reduced temperature "Hold" function. The range may be set for automatic start-up and preheating as well as automatic shut-off programs once set may also be "locked-in".

CAPACITIES OF OVENS FOR THE STANDARD
36" ELECTRIC RANGES

Pan Size	Capacity
18" x 24"	1
18" x 26"	1
12" x 20"	2
10" Pie Pans	5

CHINESE RANGES

These ranges average 30" to 45" in depth x 36" high to work top. High back shelf has rack for woks and utensils. The overall width of the range is determined by width required to accommodate number and diameter of woks and bowls desired allowing 6" space between them. Soup pot holders or two 12" open burner sections may also be included.

RANGE WIDTH BY WOK SIZE

Wok Diameter	Hole Diameter	Range Width Per Wok
16"	14"	22"
18"	16"	24"
20"	18"	26"
22"	20"	28"
24"	22"	30"
26"	24"	32"
28"	26"	34"

Up to 18" wok requires 53,000 BTU burners from 20" up requires 107,000 BTU burners.

CHINESE BARBEQUE RANGE

Size: Approximately 28" x 28" x 66" high, including legs. Full door opening for loading. Unit supplied with 12 skewers, two 15,000 B.T.U. burners (one each side). Double wall insulated construction. Large grease pan with removable splash plates in base. Available standard black enamel or stainless steel.

GYROS CONE ROASTER

Gyros (pronounced - year-rows) is a Greek specialty consisting of sliced beef and/or lamb served in a slice of pita bread complemented with tomatoes, raw onions and cucumber-yogurt sauce. The gyros meat, with a unique blend of spices and herbs, is available in conical form resembling inverted twine spools. As it is roasted on the vertically revolving skewer it may be sliced off for serving.

The roaster is an attractive display model, requiring counter space 24" wide x 30" deep and requires an exhaust hood above. Available in gas or electric, overall dimensions of either unit 17" wide x 21" deep x 48" high.

Electric model: 208 or 240 volt, 1 phase, 208 V units, 6240 watts, 240 V units, 7200 watts.

Gas model: two 18,000 BTU burners, requires 110 V connection for skewer motor.

To quote the supplier of these products, "Gyros should be eaten with the fingers . . . but preferably, the fingers should be eaten separately."

TYPICAL TACO RANGES

Width L to R	Depth	Height	Burners	BTU
18¼"	25"	30¾"	1	30,000
38¼"	25"	30¾"	2	60,000
58¼"	25"	30¾"	3	90,000
78¼"	25"	30¾"	4	120,000
98¼"	25"	30¾"	5	150,000

Accommodates heavy duty pans up to 18" x 26".

124

STEAM COOKING
STEAM COOKERS AND KETTLES

This section of Chapter 5 will cover all known steam cooking equipment. The advantages of steam cooking are basically flavor and nutrient retention, speed, energy savings and volume produced.

Sizes, styles and options vary by manufacturer. Emerging in the 80's are systems within the reach of smaller operations, plus more sophisticated replacements for the older conventional steamers.

Steamers are available in direct steam connected models, the steam must be approved for food contact and not contaminated. Transfer steam in which a heat exchanger uses impure steam to produce pure steam. Gas and electric generators that produce steam for compartment steamers and kettles if desired.

The steam produced can be used in steamers rated at 5 lbs. or 15 lbs. pressure or pressure/pressureless combination steamers. A pressureless steamer uses 0 pressure forced steam, known as convected steamer. Some units have a fan to circulate the steam around the chamber. Smaller pressureless steamers generate their own steam and are called self contained. Counter style 15 lb. pressure steamers are also available with built-in generators, both gas and electric.

Cooking temperatures of steam cooked foods vary with the style of steamer. Example:

Pressureless. . . . . 212^0
5 lb. Pressure. . . . . 237^0
15 lb. Pressure. . . . . 250^0

The charts following the different style steamers will show portions and 12" x 20" pan production per hour or per load.

▮▮▮ HELPFUL HINTS

1) Always consider water treatment for steam equipment. Many service problems could be eliminated by purer water.
2) **Most** steam cookers are operational on direct steam, when connected in this manner a steam separator should be used to separate the steam from the condensated water. It is also best to install a steam pressure gauge on the incoming steam line before the final steamer connection.
3) Most all steamers will require an indirect drain. The exceptions are manual water fill styles that drain to a pan.
4) Pressure style steamers (5 or 15 psi) cook by latent steam penetrating the food. Pressureless styles cook by movement of the steam through the chamber. At zero pressure, door can be opened and closed as needed. Frozen food cooks faster by convection because moving steam penetrates at a faster rate than the latent heat from the near motionless pressurized steam.

125

STEAM COMPONENTS

GENERATORS — A boiler that produces steam by gas or electric for a steam cooker or kettle.

HEAT EXCHANGER — A device that utilizes heat from contaminated steam line to generate clean steam compatible with food.

STEAM CONDENSER — Pressurized steamers must be vented before the compartment doors can be opened. To vent live steam having temperatures up to 250°F. would be very dangerous. The condensing units mix the live steam and cold water so that it may be safely exhausted to an indirect waste.

STEAM GENERATORS (BOILERS)

This section contains information on steam generators (boilers) operating at 15 PSI or less pressure.

Design of system and sizing of steam generator should be done by an engineer.

Installation of "direct-steam" operated equipment in institutions, military installations, hospitals, colleges, restaurants, etc. is an accepted and common practice.

In most states, steam generators operated at less than 15 PSI do not require licensed steam engineers for operating the unit.

1. Types of Steam-Operated Equipment:
    a. "Self-contained": This type has a steam generator as an integral part of the equipment. The steam generator is generally designed and fabricated for operation of the involved equipment only.
    b. "Direct-steam": This type has a separate source of steam for operating the equipment. The system basically consists of one low-pressure steam generator supplying steam to all "direct-steam" operated equipment, such as steamers, kettles, etc.
2. When to Consider a Steam Generator:
    a. When the proposed (new or renovated) **facility includes dishwashing equipment, or several pieces of steam-operated equipment,** consideration should be given to the purchase of "direct-steam" operated equipment and a steam generator.

Advantages of steam-generator:
    (1) Greater ease of operation.
    (2) Simultaneous operation of all steam-operated equipment at full capacity, if properly sized.
    (3) Instantaneous heat-up with shorter cooking time.
    (4) Greater efficiency resulting in lower operating costs.
    (5) Lower maintenance costs.

(6) Greater life expectancy.

(7) Lower initial equipment/installation cost. (Larger size operations.)

(8) Steam available for cleaning, heating water, and other uses.

b. When the proposed (new or renovated) facility **does not include dishwashing equipment or several pieces of steam-operataed equipment,** consideration should be given to the purchase of "self-contained" equipment. In general, "self-contained" equipment should be limited to those instances where equipment needs are small and limited.

3. Other Sources of Steam:

a. School Steam Generators: The school steam generator should be considered when (1) steam supply is available throughout the entire school year, (2) there is an adequate steam supply, and (3) non-toxic boiler descaling compounds are used for cleaning the boiler. If toxic cleaning compounds are used the available steam is commonly referred to as "contaminated steam." In some instances, a contaminated steam supply can be converted to a "clean steam" supply by changing to a non-toxic boiler cleaning compound. In those instances, where the school plans on continuing the use of toxic cleaning compounds, the contaminated steam may be used providing the steam is used in those pieces of equipment where the steam does not come in contact with food or table service, or a steam coil boiler is installed for converting contaminated steam into "clean steam."

b. A separate steam generator for operation of kitchen equipment is highly recommended as shown below.

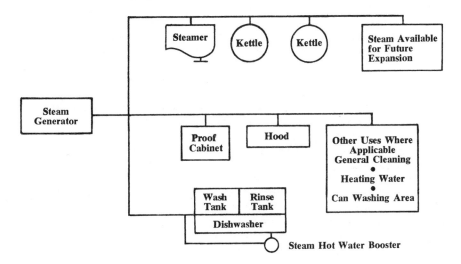

4. Boiler Horsepower Demands of Equipment:
   Boiler horsepower (BHP) demands vary with the manufacturers of food service equipment. Therefore, care should be exercised to insure that the steam generator capacity will be sufficient for the food service equipment specified plus allowance for future growth. Commonly, accepted boiler horsepower demands at equipment are as follows: (These demands are at the equipment and therefore do not reflect delivery loss to equipment due to the piping and other resistance.)

Equipment	Boiler Horsepower Demands at Equipment
Steamer	1.5 BHP per steamer compartment
Kettle	.5 BHP per each 10-gallon capacity[1]
Single-Tank Door Dishwasher	4.0 BHP per dishwasher[2]
Single-Tank Conveyor Dishwasher	9.0 BHP per dishwasher[2]
Double-Tank Conveyor Dishwasher	12.0 BHP per dishwasher[2]
Single-Tank Fight Dishwasher	13.0 BHP per dishwasher[2]

[1]The .5 boiler horsepower demand per 10 gallons of steam-jacketed kettle is sufficient to bring 70^0 F water to boil (212^0F.) in one hour. Generally, dishwashing operation and steam cooking do not occur simultaneously; therefore, the heating time can be expected to be less than one hour.

[2]The boiler horsepower demand for the dishwasher takes into consideration both wash and final rinse.

F.E.F. HUMOR

It took about ten years for any of us to look back and laugh at this one.

A hospital in our company's territory had been favoring us with an occasional small order but we could never quite gain a strong foothold with them. Finally our golden opportunity arrived. They were planning extensive renovations in their food service operation. After studying their plans we felt certain that we could greatly improve on the tray make-up and patient service system which they intended to use.

It took a lot of talking to convince them that it would be worthwhile for them to delay their project long enough for us to present a plan which we claimed would improve on a system which they had already agreed would be the best one for their operation.

They did agree to wait and when the great day for the presentation arrived, we sat face to face at the conference table with a board of directors with it clearly written on each of their faces, "This had better be good."

Our chief engineer stood up, graciously thanked them for their consideration, placed his briefcase on the table and opened it — only to find he had left the plans back in the office.

We never again received any orders from that hospital but we did establish a world record for the shortest conference ever.

STEAM VS. BOILING

This chart shows the dramatic savings of nutrients when steam is used in preference to a stock pot. There is a close relationship between nutrients, color, flavor and texture.

VEGETABLE	COOKING METHOD	LOSS OF DRY MATTER %	LOSS OF PROTEIN %	LOSS OF CALCIUM %	LOSS OF MAGNE- SIUM %	LOSS OF PHOS- PHORUS %	LOSS OF IRON %
Asparagus	BOILED	14.0	20.0	16.5	8.8	25.8	34.4
	STEAMED	7.9	13.3	15.3	1.4	10.4	20.0
Beans, String	BOILED	24.6	29.1	29.3	31.4	27.6	38.1
	STEAMED	14.2	16.6	16.3	21.4	18.8	24.5
Beetgreens	BOILED	29.7	22.2	15.9	41.6	44.9	43.1
	STEAMED	15.7	6.9	3.8	14.1	14.0	24.5
Cabbage	BOILED	60.7	61.5	72.3	76.1	59.9	66.6
	STEAMED	26.4	31.5	40.2	43.4	22.0	34.6
Cauliflower	BOILED	37.6	44.4	24.6	25.0	49.8	36.2
	STEAMED	2.1	7.6	3.1	1.7	19.2	8.3
Celery	BOILED	45.4	52.6	36.1	57.1	48.7	— —
	STEAMED	22.3	22.3	11.6	32.4	15.7	— —
Celery Cabbage	BOILED	63.2	67.1	49.7	61.6	66.1	67.6
	STEAMED	38.3	33.5	16.3	32.6	30.2	44.1
Spinach	BOILED	33.9	29.0	5.5	59.1	48.8	57.1
	STEAMED	8.4	5.6	0.0	17.8	10.2	25.7
Beets	BOILED	30.9	22.0	18.7	30.9	33.6	— —
	STEAMED	21.5	5.4	1.5	29.4	20.1	— —
Carrots	BOILED	20.1	26.4	8.9	22.8	19.0	34.1
	STEAMED	5.1	14.5	5.1	5.6	1.1	20.7
Kohlrabi	BOILED	33.6	23.2	27.8	40.4	27.7	51.7
	STEAMED	7.6	1.0	1.0	14.3	7.7	21.3
Onions	BOILED	21.3	50.2	15.6	27.8	40.2	36.1
	STEAMED	11.0	30.7	7.1	15.7	31.5	15.9
Parsnips	BOILED	21.9	13.3	11.4	46.8	23.7	27.6
	STEAMED	4.6	20.0	4.2	18.2	5.7	8.1
Potatoes	BOILED	9.4	— —	16.8	18.8	18.3	— —
	STEAMED	4.0	— —	9.6	14.0	11.7	— —
Sweet Potatoes	BOILED	29.0	71.5	38.3	45.3	44.4	31.5
	STEAMED	21.1	15.0	22.1	31.5	24.3	25.1
Rutabagas	BOILED	45.8	48.6	37.1	42.7	57.2	50.0
	STEAMED	13.2	15.7	13.4	3.4	24.6	14.3
AVERAGE FOR ALL VEGETABLES	BOILED	39.4	43.0	31.9	44.7	46.4	48.0
	STEAMED	14.0	16.0	10.7	18.6	16.7	21.3

APPROXIMATE STEAMING TIMES
(Times vary with the age, amount of moisture in the food, length of time in storage, etc.)

Food	Pounds of Food Per 100 Portions	Compartment Type Steam Cooker (5 lb. pressure)	Electric Pressure Cooker (15 lb. pressure)
Apples	30 lbs.	15 min.	10 min.
Apricots, dried	25 lbs.	25 min.	15 min.
Asparagus	36 lbs.	15 min.	8 min.
Beans, shelled lima	20 lbs.	20 min.	10 min.
Beets	28 lbs.	50 min.	30 min.
Broccoli	40 lbs.	12 min.	8 min.
Brussel Sprouts	24 lbs.	15 min.	8 min.
Cabbage	16 lbs.	20 min.	10 min.
Carrots	16 lbs.	25 min.	12 min.
Onions, dry	25 lbs.	20 min.	12 min.
Peas, green	30 lbs.	8 min.	5 min.
Potatoes, Irish	30 lbs.	30 min.	20 min.
Prunes	25 lbs.	25 min.	12 min.
Rhubarb	20 lbs.	12 min.	8 min.
Rice	26 lbs.	30 min.	15 min.
Spinach	36 lbs.	7 min.	4 min.
Tomatoes	36 lbs.	7 min.	4 min.

STEAM TEMPERATURES AT VARIOUS PRESSURES

Pounds Pressure	Deg. F.	Pounds Pressure	Deg. F.
0	212	20	259
2	218	25	267
4	224	30	274
6	230	35	281
8	235	40	287
10	240	45	292
15	250	50	298

PRESSURELESS STEAMERS - COUNTERTOP STYLE

Capacity : 1 pan - 12" x 20" x 2½". Unit is 24" wide x 25" deep, 14" high. KW 5.4, 220V, water 3/8" incoming, drain 3/4" indirect waste. Boiler built in, dial timer with indicator (on and ready) lights.

SAMPLE COOKING TIME

Product	Quantity	Timer Setting
Frozen Broccoli Spears	6-7½ lbs.	3½-4 min.
Frozen Lobster Tails	7-8 lbs.	15-25 min.*
Frozen Shrimp	8-10 lbs.	8-11 min.*
Fresh Green Beans	3-6 lbs.	15-20 min.

(Continued)

SAMPLE COOKING TIME (Cont.)

Product	Quantity	Timer Setting
Canned Vegetables	7 lbs.	5-10 min.
Cut-up Chicken	8 lbs.	25-30 min.
Fish Fillets	3 lbs.	6-10 min.
Clams Steamers	10 lbs.	12-14 min.
Lobster 1½*	2-6 doz.	12-15 min.
Crabs, Whole	4 lbs.	15-20 min.

*Depending on unit weight

PRESSURELESS STEAMER - COUNTERTOP STYLE

Capacity: 3 pans 12" x 20" x 1½" or 2 - 12" x 20" x 4". Holds up to 22 lbs. of frozen vegetables. Unit is 24" wide x 26½" deep x 29" high, KW 18 at 240V, water 1/2" incoming - drain 2" indirect waste. Boiler built in. Unit has both 15 minute and 60 minute timers. On and ready indicator lights.

COMPARTMENT STEAMERS - FLOOR MODELS
(Operating Pressure 5 lbs.)

2, 3 and 4 compartments, electric, gas or direct steam fired.

Size: 36" wide x 33" deep. Heights: Self-contained units, 2 compartment, 55"; 3 compartment, 58". Direct connected units available on legs, pedestal base, cabinet base or wall mount. Two compartment unit 55" high; 3 compartment unit 58" high; 4 compartment unit 67" high.

Incoming steam line - one BHP per compartment.

Each compartment holds 4 - 12" x 20" x 4" pans or 6 - 12" x 20" x 2½" pans.

Power requirements: Electric - 24, 36 or 48 KW generator.

Gas - 170,000 to 250,000 BTU gas generator.

Direct connected steam - 1 BHP per compartment.

SAMPLE COOKING GUIDE
(Using 12" x 20" x 2½" pans)

	Cooking Time Minutes	Size Portion	No. Portions per Compt. per Hour
MEATS, FISH POULTRY			
Fish Fillets or Steaks	10-20	5 oz.	200
Meatballs	20-30	4-1oz.	300
Turkey on Carcass	2 hrs.	3 oz.	70/2 hrs.
Turkey off Carcass	60-75	3 oz.	300
Lobster	7-9	1#	250

(Continued)

SAMPLE COOKING GUIDE
(Using 12" x 20" x 2½" pans) (Cont.)

	Cooking Time Minutes	Size Portion	No. Portions per Compt. per Hour
VEGETABLES			
Carrots - Fresh	20-30	3 oz.	500
Cauliflower - Fresh	10-20	3 oz.	500
Peas - Frozen, Defrosted	5-10	3 oz.	800
Corn - Canned	10-15	3 oz.	1350
Potaotes - Whole	20-30	4 oz.	500
Lima Beans - Frozen Defrosted	10-15	3 oz.	500
MISCELLANEOUS			
Pasta 4" Pan	20-25	8 oz.	200
Rice 4" Pan	20-25	3 oz.	650
Eggs - In Shell	8-10	1 each	1100
Out Shell	6-8	1 each	2000
Custard	10-12	5 oz.	1000

TYPICAL PER HOUR LOADS FOR 5 LB. PRESSURE STEAMERS

FOOD	No. of Loads per Hour	Approx. No. Cooked 3 oz. (85g) Servings Per Compartment Per Load	Per Hour
Frozen Vegetables Defrosted			
Asparagus	4	150	600
Green Beans	4	150	600
Lima Beans	4	150	600
Broccoli	5	120	600
Brussels Sprouts	4	150	600
Carrots	4	150	600
Cauliflower	4	150	600
Corn	4	150	600
Peas	6	150	900
Fresh Vegetables			
Green Beans	2	180	360
Beets	1	150	150
Broccoli	3	150	450
Cabbage	3	120	360
Carrots	2	210	420
Cauliflower	3	180	540
Corn on Cob	4	36	144
Onions	2	150	300
Peas	4	180	720
French Fried Potatoes - Blanch	3	300	900
Regular Cut Potatoes	2	300	600
Spinach	8	60	480
Summer Squash	4	180	720
Winter Squash	2	180	360
Turnip	2	120	240
Canned Vegetables	6	180	1080

PRESSURE COOKER - COUNTER STYLE
(15 Lbs. Steam Pressure)

Capacity: Holds 3 - 12" x 20" x 2½" pans or 2 - 12" x 20" x 4" pans. Built-in generator, electric 12 KW or gas 40,000 BTU or direct steam requiring an input of ½ B.H.P. Also available with steam generator below, for quicker .cooking and reduced pre-heat time. If properly ;sized, generator could also provide steam for kettles or other steam equipment. 18¾" wide x 31½" deep x 26" high. Drains to pan.

SAMPLE COOKING GUIDE

Product	Quantity	Timer Setting
Frozen Vegetable	19-22½ lbs.*	3-15 min.
Frozen Lobster Tails	21-24 lbs.	15-25 min.
Frozen Shrimp	24-30 lbs.	8-11 min.
Fresh Vegetables	9-30 lbs.*	5-10 min.
Cut-up Chicken	24 lbs.	20-30 min.
Fish Fillets	9 lbs.	10-15 min.
Meatballs	18 lbs.	20-25 min.
Eggs in Shell	9 doz.	9-11 min.
Rice (raw)	12 lbs.	18-22 min.

*Depends on type of vegetable

PRESSURELESS STEAMER - FLOOR MODEL

Overall size: 24" wide x 33" deep x 58" high, including base. Unit has two separate compartments, each with its own timers (15 min. and 60 min.), on and ready lights.

Capacity per compartment: six 12" x 20" x 1" pans, or
three 12" x 20" x 2½" pans, or
two 12" x 20" x 4" pans.

Unit will cook up to 45 lbs. frozen vegetables per total load.
Power Options:
Electric - 208, 240, 480 VAC, 24 or 36 KW
Gas - 170,000 BTU steam boiler
Steam Coil - supply pressure maintained at 30 PSI to 50 PSI.
Direct Steam - 2.5 BHP
Optional 48 KW or 250,000 BTU boilers available in 36" wide cabinets

Temperature (degrees F) of steam at various altitudes and pressures

Altitude	5 PSI	10 PSI	15 PSI
Sea Level	227	240	250
2,000	224	237	248
5,000	220	234	245
10,000	213	228	240

SAMPLE COOKING GUIDE

Product	Quantity Per Compartment	Minutes — Cooking Time
Frozen Vegetables	18-22½ lbs.*	12-15
Frozen Lobster Tails	21-24 lbs.	15-25
Frozen Shrimp	24-30 lbs.	11-15
Fresh Vegetables	9-30 lbs.*	18-21
Canned Vegetables	21 lbs.*	5-10
Cut-up Chicken	24 lbs.	20-30
Fish Fillets	9 lbs.	10-15
Meatballs	18 lbs.	20-25
Eggs in Shell	9 doz.	9-11
Rice (raw)	12 lbs.	18-20

*Depends on type of vegetable

PRESSURE/PRESSURELESS STEAMER
(2 Compartment Floor Model)

FEATURES:

The upper compartment of this unit is the unique feature. With a flick of the switch, the conventional 5 PSI pressure cooker can be converted to a free venting, pressureless cooker-defroster. The lower compartment is a high capacity 5 PSI pressure cooker, capable of cooking 60 pounds of fresh food at a time. That kind of capacity and versatility are especially important when you have to serve several hundred guests, but can't determine the exact number of meals in advance.

DIMENSIONS:

55" high x 36 wide x 33" deep.

Capacity (per compartment): Six 12" x 20" x 2½" pans; Four 12" x 20" x 4" pans.

Operating Pressure: 5 PSI pressure mode; 0 PSI pressureless mode

POWER OPTIONS:

Electric - 208, 240, 480 VAC, 3-phase 48 KW
Gas - 250,000 BTU steam boiler
Steam Coil - supply pressure maintained at 40 PSI to 50 PSI
Direct Steam - 6 BHP

SAMPLE COOKING GUIDE

Product	Quantity Per Compartment	Minutes — Cooking Time
Frozen Vegetables	36-45 lbs.	5-13
Frozen Lobster Tails	42-48 lbs.	15-20
Frozen Shrimp	48-60 lbs.	8-18
Fresh Vegetables	18-60 lbs.	12-20
Canned Vegetables	42 lbs.	5-8
Cut-up Chicken	48 lbs.	25-30
Fish Fillets	18 lbs.	10-15
Meatballs	36 lbs.	22-25
Eggs in Shell	18 doz.	9-10
Rice (raw)	24 lbs.	25-27

TYPICAL COOKING GUIDE

FOOD	Recommended 12" x 20" (1/1) Solid Pan	Approx. Raw Weight Per Pan	Number of Loads Per Hour	Approx. Number Cooked 2 oz. (55g) Servings Per Compartment	
				Per Load	Per Hour
Meat, Poultry, Fish					
Chicken - Cut up	1½" (65mm)	8# (3.63kg)	2	60	120
Chicken Whole - 4# (1.8kg)	4" (100mm)	12# (5.44kg)	1	60	60
Frankforts	2½" (65mm)	5# (2.27kg)	10	120	1200
Hamburgers	2½" (65mm)	5# (2.27kg)	3	75	225
Meatballs	2½" (65mm)	6# (2.72kg)	2	75	150
Meatloaf	2½" (65mm)	15# (6.80kg)	1	150	150
Pork Chops	2½" (65mm)	6# (2.72kg)	2	72	144
Sausages	2½" (65mm)	6# (2.72kg)	2	60	120
Turkey on Carcass	4" (100mm)	20-22# (9.1-10kg)	1	50	1½-2 hrs.
Turkey off Carcass	2½" (65mm)	10-12# (4.5-5.4kg)	1	180	180
Fish Fillets	2½" (65mm)	3# (1.36kg)	4	45	180
Fish Steaks	2½" (65mm)	4# (1.81kg)	3	75	225
Lobster	2½" (65mm)	10# (4.5kg)	6	30	180
Eggs out of Shell	2½" (65mm)	48 (48 each)	6	144	864
Rice	4" (100mm)	4# (1.81kg)	2	120-3 oz. (85g)	240
Spaghetti	4" (100mm)	3# (1.36kg)	2	80-4 oz. (115g)	160
Frozen Entrees	**Perforated Pan**				
Bulk Pack	2½" (65mm)	5# (2.27kg)	2	36-6 oz. (170g)	72
Individual Pouches	2½" (65mm)	3# (1.36kg)	5	18 pouches	90
Shrimp CPD	2½" (65mm)	3# (1.36kg)	4	60-2 oz. (57g)	240
Shrimp Green	2½" (65mm)	3# (1.36kg)	3	45-2 oz. (57g)	135
Lobster Tails	2½" (65mm)	6# (2.72kg)	4	36-6 oz. (170g)	144

SMALLER PRESSURE STEAMERS - 15 Lb. PRESSURE

Small, fast and space saving, these smaller steamers will require separate generators in most all models. Steam required will vary by compartment size. Using solid smaller pans, these steamers automatically defrost the food product and shift to a timed pressure cook cycle. Defrost is pressureless.

TYPICAL SIZES AND PRODUCTION

Wide	Deep	High	Pans	Servings Per Hour 2½ Oz. Frozen Vegetables
20"	22"	28"	1 - ⅓ size, 4" deep*	220-300
12"	22"	20½"	1 - ⅓ size, 4" deep	315-415
18"	22"	26"	1 - ½ size, 4" deep	680-875
24"	27"	24"	1 - full, 4" deep plus 2 - ½ size, 4" deep	675-900
18"	22"	28"	2 - ⅓ size, 4" deep	675-900
24"	22"	36"	1 - ⅓ size, 4" deep 1 - ½ size, 4" deep	990-1325
24"	22"	36"	2 - ½ size, 4" deep	1320-1750
36"	27½"	29"	2 - full, 4" pans 4 - ½ size, 2½" deep	2160-2880

*Self contained generator.

135

TIMING CHART FOR ABOVE 15 LB. STEAMERS

VEGETABLES, FRESH
Asparagus spears,
   medium.................. 2-2½ min.
Beans, green or was........ 2-3 min.
Cabbage, coarse
   shredded................ 2-2½ min.
Corn-on-cob, small.......... 3-4 min.
Onions, sliced ¼".......... 3-4 min.
Potatoes, sliced ¼"........ 4-5 min.
Spinach, leaf................. 1 min.

VEGETABLES, FROZEN
Beans, French-cut
   green....................... 1 min.
Broccoli spears........... 1-1½ min.
Brussels sprouts,
   medium................. 2½-4 min.
Carrots, baby whole...... 2½-3 min.
Cauliflower............... 1-1½ min.
Chinese pea pods........ ¼-½ min.
Corn, whole............... ½-1 min.
Mixed vegetables............. 1 min.
Peas....................... 1 min.
Yam patties, 2-oz........... 5-6 min

VEGETABLES, CANNED
Beans, green or was........ ½ min.
Carrots, baby whole........ ½ min.

Potatoes, small whole.... 2-2½ min.

SEAFOOD, FRESH OR THAWED
Clams, soft shell......... 1½-2 min.
Crab legs or claws,
   cut into pieces.............. 3 min.
Lobster tails, 5-oz.
   halved or flowered........ 3½ min.
Lobster, whole,
   1-1½ lbs. ....

Lobster, whole,
   1-1½ lbs................... 7-9 min.
Fish Fillets................. 1-3 min.
Shrimp, green,
   10-12 ct. per lb.............. 4 min.

MEAT AND POULTRY
Beef, ½" cubes,
   separate................ 30-35 min.
Chicken breasts,
   boned and rolled........... 7-8 min.
Chicken wings (precook)...... 2 min.
Spareribs (precook)....... 12-15 min.
Wieners.................. 1½-2 min.

EGGS
Eggs, hard-cooked........ 6½ min.

KETTLES

Styles available are either direct steam connected, generated steam from a boiler or self contained. The self contained style has a permanent supply of chemically pure water. No direct water connection is necessary. Sizes range from a 1 quart table top oyster cooker to 200 gallons. Electric, gas, direct steam.

Mountings available are table top, wall mount, floor style on legs, pedestals or modular in a stainless steel frame. They may be tilting style or stationary. Options are numerous among them: mixer - agitator assemblies, cooling devices for the jackets, water fill systems, vegetable strainer cooking systems that allow cooking three different products at the same time, pouring lips, pan supports, timed computer operation.

Jackets or outer shells are available, either full or 2/3. The kettles come deep or shallow style. Shallow types are used primarily for braising of meats, corn beef, soups and gravies, while deeper styles would be best for vegetables, pastas, stews, chili, turkey a la king, etc. Kettles are available modular, having steam cookers to the side or smaller kettles side by side on a base. Bases also house generators for the steam production if needed.

Sizes and capacities vary by manufacturer. Listed below are a few typical measurements, followed by some production facts.

STEAM KETTLES STYLES AVAILABLE

Capacity	Jacket Style	Mounts
1, 4, 6, 8, 10 qts.	1/2	Table top

Gallons	Jacket Style	Mounts
10	2/3	Tilt - Floor or Table Top
20	2/3 or Full	Floor - tilt
25	Full	Floor
30	2/3 or Full	Floor - Tilt
40	2/3 or Full	Floor - Tilt
50	Full	Floor - Tilt
60	2/3 or Full	Floor - Tilt
80	2/3 or Full	Floor - Tilt
100	2/3 or Full	Floor - Tilt
125	2/3 or Full	Floor
150	2/3 or Full	Floor
200	2/3	Floor

HELPFUL HINTS

Remember, kettles are available shallow and deep, with or without generators and can be joined with other steam equipment. Many kettles can be wall mounted and wall-mount tilting.

KETTLE SELECTION

Meals Per Day	Kettle Selection
100 to 250	1 - 20 gallon
251 to 300	1 - 30 gallon
301 to 350	1 - 30 gallon
351 to 400	1 - 40 gallon
401 to 450	1 - 40 gallon
451 to 500	1 - 60 gallon
501 to 600	1 - 60 gallon
601 to 750	1 - 60 gallon
751 to 1000	2 - 40 gallon
1001 to 1250	2 - 40 gallon
	or 1 - 60 gallon, 1 - 40 gallon
1251 to 1500	2 - 60 gallon

HELPFUL HINTS

These charts may be converted to tilt fry pan (braising pan) by checking production of these units.

TYPICAL SIZES OF SELECTED KETTLES

Gas and electric requirements will vary by manufacturer, amount of steam equipment to be used and in some cases, the amount of production needed. An example of product turnover would be using 36 KW generator for a kettle - steamer when the standard rating would be 24 KW. The higher rating reduces the pre-heat and recovery times resulting in higher production in less time.

Some sample sizes.

SELF CONTAINED KETTLES - ELECTRIC

Gals.	Height to Rim	Wide	Front to Back	KW at 220V
		FLOOR MODELS		
20	35½"	23¼"	27½"	12
30	38"	26¼"	30½"	15
40	40½"	28¼"	32½"	18
60	42½"	32¼"	36½"	18
80	45¾"	35¼"	39½"	18
		TILT FLOOR MODELS		
20	35½"	35"	33½"	12
30	38"	38"	37"	15
40	40½"	40"	39"	18
60	42½"	44"	43"	18
80	45¾"	47"	45"	18

MODULAR DIRECT CONNECTED KETTLES

Gals.	Height to Rim	Wide	Front to Back	BHP
10	33"	24"	33"	.75
25	33"	36"	33"	1.25
40	38"	36"	33"	2.00
60	41"	36"	33"	3.00
	TILT MODELS - DIRECT CONNECTED - MODULAR			
25	33"	36"	33"	1.25
40	38"	36"	33"	2.00
60	39"	48"	33"	3.00

GUIDE TO TRUNNION TILTING KETTLES

Capacity Gals.	Height (to kettle rim)	Width	Front to BAck	BHP, KW or BTU
5	24"	13"	14½"	1/3
10	32¼"	16"	27"	2/3
On Modular Cabinets				
5	54"	18"	33"	1/4
(2)5	54"	36"	33"	1/2
On Boilers				
5	54"	24"	33"	24 or 36
(2)5	54"	36"	33"	24, 36 or 48
5	54"	24"	33"	170,000
(2)5	54"	36"	33"	170,000 or 250,000

GUIDE TO DIRECT CONNECTED FLOOR MODEL KETTLES

Capacity Gals.	Height (to kettle rim)	Width	Front to Back (off wall)	BHP at 15 PSI
Stationary, two-thirds jacketed				
20	34½"	22"	29½"	1.27
30	36½"	25"	38½"	1.91
40	36"	27"	40½"	2.49
60	39"	31"	44½"	3.82
80	41½"	34"	47½"	5.09
100	43½"	37"	50½"	5.36
125	44½"	40"	53½"	7.95
150	46½"	43"	56½"	9.54
Stationary, full jacketed				
30	32½"	31"	44½"	3.82
40	34"	34"	47½"	5.09
60	33½"	37"	50½"	6.36
80	37½"	40"	53½"	7.95
100	39"	43"	56½"	9.54
Pedestal, tilting, 2/3 jacketed				
20	35½"	31¼"	27½"	1.27
30	35½"	34¼"	30"	1.91
40	36½"	36¼"	31¼"	2.49
60	41"	39¾"	34¼"	3.82
80	43"	43¼"	36½"	5.09
Leg-mounted, tilting, 2/3 jacketed				
20	35½"	33-3/8"	28¾"	1.27
30	35½"	36-3/8"	31¼"	1.91
40	36½"	38-3/8"	32½"	2.49
60	41"	41-7/8"	35½"	3.82
80	43"	45-3/8"	37¾"	5.09

139

BASKET COOKING SYSTEM
(For Most Steam Jacket Kettles)

This system uses 3 lightweight stainless steel baskets, held in place by a sturdy movable frame which permits each basket to be rotated to front of kettle for easy removal. Available for 20 - 30 - 40 - 60 and 80 gallon kettles.

Nylon bags are used inside of the baskets to contain small items such as corn. Use of the basket system of cooking provides lightweight handling, quick drainage and if timing is similar, 2 or 3 products may be cooked at one time.

STEAM KETTLE · TABLE TOP · COMPUTER OPERATED

Size: 20 gallon, 24" long x 16" deep x 26" high, 6.3 KW electric.
Features: Probe from computer controls temperature of product, controlled and pre-heat and cook cycle, stir signal or automatic stirring, product doneness signal, automatic probe test.

A fully automated cooking kettle for soups, chili, sauces, vegetables and other items normally cooked in double boilers or stock pots.

STEAM KETTLE PORTION GUIDE

| | Portion | No. of Portions | | | |
	Size	5 Gal.	10 Gal.	25 Gal.	40 Gal.	60 Gal.
MAIN ENTREE						
Turkey Tetrazzini	8 oz.	30	65	320	560	800
Beef Stew	8 oz.	50	150	320	560	800
American Chop Suey	6 oz.	65	150	420	735	1050
Spaghetti	8 oz.	32	65	160	280	400
Chicken A La King	4 oz.	100	225	650	1125	1600
SOUP · GRAVY · DESSERTS						
Cream or Broth Soup	6 oz.	65	150	420	735	1050
Fruit Pie Filling						
(2# per pie)	4 oz.	100	225	650	1125	1600
Chocolate Sauce	1 oz.	400	900	2500	4500	6500
Brown Gravy	2 oz.	200	450	1250	2250	3250
Cornstarch Pudding	3 oz.	135	300	850	1500	2100
MISCELLANEOUS						
Coffee - Tea - Cocoa	6 oz.	65	150	420	735	1050
Hot Cereal	6 oz.	65	150	420	735	1050
Scrambled Eggs	4 oz.	100	225	600	1000	1250
Vegetables	4 oz.	65	125	315	500	750
Rice	3 oz.	75	150	350	500	750

140

GUIDE FOR SCHOOLS SELECTING STEAM-JACKETED KETTLES AND TILTING BRAISING PANS

Number and Size of Steam-Jacketed Kettles and Tilting Braising Pans Recommended:

Number of Type A Lunches Served Daily	Number, Type and Size Equipment [1] [2]	
	Steam-Jacketed Kettles	Steam-Jacketed Kettles and Tilting Braising Pans
100–250	1 20-gallon kettle	– OR – 1 20-25-gallon tilting braising pan
251–350	1 30-gallon kettle	– OR – 1 30-35-gallon tilting braising pan
351–500	1 40-gallon kettle	– OR – 1 40-gallon tilting braising pan
501–750	2 30-gallon kettles – or – 1 60-gallon kettle [3]	– OR – 1 20-25-gallon tilting braising pan 1 40-gallon kettle
751–1000	2 40-gallon kettles	– OR – 1 20-25-gallon tilting braising pan 1 60-gallon kettle [3] OR any other workable combination
1001–1250	2 40-gallon kettles 1 20-gallon kettle – or – 1 60-gallon kettle [3] 1 40-gallon kettle	– OR – 1 40-gallon or larger tilting braising pan 1 60-gallon kettle [3] OR any other workable combination
1251–1500	3 40-gallon kettles – or – 2 60-gallon kettles	– OR – 2 30-35-gallon tilting braising pans 1 60-gallon kettle [3] OR any other workable combination

[1] A table model trunnion or stationary kettle of 5-10 gallon capacity is suggested for high schools when choice within Type A pattern and/or a la carte items are offered.

[2] Steam-jacketed kettles can be purchased as individual pieces of equipment or in a combination unit with steamer(s).

[3] Sixty-gallon kettles can be used in place of two 30-gallon kettles, or one 20- and one 40-gallon kettle, or in combinations of one 60-gallon kettle with other size kettles, e.g. 20- and 60-gallon kettles to replace two 40-gallon kettles, etc., providing the 60-gallon kettle is low profile. Otherwise, the 60-gallon kettle is apt to be too high for efficient use.

141

TYPICAL ELECTRIC TABLE TOP
40 QT. KETTLE GUIDE TO PRODUCTION

Product	Cooking Time
Water (212°F)	8-12 min.
Tapioca	1 hr.
Chocolate Pudding	13 min.
Glossy Chocolate Frosting	½ hr.
Chocolate Syrup	½ hr.
German Chocolate Icing	½ hr.
Canned Vegetables	10 min.
Frozen Vegetables	15-18 min.
Onions (3 gal.)	5 min.
Celery (3 gal.)	5 min.
Minestrone Soup	45 min.
Clam Bisque	1 hr.
French Onion Soup	2 hrs.
Cream of Potato	1 hr.
Beef Barley	1½ hrs.

Product	Cooking Time
Beef Noodle	20 min.
Split Pea	20 min.
Chicken Noodle	20 min.
Vegetable Beef	1 hr.
Pasta (9 lbs.)	10 min.
Spaghetti (10 lbs.)	8 min.
Shells (10 lbs.)	11 min.
Frozen Ravioli (60 pcs.)	22 min.
Brown Gravy	15-20 min.
White Cream Sauce	20 min.
Cheese Sauce	15 min.
Chili	1½-2 hrs.
Ground Meat (15 lbs., browned)	7 min.
Spaghetti Sauce	1 hr.

SERVING GUIDE FOR STEAM KETTLES
(Full Capacity)

Size	Usable Gallons	Full	Servings by Cup 3/4	1/2	1/4
20 Gal.	16	256	341	512	1024
30 Gal.	24	384	512	768	1536
40 Gal.	32	512	683	1024	2048
60	48	768	1204	1536	3072

STEAM KETTLE PORTION GUIDE

Size	8 oz. Serving oz.	5 oz. Serving	4 oz. Serving
10 Gal.	160	256	320
20 Gal.	320	512	640
30 Gal.	480	768	960
40 Gal.	640	1024	1280
60 Gal.	960	1536	1920
80 Gal.	1280	2048	2560
100 Gal.	1600	2560	3200
150	2400	3840	4800

NOTE: Allow approximately 15-20% less for actual usable portions of most food items

TILTING SKILLETS/FRY PANS
(Gas and Electric Available)

Styles available: table top or floor models. These very versatile cookers can braise, boil, saute, pan fry, simmer, kettle cook, steam, proof and act as a steam table. Stated another way, these units can do the work of a range, griddle, small kettle, stock pot, or frying pan. Electric table top units rated at approximately 8 KW; 23 gallon, 12 KW and 40 gallon at 21 KW. Gas; 23 gallon at 76,000 BTU and 40 gallon at 114,000 BTU.

HELPFUL HINTS

A drain trough should be placed in front of the units. It makes cleaning much easier.

TILTING SKILLET COOKING GUIDE

Item	Portion Size	Number of Portions Per Hour 23 gal.	40 gal.
BREAKFAST FOODS			
Scrambled Eggs	1½ eggs	720	1,100
Oatmeal	½ cup	1,000	2,000
Pancakes	2 each	150	250
MEAT – FISH – POULTRY			
Macaroni and Beef	6 ounces	700	1,400
Hamburgers	3 ounces	525	750
Chicken – Pan Fried	5 ounces	150	240
Minute Steaks	7 ounces	200	300
Halibut Steak	5 ounces	150	225
Chili Con Carne	4 ounces	550	1,100
MISCELLANEOUS			
Canned Vegetables	3 ounces	750	1,200
Frozen Vegetables	3 ounces	250	375
Grilled Cheese Sandwich	1 sandwich	280	400
Soups	6 ounce	375	725
Sauces & Gravies	2 ounces	1,150	2,250

TYPICAL TILTING SKILLET SPECIFICATIONS

SIZE & CAPACITIES OF 3 POPULAR FLOOR MODELS

Ft. to back of pan	25-5/8"	24-5/8"	24-5/8"
Rt. to left of pan	24-5/8"	31-5/8"	41-5/8"
Width of unit	42"	48"	59"
Pan working height	36"	36"	36"
Height with lid up	67"	67"	67"
Cubic volume 7" depth	18.1 gal.	23.3 gal.	30.8 gal.
Cubic volume 9" depth	X	30 gal.	39.6 gal.

Other sizes and wall or counter models available.

TYPICAL PRODUCTION TIMES FOR 40 GAL. TILT SKILLET

PRODUCT	QUANTITY	COOKING TIME
Steaks, 7 oz., minute	26	5 min.
Scrambled eggs	2-3 cases	5 min.
Grilled cheese sandwiches	48	7-8 min.
Hamburgers	60	5 min.
Hamburgers	700	2 hrs.
Pancakes	24	1½ min. per side
Chocolate mousse	200-300 portions	15 min.
Noodles	30 lbs.	15-20 min.
Dumplings, Bohemian	15 loaves (175 portions)	10 min.
Chocolate pudding	850 8 oz. portions	10 min.
Zucchini	300-400 portions	10-15 min.
Green peppers	5 bushels	35 min.
Crabmeat stuffing	250 servings	30 min.
Crêpes	250 (15-20 per batch)	1 hr.
Veal, sauteed	20 lbs.	25 min.
Chicken breasts, boned	120 lbs.	20-30 min.
Ribs, barbequed	500 portions	2 hrs.
Ground beef, frozen	55 lbs.	1 hr.
Taco meat	175 lbs.	1 hr. 10 min.
Refried beans	40 lbs.	2½ hrs.
Beef Ragout	90 lbs.	1½ hrs.
Ground beef cheese steaks	500 portions	1 hr.
Pepper steak	50 lbs.	1 hr.
Beef tips	50 lbs.	1 hr.
Chicken Cacciatore	500 portions	2 hrs.
Turkeys	6 at 28 lb. each	2 hrs.
Italian Beef Roasts	200 lbs.	2¼ hrs.
Pot roast	90-100 lbs.	1¾ hrs.
Salisbury steak	350 portions	1 hr.

F.E.F. HUMOR

Negotiations for a large food service installation in a local college culminated in a rather formal luncheon meeting in the faculty dining room.

Meeting with the faculty members concerned with the project were our company's chief engineer and the co-authors of this book. We apparently made a favorable impression and gained their confidence, for they awarded us the contract and gave us a check for the deposit.

Their confidence however, may have diminished slightly when upon exiting, one of us opened the door and the other two bumped him and themselves into a closet.

STEAMER ASSEMBLY FOR TILTING SKILLETS

The steamer assembly converts braising pans or tilt skillets to a pressureless steamer. Using lift out compartments you add 12" x 20" x 2½" or 12" x 20" x 4" perforated pans and as with other steamers use the same pan for serving.

TYPICAL COOKING TIMES USING BRAISING PAN STEAMER ASSEMBLY

Item	Quantity	Time	Results
Sliced Carrots (frozen)	10 lbs.	15 min.	Good color, firm texture, excellent taste.
Cut Green Beans (frozen)	10 lbs.	15 min.	Good color, firm texture, excellent flavor
Whole, white kernel corn (frozen)	10 lbs.	12 min.	Good color, firm texture, excellent flavor.
Broccoli Spears (frozen)	8 lbs.	13 min.	Good color, best way to broccoli
Potatoes, cut, peeled (frozen)	10 lbs.	25 min.	Good flavor, good texture, no discoloring.

SHOT OR PUMP STYLE - FREE VENTING STEAMERS

Manual load or automatic water feed, super heated water, converted to steam for portion reheating, 115V.

Size: approximately 12" wide x 18" deep x 12" high.

TYPICAL TIME CHART

Item	Time
Sliced Meats	10-20 sec.
Pre-cooked Hamburg	30 sec.
Hot Dogs	60-90 sec.
Bacon	45 sec.
Open Buns	10 sec.
Cooked Vegetables	45-60 sec.
Cooked Spaghetti	30-45 sec.

CHEESE MELTERS - ELECTRIC

Normally available in lengths of 2 to 6 feet. Depths and heights vary by manufacturer. Quartz heaters normally heat to 2,000° almost instantly. They may be wall mounted, table top style and pass thru. Some units are turned on by switch, others by the weight of a plate.

Grids are adjustable. These flexible pieces of equipment are being used for melting, browning, poaching and light broiling and finishing. Typical KW rating: 24" - 2.5 KW, 36" - 3.5 KW, 48" - 4.8 KW.

Melters are also available in gas.

SPECIFICATIONS

Lengths	Kilowatts	Number of Controls
24"	2600	1
36"	3900	2
48"	5200	2
60"	6500	3
72"	7800	4

Depths 16" or 18" - 208V or 240V, single phase.

These food finishers may be counter style or wall mount.

Zone control provides the most efficient use of energy. Each on-off switch controls various sets of quartz elements to give the operator more flexibility. The rack reaches 660^{0}F in the top position, 575^{0}F in the middle position and 500^{0}f on the lower position. These temperatures are constant front to rear, and side to side under each set of elements. The elements run front to back to give this exceptional zone control.

These units cook, warm, reconstitute, broil, shirr eggs, melt cheese, toast, brown, and heat; a real chef's aid.

Warm plates	Garlic Bread	Mexican Dishes
Reconstitute Food	Au Gratin Potatoes	Sea Food
Brown Souffles	Sandwiches	Heat Rolls & Pastries

SOME TYPICAL PRODUCTION TIMES FOR THE ELECTRIC QUARTZ CHEESE MELTERS
(To be used as a guide only)

	Saute	Poach	Broil
FISH:			
Salmon - ¾" thick	7-9 min.	7-9 min.	7-9 min.
Halibut ¾" thick	7-9 min.	6-9 min.	7-10 min.
Sword Fish - ¾" thick	8-10 min.	8-10 min.	8-10 min.
SHELLFISH:			
Scallops	5-7 min.	4-6 min.	
Lobster	7-8 min.	6-8 min.	8-10 min.
Shrimp, Scampi Style	5-7 min.	5-7 min.	4-6 min.
BREADS:	**Heating Time**		
Croutons	2-3 min.		
English Muffins	2-3 min.		
Toast, Texas Style	2-3 min.		
Sliced Bread	2-3 min.		
Danish	2-3 min.		

SOME TYPICAL PRODUCTION TIMES FOR THE
ELECTRIC QUARTZ CHEESE MELTERS
(To be used as a guide only)

	Heating Time
SANDWICHES, OPEN FACE:	
Grilled Cheese	2-3 min.
Ham & Cheese	3-4 min.
EGGS:	
Poached	2-4 min.
Over Easy	2-4 min.
Scrambled	2-4 min.
CHEESE TOP DISHES:	
French Onion Soup	2-3 min.
Casseroles	2-3 min.
Mexican Food:	
Chili Relleno	3-4 min.
Italian Food:	
Lasagna	2-3 min.
Canneloni	2-3 min.
Crepes	2-4 min.
Broiled Tomatoes	2-3 min.
HORS D'OEUVRES:	
Chicken Livers w/Bacon	3-5 min.
Mini Pizza	2-4 min.
Nachoes	2-3 min.
DESSERTS:	
Hot Pastry	3-5 min.
Crepes	3-5 min.
Sopapilas	2-4 min.
Heats:	
Gravies - Sauces	3-5 min.
Warms:	
Plates, Bowls, Platters	2-3 min.

RECOMMENDATIONS:
1) Use a dark-coated aluminum pan
2) Preheat pan on stovetop
3) Turn some products half way through cooking, e.g. Swordfish
4) Baste most sauteed or poached products during cooking
5) When poaching, salted water and always simmer - never boil

HIGH HEAT RADIANT OVENS
(Counter Models)

These units are heated by two plates and heaters - one each, top and bottom. Exterior cabinet is air insulated and cooled by fan. Designed to hold 12" x 20" pans. Available in two sizes. Units may be stacked. Dial temperature control.

Shallow cavity model measures 34¾" wide x 19" deep x 14" high. Cavity is 22" wide x 14" deep x 4" high. 208/240 - 1 phase 4.5/6 KW.

147

High cavity model measures 34¾" wide x 19" deep x 22" high. Cavity is 22" wide x 14" deep x 12" high, 240 Volt - 1 phase, 5 KW. The high cavity permits roasting of turkeys or with use of rack, double pie baking, etc.

AVERAGE COOKING TIME GUIDE

Product	Weight	Start Temp.	Setting	Time
Beef Stews	5 lbs.	—10°F.	750°	45 min.
Beef Stews	5 lbs.	38:	750°	25 min.
Breaded Chicken Thighs	6 lbs.	34°	700°	12-15 min.
Breaded Chicken Breasts	6½ lbs.	0°	600°	25 min.
Creamed Chipped Beef	4 lbs.	34°	700°	17-20 min.
Hamburger Patty	3 lbs.	34°	700°	10 min.
Mexican "TV" Dinner	16 oz.	0°	650°	18-20 min.
Salisbury Steak in Sauce —				
Precooked	3 lbs.	0°	750°	24-30 min.
Asparagus (Frozen)	2½ lbs.	0°	750°	7-10 min.
Corn	2½ lbs.	0°	750°	13-16 min.
French Fries	2 lbs.	0°	650°-750°	6-9 min.
Spinach	5 lbs.	0°	750°	35-40 min.
Puff Pastries	5 oz.	0°	670°	11-13 min.

Cakes, cookies & breads may be baked in the oven at 550°-600°F. in 2/3 normal bake time.

Melted Cheese Topping French Onion Soup - Crumble cheese on crouton - ¼" Tureen

Pizza	2 lbs.	38°	700°	2 min.
Pizza	2 lbs.	0°	750°	7-9 min.

SEMI-AUTOMATIC SPAGHETTI COOKER

Unit is 32" wide x 30½" deep x 36" high, not including back splash and faucet - cold water fill standard hot and cold water optional. Cooking tank holds 8.5 gal. water, 208 or 240 volt, 1 phase, 7.4 K.W. Cooking capacity: 6 lbs. dry spaghetti. Re-heat capacity: 9 portions, approx. 30 seconds.

OPERATION:
Spaghetti is cooked in timed heat controlled tank. Basket raises automatically. After rinsing, spaghetti is pre-portioned into holding cups and held in cold water in the holding tank - capacity 48 cups. At serving time, the cooking tank is re-heated and held just below boiling by thermostat. Up to 9 cups may be placed in basket and automatically lowered, re-heated and raised for plating. Unit is available without holding tank.

148

AUTOMATED HEAVY DUTY COOKING EQUIPMENT
(Large Production Capacity)

Styles available include:
- Continuous fryer
- Automatic griddle
- Automatic boiler
- Continuous pass thru convection oven
- Automatic kettle/cooker
- Rotating ovens
- Automatic steamer

The sizes and options of these specialized pieces are varied. A few charts will show some typical production. Please use our information and referral service if you need further information.

CONVEYOR BAKE OVEN: 120" wide, 49" deep, 53" high - 200,000 BTU input. Jets of hot air sweep away heavy cold air adhering to product. Faster baking at lower temperatures. Conveyor speed control or reversible. Side load option.

REVOLVING TRAY OVEN: From 8'-0" to 17'-6" wide, 5'-10" to 11'-9" deep. Bake or roast. Capacities to 240 turkeys, 2,000 potatoes or 72 large pies per load.

ROAST AND BASTE OVEN: Automatic basting conveyor oven.

CAPABILITIES

Food	Pounds	Cooking Time (Min.)
Pork Roast	280	90
Roast Beef	280-350	40-45
Beef Tenderloin	210-350	30-40
Pot Roast	280-350	120-150
Meat Loaf	350	120

CONVEYOR FRYER: Requires only one unskilled operator. Once the chef has set the time and temperature controls and check the product.

CAPABILITIES

Food	Pieces Per Hr.
Pork Chops	1100
Sausages	1200
Hamburgs	1200
Fried Fish	1000

RUN-THROUGH STEAMERS: Pressure cooker for large volume quick cooking. Holds up to 18 stainless steel 12" x 20" x 4" pans.

Food	Pounds
Green Beans	970
Carrots	970
Potatoes	1120
Peas	970
Fish	1110
Chicken	560

OTHER HIGH PRODUCTION EQUIPMENT

- Sauce and Stew Cooker with automatic stir arm
- Automatic Pasta, Dumpling and Rice Cooker
- Automatic Fryer for short fry time items, scallops, etc.
- Roasting and Grilling Machines for large pieces of meat
- Automatic Griddles
- Automatic Steamer and Boiling Pan
- Automatic Broiler
- Continuous Feed Convection Oven

Please use F.E.F. Personal Assistance Service if you desire further information on any of the above units.

POPCORN FACTS

Kettle Capacity Per Load	Produces Per Hour
8 oz.	160 oz.
12 oz.	240 oz.
14 oz.	280 oz.
16 oz.	320 oz.
20 oz.	400 oz.

Machines available in many styles and sizes.

SNACK FACTS

All weights = 100 grams (3½ oz.)	Calories	Protein Grams	Carbohydrate Grams	Fiber Grams
Plain Popcorn, popped	386	12.7	76.7	2.2
Popcorn, popped with salt and oil	456	9.8	59.1	1.7
Potato Chips, plain	568	5.3	50.0	1.6*
Ice Cream cones	377	10.0	77.9	.2
Pretzels	390	9.8	75.9	.3
Saltines	433	9.0	71.5	.4

POPCORN BUTTER DISPENSERS

12" x 12" square, 6 lbs. butter at serving temperature, 400 watts, 115 V.

COTTON CANDY MACHINE

21" long x 14" wide x 18" high, 1800-2100 watts, 115 V, produces 17 to 33 lbs. per hour.

"SPIKE" DOG MACHINE

115 Volt, plug in counter unit - 14" wide, 12" deep, 12" high.

Operation: Steaming chamber holds approx. 40 hot dogs, warming time 20 to 30 minutes. Four vertical spikes at front of unit, brushed with soft butter or margarine toast inside of uncut roll in approx. 30 seconds. Pour mustard, catsup, relish and onion into tunnel left by spike, then insert steamed hot dog.

Production: Approx. 120 hot dogs per hour.

CANDY APPLE COOKERS

16" diameter, 24" high. Gas: 39,000 BTU, Electric: 220V, 4500 watts. Compact: 110 V, 2,000 watts. 16" aluminum or copper kettle.

CARMEL DIP WARMER

12" x 20", 110 Volt unit holds two No. 10 cans - individual heat control. No. 10 can covers average 50-60 apples.

HOT DOGS

ROLLER STYLE GRILL - 110 VOLT

| Dimensions | | | | | |
Wide	Deep	High	Volts	Amps	Capacity
23½"	13½"	7¼"	120	6.4	21 Franks (420 per hr.)
37"	13½"	7¼"	120	11.3	35 Franks (700 per hr.)
15"	24½"	8"	120	6.8	21 Franks (420 per hr.)
30"	24½"	8"	120	15.	48 Franks (960 per hr.)
22½"	25"	8¾"	120	9	42 Franks (840 per hr.)
36"	19"	8¾"	120	10.5	50 Franks (1000 per hr.)
36"	25"	8¾"	120	19	70 Franks (1400 per hr.)

HOT DOG OR SAUSAGE BROILER

Stainless wire cage holds 9 hot dogs. Revolving ferris wheel style around calrod heating unit produces open-pit barbecue flavor. Produces up to 180 hot dogs per hour. Temperature control cooks slow, fast or holds.

Specifications: 115V - 1500W - 13.5 Amp. Size 14" wide, 14" deep, 13" high.

Optional roll warmer pan available for top of the unit, picks up heat from the broiler.

HOT DOG ROTISSERIE (Ferris Wheel Motion)

Available in two sizes.

	Small	Large
Cradle Capacity	56 dogs	84 dogs
Spike Capacity	54 dogs	not avail.
Bun Warmer Capacity	40	60
Width	20½"	26½"
Height	24"	24"
Depth	15½"	15½"
Wattage	1680	1880

Warmers in top of units hold 40 or 84 buns respectively.

Glass front, top load steamer, 110V, 1000 watt unit holds 150 hot dogs and 50 rolls.

BARBEQUE CHILI WARMER

12" x 12" x 13" high, 1½ quarts: 265 watts, 115V; 4 quarts: 750 watts, 115 V.

CORN DOG FRYER (Hot Dog on a Stick)

12" wide, 24" deep, 14 dog capacity, 1800 watts at 110V, 3000 watts at 220V.

NACHOS CHEESE WARMER

12" x 12" x 13" high, holds #10 cans of cheese, 400 watts, 110V (topping for tortilla chips).

PEANUT ROASTER

Sizes vary. Typical production: 25 lbs. in 20 min., 75 lbs. in 1 hour. 80,000 BTU with 110V motor drive.

CARMEL CORN STOVE

220V, 2600 watts or 33,000 BTU gas burner. Legs adjust height.

152

SLUSH MACHINE

Typical freeze time, 8 to 22 minutes from start. Production, 150 to 300 servings per hour. Typical cup sizes: 7, 9, 12, 16 oz.

ICE SHAVERS

Pounds shaved ice per hour: 300/500/900, typical cup size: 6 oz. Typical flavors: cherry, grape, strawberry, orange, lime, raspberry, pineapple, root beer.

QUICK SNACK COOKER

Pour batter into six compartment mold, add any product or seasoning of your choice — Reubens, hot dogs, potato knishs, cherries or apple — lower top mold onto product. Cooks in two minutes, baked outside, cooked inside.
21" wide x 12" deep, 9" high with legs, 120V, 2.5 KW.

RICE COOKER/STEAMER

23 cup capacity, cooking - 1600 watts, warming - 65 watts.

PRETZEL WARMERS

15" wide x 17" deep x 26 high, 115 volt. Each unit holds 48 large pretzels, revolves at 1 RPM.

GLASS FRONT HOT DOG STEAMERS

These display merchandisers steam both the hot dogs and rolls in divided compartments. The water is manually fed out heated by thermostatically controlled elements. The units are easily broken down for cleaning.

TYPICAL SIZES

Width	Depth	Height	Capacity	Power
24¼"	15¼"	16¾"	130 Hot Dogs - 90 Rolls	115 V - 1.5 KW
18"	15-5/8"	15"	150 Hot Dogs - 40 Rolls	115 V - 1 KW

DUAL WAFFLE BAKER

22" wide x 16¼" deep x 8" high, 115 or 220 volt. Produces 50 7" waffles per hour. This waffle baker features removable grids for ease of cleaning and floating hinges allowing top grid to rise when waffle expands during baking.

HEAT AND HOLD UNIT

Single opening to hold #8½ (7 qt.) or #10½ (11 qt.) round inserts. Use wet or dry. For soup, chili, gravy or thawing and holding frozen products. Unit is 12-5/8" square x 11" high, std. 120 volt plug-in cord - 1650 watts. Thermostatic control 150° to 210°. Amber and green lights indicate on and heating cycles.

EGG BOILER OR COOKER

Two styles of automatic egg cookers are available. One boils the eggs, the other steams them.

In the operation of the egg boiler up to 6 eggs are placed in each individually controlled bucket. After setting the timers, the buckets are manually lowered into the boiling water. The timers automatically lift them out. Electric timers adjustable up to 6 minutes.

Boiler Cooker Specifications

Unit	Width	Depth	Height	Total Eggs Per Load	Voltage
2 Buckets	10½"	9"	32"	12	110 - 1.8KW or 208 - 2KW
3 Buckets	15½"	9"	32"	18	110 - 1.8KW or 208 - 2KW
4 Buckets	20½"	9"	32"	24	208 - 2KW Only

In the operation of the steamer the units are divided into compartments at the top. Each compartment has a spring loaded cover and timer. Whole eggs or eggs in poaching cups are set on trays and placed into the compartments. The timer is set and the cover closed. The timer automatically releases the cover and it springs open at the end of the cooking cycle. Timers are adjustable up to 15 minutes. These units will also steam many other items such as hot dogs, cook-in-pouch foods, etc.

Steamer Specifications

Unit	Width	Depth	Height	Total Capacity Eggs Poach Cups	Voltage
2 Compt.	10½"	9"	21"	12 or 4	110 - 1.8KW or 208 - 2KW
3 Compt.	15½"	9"	21"	18 or 6	110 - 1.8KW or 208 - 2KW
4 Compt.	20½"	9"	21"	24 or 8	208 - 2KW Only
2 Large	20½"	9"	21"	24 or 12	208 - 2KW Only

All models (steam or boil) have automatic low water cut-off. Automatic water fill available for any unit. Extra poaching cups and trays for steamer suggested.

Chapter Six

COOKING
EQUIPMENT
EXHAUST
VENTILATION

The National Fire Protection Association bulletin 96 covers systems for vapor removal from cooking equipment as well as fire extinguishing system requirements for both the cooking equipment and exhaust system.

Bulletin NFPA-96 is considered as the standard for the installation of equipment designed to remove smoke and grease laden vapors from cooking equipment. Its standards significantly influence insurance underwriters.

Even though the standards set forth in Bulletin 96 are generally accepted throughout the United States, let us remind you that your local Building Codes are the ones that control your installation. Other approvals necessary may include N.S.F., U.L., or O.S.H.A.

Bulletin 96 concerns itself mainly with construction details of exhaust and fire systems. Regarding make-up air it states only that replacement air shall be adequate to prevent negative air pressure from exceeding .02" water column and that openings providing the make-up air not be restricted in any way that would reduce the exhaust system's efficiency.

Particularly in areas which require heating in winter and air conditioning in the summer, properly engineered and installed systems are not a "do it yourself" project. Codes are always being changed and updated. Your Health Department, insurance carrier and local government agencies should be contacted for up-to-date information. Considering insurance costs, safety and energy saving potentials it will be to your advantage to have exhaust and ventilation work coordinated by professionals.

We have included in this chapter some basic information to guide you in selecting equipment suited to your requirements.

First some important facts to know about the new revised edition of NFPA-96.

Requirements:

Cooking equipment that produces smoke or grease laden vapors shall be equipped with hood, duct, system, grease removal device, fire extinghishing equipment.

Hoods, ducts — grease extractors shall have a clearance of at least 18" from combustible materials, except when listed for lesser clearance and combustible material is protected to satisfaction of authority having jurisdiction.

155

If required by authority having jurisdiction, notice in writing must be given on any changes or replacement of existing systems.

CHAPTER 2 — HOODS
Construction
Hoods shall be constructed of and supported by metal not less than:

20 gauge stainless steel

18 gauge steel

or other approved material of equivalent strength, fire and corrosion resistant.

All seams and joints shall have a liquid tight continuous external weld.

IMPORTANT ADDITION TO CODE

Exception: Hoods or enclosures of listed grease extractors, and automatic damper hood assemblies that are evaluated under same fire severity as listed items shall be considered complying with above.

Canopy Hoods shall completely cover equipment plus an over-hang of at least 6" on all sides of equipment not adjacent to walls.

Distance between floor and lower edge shall not exceed 7 ft.

Depth from lower to upper edge shall be at least 2 ft.

Non canopy, prefab hoods sized according to manufacturer's specifications.

CHAPTER 3 — Duct Systems
NOTE: Exterior and interior ducts are permitted and described extensively in Bulletin.

Listed grease ducts shall be installed in accordance with terms of listing.

Other ducts shall be constructed and supported by:

16 gauge carbon steel

18 gauge stainless steel

All seams and joints shall have liquid tight continuous external weld (means for expansion of long ducts shall be provided).

Duct systems shall not be inter-connected with any other ventilating system.

Ducts shall not pass thru fire walls or partitions.

Where ducts pass thru partitions or walls of combustible materials, clearance to duct shall be not less than 18".

Except when combustible material is protected in a manner satisfactory to authority having jurisdiction.

Ducts shall be installed without forming dips or traps which might collect residues, except when clean-out traps are provided for continuous or automatic removal of residue.

Each duct system shall serve only one floor.

IMPORTANT CHANGE FROM PREVIOUS CODE

Termination of ducts shall terminate as follows:

at least 10 ft. from adjacent buildings, property lines, air intakes, etc.

with direction of air flow exhaust away from roof surface; if not possible, a metal pan shall be provided to catch residue.

with discharge at least 40" clearance from outlet to roof surface, except when permitted by authority with jurisdiction, ducts may terminate at exterior of wall provided that fire in duct cannot be transmitted to adjacent facilities.

IN ADDITION, the following exception has been added to this paragraph:

"When permitted by the authority having jurisdiction, ducts may terminate into the base of an up-discharge exhaust fan, provided the ductwork extends a minimum of 18" above the roof surface and is constructed of materials complying with the provision of Bulletin 96 and at least 40" of clearance is maintained between the exhaust fan discharge and roof surface."

CHAPTER 4 — Grease Removal Devices

Grease removal devices shall be provided and consist of one of the following:

Listed extractors

Listed filters or removal devices

Constructed of non-combustible materials

Shall be listed for use with commercial cooking equipment

Shall be easily accessible and removable

CHAPTER 5 — Air Movement

Exhaust fans shall be approved and rated for continuous operation.

All wiring and electrical equipment shall comply with NFPA-70-1975.

Shall have means for inspections, service, cleaning

Air velocity thru duct not less than 1500 ft. per minute

IMPORTANT CHANGE FROM PREVIOUS CODE

Exhaust air volumes shall be of sufficient level to provide for capture and removal of grease laden vapors. Test data or performance acceptable to authority having jurisdiction shall be provided **or** displayed upon request.

"This most important code revision should be clarified so that it is understood and properly applied."

We feel that the following factors should be used to determine air exhaust volume requirements.

WALL HOODS: (open on three sides), 100 c.f.m. per

	square feet of hood area.
ISLAND HOODS:	(open on all four sides) 150 c.f.m. per square foot of hood area.
NON CANOPY TYPE HOODS:	300 c.f.m. per lineal foot of hood except if hood is of pre-fabricated type and hood manufacturer recommends otherwise.

Replacement air quantity shall be adequate to prevent negative air pressures from exceeding .02" water column.

CHAPTER 6 — Auxiliary Equipment

Dampers shall not be installed in ducts or duct systems except when specifically listed for such use or used as part of a listed device or system.

Wiring of any type shall not be installed in ducts.

Motors, lights and other electrical devices shall not be installed in ducts or in path of exhaust except when specifically approved for such use.

IMPORTANT ADDITION TO CODE

Fume incinerators, thermal recovery units, air pollution control devices may be installed in ducts or hoods or path of travel of exhaust when specifically approved for such use and shall not increase fire hazard.

CHAPTER 7 — Fire Extinguishing Equipment

Approved fire extinguishing equipment shall be provided for duct systems, grease removal devices, hoods.

Except when acceptable to authority having jurisdiction fire extinguishing protection for ducts may be omitted when equipment is served by listed grease extractors.

Fat fryers, ranges, griddles and broilers shall also be protected.

Operation of extinguishing system shall automatically shut off all sources of fuel and heat to protected equipment or equipment located under ventilating equipment that is protected.

Review and certification may be required.

CHAPTER 8 — Procedures for the Use and Maintenance of Equipment

Exhaust systems shall be operated during all periods of cooking.

Filter equipped exhaust systems shall not be operated with filters removed.

Openings for replacing air exhausted thru ventilating equipment shall not be restricted by covers, dampers, or anything that would reduce operating efficiency of exhaust system.

Inspection of fire extinguishing system every 6 months.

important change from PREVIOUS CODE

Hood, grease removal, devices, fans, ducts shall be cleaned at frequent intervals to avoid contamination by grease and oily sludge.

NOTE: Depending on cooking equipment usage, the entire exhaust system including grease extractors should be inspected daily or weekly. When evidence of grease or residue deposits appear, system should be cleaned.

CHAPTER 9 — Minimum Safety Requirements for Cooking Equipment

Cooking Equipment shall be approved based on:

a) listings of Nationally recognized Test Laboratories.

b) test data acceptable to authority having jurisdiction.

All fat fryers shall be installed at least 16" from adjacent surface flames.

Fat fryers shall have high limit controls, and adjustable operating thermostat.

BASIC HOOD AND FILTER STYLES

1. Conventional Hoods or Canopys — either wall mounted, ceiling hung at wall or island type.
2. Ventilators — back shelf type either wall or center island installation.
3. Grill stands with built-in filters.
4. Proximity ventilators.

The old days of the pop-riveted aluminum hood with standing seams and a propeller type fan in a hole in the wall are long gone but the image still remains in the minds of many old timers who simply cannot understand why the new range hood they require costs so darn much. Many an honest salesman has lost an order because the restaurant owner knew a sheetmetal man who would do the whole job for only $500.00. The grief that can follow when the fire underwriters condemn the job is endless. We have inserted Fig. 6-1 in an endeavor to alleviate such problems. The drawing clearly shows the many requirements for installation of a range hood in a kitchen with wooden studs and ceiling joists. The drawing shows requirements for New York State at the time this book was published.

TYPICAL REQUIREMENTS FOR HOOD INSTALLATION
IN WOOD FRAME BUILDING

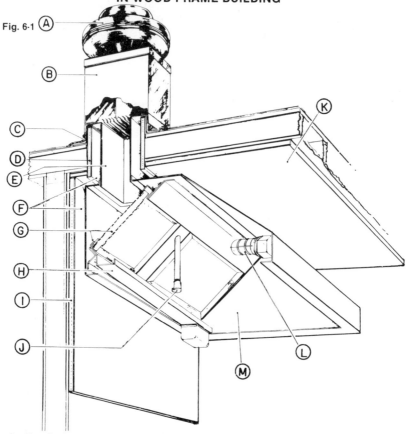

Fig. 6-1

A—Top discharge - centrifugal exhaust fan sized for required C.F.M. exhaust of air.

B—Stack - to extend exhaust to min. of 40" above surface of roof. No. 16 gauge metal, welded seams and back-draft louvers.

C—No. 16 ga. galv. welded roof curb.

D—1" thick rockwool w/wire mesh. Enclosed in 22 ga. galv. iron.

E—16 Ga. all wedled - galv. iron duct sized for C.F.M. exhaust req'd.

F—Minimum of 3" air space around duct, behind and above hood.

G—Approved filters. Grease extractors optional.

H—Grease gutter pitched to an approved, removable container.

I—1" thick rockwool w/wire mesh covered w/22 ga. sheetmetal. To be carried down to approved distance below cooking surface of ranges.

J—Typicai 'down' nozzle shown - fire protection system to be installed in accordance with all applicable codes.

K—Where top of hood is less than 18" from ceiling insulation, as in 'I'. Shall be applied to ceiling and extend 18" beyond face of hood. A minimum of 3" air space is required between hood kand insulation.

L—Vapor-proof, marine type lights.

M—Entire hood to be No. 18 ga. galv. iron or 20 ga. stainless steel with all seams welded.

160

Another quick run through of the requirements and then on to other charts and information:

1. Hood Material — 18 gauge galvanized steel or
   20 gauge stainless steel
   (Liquid tight external welds)
2. Duct Material: 16 gauge carbon steel or
   18 gauge stainless steel
   (Continuous liquid tight external welds)
3. Ducts not to be interconnected with any other building system. Must terminate a minimum of 40" above roof surface and at least 10'-0" from adjacent buildings or other air inlets.
4. Duct Air Velocity: minimum 1500 C.F.M.
5. Ducts may never be run through a fire wall.
6. Hood Dimensions: must extend a minimum of at least 6" over range battery on all sides of island installation and both ends and front of wall installation. Minimum top to bottom dimension of hood 2'-0".
7. Maximum Height: above floor 7'-0" - 6'-6" preferred.
8. Hood Lights: must be vaporproof.
9. Distance from cooking surface: lowest point of filter to be 2'-6" above a surface with no exposed flame, 3'-6" above open flames.
10. Air Velocity across Face of Hood: 100 F.P.M. for hoods exposed 3 sides, 150 F.P.M. for island type hoods exposed on all 4 sides and 300 F.P.M. for back shelf hoods. Hoods in corners or having aprons on 3 sides require only 85 F.P.M.

FAN SELECTION METHOD

Fans are rated by HP required to remove a specific volume of air (C.F.M.) against friction created by filters duct surfaces and bends. This resistance to the air flow is called static pressure measured by water column; i.e. .250 or ¼" s.p.

To select a fan let us assume we have a wall mounted hood 12'-0" long x 4'-0" front to back with the duct work running straight up to the point of exhaust and with no charbroiler broiler under the hood.

Length (12'-0") x Depth (4'-0") = 48 square feet using 100 feet per minute hood face velocity x 48 we arrive at 4800 cubic feet per minute of air to be removed. For our straight up exhaust duct using standard 2" filters a static pressure of .375 or 3/8" will suffice. Using the sample fan guide Fig. 6-2 we see that a 1 HP, 665 R.P.M. fan will do the job.

SAMPLE FAN GUIDE

Fig. 6-2

Motor H.P.	R.P.M.	Static Pressures			
		.125	.250	.375	.500
¼	425	3145	2685		
⅓	465	3300	3205		
½	525	4365	3840	3350	
¾	600	5105	4655	4270	3780
1	665	5735	5375	4945	4623
1½	755	6865	6595	6265	5895
2	830	7285	7040	6750	6375

NOTE: Two separate fans should be considered for hoods much over 10'-0" long. To size 2 fans use ½ C.F.M. (approx. 2450). Other fan charts from suppliers catalogs would give proper fan size.

In our example for fan sizing we used a tentative .375 static pressure. Actual static pressure must be determined correctly by the contractor for each installation.

DUCT SIZES BY C.F.M.

C.F.M.	Round Duct	Square Duct
2400	13"	13" x 13"
2800	15"	14" x 14"
2950	15"	14" x 14"
3500	16"	15" x 15"
3600	18"	16" x 16"
4300	20"	18" x 18"
5000	23"	21" x 21"

Our 4800 C.F.M. would require a round duct of approximately 22" diameter or a 20" x 20" square duct.

COMMON FILTER SIZES
(All 1¾" thick · commonly called 2" filters)

Height		Width	Height		Width
10"	x	16"	16"	x	20"
10"	x	20"	16"	x	25"
10"	x	25"	20"	x	16"

(Continued)

COMMON FILTER SIZES (Cont.)
(All 1¾" thick - commonly called 2" filters)

Height		Width		Height		Width
12"	x	16"		20"	x	20"
20"	x	20"		20"	x	25"
12"	x	25"		25"	x	16"
16"	x	16"		25"	x	20"

Available in aluminum, galvanized steel or permanent stainless steel mesh.

Using 20" x 20" filters our 12'-0" hood would have 7 filters.

TYPICAL C.F.M. RATINGS OF 1¾" FILTERS

Size	C.F.M.
16" x 20"	700
20" x 20"	900
20" x 25"	1100
25" x 30"	1400

HOOD LIGHTING

Vapor-proof fluorescent fixtures are available with hinged glass doors. The metal box enclosing the fixture is usually mounted outside of the hood with a tight fitting frame permitting the light to shine down on the ranges. Marine type, vapor-proof incandescent lights may be mounted with the junction boxes either inside or outside of the hood.

SOME GUIDELINES FOR MAKE-UP AIR

We have used the air velocity method across the hood face to calculate exhaust requirements. Another method is by air volume providing for from 20 to 30 complete changes of air in the room per hour. The velocity method is preferred and recommended by many local and national codes since it directly relates to the number of cooking appliances under the hood. As long as the required minimum 1500 C.F.M. duct velocity is maintained the total air removal may be reduced if the kitchen is very large in proportion to the number of cooking appliances or if the kitchen is air conditioned or if a hood system employing positive make-up air is installed. (These systems are described further on.)

On an average, local codes call for 15 C.F.M. per person of air change in an air conditioned dining room. (Check your local codes.)

In a 100 seat room there would then be an automatic 1500 cubic feet per minute of make-up air for the exhaust system. This 1500 C.F.M. is already a basic necessary load on the air conditioning system required to maintain the desired comfort level in the dining room.

Back to our example of the 12'-0" x 4'-0" hood which required 4800 C.F.M., we find 1500 C.F.M. automatically available from the dining room leaving 3300 C.F.M. which must be brought in from the outside. Make-up air is normally introduced into kitchens through supply grilles or defusers located as high as possible and across the room as far as possible from the exhaust hood. This allows the air to benefit the greater part of the kitchen. The grilles must be sized in accordance with manufacturer's specifications. Air diffusers are preferred.

Climatic conditions will dictate whether the make-up air be heated, air conditioned or both.

We told you it wouldn't be easy.

AUTOMATIC FIRE PROTECTION

N.F.P.A. is quite naturally the authority on fire system requirements. Local authorities generally incorporate their requirements. All systems should be installed by professional suppliers.

The general required components are as follows:
- First of course, a chemical tank of a capacity to cover the areas affected,
- Automatic shut-down of exhaust fans,
- Automatic shut-down of all cooking equipment, both gas and electric,
- Both automatic, by fusible links or thermal switches and manual activating devices must be included,
- Chemical spray nozzles are required over deep fat fryers and charbroilers, in regular broilers, in the hood plenum chamber and the exhaust duct.

The above general code requirements confirm with local governing agencies.

Fig. 6-3

N.F.P.A. BULLETIN "96"
AIR FLOW REQUIREMENTS

FOR WALL CANOPIES

	Exhaust requirements/CFM		
HOOD	42''	48''	54''
3' 0''	1050	1200	1350
4' 0''	1400	1600	1800
5' 0''	1750	2000	2250
6' 0''	2100	2400	2700
7' 0''	2450	2800	3150
8' 0''	2800	3200	3600
9' 0''	3150	3600	4050
10' 0''	3500	4000	4500
11' 0''	3850	4400	4950
12' 0''	4200	4800	5400
13' 0''	4550	5200	5850
14' 0''	4900	5600	6300
15' 0''	5250	6000	6750
16' 0''	5600	6400	7200
17' 0''	5950	6800	7650
18' 0''	6300	7200	8100
19' 0''	6650	7600	8550
20' 0''	7000	8000	9000
	Make-up air requirements/CFM		
3' 0''	787	900	1012
4' 0''	1050	1200	1350
5' 0''	1312	1500	1688
6' 0''	1575	1800	2026
7' 0''	1839	2100	2364
8' 0''	2102	2400	2702
9' 0''	2365	2700	3040
10' 0''	2628	3000	3378
11' 0''	2891	3300	3716
12' 0''	3154	3600	4054
13' 0''	3417	3900	4392
14' 0''	3680	4200	4730
15' 0''	3943	4500	5068
16' 0''	4206	4800	5406
17' 0''	4469	5100	5744
18' 0''	4732	5400	6082
19' 0''	4995	5700	6420
20' 0''	5258	6000	6758

Fig. 6-4

N.F.P.A. BULLETIN "96"
AIR FLOW REQUIREMENTS

FOR ISLAND CANOPIES

	Exhaust requirements/CFM			
HOOD	72''	84''	96''	108''
6' 0''	5400	6300	7200	8100
7' 0''	6300	7350	8400	9450
8' 0''	7200	8400	9600	10800
9' 0''	8100	9450	10800	12150
10' 0''	9000	10500	12000	13500
11' 0''	9900	11550	13200	14850
12' 0''	10800	12600	14400	16200
13' 0''	11700	13650	15600	17550
14' 0''	12600	14700	16800	18900
15' 0''	13500	15750	18000	20250
16' 0''	14400	16800	19200	21600
17' 0''	15300	17850	20400	22950
18' 0''	16200	18900	21600	24300
19' 0''	17100	19950	22800	25650
20' 0''	18000	21000	24000	27000
21' 0''	18900	22050	25200	28350
22' 0''	19800	23100	26400	29700
23' 0''	20700	24150	27600	31050
24' 0''	21600	25200	28800	32400
	Make-up air requirements/CFM			
6' 0''	4050	4725	5400	6075
7' 0''	4725	5512	6300	7086
8' 0''	5400	6299	7200	8100
9' 0''	6075	7086	8100	9120
10' 0''	6750	7873	9000	10132
11' 0''	7425	8660	9900	11144
12' 0''	8100	9447	10800	12156
13' 0''	8775	10234	11700	13168
14' 0''	9450	11021	12600	14180
15' 0''	10125	11808	13500	15192
16' 0''	10800	13382	14400	16204
17' 0''	11475	14169	15300	17216
18' 0''	12150	14956	16200	18228
19' 0''	12825	15743	17100	19240
20' 0''	13500	16530	18000	20252
21' 0''	14175	17317	18900	21264
22' 0''	14850	18104	19800	22276
23' 0''	15525	18891	20700	23288
24' 0''	16200	19678	21600	24300

Just a few reminders and suggestions before we move on to make-up air, custom built ventilators and complete systems.

As stated at the beginning of this chapter, exhaust and ventilation systems are not "do-it-yourself" projects, but the authors' practical experiences in the field have shown that there will always be do-it-yourselfers. A small operator may have a growing business and require a new and larger hood. His dining room may be air conditioned with small window or wall mounted units. His budget will invariably be limited. It is to this type of industrious person who may in the future, be well able to afford a completely engineered air conditioning and ventilation system with heated and/or air conditioned make-up air that we offer a few words of cautious advice. In addition to studying this chapter, your health department, insurance carrier and local governing agencies should be contacted for updated information on ever-changing national and local codes.

Make sure that all components and the entire system comply with all requirements. The biggest bugaboo usually turns out to be the problem of make-up air. N.F.P.A. Bulletin 96 states that replacement air quantity shall be adequate to prevent negative air pressure from exceeding .02" water column. At this point we caution the food service equipment dealer as well as the purchaser — any contract for kitchen exhaust systems should clearly state whether or not the supplier is responsible for adequate make-up air. It is generally not within the scope of the equipment dealer to supply air conditioning and ventilating systems. All components which they may supply must comply with all applicable codes but poorly worded contracts can lead to misunderstanding and grief.

Some facts pertaining to make-up air and fire systems will follow, but first a few hints and reminders:

• Low ceilings can cause problems. Don't forget the overall height of the hood must be 2'-0" and that the filters or grease extractors must be at an angle no less than 45° from a horizontal plane.

• Perimeter grease gutters are not permitted.

• Round exhaust ducts offer less resistance to air flow thereby reducing static pressure. If round ducts cannot be used, ducts should be kept as near to square as possible.

• Fans have many variances and options by manufacturers. Check motor heat shields or cold air vent systems, automatic belt tension devices, bird and insect screens, back-draft units, hinged roof curbs for easy service access, grease trough on roof curbing and two speed motors for slow or idle periods.

HELPFUL HINTS

As previously outlined, end panels on hoods reduce the required air velocity across the face of the hood. This could reduce heating and air conditioning costs. In addition to that, since it is usually convenient to have the chef's refrigerator or freezer at one or each end of the range battery, if the end panels attached to the hood were of double wall construction with 1" of rock wool with wire mesh between or otherwise fireproof insulated, it would provide heat protection for the refrigerated units. The panels could be wall mounted and kept 10" or 12" above the floor for ease of cleaning.

GRIDDLE STANDS

These units designed with various type bases to hold short order cooking appliances, still require all of the aforementioned considerations but on a much smaller scale. They require equal fire extinguishing protection but the C.F.M. required for exhaust air is much lower. The units come with back shelf style hoods, filters and grease gutters with removable containers. The duct opening is provided in the unit. Ductwork and exhaust fan must be installed. Some common sizes are listed below.

Length	Duct Size	C.F.M. Air
4'-0"	8" x 15"	800
5'-0"	8" x 18"	1000
6'-0"	8" x 24"	1200
7'-0"	8" x 30"	1400
8'-0"	8" x 36"	1600
9'-0"	8" x 36"	1800
10'-0"	8" x 40"	2000

Depth available 24", 27" or 30", height 68" or 72".

Check requirement with local authorities. Charbroilers could increase required exhaust C.F.M.

Some options to consider for griddle stands:
- Order slip holders
- Removable cutting boards
- Plate shelves (on some styles)
- Built-in electrical outlets for equipment
- Open or closed bases (doors or drawers)
- Stainless steel or decorator panel finishes
- Refrigerated bases - self contained or remote
- Refr. bases with doors or drawers or both
- Stands with built-in recessed equipment with controls under cutting board

Some available with down-draft exhaust provisions. Options and dimensions vary by manufacturer.

PROXIMITY VENTILATORS

These units measuring 48" high x 18" wide and 30" deep are equipped with a fan and motor to pull exhaust air through one or both sides downward and out of the back of the unit. The exhaust air may then be ducted through outside wall or vertically through the roof. The ductwork must be engineered and installed in accordance with applicable codes. The units have built-in stainless steel filters and a grease receptacle which are easily removed through the door on the front of the unit for cleaning. The air intake vent is protected with a fusible link for fire protection.

The flat top provides a handy shelf beside the range. Since the effective exhaust collecting area extends only 24" to each side of the unit their application is somewhat limited. They could however be an ideal solution to the problem of adding more cooking equipment to an existing system. They could also be installed where remote cooking equipment is desired; i.e., at tableside.

SIZES OF DRY CHEMICAL TANKS

Height	Diameter	Pounds of Chemical	Cu. Ft. Area Covered
15-7/8"	5¼"	8½	500
17¾"	6¾"	17	1000
24"	6¾"	25	1500
24½"	7¾"	33	2000

(Tanks interconnect for larger areas as required.)

Two common types of fire extinguishing systems in use today have certain advantages and disadvantages.

DRY CHEMICAL EXTINGUISHERS are equipped with tanks containing a dry chemical, pressureized by an inert gas. The dry chemical is usually sodium bicarbonate or one with similar extinguishing properties. When the chemical is released it smothers the fire and soponifies on contact with the hot grease forming a soap-like blanket which prevents re-ignition. The chemical is pure and non injurious to workers in the area. The main disadvantage of this system is the "mess" it creates and all food contacted must be disposed of.

INERT GAS SYSTEMS usually carbon dioxide, instantly smothers the fire by cutting off the supply of oxygen. The suddenly expanded gas will have a cooling effect on the surface burning. Carbon dioxide has absolutely no effect on food or grease and leaves no mess. However, the carbon dioxide gas may dissipate and permit re-ignition from retained heat.

Many authorities prefer thermal switches over fusible links for activating fire systems. Fusible links can sometimes be carelessly left wired solidly together after a systems test or by hood cleaning crews. This defeats the whole purpose of the system.

169

Fire extinguishing systems should be completely and thoroughly inspected at least every 6 months.

SPECIAL NOTE:

At this time there is much experimentation being done with high pressure, atomized water for fire protection systems. Acceptance by governing authorities is slow. You may wish to inquire from local insurance code authorities.

The authors are keeping track of this and will answer your queries in the future.

LET'S TOUCH ON THE BIGGIES AND CLOSE THIS CHAPTER

Consultants for the food service industry, when designing and coordinating equipment installation for the larger establishments, colleges or institutions would almost certainly specify one of the many complete ventilating systems available. With the ever rising costs of energy and labor these units can quickly convert their initial cost to profits.

It is not within the scope of this publication to become involved with the engineering required for some of these systems. We leave that to the consultants. Neither is it our intent or purpose to recommend any system over any other. We will describe briefly the functions of each system in a manner that may aid you in selecting the proper unit for your needs.

Again, if you have questions, F.E.F. Personal Assistance Service will deliver the answers.

DUAL AIR HOODS

These hoods which are of approximately the same proportions as conventional canopy hoods are factory built and engineered complete systems for exhausting cooking fumes and supplying tempered make-up air. The hoods are in effect a hood within a hood. The interior hood contains all standard required components and duct work. Surrounding the up-draft duct is a down-draft duct for make-up air. The make-up air chamber envelops the plenum chamber and the return air is released downward through a slot running along the front of the hood forming an air curtain at the cooking battery and at the same time supplying up to 88% of the required make-up air.

The exhaust fan housing, mounted on the roof, is supplied with a duct take-off which extends the required distance from the exhaust outlet to bring in make-up air. Constructed within this duct is the return air fan and air heating unit. The return air may be heated by electricity direct fired, indirect fired, natural or LP gas, steam or hot water coils or fuel oil. The heating unit may be omitted.

The hood sections are of modular construction adaptable to any length from approximately 6'-0" upward.

There are many options and specifications vary by manufacturer.

VENTILATOR HOODS

The term "ventilator hood" is applied to the back shelf type used on the familiar griddle stand. Those for heavy duty cooking appliances are of course larger. They usually extend 18" to 22" from the back of the cooking equipment. The bottom of the hood should be located from 18" to 24" above the cooking surface. The type of appliance, hood design and location determine air flow which may vary from 200 to 350 F.P.M. Total air volume may be less than that required for conventional canopy type hoods due to the higher air velocity required for the ventilator hood but the same considerations for replacement air must be taken into account.

Special ventilator hoods are available for installation over upright broilers, ovens, steamers, etc.

Ventilator hoods are available with automatic wash-down systems, filters or grease extractors and with electrostat precipitator cells, for smoke removal, installed in the duct above the grease removal chamber.

Options and dimensions vary by manufacturer.

SOME AVERAGE VENTILATOR HOOD SPECIFICATIONS

Fig. 6-5

Length	C.F.M.	Duct Sq. Inches	Duct Size	
3'-0"	750	72	6" x 12"	
3'-6"	875	84	7" x 12"	
4'-0"	1000	96	8" x 12"	
6'-6"	1125	96	8" x 12"	
5'-0"	1250	120	10" x 12"	
5'-6"	1375	120	10" x 12"	
6'-0"	1500	144	12" x 12"	
6'-6"	1625	144	12" x 12"	
7'-0"	1750	144	12" x 12"	
7'-6"	1875	180	12" x 15"	
8'-0"	2000	180	12" x 15"	(Continued)

SOME AVERAGE VENTILATOR HOOD SPECIFICATIONS (Cont.)

Length	C.F.M.	Duct Sq. Inches	Duct Size
8'-6"	2125	180	12" x 15"
9'-0"	2250	216	12" x 18"
9'-6"	2375	216	12" x 18"
10'-0"	2500	216	12" x 18"
10'-6"	2625	216	12" x 18"
11'-0"	2750	264	12" x 22"
11'-6"	2875	264	12" x 22"
12'-0"	3000	264	12" x 22"

COMPENSATING HOODS

Similar in principal to the dual air hood previously described, these hoods more resemble ventilator hoods in cross section with one major difference. The double wall back section extends down below the cooking surface, then turns sharply upward to a point just above the cooking surface.

These hoods are designed to supply from 60% to 80% of make-up air requirements. In general 20% of the air supplied will be forced through the double wall at the front of the hood and be directed toward the filters. The remaining 60% being forced down through the double wall at the back and out through the upward turned opening just above the cooking surface. This strong upward jet flow of air draws the heat and fumes from the cooking surface by venturi action. The remaining 20% of required make-up air must be supplied from the kitchen.

AUTOMATIC WASH SYSTEMS

Ventilator hoods and some others are available with automatic wash-down systems to provide thorough cleansing of the grease extraction chamber.

In brief, the hood is designed for and provided with properly positioned spray nozzles for cleaning and a drain connection. Safety devices are incorporated which damper the hood and shut off the exhaust fan. For wash-down cycles the fan must be furnished with a magnetic starter having a 120V starter coil with holding circuit interlock.

An emergency fire switch is provided for remote location in the path of fire exit. The wash system is controlled from a remote cabinet which may be wall mounted or built into any convenient location. The system operates with from 104⁰ to 180⁰ hot water. Detergent is injected into the water line at the control cabinet. The cabinet houses the shut-off valve, line strainer, pressure switch, solenoid valve, detergent injection system, detergent container, water piping, solid state controller and special safety device for closing damper in the event of power or water failures.

The hood sections are of modular construction adaptable to any length requirements.

Customization of standard units may be obtained.

Systems vary by manufacturer.

F.E.F. HUMOR

Things were quiet in the engineering room. Plans were being drawn, specs written and shop drawings being checked. Our shipper knew we would be glad to know that an urgently needed shipment had arrived, so he stuck his head in the door just long enough to announce, "The bar stools for the elks just came in."

I can still picture all those beautiful animals sitting around the bar clicking their horns together.

— NOTES —

Chapter 7

HOLDING
TRANSPORTING
AND
SERVING

In this chapter we start in the kitchen area from the time food is prepared on into the holding operation. A quick look at pantry areas and then on into back bar areas for coffee shops.

Other areas of interest in this chapter will be banquet equipment; also school and hospital food service. The last half of the chapter will deal with beverage systems, ice machines, toasters, trucks, warmers and other related equipment that would be applicable to all commercial food operations. If we miss an item of interest please check index for another chapter or drop us a line and we will insert the information ASAP.

HOLD TEMPERATURE GUIDE FOR HOT FOODS
(Moist and Crisp)

The following charts are based on the use of well insulated, thermostatically controlled holding equipment. Other types of holding equipment will be discussed later on in this chapter.

MOIST FOODS

		HOURS ITEM MAY BE HELD	
Food Product	Temp. F.	Suggested Limit	Max. Limit
Baked Beans	175-200°	4	8
Baked Lobster	175-200°	2	3
Biscuits	150-175°	½	1
Casseroles - No Crust	175-200°	3	8
Chop Suey	200°	4	6
Deviled Crabs	175-200°	3	5
Hot Dog Rolls	160-175°	3	6
Hash	175-200°	2	4
Puddings	150-200°	4	6
Mashed Potatoes	160-180°	2	3
Ready Meats	175-200°	2	4
Muffins	140-150°	3	8
Soft Rolls	120°	4	12
Stews	175-200°	2	4
Sweet Rolls	140-150°	2	4
Pork Chops - Stuffed	175-200°	2	4
Vegetables	175-200°	2	6
Turkey/Dressing	175°	2	3

CRISP/DRY FOODS

Food Product	Temp. F.	HOURS ITEM MAY BE HELD Suggested Limit	Max. Limit
Baked Potatoes	175-200⁰	½	2
Corn Sticks	140-150⁰	1	2
Crackers	140-150⁰	5	8
Chicken Pie	175-200⁰	3	6
Wrapped Sandwiches	160⁰	½	1
Fried Chicken	175-200⁰	3	6
Fried Sea Food	175-200⁰	3	6
Hard Rolls	140-150⁰	4	8
Apple Pie	160⁰	4	6
Meat Pie	175-200⁰	3	6
Popcorn	150⁰	5	10
Potato Chips	150⁰	5	10
Popovers	140-150⁰	1	2

Approximate food holding times for heat lamps and enclosed counter warmers.

Food Product	HEAT LAMP Time	ENCLOSED WARMER Time	Moisture Level
Wrapped Sandwiches (hamburger, sliced meat, etc. with no dressing or pickles). Fresh or premade commercial type	45 min.	4 hrs.	Medium
Wrapped Pastry	1½ hrs.	4 hrs.	Medium
Open Pastry or Pie (unwrapped)	45 min.	2 hrs.	High
Pretzel	1½ hrs.	3 hrs.	Low
French Fries (open) (Completely dry oven)	10 min.	30 min.	Low
Onion Rings & Stix	15 min.	45 min.	Low
Egg Rolls (open)	1 hr.	2 hrs.	Medium
Chicken (open)	1½ hrs.	4 hrs.	High
Ribs	1½ hrs.	4 hrs.	High
Meat Turnover or Meat Pie (open)	45 min.	2½ hrs.	Medium
Juicy Joe	45 min.	4 hrs.	Medium
Corn on the Cob (in bag made)	30 min.	3 hrs.	Medium
Pronto Pup (baked) (Chicken and meat)	30 min.	3 hrs.	Medium
Fruit Turnover	20 min.	1½ hrs.	Low
Pizza — Thin crust	20 min.	1 hr.	Medium
Thick crust	20 min.	2 hrs.	Medium
Fish	20 min.	2 hrs.	High
Entree (stews, creamed sauces or gravies)	30 min.	2 hrs.	High
Bagels	1 hr.	2 hrs.	High
Burritos	30 min.	2½ hrs.	Medium

THE CHEF'S TABLE

The first item after preparation and cooking will be the chef's table. This can vary from a standard steam table unit with a work table placed beside it, to a well planned and very elaborate factory constructed unit. Below are options to consider when planning a chef's table. A chef's table would never require all of the items listed but a careful study of them will help you plan for your individual requirements. Following the list is an illustration of a typical unit embodying many of the items most common to chef's tables.

Many of the components are described in this chapter. Refer to index for others which may be in other chapters; i.e., drop-in warmers, hardware, refrigeration, etc.

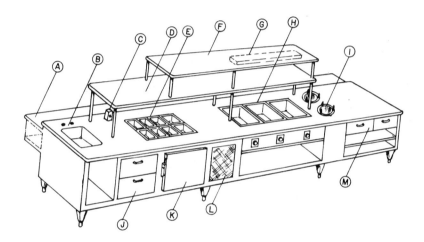

CHEF'S TABLE

A—Tray rest with plate shelf under
B—Sink and faucet holes
C—Electric outlet
D—Space for microwave oven (top shelf cut short)
E—Cold pan or sandwich unit inserts
F—Top shelf
G—Heat lamp
H—Hot food wells
I—Plate elevators
J—Bread drawers
K—Refrigerated base
L—Compressor
M—Tool drawers

A LOOK AT THE OPTIONS

Plate storage cabinets
   (heated or not)
Lowerators for plates
   (heated or not)
Sliding Door Cabinets
Heat Lamps
Over Shelves
Sinks and Pipe Chase
Refrigerated Base
Refrigerated Top
Refrigerated Drawers
Freezer Base
Hot Food Wells
Hot Food Bain Marie
Roll Warmers
Soup Warmers
Ice Bins
Dish Shelves
Tray Rails

Tray Storage
Carving Boards
Slicer Space
Pan Storage
Toaster Area
Microwave on Shelf or under
Electrical Outlets
Bread Dispenser
Hot Food Drawers
Space for Mobile Lowerators
Call Systems
Order Holders
Factory Pre-wired
Factory Pre-plumbed with shut-off
   valves and common drain
Tile base at site
Open Base (on legs)
Closed Base

PANTRY AREA

Before moving on to descriptions of individual items let's brainstorm on pantry areas.

In hospital, large hotel and many institutional food service facilities pantry areas are clearly defined sections of the total operation. Large full service restaurants will usually have separate sections, set aside from the main cooking area, for the preparation of desserts, salads and sometimes complete clam and oyster bars. These separate units will be operated by individuals who will plate the orders for the serving personnel. The next step down will be a separate area housing such items as coffee, beverages, soup, dessert, ice cream, etc. where the serving personnel prepare and serve the items themselves.

All pantry areas should be carefully designed with the intent to reduce kitchen traffic, relieve the chef of unnecessary work, improve customer service and still control portions and quality.

Listed below are most of the items which should be considered in planning efficient pantry areas. Many will be discussed in this chapter. Refer to the index for items described in other chapters such as ice cream cabinets, sinks, refrigerator capacities, etc.

Soup Warmers	Microwave Ovens	Toasters
Salad Prep.	Ice Cream Cabinet	Oyster & Clam Bar
Desserts	Coffee Equipment	Egg Cookers
Refrigerators	Sinks	Water and Ice
Milk	Dry Storage	Bread Drawers
Cereal	Linen Basket	Roll Warmer
Juices	Waste Basket	China & Glass Stge.

Pantry areas often bleed over into waitress stations or combine as one unit out in the dining area. When kitchen space limitations make this necessary, serious consideration should be given to shielding the area with partitions or stub walls approximately 5'-0" high. Some of the necessary equipment can be located against the stub wall with an ample aisle between it and the remaining equipment against the back wall. This design will reduce noise and visual distraction in the dining room and conceal the untidy mess that a pantry area can easily become during rush periods. Separate waitress station items will be discussed later in this chapter.

Don't forget to provide a space for highchairs. An isolated spot for off-duty waitresses is a must too. Nothing steams up a patron who is waiting for service more than sitting and watching two waitresses idly chatting in a corner booth. Remember he has no way of knowing they are off-duty.

REFRIGERATED SPECIALTY UNITS

Many styles of work-top and undercounter refrigerators and freezers are available. Most of the options listed for reach-in refrigerators in Chapter 3 will apply. Some average specifications for typical units are listed below. They apply to self-contained models. The cu. ft. content of similar width remote units will increase by an average of 8 to 11 cubic feet.

Fig. 3-17

COUNTER OR WORK TOP UNITS (34" to 36" high plus legs)					
Doors	Cu. Ft.	Width	Depth	Refr. HP	Freezer HP
1	10	4'	18"	1/4	1/3
1	12	4'	23"	1/4	1/3
1	14	4'	27"	1/4	1/3
1	16	4'	30"	1/4	1/3
2	18	6'	18"	1/4	1/3
2	21	6'	23"	1/4	1/3

(Continued)

COUNTER OR WORK TOP UNITS (Cont.)
(34" to 36" high plus legs)

Doors	Cu. Ft.	Width	Depth	Refr. HP	Freezer HP
2	24	6'	27"	$1/4$	$1/3$
2	27	6'	30"	$1/3$	$1/2$
3	26	8'	18"	$1/4$	$1/3$
3	30	8'	23"	$1/4$	$1/3$
3	34	8'	27"	$1/4$	$1/3$
3	38	8'	30"	$1/3$	$1/2$
4	34	10'	18"	$1/3$	$1/2$
4	39	10'	23"	$1/3$	$1/2$
4	44	10'	27"	$1/2$	$3/4$
4	49	10'	30"	$1/2$	$3/4$

NOTE: Many manufacturers do not build 18" deep models.

REFRIGERATED UNDER COUNTER UNITS
(27" high plus legs- Choice of Tops or Unfinished)

Doors	Cu. Ft.	Width	Depth	Refr. HP	Freezer HP
1	8	4'	23"	$1/4$	$1/3$
1	10	4'	27"	$1/4$	$1/3$
1	12	4'	30"	$1/4$	$1/3$
2	12	6'	23"	$1/4$	$1/3$
2	12	6'	23"	$1/4$	$1/3$
2	14	6'	27"	$1/4$	$1/3$
2	16	6'	30"	$1/4$	$1/3$
3	22	8'	23"	$1/4$	$1/3$
3	26	8'	27"	$1/4$	$1/3$
3	30	8'	30"	$1/3$	$1/2$
4	29	10'	23"	$1/4$	$1/3$
4	34	10'	27"	$1/3$	$1/2$
4	39	10'	30"	$1/3$	$1/2$

The above charts show typical specifications only. These units can vary considerably both in dimensions and options.

May we remind you of our offer to assist. A stamped self-addressed envelope will bring an answer to your equipment problems.

STEAM TABLES - GAS AND ELECTRIC

Styles available: free standing, drop ins, counter top, single or double 12" x 20" openings.

Opening type: round and rectangular. Pans and capacities discussed later in this chapter.

BRAINSTORMING STEAM TABLES

- Heated Base
- Wheels
- Overshelves
- Glass Protector
- Plate Shelves
- Cutting Boards
- Condensation Frame

- Dry or wet wells
- Open water style or
- Separate Heat Wells
- With or without drains
- Tray Rail
- Round or rectangular pans

COMMON SIZE STEAM TABLES - GAS AND ELECTRIC
(Depths vary with accessories)

GAS

Number of 12" x 20" Openings	Length Typical	Average BTU'S
2	2'-6"	7,200
3	3'-8"	10,800
4	4'-10"	14,400
5	6'-0"	18,000
6	7'-2"	21,600

Electric

Number of 12" x 20" Openings	Typical Length	Average K.W. Req'd.
2	2'-6"	2
3	3'-8"	3
4	4'-10"	4
5	6'	5
6	7'-2"	6
7	8'-4"	7

NOTE: 1 to 3 wells, 115 Volt available. Above 3 use 208/220 Volt. Check phase — many not available 3 phase.

OVEN STYLE - TRIPLE WALL HOLDING UNITS

The unique principle of these holding units is that they are of triple wall construction. The outer stainless steel wall is integrally welded to the interior stainless steel shell. In between is 1½" fiber-

181

glass insulation. A third wall of stainless steel forms the food holding compartment. This compartment is suspended, leaving air space around all sides between the inner shell and the holding chamber itself. The thermostatically controlled heating elements are at the base of this air chamber. The heated air in the outer chamber wraps around the inner compartment and radiataes heat into the holding compartment bringing it up to the selected temperature. There is minimal air movement in the holding chamber. All fluctuations occur in the outer area.

Due to the relatively small compartment size, moisture released from the food quickly saturates the compartment atmosphere holding the residual within the food products. Individual moisture dampers are provided for each compartment. The manufacturer claims this principle extends holding quality over any other method. The holding compartment is easily removed, exposing the snap-out sheath type heating elements if replacement is required.

The food pans are supported within the chamber by removable angle glides. There are many optional combinations in which the holding units may be ganged in groups, built in-line or stacked to form complete units. Grouped units may have 1 thermostat each compartment or 1 thermostat per unit.

Units may be free standing on legs or have casters for mobility. They may be built into walls or under counters as pass-through units. Glass door panels are available.

The overall sizes of the units depends upon the individual size of the compartments selected.

They may be ordered custom built to fill special requirements.

The following charts may aid in selecting which unit or combination of units you may require.

First: Determine the maximum number of pans of each food item to be held in each chamber.

Second: Determine the number of different foods to be held. This will give you a reliable indication of the number of compartments you require in any one location.

Third: Consider the many options.

Capacity Per Individual Compartment portion approx. 4 ozs.	6 – 12" x 20" x 2" or 4 – 12" x 20" x 4" or 2 – 12" x 20" x 8" pans 3 – 18" x 26" pans on 3" centers	Approx. 42 quarts or 336 portions	3 – 12" x 20" x 2" or 2 – 12" x 20" x 4" or 1 – 12" x 20" x 8" pans	Approx. 21 quarts or 168 portions
Dimensions of Individual Compartment	▶ 9" high x 22" wide x 28½" deep		9" high x 14" wide x 23½" deep	

Capacity Per Individual Compartment portion approx. 4 ozs.	14 – 12" x 20" x 2" or 8 – 12" x 20" x 4" or 4 – 12" x 20" x 8" or 7 – 18" x 26" pans on 3" centers	Approx. 98 quarts or 784 portions	10 – 12" x 20" x 2" or 6 – 12" x 20" x 4" or 4 – 12" x 20" x 8" or 5 – 18" x 26" pans on 3" centers	Approx. 70 quarts or 560 portions
Dimensions of Individual Compartment	▶ 21" high x 22" wide x 28½" deep		16¾" high x 22" wide x 28½" deep	

(Continued)

182

(Cont.)

| Capacity Per Individual Compartment portion approx. 4 ozs | 18 – 12" x 20" x 2" or 8 – 12" x 20" x 4" or 6 – 12" x 20" x 8" or 9 – 18" x 26" pans on 3" centers | Approx. 126 quarts or 1008 portions | 6 – 12" x 20" x 2" or 4 – 12" x 20" x 4" or 2 – 12" x 20" x 8" pans | Approx. 42 quarts or 336 portions |
| Dimensions of Individual Compartment | ▶ 27" high x 22" wide x 30½" deep | | 9" high x 29" wide x 23½" deep | |

DROP-IN STEAM TABLE UNITS

These units are designed for insertion into existing counters or to be fabricated into new units. Each 12" x 20" opening may be used as either wet or dry heat. Wells have ½" drain nipples. Factory pre-plumbing to a common manifold with shut-off valve is optional. The units are pre-wired to a single control panel housing an individual thermostatic control with off light for each well and a master on/off disconnect switch. The drop-in units are 23½" front to back and measure 9½" from the supporting flange to the bottom of the unit. The control panels are approximately 6" high x 3" deep. These units are also available without drains.

SPECIFICATIONS

Openings	O.A. Length	Voltage	Phase	K.W.	Control Panel Length
2	29½"	108/240	1	2.4	14"
3	43¾"	208/240	1	3.6	18"
4	57¾"	208/230	1 or 3	4.8	18"
5	71¾"	208/230	1 or 3	6.0	36"

(Dimensions and specifications vary by manufacturer.)

HEATED/HUMIDITY HOLDING CABINET
(Counter Top Model)

Thermostatically controlled heat and automatic water filling plus recirculating fan keeps food hot and juicy. Up to 200°F, excellent for ribs, rolls - chicken. Humidity level adjustable to 50%. Three drawer unit is supplied with wire baskets and magnetic drawer gaskets. Will accommodate standard 12" x 20" pans. May also be used dry. Standard 115 Volt, 842 Watt plug-in. Requires 1/4" water line.

Size: 18" wide, 25-1/8" deep, 21" high.

PORTABLE, COUNTER TOP UNITS

These units accept any standard 12" x 20" pan combination. Single opening unit is 14¾" wide x 23-9/16" deep x 8" high. Standard 115 V. cord and plug - 1000 watts. Thermostat control with indicator light. Wet or dry heat.

Double opening unit is 29-9/16" wide x 23-9/16" deep x 8" high. 4" high legs optional. Wells have drains with caps. Standard 115V cord and plug - 1650 watts. Each well individually thermostatically controlled with indicator light, wet or dry heat.

BAIN MARIES OPEN
(Non Cooking)

Open Bain Maries are used when you desire to go from range to holding in the same pot rather than transfer to steam tables. Smaller menus and restaurants that use many sauces frequently use these pieces of equipment. Available free standing or drop in style.

Standard sizes free standing units: Lengths - 2', 3', 4', 5' or 6'; width - 24", 30" or 36"; pan depth - 6" to 9".

ELECTRIC BAIN MARIES

Typical Opening	K.W. Required
24" x 24"	3
30" x 30"	4.5
36" x 36"	6.5
24" x 48"	6.5
30" x 60"	9.5
30" x 72"	9.5

(Also available with gas heat.)

Rapid boil capacity for above would require 2½ times above KW.

OPTIONS FOR BAIN MARIES

- Stainless Steel Covers
- Undershelves
- Insulated Housing
- Overflow protection
- All Stainless Steel Legs
- Water Fills
- Thermostats
- Above water Level Faucet

BAIN MARIE HEATING TIMES

MINUTES TO HEAT
(750 Watts Per Square Foot 6" Deep Water)

Incoming Water Temp.	TEMPERATURE WATER HEATED TO											
	70	80	90	100	110	120	130	140	150	160	170	180
60	8	15	23	31	40	48	57	67	77	90	108	140
70		8	16	24	33	40	49	59	70	83	100	133
80			8	16	25	33	41	51	62	75	92	125
90				8	17	23	33	43	54	67	84	117
100					9	17	25	35	45	59	76	109
110						8	17	27	37	44	68	100
120							9	19	29	42	60	92
130								10	21	34	51	84
140									11	24	41	74
150										13	31	63
160											17	50
170												33

HEAT LAMPS

CHECKLIST:
1) Element - quartz or metal sheath. Four basic styles:
   Bulb: Basically the same as illuminating bulbs but with lower filament temperature.
   Glass Tube: The heating filament is encased in a specially processed glass tube.
   Metal Rod: The filament is encased with stainless steel or nickel alloy. These are less efficient but much more durable.
   Quartz Tube: Natural quartz crystals are fused together to form the heating element. Though delicate and easily broken the quartz crystals are up to 20 times more efficient than other heating sources. They are also much more resistant to thermal shock and will stand rapid, extreme temperature changes without breaking or cracking.
2) Control - On/off or dial the heat.
3) Length - width - single or dual. Dual can be joined end to end or side by side.
4) Voltage
5) Mounting
   a) Counter unit with stand
   b) Mounting legs for over a counter or shelf
   c) Tabs for undershelf mount
   d) Wall mounting
   e) Chains for ceiling mount (or post)
6) Maximum distance from food 12". 9" would be optimum.

HEAT LAMPS - TYPICAL SIZES

Length	Watts	Watts with Built-in Lights
24"	375	450
36"	575	655
48"	750	830

PAN CAPACITIES BOTH ROUND AND RECTANGULAR

Using most all combinations possible — match these pans with all other equipment needed in transporting, holding and serving. This could include trucks, steam tables, transport equipment, shelving and refrigeration.

ROUND INSERTS IN A STANDARD 12" x 20" OPENING

A = 1 - 10½" pan = 11 quarts ea.
     1 - 8½" pan = 7 quarts ea.

B = 3 - 6½" pans = 4 quarts ea.

C = 2 - 8½" pans = 7 quarts ea.

D = 3 - 5" pans = 2½ quarts ea.
     2 - 6½" pans = 4 quarts ea.

E = 6 - 5" pans = 2½ quarts ea.

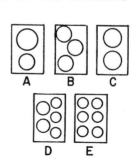

TYPICAL 12" x 20" PAN OPENING POSSIBILITIES

A. Full size pans 12" x 20" x 2½" - 4" - 6" or 8" deep. Capacities as follows.

QUICK REFERENCE CHART FOR PAN CAPACITIES

NOTE: Quantities shown are average usable space in pans. Filled to overflowing slightly higher.
Total volume shown is in usable fluid ounces.

Pan Depth	Full Size	2/3 Size	1/2 Size	1/3 Size	1/4 Size	1/6 Size
2½"	240	216	136	96	80	44
4"	464	320	208	140	108	64
6	704	464	352	212	152	90
8	992		460			

To determine number of portions, divide total volume of pan by the number of ounces in portion served.
EXAMPLE: 8 oz. portions to be served
4" deep ½ size pan holds 208 oz.
208 divided by 8 = 26 portions

DINING ROOM WAITRESS STATIONS
(Sometimes called Service Stands)

Standard wood grain finish (formica or vinyl) stands are usually 24" deep and 34" or 36" high to countertop. Lengths vary by manufacturer from 2'-0" up to 6'-0" (some larger). 4" backsplashes are usually standard - end splashes optional.
Below are options most manufacturers will supply.

- Water station with drain and ice storage bin
- Butter pan insert
- Bread Drawers
- Coffee Warmers
- Cup Rack Glides under
- Open shelving under
- Open shelving over
- Sliding or hinged doors
- Cut-outs for dish elevators
- Cold pans, scrap chutes, sinks, etc.
- Silver storage
- Glass storage
- Racks glides under
- Napkin storage
- Drop-in soup stations
- Menu holders
- Back panels with shelving
- End splashes or enclosures

Larger metal units for coffee shop back bar installation to follow.

186

BACK BAR EQUIPMENT · COFFEE SHOP STYLE

Back bar equipment is available in various lengths and depths, in stainless steel, formica and as many combinations as there are manufacturers. The components we show below will allow you to brainstorm before or during layout and design. Refer to other chapters for specific production of items not in this chapter, such as undercounter dishwashers, Chapter 9, etc.

- Soda fountain
- Bobtail fountain
- Dipper wells
- Fountainettes
- Ice Cream cabinets
  plain or w/syrup rails
- Beverage stations, provide
  for syrup tanks if not
  built-in
- Sandwich Units
- Refrigerators
  upright, under counter
- Freezers
  upright, under counter
- Refrigerated display cases
- Wall display cases

- Urn stands
- Shelving units
- Grill stands
- Dishwasher stands
- Roll warmer stands
- Compressor stands
- Plate lowerators
- Water stations
- Ice chests
- Bread boxes
- Cup and glass rack glides
- Scrap chutes w/trash can
  concealed
- Soup kitchens
- Specialty items as candy -
  cereal

BACK BAR EQUIPMENT

For the sake of consistency the authors will select a manufacturer who produces a full line of equipment for the various areas discussed and use their sheets to describe the individual items. Usually only slight variances will be found in similar items by another manufacturer. If there is a very unique item available it will be included or noted.

SODA FOUNTAIN BOBTAIL UNITS

26½" or 30" deep x 36" long - self contained or remote 1/3 HP.

FEATURES:
Refrigerated storage with flip-flop cover, dipper well w/faucet, scrap chute, 2 draft arms (plain and carbonated), either 5 or 8 syrup wells. Built-in carbonator optional extra. Front finish S/S, woodgrain or color panels. This applies to all units.

5'-6" long x 30" only deep unit - self contained or remote 1/3 HP.

FEATURES:
Basically same as 36" model with 3 compartment sink, ice bin and spoon holder added.

SINK UNITS

26½" or 30" deep x 36" long - contains 3 compartment sink with faucet. Backsplash - glass drainer space behind sinks.

ICE CREAM CABINETS

26½" or 30" deep - remote or self contained.

Lengths	Gallon Capacity Remote Units	Gallon Capacity S/C Units	Average HP for Units
1'-6"	10	5	1/4
2'-6"	20	15	1/4
3'-6"	30	25	1/4
4'-6"	40	35	1/3
5'-6"	50	45	1/3
6'6"	60	55	1/2

There are drop-in fountainette units which fit into one hole of the cabinet and provide various fruit wells and syrup pumps. The 30" deep units may be ordered with syrup rails at the back.

SODA FOUNTAIN UNITS

These units, usually all 30" deep are available with many variable features in different arrangements. They may have remote or self contained compressors, refrigerated as well as ice cream storage, dipper well and scrap chute, sink, carbonator, water cooler, soda systems incorporated and some are available with ice machines.
Average size and ice cream capacity of 4 units shown below.

5'-0"	20 Gal. I.C.	½ HP compressor
6'-0"	30 Gal. I.C.	½ HP compressor
7'-0"	40 Gal. I.C.	¾ HP compressor
8'-0"	50 Gal. I.C.	¾ HP compressor

Separate ice maker units available with water stations, or soda systems built-in. Average length 42".
The following items available in depths and finishes to match the preceeding fountain units.

188

TYPICAL SANDWICH UNITS

Length	Comp.	Cu. Ft. Storage Under
2'-6"	1/4 HP	7
4'	1/4 HP	12
5'	1/4 HP	12
6'	1/3 HP	19
7'	1/3 HP	20

Available S/C or remote. Options: refrigerated drawers, bread drawers, toaster space, various pan styles.

BACK BAR LOW BOY REFRIGERATORS

Length	Average C.F. Capacity	Available S/C or Remote
2'-0"	5½	1/4 HP Recommend
2'-6"	7	1/4 HP Recommend
4'-0"	12½	1/4 HP Recommend
5'-0"	12½	1/4 HP Recommend
6'-0"	19½	1/3 HP Recommend
7'-0"	19½	1/3 HP Recommend

Also available freezer low boys or dual temperature units.

BREAD BOXES

Lengths: 18", 24" or 30" - 1 or 2 drawers - Wood or S/S Tops.

GRILL STANDS - TYPICAL SIZES
(See Ventilation, Chapter 6 for more details)

Length	Venting CFM	Duct Collar Size	
4'-0"	900		6" x 36"
5'-0"	1400		6" x 36"
6'-0"	1800		6" x 48'
7'-0"	1900		6" x 60"
8'-0"	2300		6" x 72"
9'-0"	2500	(2)	6" x 36"
10'-0"	2700	(2)	6" x 36"

BACK BAR SINKS - CABINET STYLE

Length	Bowl Sizes
1'-6"	12" x 14" x 10" deep
	or
2'-6"	9" x 14" x 10" deep
4'-0"	Many sizes and arrangements of sink compartments available.

REFRIGERATED DISPLAY CASES
(Self contained)

Wall mount on counter or with legs. Average sizes: 18" to 22" high, 16" to 20" deep, 4'-0" or 5'-0" long. 1/4 HP compressor. All have glass sliding doors. Pass through models available. Similar units available not refrigerataed.

FLOOR MODEL DISPLAY CASES

These standard "lunch counter" units are available self-contained or remote. Finishes and depth to match other back bar units. Top of base fitted with pans.

Length	Depth	Base C.F. Capacity	Compressor
3'-0"	26½"	10"	1/3 HP
3'-0"	30"	12"	1/3 HP
4'-0"	26½"	14"	1/3 HP
4'-0"	30"	16"	1/3 HP
5'-0"	26½"	18"	1/3 HP
5'-0"	30"	20½"	1/3 HP
6'-0"	26½"	22"	1/2 HP
6'-0"	30"	25"	1/2 HP

Lighted, mirrored back superstructure - 4 shelf unit 38" high above counter top - 2 shelf unit 22" high.

The above units are obtainable as double sided units. By adding 12" to the length they may have refrigerated water stations with glass storage shelving above for either back wall or double sided units.

UTILITY URN OR FILLER SECTIONS
(Available from 1'-6" to 8'-0" in length)

Options for above stands:
- Drop in sink
- Drop in soup warmer
- Drop in coffee warmer
- Drop in hot plate
- 12" x 20" warmer
- Ice chests
- Water stations
- Dish dispenser
- Cup dispenser
- Egg dispenser
- Napkin dispenser
- Roll warmers
- Ice stations
- Outlets - electric
- Back glides

Finishes and depths to match other units.

OTHER BACK BAR EQUIPMENT

COMPRESSOR HOUSINGS
1'-6", 2'-0" wide for 1/4, 1/3, 1/2 HP compressors.

DISH LEVELERS
1'-0" to 4'-0" long — See lowerators

DISHWASHER STANDS
3'-0" to 5'-0" long. House under counter dishwashers and may have sink and scrap areas.

WATER STATIONS
2'-0" long - compressor or ice cooled.

ICE MAKER WITH STORAGE BIN
3'-0" long, makes up to 200 lbs. cubed or 600 lbs. flaked ice per day.

SODA STATIONS
Pre-mixed soda available with ice makers and storage, 3' to 6' long. See Beverages for post mix and more.

MORE OPTIONS TO BACK BARS
- Lights
- Soffits
- Wall panels
- Register cut out
- Built in chutes
- Pass thru windows
- Ice pan tops
- Frost tops
- Built in silver bins
- Wall shelving

DELICATESSEN AREAS

Using many of the back bar components described we may add these options to create a deli line up.
1) Glass enclosures
2) Display shelves
3) Refrigerated shelves
4) Deli steamer
5) Pastrami warmers
6) Pan cut outs in refrigerated bases
7) Drop in removable cutting boards
8) Register cut out
9) Tray rails
10) Base enclosures
11) Slicer area

CAFETERIA EQUIPMENT

Styles available include mobile, fixed modular or custom fabricated.

BRAINSTORMING THE COMPONENTS OF CAFETERIAS

- Hot food tables
- Cold food tables
- Cold pans - frost tops
- Sandwich units
- Salad and dessert cases
- Silver trays and cylinders
- Tray trucks
- Cashiers stand
- Refrigerated base
- Hot base
- Glass protectors
- Tray rails
- Milk dispensers
  (Ice cream cabinets)
- Grilled foods section

- Made to order section
- Heat lamps
- Over shelves
- Beverage station
- Toast station
- Cup dispensers
- Plate dispensers
- Saucer dispensers
- Urn section
- Mobile dish units when
  employees serve
- Bulletin boards
- Product elevators
  (Ice - milk cartons)
- Ice dispensers

Many of the components for cafeteria counters are listed in this chapter. Check index for others. Power systems in Chapter 14 should be considered. For school installations the components are to a great extent standardized. Large installations usually require Food Service Consultants or the design service of a competent equipment dealer. Space must be carefully allocated. Straight line, double sided service units, scatter systems and checking systems must all be taken into account. Grill and sandwich "made-to-order" sections can cause jam-ups. Beverage sections often require much more space than originally anticipated.

Before moving on to cafeteria components, let us discuss a relatively new innovation.

THE REVOLVING CAFETERIA

These units are positioned in the wall between the kitchen and the customer area. The revolving portion is approximately 86" in diameter and 75" high. The bottom shelf is at counter height. Heat lamps above this shelf keep foods at serving temperatures. Three more shelves are mounted on the back superstructure. The top one has an angled mirror to enhance dessert display. The two intermediate shelves may display salads, wrapped sandwiches, etc. Trays are stored below six segment tray rail on the customer side. The unit turns at the rate of one revolution per minute. Selected items are freshly plated and replaced by employees as the shelf segments revolve through the kitchen area. Six to eight patrons may be served simultaneously and proceed to the beverage and cashier stations.

The unit is ideally suited for institutional service, in-plant snack bars, airport and highway cafeterias where items are limited. The basic principle of the unit is that since the cafeteria moves past the customer, the entire line is not forced to move at the pace of the slowest person.

Manufacturers claim that the unit occupies from 35% to 50% less floor space than conventional units and that with 2 or more fewer serving personnel, 8 to 12 meals may be served per minute.

SPACE ALLOCATIONS FOR CAFETERIAS
(College, Industrial and Commercial)

TYPICAL STATION REQUIREMENTS FOR PUBLIC CAFETERIAS

Station Requirements	TOTAL PATRONS PER MEAL					
	500	1000	2000	3000	4000	5000
Tray Dispensers (No. of Locations)	2	4	8 (2)	12 (2)	18 (3)	22 (3)
Cold Food	1-10 ft.	1-12 ft.	2-10 ft.	2-16 ft.	3-15 ft.	3-18 ft.
Made-to-Order Sandwich	1-6 ft.	1-6 ft.	2	3	3	4
Hot Carved Sandwich	1-6 ft.	1	2	2	3	3
Grilled Food	1-6 ft.	1-6 ft.	3	4	5	6
Hot Food	1-10 ft.	1-14 ft.	2-12 ft.	2-18 ft.	3-15 ft.	4-15 ft.
Beverage Counter	1-16 ft.	1-16 ft.	2-16 ft.	2-24 ft.	3-20 ft.	4-18 ft.
Cashiers	1	1 + 1 PT	2 + 2 PT	3 + 2 PT	4 + 2 PT	6 + 3 PT

TYPE A SCHOOL LUNCH - NET SQUARE FOOT AREAS FOR SIZING A MANUAL KITCHEN

	NUMBER OF A LUNCHES SERVED DAILY				
Space Description	250 Sq.Ft.	500 Sq.Ft.	1000 Sq.Ft.	1500 Sq.Ft.	2000 St.Ft.
Truck Dock	50	80	120	120	120
Receiving Room	50	75	100	150	150
Trash Room	60	75	75	100	150
Staff Lockers & Toilets	50	120	180	220	300
Mop Closet	5	10	20	20	20
Manager's Office	35	60	90	120	120
Walk-in Cooler (38ºF.)	—	80	120	180	240
Walk-in Freezer (-5ºF)	—	80	120	150	180
Food Preparation/Cooking	450	600	1000	1200	1500
Dishwashing	120	200	350	500	600
Dry Food Storage & Supplies	225	250	400	750	1000
TOTAL NET* SQ. FT.	1045	1630	2575	3510	4380

*Net square feet does not include allowance for walls or corridors. Dry Storage space must be subdivided to separate soaps and cleaning agents from all food storage.

SERVING LINES REQUIRED

1. FACTORS AFFECTING SERVING LINES:
   The planning of a serving line requires consideration of many factors. Each item must be carefully analyzed and its relationship to related factors understood before a decision is made. The following factors should be considered:
   a. Length of Serving Time: When the serving time is decreased for a fixed number of students, additional serving lines or serving line equipment is generally required.
   b. Menu: Where choice within the Type A pattern or a la carte service is offered, an additional or longer serving line may be required.
   c. Degree of Self-Service: Self-service can advantageously or adversely affect the serving line rate, depending upon age of students, food items to be picked up, location of serving line, etc.
   d. Table Service: The type of table service (compartment trays versus serving trays with plates) effects the support equipment for the serving line.

2. DEFINITIONS:
   A. Student Lunch Period: The length of time established for a student to proceed to the dining area, be served, consume the meal, and exit.
   b. Seating Time: The average time a student occupies a seat while in the dining area.
   c. Serving Time: The total length of time required to serve all students during an established school lunch period.
   d. School Lunch Period: The total time the dining area is required to be in service to accommodate all the student lunch periods.
   e. Total Serving Line Rate: The total number of students served per minute from all serving lines.

3. HOW TO COMPUTE NUMBER OF SERVING LINES FOR CONTINUOUS LUNCH PERIOD:
   Step 1 Determine the **serving time** by subtracting the seating time from the school lunch period.

School Lunch Period	90 Min.
Seating time	— 20 Min.
Serving time	70 Min.

   Step 2 Determine the **total serving line rate** by dividing the school enrollment by the serving time.

   $$\text{Total Serving Line Rate (1)} = \frac{700 \text{ Enrollment}}{70 \text{ Serving Time}}$$

194

Step 3 Determine the **number of serving lines** by dividing the total serving line rate by the following acceptable individual serving line rates for the various types of food service.

Type A without choice   10 Meals per min.
Type A with choice   7-8 Meals per min.
Type A plus a la carte   5-6 Meals per min.

When the computation results in a **fraction** of a serving line, an **additional serving line** should be considered. Such factors as the length of the school lunch period, and/or reduction in a la carte items (when applicable) should be weighed before deciding on an extra line.

SCHOOL LUNCH FACTS AND FIGURES

COUNTER LENGTHS
(Typical Size Per Mea'   ~ved)

Meals Served	Serving Counters
100 to 200	1 - 12' to 15' unit
200 to 350	1 - 15' to 20' unit
350 to 500	2 - 15' to 20' units
500 plus	2 or 3 15' to 20' units

HOT/COLD FOOD · TYPICAL ALLOCATION OF SPACE

Meals Served	12" x 20" Opening Hot Foods	Cold Foods
100 to 200	4	4' to 6'
200 to 350	4	6'
350 to 500	4	6' per counter
500 plus	4	6' per counter

SCHOOL LUNCH UTILITY SECTIONS

Meals Served	Utility Area
100 to 200	3' to 5'
200 to 350	3' to 5'
350 to 500	3' to 5' ea. counter
500 to 750	3' to 5' ea. counter

Add to hot, cold and utility areas milk, ice cream, tray and silver equipment.

Flow rate: average school lunch line 10 to 12 pupils per minute.

For large schools and varied menus, your designer should consider the scramble system, ala carte line, and if space permits, consider "L" or "U" shaped lines.

CAFETERIA FACTS

SILVER HOLDERS

Round Cylinder Capacities Each

Knives	Forks	Spoons
60	42	42

1/3 size 6" deep stainless steel pans hold approximately 9 dz. each of knives, forks or spoons.

TRAY TRUCKS - FLAT STYLE

Length	Width	Height
23½"	17½"	30"

Hold 120 - 14" x 18", 15" x 20" or 16" x 22" trays.

SELF-LEVELING TRAY TRUCKS

Length	Width	High	Amount Trays
25"	20"	36"	100 - 14" x 18"
29"	23"	36"	100 - 15" x 20"
29"	23"	36"	100 - 16" x 22"

SILVER BIN SYSTEM - HANDLING

Bins for this system are 10-1/8" long x 4-1/8" wide x 7" high, impact proof plastic, holding 75 pieces of silver each bin.

COMPONENTS

Tote Tray: holds 4 bins, 300 pieces or holds 3 bins, 225 pieces.
Counter Rack: holds 3 or 4 bins
Storage Truck: holds 32, 40 or 48 bins, 3200 to 4800 pieces of silver. Largest truck is 31-7/8" long x 22-1/8" wide x 33¾" high.
Self level dispenser: capacity in bins 300 pieces, 12-1/16" long, 6-1/8" wide x 31-1/8" high.
Dispenser cart: 4 sizes hold 4, 5, 6 or 8 bins. Tray rail optional, mobile. Largest dispenser cart: 45-5/8" long, 17" wide, 38" high.

SANDWICH RACKS

Used to hold bagged or wrapped sandwiches, keeping them warm. Typical lengths: 25" holding 5 rows, 35" holding 7 rows and 45" holding 9 rows. Depths 24" height at rear of all models 11" tilting forward to 2".

Units are all 115 Volt with cord set. Individual radiant strip heaters mounted under each compartment are thermostatically controlled. 25" units are 1.25 KW, 35" units 1.70 KW and 45" units 2.25 KW.

FAST FOOD PIE DISPLAY UNIT

Heats and displays deep fried pies. Displayed items rotate ferris wheel style and are kept hot and fresh looking by a heat lamp behind the lighted full color transparency on the top of the unit.

500 Watt unit is 22" Wide x 12½" deep x 33" high.

400 Watt unit is 12½" wide x 13½" deep x 26¼" high.

TRAY RAILS

Styles: solid, 3 bar or 4 bar, normally 34" above floor, 12' wide. Mounted 30" above floor for elementary schools.

DISPLAY SHELVES OR BREATH PROTECTORS

Styles: cold food shield 14" high, 10" wide top shelf, fixed or adjustable, flat or curved glass shield.

Two Shelf: 23" high, 16" wide top shelf and 1 intermediate shelf, fixed or adjustable flat or curved glass shields.

Three Shelf: 30" high, 16" wide top shelf and 2 intermediate shelves, approximately 9" apart by 10" wide, fixed or adjustable flat or curved glass shields.

Many styles and designs by various manufacturers.

CAFETERIA COLD PAN SECTIONS

Length	Comp. Size Pan Only	Comp. Size w/Refr. Base
46"	1/4 HP	1/4 HP
63"	1/4 HP	1/3 HP
79"	1/4 HP	1/3 HP

TYPICAL ICE CREAM ELEVATOR, DISPENSER

Length	Aprox. Size Width	Capacity	HP
36"	28"	538 - 3 oz. cups	1/4
		352 - 5 oz. cups	

These units vary by manufacturer, particularly in design of compressor housing.

MILK ELEVATOR DISPENSERS

Length	Width	Milk Capacity	HP
49"	28"	450 flat top 376 peak top	1/4
63"	28"	720 flat top 564 peak top	1/4

MILK COOLERS
(Mobile)

These units, particularly suited to school use are approximately 39" high x 30" wide. One half of top flips open and one half of front drops down when open for use. Also available double side opening.

CASE CAPACITY

Case Length	HP	13" x 13" x 11" H	19" x 13" x 11" H
36"	1/5	8	4
48"	1/5	12	8
63"	1/3	16	12

		Cartons Flat		Peak Cartons	
		1/2 Pt.	1 Pt.	1/2 Pt.	1 Pt.
36"	1/5	864	432	680	430
48"	1/5	1368	684	1020	645
63"	1/3	1800	900	1360	860

MOBILE CAFETERIA OR BUFFET UNITS

Take most any 24" deep 4' or 5' standard component of a cafeteria counter, i.e. flat top section, cold pan unit, 4 or 5 compartment hot food unit, dress them up with an unlimited choice of decorator panels, add breath protectors, display shelves, heat lamps, etc. and put them on casters and you have mobile buffet or cafeteria counters. The buffet units would have drop down plate shelves on each side. The cafeteria units would have tray rails on one side and plate shelves or cutting boards on the other. Matching tray and silver stands, cashier stands, special meat carving sections and 90° interior or exterior corner sections are available. Many styles and variations available.

Units that accept standard hot food, hand carry, transport units, from which the food may be served directly, are available for school feeding and similar institutional service.

HOSPITAL PATIENT FEEDING

Many methods and systems are available for the transporting of food from the kitchen to bedside. For new buildings the system selection, details of design and installation will be coordinated by the consultant. When major changes are planned for existing hospitals consultants may be employed to work with the dietary staff. In other circumstances the hospital staff may work with the food service equipment supplier in planning systems changes. The authors role in writing F.E.F. is limited to briefly describing the various systems and presenting facts pertaining to the various components. Nearly all of these components are detailed in this chapter. Check the index for others such as dumb waiters in Chapter 13, roll-in refrigerators in Chapter 3, conveyors in Chapter 9, etc. F.E.F. has many back-up sheets and typical layout plans for various systems available. Should you desire these or more specific and detailed information on any components, please use our Personal Assistance Plan outlined in the front of the book.

The central tray make-up system is the most commonly employed system of meal distribution. It involves some means of moving the serving tray past employees who place diet cards, utensils, condiments, food and beverages on the tray. The trays are then transported to the patients. Soiled items are later transported to warewashing areas.

The alternative is to transport the hot food in bulk to pantry-serving areas located in various wards. Such pantry areas might house all or any of the following: china, glassware, flatware, trays and warewashing facilities, as well as hot and cold beverages, ice facilities, refrigeration, toasters, blenders, hot plates and microwave ovens. In using the pantry-serving system the main concern is in deciding which of the required components are to be housed in the pantry area and selecting transport items for those which are not.

Now, back to the central tray make-up system. In its basic form it sounds simple enough. The complicated part is the proper sizing of the various components. The really complicated part is in choosing which method of plating, holding and transporting is to be used. To list a few, which are described later in this chapter, insulated trays with insulated covers, insulated plate underliners and covers use preheated plates, peletized plates with insulated covers, pellet systems to keep serving plates hot and rethermalization trays. Moving on to descriptions of individual components we start with the most basic, the tray conveyor.

TRAY CONVEYORS (MANUAL)

All conveyors must of course, be sized to the width of trays to be used.

The simplest form of conveyors are the skate-wheel or roller type.

The trays are pushed manually from station to station. A small skate-wheel model is available which may be mounted on a 3 or 4 hole hot food unit. It would be appropriate for nursing homes of approximate 100 bed capacity. Skate-wheel conveyors are for use with flat bottom trays only. Either skate-wheel or roller conveyors are available in any length as free standing units. Legs may have locking casters. Conveyor may be fitted with U.L. approved wireways and outlets for adjoining components. Over shelves and clip-on work shelves for the sides of the conveyors are optional.

MOTOR DRIVEN CONVEYORS

These units, sized to requirement are available with the following options:
1) Built-in wireways with outlets and separate circuit breakers for adjoining equipment. This feature could appreciably reduce building construction costs.
2) Either lexan or solid plastic conveyor belts.
3) Variable speed control on belt drive.
4) Stationary or legs with locking casters.
5) Skirting for sides of conveyor bed.
6) Over or side mount shelves.
7) Automatic belt wash for stationary units.
8) Stationary models available in "L" or "U" serpentine shapes to circumvent columns or to accommodate irregular shaped areas.
9) The horizontal conveyor can be combined with vertical transport systems for tray delivery to patients' floors.

CHAIN DRIVE TRAY CONVEYOR

This style conveyor is mounted on an elongated pedestal. The trays are carried in pans at a height of 46" above the floor. These tray pans rest on a shelf-like extension around the entire perimeter of the pedestal. These pans are powered around the unit by a chain drive concealed within the top of the unit. The base of the pedestal can contain power outlets for support units. The base may be extended outward on all sides of the pedestal approximately 30" to a height of 34" forming a flat work surface around the entire unit. Refrigerated cold pans, hot food wells and some other items may be incorporated into the work surface. Either the pedestal or table base unit can set on masonry bases or made mobile by casters.

RETHERMALIZATION SYSTEM

Basically this system consists of three components. Insulated plastic compartment trays and covers, automatic mobile rethermalization carts which hold 24 meal trays each and specially constructed roll-in refrigerators for the carts. The trays are constructed with three compartments for hot foods on one side and a compartment large enough to hold 3 cold food items on the other. These four compartments fit under the insulated cover. The "L" shaped compartment at the end remains uncovered and is for beverages, menu, flatware, napkins and condiments.

The principle involved is that the plated meal on the covered tray is placed on shelves in the mobile unit. The unit is rolled into the refrigerator and connects with electric circuitry. The complete meals are kept under refrigeration at 40°F. About 35 minutes prior to serving time the refrigerator's timer activates the heating units in the cart. Only the food items intended to be served hot are heated. For cold meals the trays are placed on the shelf backwards which prevents tripping the activator switch which would heat the shelf. Empty shelves do not heat.

The manufacturers of this system state that it enables the staff to prepare all three meals for the day at one time and hold them until serving time. Some menu adjustments are necessary and the manufacturer will supply some 300 recipe cards and offers to train production workers.

INTEGRAL HEATING SYSTEM

For use with the cook and chill principle which allows for preparation of all three meals at one time.

The unique advantage of this system is that the food to be reheated for serving is heated directly by the dish in which it is to be served. Two styles of dishes are provided. Serving plates for entree selections and bowls for soups, casseroles, etc. The dishes consist of a porcelain ceramic inner dish with a special resistive coating fused to its underside. The dish in turn is hermetically sealed in an outer polymer shell. Metal buttons built into the shell provide electrical contact for the resistors to heat the plate. Built-in sensors control delivery of heat to the food. Reusable thermoplastic covers for the dishes hold the heat in. The polymer shell remains cool enough for safe handling. The dishes are capable of heating the food to serving temperature in 18 minutes, then automatically switch to "hold" to prevent burning or drying out. Since only the dish and food are heated, this system is rated at 90% energy efficient.

Two companion units for the systsem are available. A module with top mounted controls measures 23" wide, 36" high and 21" deep. This unit will hold 24 dishes (plates or bowls). Holding racks provide electrical contact. Automatic shut-off when door is opened. 220 volt, 20 amp plug-in unit. Maximum power consumption 3.5 KVA fully loaded.

The other companion unit is a mobile serving cart designed to hold complete meals on specially designed 14" x 18" trays which accommodate the heating bowls and plates as well as the other items, i.e. desserts, beverages, flatware, etc. After loading the carts may be rolled to the serving areas where they will be plugged into the system's power supply units for re-heating of the hot food items when required.

The manufacturer of this system will supply complete information, demonstrations, engineering, training and follow-up service for their installations.

HOSPITAL - NURSING HOME AND EXTENDED CARE SPECIALTY ITEMS

- Flexible pastic straws
- Disposable carafes/pitchers
- Spill proof cups
- Plate food guards

- All purpose scoop plates
- Deep suction type plates
- Padded handle silverware

COLOR CODED DIET KITS

Type Diet	Color Code	Contents
Regular	Green	Salt, pepper, sugar
Regular dbl. sugar	Blue	salt, pepper, 2 sugar
Bland	Pink	Sugar, salt
Sugar free	Yellow	Salt, pepper, sugar substitute
Low Sodium	Grey	Sugar, salt substitute, pepper
Bland dbl. sugar	2" Pink	2 sugar, salt
Sugar free dbl. sugar sub.	2" Yellow	Salt, pepper, 2 sugar substitute
Low Sodium dbl. sugar	2" Grey	2 sugar, salt substitute, pepper
Sugar free	2" Orange	2 substitute sugar
Low Sodium	No Code	Substitute salt
Dbl. sugar substitute	No Code	Substitute pepper

TRAY STARTER UNITS

These mobile units straddle the lead end of the tray conveyor. The lower of two overshelves is provided with insert pans for wrapped silverware and condiments. The upper flat shelf is for napkins, placemats, etc. The operator would normally face this unit and the end of the conveyor with a tray dispenser at one side and a tote box for other items on the other.

Other combination starter units are available for smaller operations.

TRAY MAKE-UP EQUIPMENT
(Typical 300 Meal Service)

1) Starter unit for trays, silver and napkins
2) Heated plate truck, plate truck only, heated bases for plates or pellet ovens for plates using pellet bases. (A pellet is hot metal disc used to heat plate placed above it.)
3) Cold food truck or mobile refrigerator
4) Beverage unit, juice, milk, coffee
5) Hot food truck
6) Dish dispensers as needed
7) Toaster truck
8) Conveyor

Probable Servers: 7 to 8 employees.

CENTRAL TRAY MAKE-UP (Expressed in Sq. Ft. Required)

NUMBER OF BEDS	50	100	200	400
Main Kitchens	300/375	500/625	750/1000	1500/1800
Tray Assembly	100/150	200/250	300/400	500/750
Truck Storage	100/150	175/250	275/375	500/750
Dishwashing	130/175	250/300	350/375	500/800

Use as a guide only - many variables. See Chapter 9 for dishwasher information.

Pellet oven . . . . 6 KW   Toaster . . . . 4 KW
Lowerator . . . . None   Conveyor . . . . 1 KW
Coffee urn . . . . 7-10 KW   Cold Foods . . . . None
Hot Foods . . . . 5 KW

HOT FOOD TRUCKS

These mobile units, designed specially for tray make-up service are available in 2, 3 or 4 well sizes. The 12" x 20" wells may be arranged side-by-side as in normal steam tables or end-to-end for slim-line serve over units. All units come with cord sets. Outlets can be built into the other end of the units for series connections.

Options are:
1) Heated cabinet bases for storage of back-up food pans
2) Open bases
3) Shelves for open base units
4) Serving or plate shelf
5) Push handle
6) Overhead infrared warmers - not recommended for units to be used as serve-over
7) Removable stainless steel well liners for ease in cleaning.

PELLET OVENS

These ovens are used primarily in hospital and nursing home food operations. The pellet (a heated metal disc) is placed in a metal base. The plated meal is placed over the base and covered. The hot metal pellet will generate heat, holding the meal at serving temperature for at least 45 minutes.

TYPICAL ELECTRIC PELLET OVENS
(Depths 18")

Width	Height	Pellet Capacity	Watts
16"	29¾"	30	600
16"	29¾"	60	1200
16"	37¼"	90	1750
27"	29"	120	2400
27"	37"	180	3500
53"	29"	240	4800
53"	37"	360	7000

Normally 220 volts.

A pellet loading gun is available for removing hot pellets and placing them in the base.

Available options include stands with plate holder storage and an oven stand turntable which rests on the stand permitting rotation of the pellet oven.

A new stainless steel underliner and cover is available which retains proper serving temperature up to 25% longer. The base is double walled with a wax-like substance hermetically sealed into the bottom.

CHECK LIST FOR TRUCK SELECTION
(Hospital Food Service)

1) What size tray
2) Total capacity needed
3) Type truck:
   - Heated
   - Unheated
   - Refrigerated dual temp.
   - Insulated - non insulated
4) Any doors, elevators, halls to limit size of truck length - width
5) How and where will truck be moved — ramps - elevators
6) Casters — diameter, width, swivel, brakes, locking casters
7) Handles — bumpers, corner guards

TRAY DELIVERY TRUCKS - SAMPLE CAPACITY

NOTE: The trucks are so varied, we dare only give a few capacities and not dimensions.

Style: using dome covers and 15" x 20" or 16" x 22" trays, closed truck.

Standard sizes available to hold 14, 16, 20, 21, 24 or 30 trays per truck.

Style: unheated for 14" x 18" — 15" x 20" or 16" x 22" ttrays

TRAY TOTALS PER TRUCK
(By spacing clearance)

Doors	3 "	4½"	5½"	6"
2	16	14	12	10
2	22	18	16	14
3	24	21	18	15
2	28	22	20	16
3	33	27	24	21
3	42	33	30	24

HOSPITAL TRAY TRUCKS - SELECTED SIZES
(Side Load 15" x 20" Trays)

Truck Height	Spacing	CAPACITY	
		1 Door	2 Door
45½"	5½"	12	24
54½"	5½"	14	28
56½"	5½"	16	32
63½"	5½"	18	36

FRONT LOAD - 14" x 18" TRAYS

Truck Height	Doors	Capacity
59"	1	24
59"	2	48
64"	1	20
64"	2	40

INSULATED TRAY - INSULATED COVERS

This system requires no special trucks to deliver as trays are nesting and stackable. Many style wells are available. Inserts can be thermal ware - china or disposables. Thermal and china plates for hot entrees are heated to 180° before loading and covering. The following chart illustrates temperature drop in this system.

INSULATED MEAL SERVERS
(Chart based on 180° temperature at loading time)

Lapsed Time Minutes	Thermal Plate	China	Disposable
10	170°	165°	160°
20	165°	158°	150°
30	160°	155°	144°
40	156°	150°	140°
50	152°	148°	138°
60	150°	145°	135°
70	149°	142°	132°
80	148°	140°	130°

Approximate times only to illustrate the feasibility of using various components to this system. Many foods retain heat for much longer periods than others.

See index for all other standard items related to hospital food serving equipment. Most will be found in this chapter.

AIRLINE INFLIGHT CATERING OPERATIONS
KITCHEN EQUIPMENT

Typical pieces — no sizes
1) Carrier carts - Food modules
2) Breakdown truck - silver, china and trays
3) 3 Shelf storage trucks - for bulk baskets - pots, pans, tools
4) Food module truck for ovens and bulk storage module
5) Hot - cold preparation table
6) 4 Compartment tray handling trucks, trays for empty, clean trays
7) Tray truck airline trays - 52" long truck accommodates to 1250 trays
8) Dry ice chest
9) Module - food and beverage to truck or plane truck
10) Standby holding hot meal trucks
11) Final tray make-up tables — shelf over - tray rail on front, modular to conveyors
12) Tier shelving trucks adjustable stationary and mobile to bank in with other in flight equipment

13) Also available modular pan trucks, portable sinks and other complimenting equipment from other chapters F.E.F.

Lest we be accused of over simplifying this or other types of commercial feeding, one must remember we are discussing facts and brainstorming and not on the drawing board dealing with systems approaches.

CATERING QUICK CHECK LIST

☐ Silverware
☐ Serving spoons
☐ Punch bowl - ladle
☐ Fountain cups
☐ Candelabra
☐ Table skirts
☐ Tent
☐ Serving display trays
☐ China
☐ Salt and peppers
☐ Coffee pots
☐ Water pitchers
☐ Bus boxes
☐ Chafing dish
☐ Candles

☐ Flowers
☐ Table cloths
☐ Ice scoops
☐ Portable bar
☐ Trash cans
☐ Napkins
☐ Juice glass
☐ Water glass
☐ Bar glass
☐ Extra sterno
☐ Cocktail picks
☐ Condiments
☐ Bus trays
☐ Ice molds
☐ Portable counter steam table (2 - 12" x 20" openings)

BANQUETS - IN HOUSE OR REMOTE AND RELATED SERVING

Typical equipment may include the following mobile equipment:
1) Steam tables
2) Flat top dish up table
3) Bulk storage truck (heated - refrigerated or freezer)
4) Heated dish dispensers
5) Mobile trucks for pre-plated covered meals
6) Ice storage trucks
7) Tray trucks
8) Silver transport trucks
9) Mobile bar
10) Dirty dish busing truck
11) Utility trucks (condiments)
12) Angle ledge carts

BANQUET SERVING
(Probable Employees and Time)

No. of Meals	Dish up Servers	Lapsed Time
100	2	20 min.
300	3	35 min.
500	6	45 min.
750	8	35 min.
1000	13	25 min.

TYPICAL BANQUET TRUCKS
(Dimensions and Capacities)

30" deep. Style: insulated and heated.

No. Plates Using Stacker Device	Width	Height
48	31½"	48"
60	31½"	56"
72	42½"	48"
90	42½"	56"
120	53¾"	56"
144	53¾"	66"
180	64¼"	66"
200	64¼"	72"

Also available not insulated or not heated. Remember this is a guide and many manufacturers trucks vary.

BANQUET MAKE UP TABLE · ELECTRIC · MOBILE

30" - 36" wide x 8' long x 36½" high.

A unique approach to volume and banquet feeding. Entire top can be heated to allow your pans to keep warm without transfer to other equipment.

FACTS:
1) Open construction, other trucks fit under
2) Internal power system for support equipment as heat lamps, slicers, dish carts, etc.
3) Ground fault protection
4) Quick disconnects available
5) Recessed controls, breakers and outlets

MOBILE HOT FOOD TRUCKS
(For 12" x 20" pans · Insulated or Heated)

All 26" in depth

Wide	High	No. Doors	Truck Capacities by Pan Depths		
			2½"	4"	6"
24"	36"	1	8	4	2
24"	42"	1	10	5	3
24"	55"	1	15	7	5
41"	42"	2	20	10	6
41"	55"	2	30	14	10
58"	55"	3	45	21	15

Can be adapted for 1/2 and 1/3 size pans.

ROUND INSULATED CONTAINERS FOR TRANSPORT

Common capacity without pans: 3, 4¾, 6½ and 11 Gallons.

CAPACITY WITH PAN ASSORTMENTS

No. of Pans	Qts. Per Pan	Total Gals.
2	16	8
4	8	8
1 large	16	
1 small	8	8
2	8¾	4-3/8
4	4-3/8	4-3/8
1 large	8¾	
1 small	4-3/8	4-3/8
2	6	3
4	3	3
1 large	6	3
1 small	3	3
2	4	2
4	2	2
1 large	4	2
1 small	2	2

HAND LIFT TRANSPORTS FOR 12" x 20" PANS
(Non-insulated - No covers)

Wide	Deep	High	2½" Deep Pans
15"	23½"	25½"	8
15"	23½"	19½"	6
15"	23½"	13½"	4

HOT FOOD TOTES
(Boxes, Trucks, Hand Lifts)

GUIDE TO SELECTION:
1) Number to be served
2) Pan or meal pack size
3) Heated, unheated, insulated or non-insulated
4) Heat by electric, sterno, car lighter
5) Cold pack — freeze first then put in transport to cool food products. Excellent for salads, dairy products.
6) See pan capacities for portions per pan or pizza pan sizes

HAND LIFT TRANSPORT CABINET
(Insulated pans - with covers)
Size: 18" wide, 27 deep, 27" high

CAPACITY

2 - 12" x 20" x 2½" Pans
plus
3 - 12" x 20" x 4"   Pans
or
4 - 12" x 20" x 4"   Pans
or
5 - 12" x 20" x 2½" Pans

Capacity approximately 100 meals per cabinet. Carriers may be insulated or non-insulated, or electrically heated, and are normally made of aluminum or stainless steel. Non-heated insulated units also available in various plastic materials in decorator colors.

INSULATED
HAND LIFT CAPACITY - TOTAL PANS AND PORTIONS
(Using 12" x 20" Transport Pans)

Pan Depth	Pans Per Lift	2 oz.	Total Portions 2-2/3 oz.	4 oz.	8 oz.
2½"	5	400	300	200	100
4"	3	480	360	240	120
6"	2	512	384	256	128

Food
Put in at 170° at 1:00 P.M.

By	It will be
2:00	168°
3:00	164°
4:00	160°
5:00	158°
6:00	156°

NUMBER OF SERVINGS BY PORTIONS
(Using Food Transport Pans 12" x 20" sizes)

Pan Depth	1/4 Cup #16 Scoop 2 oz.	1/3 Cup #12 Scoop #8 Scoop 2-2/3 oz.	1/2 Cup 4 oz.	1 Cup 8 oz.
2½"	80	60	40	30
4"	160	180	80	58
6"	256	192	128	88

COMMON HAND LIFTS
(Cabinets for 18" x 26" Pan)

Wide	Deep	High	Pan Capacity	Slides
19-5/16"	27-3/8"	11-3/4"	3	Angle
19-5/16"	27-3/8"	19-1/4"	5	Angle
19-5/61"	27-7/8"	11-3/4"	6	Corrugated
19-5/16"	27-7/8"	19-3/4"	11	Corrugated

FOAMED STYLE TRANSPORT EQUIPMENT

Heavy approved plastic outer shells foamed in place, insulated, seamless interiors.

AVAILABLE ITEMS

ICE CHESTS with swivel caster dolly, available 30, 100, 200 lb. capacity. Hold ice up to 90 hours.

HAND TOTES for 1/4 size pans

CAPABILITIES

Overall Size	Holds
13½" x 13½" x 20" high For hot or frozen foods	Holds seven 2½" deep pans @ 40 fl. oz. each (280 fl. oz. capacity) Holds four 4" deep pans @ 64 fl. oz. each (256 fl. oz. capacity) Holds three 6" deep pans @ 96 fl. oz. each (288 fl. oz. capacity)
15½" x 12½" x 13¾" high For hot or frozen food	Holds four 2½" deep pans @ 40 fl. oz. each (160 fl. oz. capacity) Holds two 4" deep pans @ 64 fl. oz. each (128 fl. oz. capacity) Holds one 6" deep pan @ 96 fl. oz. and one 2½" deep pan @ 40 fl. oz. (136 fl. oz. capacity)
13½" x 13½" x 20½" high Insulated divider between compartments - Hot food top, frozen food in bottom	Compartment #1 holds the same capacity as 13¾" high model Compartment #2 holds 2½" deep pans @ 40 fl. oz. each or on 4" deep pan @ 64 fl. oz. (240 fl. oz. transporter total capacity)

TRANSPORTERS
(Senior Citizens, Day Care Centers and other remote feeding)

Uses disposable containers - small units available side or top load Large unit side load only.

MEALS PER TRANSPORTER

Container Brand	Container Size	Small Units	Large Units
Amoco	8-1/2" x 7-1/4" x 1-1/2"	10	16
Amoco	8" x 8-1/2" x 2-1/4"	7	—
Ekco	8-1/2" x 6-1/2" x 1-1/2"	20	24
Kaiser	8-1/2" x 6-1/2" x 1-1/2"	20	24
Keyes Fibre	8-1/2" x 7-1/2" x 1-7/8"	8	12
Keyes Fibre	5" x 9-1/8" x 1-7/8"	24	18
Polytherm	9-1/4" x 6-3/4" x 2-7/8"	10	8
Polytherm	8'" x 6-3/4" x 1-1/4"	24	30
Reynolds	7-7/8" x 5-1/8" x 1-3/8"	30	36
Reynolds	8-1/2" x 6-3/8" x 1-15/32"	20	24

COMMISSARY AND SATELLITE FOAM STYLE BULK TRANSPORTERS

Holds to 140^0 hot foods for 5 hours, or ice cream for 20 hours at 85^0 outside temperature.

TWO TYPICAL SIZES OF MOBILE UNITS

Dimensions (Inches)	Description	Empty Wt. (Lbs.)
O.D. 28 x 19 x 28 H I.D. 23 x 14 x 23 H	Up to 200 lb. food capacity or 325 ice cream cups; 375 milk ½ pints. Holds 5 wire baskets	40
O.D. 21 x 21 x 20 H I.D. 17 x 17 x 16 H	Up to 100 lbs. food capacity or 7 pizzas 16" size. Holds 3 wire baskets.	25

SOUP OR BEVERAGE CARRIERS
(Stainless Steel)

Height	Width (Diameter)	Ship. Weight	Capacity
13"	9¾"	14 lbs.	1 Gal.
23"	9¾"	17 lbs.	2 Gal.
29"	9¾"	19 lbs.	3 Gal.
18¾"	13¼"	25 lbs.	3 Gal.
23½"	13¼"	37 lbs.	5 Gal.
35½"	13¼"	40 lbs.	7½ Gal.

FUN FACT: The average heat loss in a well insulated soup or beverage container is from 2.5^0 to 4.5^0 per hour.

SOME COLD FACTS

The ideal drinking temperature for ice tea, water, highballs, etc. is between 38° and 42°. Drinks become increasingly flat above 42°. Taste buds are affected at temperatures below 38°, decreasing the full flavor of the beverage. Full size cubes will cool a drink in approximately 90 seconds. They melt slower, therefore last longer without over-cooling the drink. Crushed ice will drop the temperature of a drink to almost 32° in 60 seconds. Excellent for chilling soft drinks, mixing cocktails, serving or displaying cocktail foods and desserts.

Since there are many variables connected with ice consumption and production, sizing charts as shown above should be considered as an average guide only. Consumption varies considerably with weather changes. Menu changes and the addition of a salad display bar can add quite a load on an ice machine. The machine production varies by changes of incoming water and room temperatures. An average air cooled ice machine capable of producing 400 lbs. in 24 hours with incoming water at 60° and room temperature at 70° will produce only 335 lbs. in 24 hours, if the incoming water rises to 80° and the room to 90°.

A general rule of thumb for estimating ice requirements in dining areas is 5 full size cubes per person per day. 20 full size cubes = 1 pound. Estimated requirements for cocktail areas, salad bars, etc. would be added.

Full size cubes are 1¼" x 1¼" x 1¼" — half cubes 1¼" x 1¼" x 5/8" — mini cubes 5/8" x 5/8" x 1¼". (Many other sizes and shapes are produced by other manufacturers.)

Many health codes require scoops with approved holders in ice storage units. For glass filling at soda stations and cocktail bars, a 9" cast aluminum scoop kit is available with a deep plastic holder for covered ice bins and a shallow holder for open bins. For pitcher filling, a large plastic scoop, 8¼" x6" x5", with holder for mounting in large ice bins. The kits come with theft protection, nylon covered cables for securing scoops to bin.

ICE CHART - POUNDS OF ICE = VARIOUS CUBES
(Using 1½" x 1½" x 1½" Full Size)

Pounds/24 Hrs.	Full Cubes	1/2 Cubes	Mini Cubes
110	1,485	2,970	5,940
300	4,050	8,100	16,200
400	5,400	10,800	21,600
600	8,100	16,200	32,400
800	10,800	21,600	43,200
900	12,150	24,300	48,600
1200	16,200	32,400	64,800
1600	21,600	43,200	86,400
2000	27,000	54,000	108,000

APPROXIMATE ICE REQUIREMENTS
FOR VARIOUS OPERATIONS

Fig. 7-

FACILITY		Lbs. of Cubes	Lbs. Crushed
HOTEL OR MOTEL	50	600-800	200-400
	100	1000-1200	200-400
BY	150	1400-1600	400-600
NUMBER OF ROOMS	200	1800-2000	600-800
(Includes Bar & Rm. Service)	250	2200-2400	800-1000
	250	200-400	200-400
	500	200-400	200-400
RESTAURANTS	750	400-600	400-600
BY	1000	600-800	400-600
MEALS PER DAY	1250	600-800	600-800
	250	800-1000	200-400
	500	1000-1200	200-400
HOSPITALS	750	1400-1600	200-400
BY	1000	1600-1800	400-600
MEALS PER DAY	1250	2000-2200	400-600
	250	200-400	200-400
EMPLOYEE	500	200-400	400-600
FEEDING	750	200-400	400-600
BY	1000	200-400	400-600
MEALS PER DAY	1200	200-400	600-800
	1000	200-400	200-400
	2000	200-400	200-400
COLLEGES	3000	200-400	200-400
BY	4000	400-600	200-400
MEALS PER DAY	5000	400-600	200-400
	250	600-800	200-400
	500	800-1000	200-400
CLUBS	750	1200-1400	200-400
BY	1000	1600-1800	400-600
MEALS PER DAY	1200	1800-2000	400-600

NATIONAL AVERAGE ICE USAGE*

Type Establishment	lbs/24 Hrs.	Type Establishment	lbs./24 Hrs.
Restaurants (Table Cloth)/Customer	3	Hotels/Guest	5
Cafeterias/Customer	2	Motels/Guest Room	4
Drive-In Restaurants/Customer	1	Hospitals/Bed	10
Bars & Cocktail Lounges/Customer	2½	Nursing Homes/Bed	6

*National average ice usage only. Actual ice usage will vary with climatic conditions and practices of the individual establishment.

ICE MACHINES

GENERAL NOTE: Ice machines require air space at rear and sides. Indirect wastes are mandatory.

SIZE: 24" wide, 17" deep, 34" high - 1/5 HP air cooled compressor, capacity 75 lbs./24 hr. - 2025 - 1/2 size cubes only.

NOTE: All machines listed below may be adapted to produce full size - half size or mini cubes. The full size capacity only is shown. Half size would be double the amount, mini cubes 4 times the number of full size (i.e. 1,485 - 2,970 or 5,940).

SIZE: 30" wide, 24" deep, 34" high without legs (fits under bars or high counters), legs available - 1/3 HP water or air cooled compressor, 110 lb./24 hr. capacity - 1485 full cubes. Bin holds 65 lbs.

SIZE: 28" wide, 32" deep, 72" high (narrow width for installation where space is limited), 1 HP compressor, water cooled only. Capacity 400 lbs. - 5,400 full cubes. Bin holds 340 lbs.

SIZE: 28" wide, 31" deep, 51" high on 200 lb. bin, 28" deep, 39" high on 175 lb. bin. 6" legs available - 3/4 HP water or air cooled compressor - 200 lb. capacity - 2700 full cubes.

NOTE: All of the following ice cube units are of modular construction, designed to set on the various bins listed next in this chapter. The ice units may be stacked up to 5 high on the 1000 lb. bin. Ice crusher units or bin sleeves or bin extension units with hinged doors are available to mount between the ice units and the bins, singularly or in any combination. Bin sleeves with door add 20" to overall height. The other units add 16". A bin stand 15" high is available for stacks of units not using slope front.

The ice crushers are adjustable for fine or coarsely crushed ice. Deflectors permit storage of both cubes and crushed ice in divided bins.

300 lb. Capacity Ice Cube Unit — 42" wide, 25" deep, 16" high, air or water cooled 3/4 HP compressor - 4,500 full cubes.

400 lb. Capacity Ice Cube Unit — 42" wide, 25" deep, 16" high, air or water cooled 1 HP compressor - 5,400 full cubes. NOTE: Air cooled units have cooling fins extending approximately 7" outward at back of units.

500 lb. Capacity Ice Cube Unit — 42" wide, 24" deep, 16" high, water cooled only, 1 HP compressor - 12,960 full cubes.

700 lb. Capacity Ice Cube Unit — 42" wide, 25" deep, 31" high, water cooled only. Equipped with 2 separate ice making units, 2 water cooled condensers and 1 compressor 14,000 B.T.U., 208/220 volt, single phase.

Remote compressor units with pre-charged lines are available for the above ice cube machines.

Study the options and variables to pick the unit best suited to your needs.

NOTE: The ice machines described in this chapter are representative units available from most manufacturers. Specifications, capacities and dimensions will vary. Some much larger units are available. The shapes and sizes of ice cubes produced vary considerably but the capacities will be quite similar.

ICE STORAGE BINS

APPROX. BIN SIZE			CAPACITY - POUNDS		
Width	Depth	Height	Cubes	Flake Ice	Style
3'-6"	2'-1"	1'-8"	235	190	A
3'-6"	2'-1"	2'-11"	445	355	A
3'-6"	2'-8"	2'-11"	540	430	B
3'-6"	2'-1"	4'-3"	725	580	C
3'-6"	2'-8"	4'-3"	750	595	D
5'-4"	2'-10"	3'-10"	1000	790	E
7'-6"	2'-10"	3'-10"	1500	1135	F

KEY TO STYLES:
A — Straight front, full width swing out door, hinged at bottom.
B — Front slants out at top with sliding plexiglass doors, front below doors slants back inward.
C — Same as "A" but with two doors.
D — Same as "B" with straight bin extension above doors.
E — Bin designed to support single stack of ice machines. Extends beyond ice units each side. Top of front slants out with two sets of sliding plexiglass doors. Front below doors is straight with two solid doors side hinged.
F — Same configuration as "E" but designed to support two stacks of ice machines.

ICE CRUSHER

A separate ice crushing unit which may be located beside your cuber, on 18" high legs measures 18½" wide x 21½" deep x 21½" high is available. Hopper measures 7½" x 6¼" x 10" deep. Crushed ice empties into container of your choice. Drive motor 1/3 HP. Fineness of crushed ice produced may be adjusted from approximately 1/8" to 1/2" size even while machine is running.

SELF CONTAINED STORAGE BINS

Ice storage bins are available with freezer coils and compressors built-in. These units are ideal for resort and other areas, where the demand for ice may be heavy on weekends. The overflow from the normal ice production during the week may be transferred and held in these freezer/storage units.

The units range from 600 to 4000 lb. capacities, in increments of approximately 100 lbs.

ICE STORAGE BINS - FREE STANDING
(Typcal Capacities)

SLOPE FRONTS

Lbs. Cube Capacity	Lbs. Flake Capacity	Cu. Ft. Ice
600	500	20.3
770	650	25.9
725	615	24.4
920	780	31.1
1025	870	34.6

UPRIGHTS

865	735	29.2
1120	950	37.8
1300	1100	43.8
1400	1190	47.6
1680	1425	56.6
1935	1640	65.3
2020	1715	68.1
2350	1995	79.2
2865	2435	96.5
3470	2945	116.9
4080	3465	137.5

ICE CUBE DISPENSERS

Ice dispensing to hold previously discussed ice cube machines of 300, 400 or 500 lb. capacity are available. The dispensing spout is U.S. Public Health approved. Dispenser motor is 1/3 HP, delivery rate to 1 lb. per second. Overall height of dispensing unit is 56" w/legs. Available with standard drip basin or tilt back basin for ice bag filling. Push-back water faucet optional extra.

HOSPITAL OR CAFETERIA STYLE UNIT

Width 32", depth 29", height 76", production 225 lb., 1/2 HP or 400 lb. 1 HP water cooled ice cubers - full, 1/2 or mini cubes. Dispenser motor 1/4 HP. Optional extras: water station, portion control with water station, electric eye ice saver, key or coin operation.

MOBILE DISPENSING UNIT

Width 29", depth 24", height 38" with casters - 115V plug-in unit, non-refrigerated. Bin holds approximatly 120 lbs., drip pan under. Optional portion control. 14" high stand available if mobility not required.

DECORATOR DESIGN MAKER DISPENSER

Attractively designed with sign for hotel, motel or institution use, 40" wide, 30" deep and 84" high. The unit is available with ice makers ranging from 250 lb. to 650 lb. capacity. Compressors range from 3/4 HP and 1 HP, 115 V to 2 HP, 208 volt units. Bin 300 lb. capacity. Portion control feature standard options: key, token or coin operation. Air or water cooled compressors, stainless steel cabinet without lighted sign.

FLAKE ICE DISPENSERS

The many different designs, capacities and styles available insure the prospective user of being able to find exactly what he requires. That's a reassuring fact, but it makes it impossible for us to list them all. Generalities for brainstorming are listed below:

The flake ice units are an integral part of the dispenser. Units to approximately 750 lb. capacity with bins up to 100 lb. capacity are available as counter models or free standing on bases which could house cooling units and carbonators for beverage systems. The optional beverage system dispensing heads may be mounted with the ice and water spouts on the upper unit. The beverage system can be incorporated into the counter model also.

PEBBLED ICE DISPENSERS

As above these units are available in sizes, capacities and styles to fill almost any requirements. The principle difference being that the ice making unit is remote, up to 20 ft., from the storage and dispensing unit. The ice is delivered to the storage bin through an auger powered tube.

See page 396 for energy costs for ice cube machines.

217

ICE DISPENSER SELECTION CHART

TIME	AMOUNT OF ICE DISPENSED (PER PERSON)			SUGGESTED DISPENSER
SERVING HOURS	2 OZ.	3 OZ.	4 OZ.	SIZE IN LBS. PER HR.
	NUMBER OF PEOPLE SERVED			
1 HOUR	420	310	210	50
	800	600	400	100
	1260	940	630	200
	1380	1020	690	200 Dual Feed
2 HOURS	550	400	270	50
	920	690	460	100
	1380	1030	690	200
	1620	1180	810	200 Dual Feed
3 HOURS	670	490	330	50
	1050	780	520	100
	1500	1120	780	200
	1860	1340	930	200 Dual Feed

NOTE: Above calculations are averages based on storage module that is full at the beginning, and empty at the end of the meal. Automatic filling is at the rate of 16 lbs. per hour for the next meal.

COFFEE FACTS

We examine sample urn production and sizes, expresso machines, grinders and dispensers.

Urn styles: gas, electric, steam; manual or automatic, kettle style, 10-12 cup brewers and instant-freeze dried style.

BREWING FACTS

- 6 to 8 oz. ground coffee to 1 gal. brewed
- Every gallon = 16 to 20 cups
- Every 1 pound coffee = 2½ gals. or 50 cups

Servings Per Lb.	6 Oz.	Glass Bowl Coffee Brew 1¾ Gal. Water to Lb. Coffee 35	2 Gal. Water Per Lb. 40	Urn Coffee 2½ Gal. Water Per Lb. 50	3 Gal. Water Per Lb. 60
Cost per	$2.00 lb.	5.8¢	5¢	4¢	3.4¢
serving with	$3.00 lb.	8.7¢	7.5¢	6¢	5.1¢
coffee at . . .	$4.00 lb.	11.6¢	10¢	8¢	6.8¢

The above comparison of course, varies with portions and coffee cost. We thought it interesting.

AUTOMATIC ELECTRIC PERCOLATORS

Standard Sizes

24 Cup	55 Cup	90 Cup
36 Cup	72 Cup	100 Cup

218

PAPER FILTERS
TYPICAL SIZES (URN STYLE)

Gals.	Top Diam.	Flare Height
2	16½"	6"
3	18"	6"
3	18"	7½"
5-6	20"	8"
9-10	23"	8"
10	25"-29"	11"

BREWER STYLE FILTERS 8-12 CUP

Size of Unit	Bottom Diam.	Flare Height
8-10 Cup	3"	3"
12 Cup	3½"	3-1/8"
12 Cup	4½"	2-5/8"

URN BAGS
(The diameter of the bag is used as the size number, I.e. the proper bag to order for a 6 gal. urn would be No. 13.)

Bag Diameter	Gals.	Bag Diameter	Gals.
9"	2	15"	10
10"	3	16"	12
11"	4	18"	15
12"	5	20"	18
13"	6	30"	20
14"	8		

URN RINGS
(Diameter = Gals)

10"..... 3 Gal.		14"..... 8 Gal.	
11"..... 4 Gal.		15".... 10 Gal.	
12"..... 5 Gal.		16".... 12 Gal.	
13"..... 6 Gal.		18".... 15 Gal.	

URN FACTS · TYPICAL SIZES

Single Urn	Water Capacity	Twin Urn	Water Capacity
3 Gal.	8 Gal.	2 - 3 Gal.	13 Gal.
5 Gal.	11 Gal.	2 - 5 Gal.	20 Gal.
6 Gal.	10 Gal.	2 - 6 Gal.	18 Gal.
		2 - 9 Gal.	26 Gal.

Manual or automatic will determine exact production per hour. See next chart for automatic urn production.

AUTOMATIC CREAMER

This unit may be attached to existing or new coffee urns. As coffee is drawn the cream is automatically mixed with it. Proportion adjustable, ideal for bulk feeding.

TYPICAL URN PRODUCTION
(Automatic Gas or Electric)

Size	Gals. Per Hr.	Cups Per Hr.	Recommended for Users of Pounds
Single - 3 Gal. Elec.	18	432	30 - 100 lbs.
Twin - 3 Gal. Elec.	25	600	50 - 150 lbs.
Twin - 3 Gal. Gas	15	360	50 - 150 lbs.
Twin - 6 Gal. Elec.	30	720	100 - 250 lbs.
Twin - 9 Gal. Elec.	45	1080	150 - 300 lbs.

NOTE: Above guide has many variables, such as BTU's or KW. temperature of the incoming water and water flow.

See next chart for incoming water temperature effects on production.

Unit	Coffee Capacity Ea. Liner	Incoming Water Temperature	Brews Per Hour	Gallons Per Hour	5 Oz. Cups Per Hour
6 KW Twin 3 - Elec.	3 Gal.	70^0	4.2	12.6	322
		140^0	7.0	21.0	538
		180^0	10.0	30.0	768
10 KW Twin 3 - Elec.	3 Gal.	70^0	6.2	18.6	476
		140^0	9.5	28.5	730
		180^0	10.0	30.0	768
6 KW Twin 6 - Elec.	6 Gal.	70^0	2.1	12.6	322
		140^0	3.5	21.0	538
		180^0	5.0	30.0	768
10 KW Twin 6 - Elec.	6 Gal.	70^0	3.1	18.6	476
		140^0	4.7	28.2	722
		180^0	6.8	40.8	1044
10,010—10E 10 KW Twin 10 - Elec.	10 Gal.	70^0	2.0	20.0	512
		140^0	3.1	31.0	794
		180^0	4.7	47.0	1203

TWIN COFFEE BREWER WITH REMOVABLE INSULATED URNS

Each insulated, removable container, with site glass and faucet will hold 36 cups and maintain temperature for 2 hours. The brewing unit has two brewing heads with full pattern spray heads. Regular and decaffeinated coffee may be brewed simultaneously. Hot water spout is provided. Brews up to 400 cups per hour. Any number of insulated dispensing units may be used depending on amount of service stations required. The unit is 18" wide, 16½" deep, 29" high, standard 220 Volt, 6.3 KW, 29 Amps. The portable dispensers are 9" square and approx. 12" high. Separate bases are available for these dispensers.

URN PRODUCTION - SUPER BANQUET SIZES
(From 1500 to 4000 cups - Electric)

Total Coffee Capacity Held	60 Gals. One Twin	80 Gals. One Twin	120 Gals Two Twin	160 Gals. Two Twin
Brewing Urn(s)	10 Gal.	10 Gal.	10 Gal.	10 Gal.
Brewing Urn Holding Capacity	20 Gals.	20 Gals.	40 Gals.	40 Gals.
Holding Urn Capacity	40 Gals.	60 Gals.	80 Gals.	120 Gals.
Total Capacity Brew Time	45 Min.	60 Min.	45 Min.	60 Min.
Transfer Time	10 Min.	15 Min.	10 Min.	15 Min.
Total Preparation Time (No Heat Up)	55 Min.	75 Min.	55 Min.	75 Min.
Equivalent No. 5 oz. Servings	1500	2000	3000	4000
Equivalent No. 6 oz. Servings	1250	1700	2500	3300

Based on spraying over 10.5 gallons water each batch.
Based on simultaneous 2-side brewing.
Based on connection to 140° F. hot water supply.
60 Gal. and 80 Gal. units are 15 KW. 120 Gal. and 160 Gal. units are 30 KW.

10 to 12 CUP BREWER - DECANTER STYLE COFFEE MAKERS

Hundreds of styles of bottle brewers are available. They range from a manual fill style using cold water and requiring 115 volts to fully automated high production units with up to 5 built-in coffee warmers, rated at 220 volt.

They can be coin operated, have separate hot water faucets, and newer styles are available with reservoirs to store coffee for fast turnover periods. Some styles can use instant freeze dried coffee. Many models are modular, allowing banking in of warmers next to the maker as needed. Optimum operating water temperature is 205° and actual brew times vary from 3 to 4½ minutes per bowl. Many of these coffee makers are rated at 250, 350 and 500 cups per hour. Below are some typical facts for these popular brewers.

HELPFUL HINTS

Decanter style coffee brewers of course, vary by manufacturer, but some models are available as automatic, and in case of failure can continue to be used manually. Another point to consider is flexibility of brewing. Some manufacturers offer both conventional open type brewing using paper filters and pre-packaged coffee pouch brewing requiring no filters.

Typical size of a manual fill pour-over coffee maker is 9" wide, 15" deep and 18½" high, 1700 watts at 115 volts, available with or without top warmer.

Typical size full size automatic coffee maker — 24" wide, 18½" deep, 21½" high, 4600 watts at 220 volts. Warmers are rated at 535 watts each with high, medium and low settings.

Warmers and ranges with boil settings are available from 1 to 4 pot capacity.

221

COFFEE GRINDERS AND DISPENSERS

Grinder-Dispenser: 9" wide, 15" deep, 21" high, 1/3 HP motor. Hopper capacity 8 lbs., grinds and dispenses from 1 oz. to 1 lb. portions.

MANUAL COFFEE DISPENSER

Storage capacity 7 lbs., adjusts and dispenses in 3/4 oz. increments from 1½ to 3½ oz. portions.

ESPRESSO AND CAPPUCCINO

Espresso is coffee made from selected blends of coffee beans freshly ground. The brewing is done under pressure after the machine boiler reaches temperature.

Cappuccino is the combination of "espresso" coffee and steamed milk. The coffee is automatically brewed by the "espresso" coffee machine and the milk is doubled in volume by "exploding" it with live steam from the "espresso" machine into a pitcher. The superheated steam fills the milk with millions of tiny air bubbles without adding excess liquid. Finally, the steamed milk is floated onto the "espresso" and the result is a perfect "cappuccino."

AUTOMATIC ESPRESSO - CAPPUCCINO MACHINES

Width	No. of Brewers	Volts	Watts	Boiler Capacity
20"	1	220	1800	1½ Gal.
29½"	2	220	2600	3 Gal.
39"	3	220	3700	4 Gal.
48¾"	4	220	5000	5½ Gal.

Cup warmers above. Volume selector to 13 oz. portions maximum. Available semi-automatic and manual.

UNDER COUNTER AND MOBILE COFFEE DISPENSERS

A vacuum type insulated container holding up to 11 gallons is available with a caster base and a small pump. Rolled under a counter and plugged in, the hose from the pump connects to a dispensing faucet in the counter top.

A self contained mobile cabinet which houses cups and spoons is available for the same unit. A thermostatically controlled heating unit is also available. The system works well for cold beverages also.

TOASTERS

Pop-up Style: 2 slice 6-5/8" wide, 4 slice 12-5/8" wide, both 12-5/8" deep x 7¾" high.

SPECIFICATIONS

Style	K.W.	Production - Slices/hour		
		Light Set	Medium Set	Dark Set
2 Slice	1.4	265	190	125
4 Slice	2.8	530	380	250

CONVEYOR STYLE TOASTERS

Selection Guide - using toaster K.W. to production in minutes.

Hospitals, Nursing Homes (2 slices/bed)	Serving Time		Schools 1 Slice/Student	Serving Time	
	4 KW	5 KW		4 KW	5 KW
50 bed	9 min.	7 min.	100	9 min.	7 min.
100 bed	18 min.	14 min.	200	18 min.	14 min.
150 bed	26 min.	20 min.	300	26 min.	20 min.
200 bed	35 min.	25 min.	400	35 min.	25 min.
250 bed	43 min.	33 min.	500	43 min.	33 min.

RESTAURANT TIME GUIDE FOR BUN TOASTING

Time in Min.	Complete Buns		3 Decker Buns
	3 KW	4 KW	5 KW
3	15	22	17
5	30	44	36
7	45	66	51
9	60	88	68
11	75	110	85

WALL MOUNTED CONVEYOR TOASTER

20" wide, 24½" deep, 17" high. Typical production will depend on number of elements in unit and color desired.

Product	Watts	Per Hour Production
Buns	1800	800 Bun halves
Bread	2400	540 Bread slices
Buns	1200	445 Bun halves

CONVEYOR TOASTER FACTS
(Note: production differs with KW and color setting)

Style: low profile, produces 720 to 1000 bun halves or slices toast per hour or 500 bagel halves.

Upright conveyor toasters average 30" high, at 2 wide, 800 slices per hour; at 3 wide, 1200 slices per hour; at 4 wide, 1600 slices per hour.

CONVEYOR TOASTER
RATED BY THE MINUTE · COLOR VARIES PRODUCTION

K.W.	Product	Per Min.
3.2	Buns	12
4.0	Bread or Buns	15
4.3	Buns	22
5	Bread or Buns	16
5	3 Part Buns	25

BATCH BUN TOASTERS

Twelve bun or english muffin halves, placed on a tray in these units may be toasted in 30 to 45 seconds. Production up to 400 buns per hour. Instant-on quartz lamps permit up to 50% energy savings. Units are available with color-optic control which signals when pre-selected color is reached.

Available for 115 Volt or 208-220 Volt, 1 phase - 13 to 15 Amp avg. Approximate sizes 12" high, 24" wide, 20" deep.

TRUCK SELECTION

The fact that there are hundreds of styles and sizes of trucks available makes this section most important. Use the following Brainstorming List.

1) What size pan, tray or product is to be moved or stored.
2) What capacity will be needed.
3) In ledges what spacing is required.
4) Type of ledges — narrow, wide, corrugated.
5) Ledge fixed or removable.
6) End load or side load of pan.
7) Open or closed.
8) Heated, unheated, insulated, not insulated, proofing, refrigerated.
9) Bumpers, handles, brakes, pan stops, revolving or vertical bumpers.
10) Special wheels.
11) Thermometers.
12) Will truck be used as roll-in.
13) Assembled or knocked down.
14) If heated bottom, convected heat or forced air heat ducts.
15) Cord reel sets attached.
16) Locks
17) Straps
18) Glide out shelves
19) Foot treadle

ANOTHER FORM WHICH MAY AID SELECTION

1. TRAY/PAN SIZES:

18 x 26	15 x 20
12 x 20	Other
14 x 18	

2. CAPACITY REQUIRED:

3. TYPE CART REQUIRED:

Unheated	Insulated
Heated	Non-insulated
Refrigerated	

4. CART SIZE LIMITS (Check Travel Path, Doorways, Elevators, Etc.):
    "H x   "W x   "L

5. CART CONSTRUCTION:

a. transported on trucks	Yes	No
b. moved on ramps	Yes	No
c. elevator, system	Yes	No
d. towed	Yes	No
e. rough travel surfaces	Yes	No
f. cart wash	Yes	No

6. CASTER SELECTION:

a. Diameter	5"	6"
	8"	Other
b. Tread Width	¾"	1¼"
	2"	Other
c. Tread Material	Std.	
	Polyurethane	
	Semi-pneumatic	
	Pneumatic	
d. No. Swivel	No. Fixed	
e. Number of brakes		
f. Swivel locks	Yes	No
g. Sealed bearings	Yes	No

7. SPECIAL AUXILIARY FEATURES

a. top storage racks
b. folding side shelves
c. insulated divider sections
d. custom shelves, racks
e. custom color vinyl laminates
f. menu/I.D. card holders

TRAY CAPACITY CHART

Item		Space Between Slides (Inches)	Tray Capacity	
			14" x 18"	18" x 26"
PAPER PORTION CUPS	1/2 oz.	1	88	187
	3/4 oz.	2	88	187
	1 oz.	2	63	150
	2 oz.	2	42	84
	2-1/2 oz.	2	35	77
	4 oz.	2	24	54
	6 oz.	2	12	28
	8 oz.	3	12	28
	10 oz.	3	12	24
MILK CARTON, 1/2 pint	2-7/8" square	4	20	40
MILK CARTON, 1/2 pint	2-1/4" square	4	35	70
MILK CARTON, 1/3 quart	2-1/4" square	5	35	70
JUICE GLASS	5 oz.	4	35	84
WATER GLASS	10 oz.	5	20	40
GLASSWARE	2-7/8" Sherbet	3	20	40
	3-7/16" Sherbet	3	12	28
	4-11/16" Fruit Nappie	—	6	15
	3-9/16" Supreme Insert	3	12	28
	5-3/4" Supreme Insert	3	5	8
DISHES	5-1/2" Bread and Butter	—	6	12
	6-3/8" Salad	—	5	11
	7-3/8" Dessert	—	4	8
	4-9/16" Fruit Nappie	—	12	24
	4-5/8" Fruit Nappie	—	8	21
	3" Custard Cup	3	20	40
	3-3/4" Bouillon Cup	3	12	28
	5" Soup	—	5	15
	5-7/8" Salad Bowl	—	5	11
	5-11/16" Salad Bowl	—	5	11

TRAY CAPACITY CHART (Cont.)

	Item	Space Between Slides (Inches)	Tray Capacity 14" x 18"	18" x 26"
	#12 Scoop in 4-5/8" Nappie	3-4	8	21
	#8 Scoop on 7-3/8" Plate	3	4	8
FOOD	Gelatine Salad on 6-3/8" Plate	3	5	11
ITEMS	Pie Wedge on 6-3/8" Plate	2	5	11
	Cake Wedge on 6-3/8" Plate	3-4	5	11
	1/6 Cantaloupe on 7-3/8" Plate	3-4	4	8

FOOD SERVICE CASTER AND WHEEL RATINGS

Type	Dia. Inches	Face Inches	Wheel	Rating Per Caster Lbs.	Weight Per Caster Lbs.
Stem/Swivel	5	1¼	Resilient	175	2½
Stem/Rigid	5	1¼	Resilient	175	3½
Stem/Brake	5	1¼	Resilient	175	2¾
Stem/Swivel	5	1¼	Urethane	210	2¾
Stem/Rigid	5	1¼	Urethane	210	3¾
Stem/Brake	5	1¼	Urethane	210	3
Swivel	3	1¼	Hard Rubber	225	1¼
Brake	3	1¼	Hard Rubber	225	1½
Swivel	5	1¼	Resilient	175	2½
Brake	5	1¼	Resilient	175	2¾
Swivel	5	1⅛	Resilient	200	2½
Brake	5	1⅛	Resilient	200	3¼
Swivel	5	1½	Urethane	300	5¼
Brake	5	1½	Urethane	300	7
Swivel	5	2	Urethane	1000	5½
Brake	5	2	Urethane	1000	6
Swivel	6	2	Resilient	500	5½
Brake	6	2	Resilient	500	6¼
Swivel	6	2	Resilient	400	6½
Brake/Lock	6	2	Resilient	400	7¾
Swivel	6	2	Hard Rubber	500	6½
Brake/Lock	6	2	Hard Rubber	500	7¾
Swivel	6	2	Urethane	850	5¾
Brake/Lock	6	2	Urethane	850	7¼
Swivel	8	2	Urethane	850	6½
Brake/Lock	8	2	Urethane	850	9

226

TRUCK CHECK LIST

1. What is to be stored? _____ pans, _____ trays, _____ tote boxes.

2. What size? Actual measured length _____, width _____, depth _____.

3. What capacity per rack (or cabinet)? _____

4. Spacing between ledges? _____

5. End loaded _____ or side loaded _____.

6. Material? Aluminum _____, Stainless Steel _____, Vinyl _____.

7. Open rack _____ or closed cabinet _____.

8. If rack, Uniledge _____ or angle _____.

9. If angle, set up _____ or knocked down _____.

10. How many sections? Single _____, Double _____, Triple _____.

11. If cabinet, heated _____, 110 volts _____, 220 volts _____, unheated _____, insulated _____, or uninsulated _____.

12. Quantity? _____

13. Accessories? List _____

ACCESSORIES

Cabinets are available with the following optional accessories:
- Wrap Around Bumpers
- Caster Brakes
- Push Handles
- Pass-through door
- External Thermometer

Racks are available with optional accessories, such as:
- Vertical Bumpers
- Revolving Bumpers
- Caster Brakes
- Rear Pan Stops
- Center Pan Stops — for double loading per ledge
- Side Enclosures

PAN AND TRAY TRUCKS · SELECTED RATINGS

ALL PURPOSE RACKS · WIDE ANGLE SHELF SUPPORTS

25" wide, 28" deep, 67" high, ledges normally removable and adjustable. Holds following pans:

Pan Size	Description
* 10-7/8 x 19-3/4 x 2-1/4	Baking Pan
* 10-7/8 x 19-3/4 x 3-1/2	Baking Pan
* 11-1/8 x 20 6-1/2	Deep Roast Pan
* 12 x 20 x 2-1/2	Steamtable Pans
* 12 x 20 x 4	Steamtable Pans
* 12 x 20 x 6	Steamtable Pans
* 12 x 18 x 2-1/2	Steamtable Pans
* 12 x 18 x 4	Steamtable Pans
* 12 x 18 x 6	Steamtable Pans
* 14 x 18	Service Tray
15 x 20	Service Tray
20 x 20	Cup & Glass Rack
22-1/2 x 20-1/2 x 6-1/2	Deep Roast Pan
20 x 22 x 1-1/4	Roast & Bake Pan
20 x 22 x 2-1/4	Roast & Bake Pan
20 x 22 x 3-1/2	Roast & Bake Pan
18 x 26 x 1	Bun Pan
18 x 26 x 1-3/16	Roast & Bake Pan
18 x 26 x 3-1/2	Roast & Bake Pan
18 x 26 x 4	Wire Basket
18 x 26	Economy Pan
18 x 26	Wire Screen
* 18 x 13 x 1	Half Size Bun Pan
* 18 x 13 x 4	Half Size Wire Bsk.

* Two Trays or Pans on an Angle per set of slides.

TYPICAL END LOAD TRUCK CAPACITIES

ANGLE SPACING	TYPE LEDGES	PAN SIZE	TYPE LOADING	CAPACITY	HEIGHT	WIDTH	DEPTH
$2\frac{1}{4}''$	$1\frac{3}{16}''$	18x26	End	10	$37''$	$20\frac{1}{2}''$	$27''$
$2\frac{1}{4}''$	$1\frac{3}{16}''$	18x26	End	18	$54\frac{1}{2}''$	$20\frac{1}{2}''$	$27''$
$2\frac{1}{4}''$	$1\frac{3}{16}''$	18x26	End	22	$63\frac{1}{2}''$	$20\frac{1}{2}''$	$27''$
$2\frac{1}{4}''$	$1\frac{3}{16}''$	18x26	End	26	$72\frac{1}{2}''$	$20\frac{1}{2}''$	$27''$
$1\frac{3}{8}''$	$\frac{9}{16}''$	18x26	End	18	$37''$	$20\frac{1}{2}''$	$27''$
$1\frac{3}{8}''$	$\frac{9}{16}''$	18x26	End	32	$54\frac{1}{2}''$	$20\frac{1}{2}''$	$27''$
$1\frac{3}{8}''$	$\frac{9}{16}''$	18x26	End	39	$63\frac{1}{2}''$	$20\frac{1}{2}''$	$27''$
$1\frac{3}{8}''$	$\frac{9}{16}''$	18x26	End	46	$72\frac{1}{2}''$	$20\frac{1}{2}''$	$27''$
$1\frac{3}{8}''$	$\frac{9}{16}''$	20x24	End	18	$37''$	$22\frac{1}{2}''$	$27''$
$1\frac{3}{8}''$	$\frac{9}{16}''$	20x24	End	32	$54\frac{1}{2}''$	$22\frac{1}{2}''$	$27''$
$1\frac{3}{8}''$	$\frac{9}{16}''$	20x24	End	39	$63\frac{1}{2}''$	$22\frac{1}{2}''$	$27''$
$1\frac{3}{8}''$	$\frac{9}{16}''$	20x24	End	46	$72\frac{1}{2}''$	$22\frac{1}{2}''$	$27''$

TRAY CAPACITY FOR CABINETS
Bun pan Cabinets, side loading
cabinets, hospital tray, single section*

Angle Spacing	Overall Cabinet Height			
	$72\frac{1}{2}''$	$63\frac{1}{2}''$	$54\frac{1}{2}''$	$37''$
$1\frac{3}{8}''$	44	37	31	18
$2\frac{1}{4}''$	26	22	18	10
$2\frac{1}{2}''$	24	20	16	9
$2\frac{3}{4}''$	22	18	15	8
$3''$	20	17	14	9
$3\frac{1}{4}''$	18	15	13	7
$3\frac{1}{2}''$	17	14	12	7
$3\frac{3}{4}''$	16	13	11	6
$4''$	15	12	10	6
$4\frac{1}{4}''$	14	12	9	5
$4\frac{1}{2}''$	13	11	9	5
$4\frac{3}{4}''$	12	10	8	5
$5''$	12	10	8	4
$5\frac{1}{4}''$	11	9	8	4
$5\frac{1}{2}''$	10	9	8	4
$5\frac{3}{4}''$	10	8	7	4
$6''$	10	8	7	4
$6\frac{1}{4}''$	9	8	6	3
$6\frac{1}{2}''$	9	7	6	3
$6\frac{3}{4}''$	8	7	6	3

TRAY AND PAN TRUCKS - BY SIZE AND CAPACITY

TYPICAL CAPABILITY

ANGLE SPACING	PAN SIZE	TYPE OF LOADING	CAPACITY	HEIGHT	WIDTH	DEPTH	TYPE LEDGES
2¼″	10x14	Side	24	36½″	17½″	21″	1-3/16″
2¼″	12x20	End	5	36½″	17½″	21″	1-3/16″
2¼″	14x18	End	12	36½″	17½″	21″	1-3/16″
2¼″	14x18	Side	12	36½″	21½″	21″	1-3/16″
2¼″	15x20	End	12	36½″	18½″	21″	1-3/16″
2¼″	18x26	Side	12	36½″	29½″	21″	1-3/16″
2¼″	10x14	Side	40	54½″	17½″	21″	1-3/16″
2¼″	12x20	End	9	54½″	17½″	21″	1-3/16″
2¼″	14x18	End	20	54½″	17½″	21″	1-3/16″
2¼″	14x18	Side	20	54½″	21½″	21″	1-3/16″
2¼″	15x20	End	20	54½″	18½″	21″	1-3/16″
2¼″	18x26	Side	20	54½″	29½″	21″	1-3/16″
2¼″	10x14	Side	48	63½″	17½″	21″	1-3/16″
2¼″	12x20	End	11	63½″	17½″	21″	1-3/16″
2¼″	14x18	End	24	63½″	17½″	21″	1-3/16″
2¼″	14x18	Side	24	63½″	21½″	21″	1-3/16″
2¼″	15x20	End	24	63½″	18½″	21″	1-3/16″
2¼″	18x26	Side	24	63½″	29½″	21″	1-3/16″
2¼″	10x14	Side	56	72½″	17½″	21″	1-3/16″
2¼″	12x20	End	13	72½″	17½″	21″	1-3/16″
2¼″	14x18	End	28	72½″	17½″	21″	1-3/16″
2¼″	14x18	Side	28	72½″	21½″	21″	1-3/16″
2¼″	15x20	End	28	72½″	18½″	21″	1-3/16″
2¼″	18x26	Side	28	72½″	29½″	21″	1-3/16″

ANGLE SPACING	TYPE LEDGES	TRAY SIZE	TYPE LOADING	CAPACITY	HEIGHT	WIDTH	DEPTH
5½″	1³⁄₁₆″	14x18	end	7	54½″	16¾″	21¾″
		15x20				17¾″	21¾″
		16x22				18¾″	23¾″
5½″	1³⁄₁₆″	14x18	end	9	63½″	16¾″	21¾″
		15x20				17¾″	21¾″
		16x22				18¾″	23¾″
5½″	1³⁄₁₆″	14x18	end	14	54½″	43¼″	25½″
		15x20				45¼″	25½″
		16x22				47¼″	27½″
5½″	1³⁄₁₆″	14x18	end	18	63½″	43¼″	25½″
		15x20				45¼″	25½″
		16x22				47¼″	27½″
5½″	1³⁄₁₆″	14x18	end	21	54½″	60″	25½″
		15x20				63″	25½″
		16x22				66″	27½″
5½″	1³⁄₁₆″	14x18	end	27	63½″	60″	25½″
		15x20				63″	25½″
		16x22				66″	27½″

UNIVERSAL LEDGE TRUCKS - ADJUSTABLE LEDGES

Following pans fit universal rack trucks:
  Column 1 — 69" high, 13 ledges standard
  Column 2 — 63" high, 12 ledges standard
  Column 3 — 58" high, 11 ledges standard
Truck is 24-3/4" wide, 27" deep. Additional ledges can be added and are adjustable on 1-1/2" centers.

Pan Size	Pan or Tray Description	Capacities 69"H	63"H	58"H
18 x 26 x 1	Bun Pan	13	12	11
18 x 26 x ¼	Roast & Bake Pan	13	12	11
18 x 26 x 3 ½	Roast & Bake Pan	13	12	11
18 x 26 x 4	Wire Basket	13	12	11
18 x 22	Economy Pan	13	12	11
18 x 26	Wire Screen	13	12	11
*18 x 13 x 1	½ Size Bun Pan	26	24	22
*18 x 13 x 4	½ Size Wire Bsk	26	24	22
20 x 20 x ½	Roast & Bake Pan	13	12	11
20 x 22 x 1 ¼	Roast & Bake Pan	13	12	11
20 x 22 x 2 ¼	Roast & Bake Pan	13	12	11
20 x 22 x 3 ½	Roast & Bake Pan	13	12	11
20 x 24 x 3 ½	Roast & Bake Pan	13	12	11
20 x 24	Maxi-Pan	13	12	11
22 ½ x 20 ½ x 6 ½	Deep Roast Pan	9	8	7
20 x 20	Cup & Glass Rack	13	12	11
15 x 20	Service Tray	13	12	11
*14 x 18	Service Tray	26	24	22
*12 x 20 x 2 ½	Steamtable Pan	26	24	22
*12 x 20 x 4	Steamtable Pan	26	24	22
*12 x 20 x 6	Steamtable Pan	18	18	16
*12 x 18 x 2 ½	Steamtable Pan	26	24	22
*12 x 18 x 4	Steamtable Pan	26	24	22
*12 x 18 x 6	Steamtable Pan	18	18	16
11 ⅛ x 20 x 6 ½	Deep Roast Pan	18	18	16
*10 ⅞ x 19 ¾ x 2 ¼	Bake Pan	26	24	22
*10 ⅞ x 19 ¾ x 3 ⅓	Bake Pan	26	24	22

*Rack carries two trays or pans on same set of ledges.

SELF STACKING PANS

These 18" x 26" pans are designed so that they may be loaded with plated salads, desserts, etc. and stacked in locked position on top of each other. When stacked on a dolly designated to receive them, they may be rolled to serving or storing position.

PROOFING TRUCKS

Angle Spacing	Type Ledges	Pan Size	Type Loading	Capacity	Height	Width	Depth	Proofing Unit
$2\frac{1}{4}''$	1-3/16″	18x26	End	19	$63\frac{1}{2}''$	21″	31″	Electric
$2\frac{1}{4}''$	1-3/16″	18x26	End	23	$72\frac{1}{2}''$	21″	31″	Electric
$1\frac{3}{8}''$	9/16″	18x26	End	32	$63\frac{1}{2}''$	21″	31″	Electric
$1\frac{3}{8}''$	9/16″	18x26	End	38	$72\frac{1}{2}''$	21″	31″	Electric

PROOF BOX DEFINITION

A proof box is a heated humidity controlled box used to raise dough without drying it out. The temperature should be maintained between 90° and 100°F. The humidifier maintains between 80 and 85% relative humidity. Mobility is desirable, therefore most units operate on electricity. Gas or steam models are also available.

HEATED STACKING CABINETS

Angle Spacing	Angle Ledge	Tray Size	Load	Capacity	Height	Width	Depth
$1\frac{3}{8}''$	9/16″	18x26	end	12	$21\frac{1}{2}''$	$20\frac{1}{2}''$	$27\frac{1}{2}''$
$1\frac{3}{8}''$	9/16″	12x20	end	6	$21\frac{1}{2}''$	$15\frac{1}{2}''$	$22\frac{1}{4}''$
$1\frac{3}{8}''$	9/16″	12x20	side	12	$21\frac{1}{2}''$	$23\frac{1}{2}''$	$27\frac{1}{2}''$
$2\frac{1}{4}''$	1-3/16″	18x26	end	6	$21\frac{1}{2}''$	$20\frac{1}{2}''$	$27\frac{1}{2}''$
$2\frac{1}{4}''$	1-3/16″	12x20	end	4	$21\frac{1}{2}''$	$16\frac{1}{2}''$	$22\frac{1}{4}''$
$2\frac{1}{4}''$	1-3/16″	12x20	side	7	$21\frac{1}{2}''$	$24\frac{1}{2}''$	$27\frac{1}{2}''$

HOSPITAL TRAY CABINETS

Angle Spacing	Angle Ledge	Tray Size	Load	Capacity	Height	Width	Depth
$5\frac{1}{2}''$	1-3/16″	15x20	side	12	$45\frac{1}{2}''$	$22\frac{3}{4}''$	$31\frac{3}{4}''$
$5\frac{1}{2}''$	1-3/16″	15x20	side	14	$54\frac{1}{2}''$	$22\frac{3}{4}''$	$31\frac{3}{4}''$
$5\frac{1}{2}''$	1-3/16″	15x20	side	16	$56\frac{1}{2}''$	$22\frac{3}{4}''$	$31\frac{3}{4}''$
$5\frac{1}{2}''$	1-3/16″	15x20	side	18	$63\frac{1}{2}''$	$22\frac{3}{4}''$	$31\frac{3}{4}''$
$5\frac{1}{2}''$	1-3/16″	15x20	side	24	$45\frac{1}{2}''$	$45\frac{1}{2}''$	$31\frac{3}{4}''$
$5\frac{1}{2}''$	1-3/16″	15x20	side	28	$54\frac{1}{2}''$	$45\frac{1}{2}''$	$31\frac{3}{4}''$
$5\frac{1}{2}''$	1-3/16″	15x20	side	32	$56\frac{1}{2}''$	$45\frac{1}{2}''$	$31\frac{3}{4}''$
$5\frac{1}{2}''$	1-3/16″	15x20	side	36	$63\frac{1}{2}''$	$45\frac{1}{2}''$	$31\frac{3}{4}''$

NON-HEATED

CABINETS FOR 18x26 BUN PANS, END LOADING

ANGLE SPACING	TYPE LEDGE	PAN SIZE	TYPE LOADING	CAPACITY	HEIGHT	WIDTH	DEPTH
2¼"	1³⁄₁₆"	18x26	End	10	37"	23 ½"	32"
2¼"	1³⁄₁₆"	18x26	End	18	54½"	23 ½"	32"
2¼"	1³⁄₁₆"	18x26	End	22	63½"	23 ½"	32"
2¼"	1³⁄₁₆"	18x26	End	26	72½"	23 ½"	32"
1⅜"	⁹⁄₁₆"	18x26	End	19	37"	23 ½"	32"
1⅜"	⁹⁄₁₆"	18x26	End	31	54½"	23 ½"	32"
1⅜"	⁹⁄₁₆"	18x26	End	37	63½"	23 ½"	32"
1⅜"	⁹⁄₁₆"	18x26	End	43	72½"	23 ½"	32"

CABINETS FOR 12x20 PANS, END LOADING

ANGLE SPACING	TYPE LEDGE	PAN SIZE	TYPE LOADING	CAPACITY	HEIGHT	WIDTH	DEPTH
3"	1³⁄₁₆"	12x20	End	8	37"	19 ½"	26"
3"	1³⁄₁₆"	12x20	End	14	54½"	19 ½"	26"
3"	1³⁄₁₆"	12x20	End	17	63½"	19 ½"	26"
3"	1³⁄₁₆"	12x20	End	20	72½"	19 ½"	26"
1⅜"	⁹⁄₁₆"	12x20	End	9	37"	18 ½"	26"
1⅜"	⁹⁄₁₆"	12x20	End	15	54½"	18 ½"	26"
1⅜"	⁹⁄₁₆"	12x20	End	18	63½"	18 ½"	26"
1⅜"	⁹⁄₁₆"	12x20	End	21	72½"	18 ½"	26"

CABINETS FOR 12x20 PANS, SIDE LOADING, TWO PER LEDGE

ANGLE SPACING	TYPE LEDGE	PAN SIZE	TYPE LOADING	CAPACITY	HEIGHT	WIDTH	DEPTH
3"	1³⁄₁₆"	12x20	Side	16	37"	27 ½"	32"
3"	1³⁄₁₆"	12x20	Side	28	54½"	27 ½"	32"
3"	1³⁄₁₆"	12x20	Side	34	63½"	27 ½"	32"
3"	1³⁄₁₆"	12x20	Side	40	72½"	27 ½"	32"
1⅜"	⁹⁄₁₆"	12x20	Side	18	37"	26 ½"	32"
1⅜"	⁹⁄₁₆"	12x20	Side	30	54½"	26 ½"	32"
1⅜"	⁹⁄₁₆"	12x20	Side	36	63½"	26 ½"	32"
1⅜"	⁹⁄₁₆"	12x20	Side	42	72½"	26 ½"	32"

HEATED INSULATED CABINETS

CABINETS FOR 18x26 BUN PANS, END LOADING

ANGLE SPACING	TYPE LEDGE	PAN SIZE	TYPE LOADING	CAPACITY	HEIGHT	WIDTH	DEPTH
2¼″	1³⁄₁₆″	18x26	End	8	37″	22½″	31″
2¼″	1³⁄₁₆″	18x26	End	16	54½″	22½″	31″
2¼″	1³⁄₁₆″	18x26	End	20	63½″	22½″	31″
2¼″	1³⁄₁₆″	18x26	End	24	72½″	22½″	31″
1⅜″	⁹⁄₁₆″	18x26	End	15	37″	22½″	31″
1⅜″	⁹⁄₁₆″	18x26	End	27	54½″	22½″	31″
1⅜″	⁹⁄₁₆″	18x26	End	33	63½″	22½″	31″
1⅜″	⁹⁄₁₆″	18x26	End	39	72½″	22½″	31″

CABINETS FOR 12x20 PANS, END LOADING

ANGLE SPACING	TYPE LEDGE	PAN SIZE	TYPE LOADING	CAPACITY	HEIGHT	WIDTH	DEPTH
3″	1³⁄₁₆″	12x20	End	6	37″	17½″	25″
3″	1³⁄₁₆″	12x20	End	12	54½″	17½″	25″
3″	1³⁄₁₆″	12x20	End	15	63½″	17½″	25″
3″	1³⁄₁₆″	12x20	End	18	72½″	17½″	25″
1⅜″	⁹⁄₁₆″	12x20	End	7	37″	17½″	25″
1⅜″	⁹⁄₁₆″	12x20	End	13	54½″	17½″	25″
1⅜″	⁹⁄₁₆″	12x20	End	16	63½″	17½″	25″
1⅜″	⁹⁄₁₆″	12x20	End	19	72½″	17½″	25″

CABINETS FOR 12x20 PANS, SIDE LOADING, TWO PER LEDGE

ANGLE SPACING	TYPE LEDGE	PAN SIZE	TYPE LOADING	CAPACITY	HEIGHT	WIDTH	DEPTH
3″	1³⁄₁₆″	12x20	Side	12	37″	24½″	31″
3″	1³⁄₁₆″	12x20	Side	24	54½″	24½″	31″
3″	1³⁄₁₆″	12x20	Side	30	63½″	24½″	31″
3″	1³⁄₁₆″	12x20	Side	36	72½″	24½″	31″
1⅜″	⁹⁄₁₆″	12x20	Side	14	37″	24½″	31″
1⅜″	⁹⁄₁₆″	12x20	Side	26	54½″	24½″	31″
1⅜″	⁹⁄₁₆″	12x20	Side	32	63½″	24½″	31″
1⅜″	⁹⁄₁₆″	12x20	Side	38	72½″	24½″	31″

THE CONVERTIBLE HEATED OR REFRIGERATED HOLDING TRUCK

28" wide, 35½" deep, 66" high.

Facts: 750 watts for heat, 16½ cu. ft. for refrigeration, 1/4 HP compressor. Holding only, heat gain 1° per hr. for cold food; heat loss 2° per hr. for hot food.

TYPICAL HOLDING CAPACITY

Pan Size	Ledge Centers	Total Amount Pans
18" x 26"	3-1/8"	12
12" x 20" x 2½"	3-1/8"	24
20" x 24"	3-1/8"	12

TYPICAL 18" x 26" PAN CAPACITY OF OPEN TRUCKS END LOADED (Narrow)

Angle Spacing	Overall Rack Height			
	72½"	63½"	54½"	37"
1⅜"	47	40	33	19
2¼"	28	24	20	12
2½"	25	21	18	11
2¾"	23	19	16	10
3"	21	18	15	9
3¼"	19	16	14	8
3½"	18	15	13	8
3¾"	17	14	12	7
4"	16	13	11	7
4¼"	15	13	11	6
4½"	14	12	10	6
4¾"	13	11	10	6
5"	13	11	9	6
5¼"	12	10	9	6
5½"	12	10	8	5
5¾"	11	10	8	5
6"	11	9	8	5
6¼"	10	9	7	5
6½"	10	8	7	4
6¾"	10	8	7	4

MULTIPURPOSE SLANT SHELF TRUCK
(For holding, transporting or dispensing)

This tubular frame unit measures 39½" wide x 27¼" deep x 40¼" high overall. Mounted on 4 swivel casters, the unit has an under-shelf. Above the shelf and 19" above the floor level is the slant shelf storage unit. This unit is all stainless steel with coved interior corners. The storage compartment may be ordered open front or with double hinge cover. A very versatile unit, it may be used to hold and transport the following quantities of items.

300 - 9" or 10" plates
600 - 7" plates
750 - 6" plates

192 cups on 24
9" x 18" plastic cupsaver
Trays

120 cups or 216 glasses
in 10" x 20" racks

160 trays in sizes
up to 16" x 22"

126 cups in 7 dishwasher racks 20" x 20" plus
126 saucers stacked in space beside racks.

The cup and glass racks may be placed on the undershelf as they are emptied.

The unit is available with 1,000 watt heater and 6'-0" cord and plug. Plastic cup trays cannot be used in heated units.

UNDER COUNTER SLANT SHELF UNITS

These trucks are designed for transporting, holding and then dispensing plates, saucers, cups, etc. from under counters, urn stand or chef's table. The units are only 31" high. The slant shelf holding compartments are all stainless steel construction with interior corners coved. The units are of tubular frame construction with 4 swivel casters and are available single or double sided. May be open or enclosed with double hinged doors. Heating elements and cords optional.

Single sided units available either 23-5/8" or 33-5/8" wide x 15-3/8" deep.

		9" Plates	7" Plates	6" Plates	5" Plates
Typical	23-5/8" Unit	80	120	120	160
Capacities	33-5/8" Unit	120	160	200	240

Double sided units also available 23-5/8" or 33-5/8" wide x 26" deep.

Typical	23-5/8" Unit	112 cups or 240 saucers
Capacities	33-5/8" Unit	168 cups or 112 cups and 160 saucers

Used in pairs of units many combinations possible.

NOTE: The bin sizes of double or single sided units of the same length are the same size. The plate or cup capacities apply to either unit.

PAN AND TRAY TRUCKS
(Vertically held pans)

These trucks are ideal for the larger volume feeding establishments. Pans, lids or trays are held in a vertical position. Air space between the items promotes drying and improves sanitation. Ideal for storing, drying, transporting and dispensing. Available in many sizes up to a maximum of 84" high and 60" wide. Shelf spacing customized to accommodate most plastic or metal trays and steam table pans and lids. 5" neoprene tread casters provide easy mobility. Trucks available in aluminum or stainless steel. Slotted shelves hold pans and trays by the edges. Intermediate shelves are in fact two shelves back to back. The spacing between the shelf ledges is 1-3/8". The ledges are 9/16" high. Below are typical capacities for units with 21" deep shelving. 27" deep shelving is available.

Number of Tray Sections	Tray Size	Type of Loading	Capacity	TRUCK Height	TRUCK Width
2	10½x14"	Side	80	63½"	36"
2	11⅝x15½	Side	80	63½	36
2	14x18	End	40	63½	36
2	15x20	End	40	63½	36
2	18x26	Side	40	63½	36
3	10½x14	Side	120	59¾	36
3	11⅝x15½	Side	120	65¾	36
3	14x18	End	60	59¾	36
3	15x20	End	60	64¼	36
2	10½x14	Side	120	63½	48½
2	11⅝x15½	Side	120	63½	48½
2	14x18	End	60	63½	48½
2	15x20	End	60	63½	48½
2	18x26	Side	60	63½	48½
3	10½x14	Side	180	59¾	48½
3	11⅝x15½	Side	180	65¾	48½
3	14x18	End	90	59¾	48½
3	15x20	End	90	64¼	48½
2	10½x14	Side	156	63½	60½
2	11⅝x15½	Side	156	63½	60½
2	14x18	End	78	63½	60½
2	15x20	End	78	63½	60½
2	18x26	Side	78	63½	60½
3	10½x14	Side	234	59¾	60½
3	11⅝x15½	Side	234	65¾	60½
3	14x18	End	117	59¾	60½
3	15x20	End	117	64¼	60½

OTHER TRUCKS · SPECIALTY STYLES

Mobile syrup tank truck: 48" wide, 27½" deep, 52" high. Two levels hold 5 rows of 3 tanks each — total 30 tanks full size.

PAN DOLLIES

Pan dollies normally hold 144 - 18" x 26" pans per dollie.

POKER CHIP DISH DOLLIES

Average unit 27" square by 31" high built to accommodate 4 stacks of 9" to 10" plates, has available bin dividers to convert to 8 or 12 stacks. Typical capacities below:

No. of Stacks	Plate Size	Total Capacity
12	4½" to 5½"	625
8	6½" to 7"	416
4	9" to 10½"	212

237

Many configurations available. Units generally constructed with 4 stacking bins. Optional bin dividers permit dividing any or all 4 bins to hold 3 stacks of 4" or 5" dishes or 2 stacks 4" dishes and one stack of 6" to 6¾" plates. Use the chart below to help select the unit you need.

Dish Size	Capacity per Stack
4" vegetable	50
5" cereal	40
5" plate	60
6¾" plate	60
10" to 10½" plate	60

Non-adjustable units available with various size 4 stack or 8 stack dividers.

DISH ELEVATING DISPENSERS
(Typical Sizes)

Styles: mobile, drop in, open frame, enclosed, heated, unheated, adjustable by weight. Some adjust to plate size.

Normal capacities per opening: Bowls - 3 dz.; plates, saucers, cups, glasses - 6 dz. per opening. Cups and glasses on round trays.

DISH RACK ELEVATORS

Cup and glass using 19¾ x 19¾. Dish machine racks hold approximately 18 dozen pieces per opening.

OPTIONS

Many of the styles listed above may be ganged together in 2's, 3's or 4's in open frame mobile units or in cabinet style mobile units either stainless steel or in decorator finishes.

Many styles of combination cup and saucer elevator units available.

MISCELLANEOUS STYLE ELEVATORS

Bread Elevator: approximately 1½ pullman loaves per opening.
Napkin elevator: approximately 500 napkins per opening.
Egg elevator: approximatly 18 dz. eggs per opening on 12" x 12" flats.

ROLL WARMERS

One, two or three drawer units available. Each drawer has 12¼" x 20¼" x 6½" deep removable pan which will accommodate standard insets full or fractional, up to 6'' deep. Single drawer unit has suction cup feet and 3' cord set. Two and three drawer units have 6' cord set and either 4'' or 18'' legs are optional. The 3 drawer unit may be fitted with optional mobile kit, 4 - 5'' casters (2 swivel - locking), corner bumpers and a handlebar. Any unit may be ordered as built-in model.

Each draw on these units has its own individual temperature and humidity control.

SIZES AND AVERAGE CAPACITIES

No. of Drawers	Height	Width	Depth	Doz. Rolls	Watts
1	10-7/8''	29-1/4''	22''	8	450
2	21''	29-1/4''	22''	16	900
3	31-1/8''	29-1/4''	22''	24	1350

FLAT SHELF UTILITY TRUCKS
(Typical tubular construction trucks)

Features	2 Shelf Unit	3 Shelf Unit
Shelf Size	16 x 24''	16 x 24''
Between Shelves	18-3/4''	8-5/8''
Overall Height	34-1/2''	34-1/2''
Overall Length	32''	32''
Load Cap. (lbs.)	400	400
Diameter of Casters	4''	4''
Swivel Casters	4''	4''
Weight lbs.	35	41
Shelf Size	21 x 33''	21 x 33''
Between Shelves	18-3/4''	8-5/8''
Overall Height	36-1/4''	36-1/4''
Overall Length	40-1/2''	40-1/2''
Load Cap. (lbs.)	500	500
Diameter of Casters	5''	5''
Swivel Casters	4	4
Weight lbs.	48	66

TYPICAL ANGULAR FRAME UNITS AVAILABLE

No. of Shelves	3	3	3	3	3	6
Shelf Size	17¾x27''	17¾x27''	15½x24''	21x35''	21x35''	21x35''
Between Shelves	13¾''	13¾''	13¼''	13¼''	13¼''	7½''
Overall Height	33¾''	34-7/8''	32-5/8''	33¾''	34¾''	50''
Overall Length	30-7/8''	30-7/8''	27½''	27½''	39¼''	39¼''
Load Capacity (lbs.)	300	400	300	400	500	500
Bumpers*	2*	2*	2*	2*	4*	Wrap Around*
Swivel Casters	4	4	4	4	4	4

(Continued)

TYPICAL ANGULAR FRAME UNITS AVAILABLE (Cont.)

No. of Shelves	3	3	3	3	3	6
Diameter of Casters	3½"	4"	3½"	4"	5"	5"
Wt. lbs.	30	37	26	29	69	105

*Plus handle bumpers.

LOBSTER FACTS

Size Lobster	Common Name
1 lb.	Chix or Chicken
1-1/8 lb.	Eights
1-1/4 lb.	Quarters
1-1/2 lb.	1-1/2 Selects
1-3/4 lb.	Selects
3-4 lb.	Jumbos

TYPICAL DISPLAY TANKS

Length	Unit Size Width	Height	Capacity	Remarks
49"	25"	47"	75 lb. Lobsters	Wide choice of decorator finishes
80"	30"	47½"	75 lb. Lobster— 50 - 12" Trout	Water tank is divided in half. Fresh water in trout end.
57"	25"	57"	75 lb. Lobster	Water wheel type aerator.
57"	36"	57"	50 lb. Lobster— 40 Trout	Tank divided longitudinally. Waterwheel aerator each side.

FISH MARKET TANKS

Lobster tanks with extremely large capacities are available. Some may be 8 feet wide and 12 feet long and may be up to three tiers high. The compressors, aerators, pumps, filters and saline control systems are large, complicated and usually require factory installation. If interested please use F.E.F. Personal Assistance Service.

CONDIMENT DISPENSERS - ELECTRIC 115V, 3.5 Amps

8½" wide, 15¼" deep, 16½" high. Place 1 gallon container in unit, dispenser pumps mustard, ketchup or salad dressings not requiring refrigeration. Unit can be used in kitchen or on cafeteria line. 115 Volt plug-in units.

FRESH WHOLE ORANGE JUICE SQUEEZER DISPENSER - MERCHANDISER

FACTS:
- Space required: 6 sq. ft.
- Squeeze rate: 14 oranges a minute or 1 qt. minute - 60 qts. hour

240

- Hopper capacity: 48 lbs. - 1 ctn. fruit
- Reservoir capacity: 8 qts. juice
- Fruit size: up to 3½" diameter
- Yield: 7-10 qts. per ctn. fruit

Plastic bottles available for above program: 8, 16, 32, 48 or 64 oz.

HOT CHOCOLATE DISPENSER

Piped in water style: using powder chocolate base, or #10 cans of syrup, 9" wide, 26¾" deep, 21¾" high.

Typical production: 2 - 6 oz. cups per minute; 120 cups per hour; 1.5 gallon water storage. 115V plug-in unit.

Manual load style: 9" wide, 16" deep, 16" high, 3 gallon capacity, 700 watts, 115 V.

HOT WATER DISPENSERS

1) Heats to approximately 200°C, 7" wide, 10" deep, 23" high, 1/4" cold water inlet, 2 gallon capacity, 1765 watts, 115 V.
2) Also available manual fill 4 qt. capacity, cold water in, hot water available at once, 115 Volt.
3) Under counter style: Spigot only extends above counter. Thermostatically controlled heating unit mounted under counter top. 2.5 quart tank delivers up to 100 cups per hour. Water inlet 1/4" 115 or 220 Volt.

ROLL AND POTATO WARMER - COUNTER STYLE

25" wide, 18" deep, 27" high, 115 V. Chute style top load, product is removed from front.

CAPACITY

Rolls	Potatoes
10 to 12 dz. dinner	40 to 50

REFRIGERATED SALAD CRISPER AND DISPENSER

25-1/8" wide, 22½" deep, 36½" high, bin capacity 50 heads leaf or shredded lettuce, 115 V plug-in unit. Finish stainless steel or wood grain.

MILK BASE SHAKE MACHINE

16" wide, 18" deep, 25½" high, counter style, 115 Volt or 220 Volt, 450 watts. Beverage capacity 8 Gallons. Mixes, cools, circulates

241

and whips. Using dry powder or liquid mix, unit cools to 33°-35° manual load.

JUICE DISPENSER

7¾" wide, 17" deep, 26½" high, 115 Volts, plug-in unit, 300 watt. 5 gallon capacity sprays and refrigerates product, manual load.

DUAL DISPENSER

16" wide, 16" deep, 27¼" high, 115 Volts, plug-in unit, 500 watt. Twin 5 gallon capacity, 1 or 2 whippers. Product can be sprayed or circulated. Used for juice, chocolate drinks, sours, daiquiris and pina colada. Manual feed.

BEVERAGE DISPENSERS - LARGE SPRAY STYLE

Eight Gallon: 16" wide, 18" deep, 26" high, 115 Volts at 475 watts. Chills, sprays, circulates juices. Manual fill.
Fifteen Gallon: 16" wide, 18" deep, 31" high, 115 Volt at 500 watts. Typical capacity: 320 - 6 oz. drinks. Chills, sprays, circulates, juices. Manual fill.

PROFIT CHART - JUICE CONCENTRATE
(Manual Fill Dispensers)

VERY PROFITABLE!

Size of drink you serve, not including ice	Number of drinks per case of concentrate	GROSS RETURN PER CASE AT THESE SELLING PRICES			
		20¢	25¢	30¢	35¢
3 oz.	1,104	$220.80			
4 oz.	828	165.60	207.00	248.40	289.80
5 oz.	662	132.40	165.50	198.70	231.70
6 oz.	555	110.40	138.00	165.60	193.20
7 oz.	472	94.40	118.00	141.70	165.20
8 oz.	414	82.80	103.50	124.20	144.90

Deduct cost of one case of concentrate to determine approximate profit (not including labor and cost of ice).

BUN AND CHIP DISPLAY AND WARMER UNITS

Either 12" or 15" wide, 33" deep, 43" high, 1200 watts, 115 Volt. Volume of food: 3.4 or 4.4 cu. ft.

This unit is designed to hold warm rolls, buns, popcorn, taco chips, bread sticks and other Happy Hour Snacks. Different style front chutes available. Chips or buns fall to front, operator lifts up door and slides food into basket or serving dish.

REFRIGERATED MIXER/DISPENSER
(For Frozen Desserts)

Countertop unit 20" wide, 33" deep, 63" high, compressor 1½ HP, beater ¾ HP, rated at 2-5¢ per 4 oz. serving cost.

Typical frozen desserts: Unit will blend, mix, chill or freeze.

SAMPLES

- Pumpkin Mousse
- Prune Whip
- Iced Coffee Souffle
- Mocha Delight
- Banana Creme
- Orange Frost
- Apricot Whip
- Hawaiian Sherbet

SOFT ICE CREAM MACHINES

Soft ice cream machines are available single flavor, two flavor or twist style, combining two flavors. The versatility of these machines include making and dispensing sherbets, ices, and yogurts. Also available are dual or combination units that will dispense soft ice cream and soft shakes. Design features and production vary. Check carefully your power requirements and ease of cleaning. Counter models available from some manufacturers.

The authors have found the best way to become educated in this area of fun foods is to visit on site a recent installation with your supplier.

SOFT ICE CREAM AND SHAKE MACHINES

SOFT ICE CREAM MACHINE SINGLE HEAD
20" wide, 28"-32" deep, 57" high. Motor HP: beater 1½, condenser 1 to 2 HP. Mix tank capacity 30 qts.

SOFT ICE CREAM MACHINE DOUBLE HEAD
32" wide, 36" deep, 57" high. Motor HP: beater 2-1½ HP, condenser (2) 1 to 2 HP. Mix tank capacity 30 qts. each side.

SOFT ICE CREAM MACHINE AND SHAKE COMBINATION

32" wide, 32" deep, 57" high. Motor HP: beater (2) 1½ HP, condenser (2) 1 to 2 HP. Mix tank capacity 30 qts. Shake machine capacities from 350 to 600 per hour.

SHAKE MACHINES · PER HOUR PRODUCTION
(Selected Sizes)

SPECIFICATIONS

Motor H.P.		Shakes Per Hour	Mix Tank Capacity	Dimensions		
Beater	#Condenser			W	D	H
3/4	1	360	30 qt.	32"	24"	33"
3/4	1	360	30 qt.	32"	16"	33"
3/4	1	360	30 qt.	32"	24"	57"
1-1/2	2	600	30 qt.	38"	24"	57"
3/4	1	360	30 qt.	32"	16"	57"
1-1/2	2	600	30 qt.	38"	16"	57"

BULK MILK DISPENSERS · TYPICAL

18" deep, 40" high, lengths - 14-1/8" - one container
25-1/8" - two containers
36-1/8" - three containers

These units hold 3 or 5 gallon dispenser cans or 3, 5 or 6 single service bags or box containers.

Options: drip trays, shelves, stands, malt mixer attachment on door, turntables, refrigerated bases, display case fronts, push or lift dispensing valves.

INSTANT MASHED POTATO DISPENSER

9" wide, 20" deep, 22" high, 115 or 220 V at 1,720 watts.
Potato sizes: 3 to 6 oz. single serving or 16 oz. family size portion.
Number - 3.5 oz. servings = 4 per minute
Number - 16 oz. Servings = 1¼ minutes each
Peak rates: 6 servings a minute for 7 minutes of 3.2 oz. portions.
Sizes and capacities vary by manufacturer.

INSTANT ICE TEA DISPENSER

9" wide, 18½" deep, 20¼" high. Use hot or cold ¼" incoming water line, continuous flow valve, 115 Volts at 1400 watts.

FREEZE DRIED COFFEE MACHINE

9" wide, 26¼" deep, 21¾" high, ¼" incoming water, 220 V at 3100 watts. Dispenses cups from 4½ to 8 oz. or pots 40 to 75 oz. 4 cups per minute - peak rate 6 cups per minute for 8 minutes.

WATER COOLERS

Water coolers are generally rated on gallon production per hour based on ambient temperature of 90° with water temperature drop from 80° to 50°.

Many styles and capacities available. Some available with instant hot water faucet for instant tea or coffee, etc. They are also built to hold and cool bottled spring water.

Average water coolers are rated at 5, 10 or 14 gallons per hour. Larger units available.

To estimate your requirements figure 10 oz. per person. One gallon is 128 oz. x 5 gal. rating = 640 oz. or 64 persons per hour accommodated. 10 gal. rating would serve 128 - 14 gal. rating would serve 179 persons.

SELECTION GUIDE FOR WATER COOLERS

Cooler Rating Gallons Per Hour	Approx. No. of Persons Served
4	48
6	72
8	96
10	120
12	144
20	240
22	260

BEVERAGE SYSTEMS

POST-MIX BEVERAGE SYSTEM:

The Post Mix System combines syrup with city water to make a soft drink beverage. The water is first purified by filtering, then carbonated, chilled either by a mechanical cooler or an ice cooled cold plate. The carbonated, chilled water is mixed with the syrup in the dispensing unit. The syrup is propelled through the lines by the pressure of the carbon dioxide gas from the tank which also supplies the carbonater. Pressure regulating valves carefully control all pressures to the dispensing head. The syrup lines are chilled in the same manner as the carbonated water. The dispensing head mixes the water and syrup in the proper proportions. The regulated pressure permits fast flow without foaming. The dispensing valves are adjustable.

PRE-MIX BEVERAGE SYSTEMS:

These are exactly what the name implies. In place of syrup, the tanks contain pre-mixed carbonated beverages. The dispensing and cooling system remains essentially the same. The only items to be eliminated are the mixing type dispensing valves. Carbonated water is nearly always required and the CO_2 tank is required to propel the soda through the lines. Pre-mix systems are less critical since the beverage is already mixed in the exact proportions.

All beverage systems have many options. Small complete units averaging only three feet in width are available for cafeteria counter, soda fountain or similar installation. Small carbonation and cooling units may be installed under counters or bars with dispensing towers above. So called "soda factories" which house all of the mechanical components required to deliver the product to the dispensing valves are available in various sizes. These units, properly sized, may deliver soda to various, interconnected dispensing stations. Heavily insulated multiple product delivery lines called "trunk pythons" are available with quick-disconnect couplings.

Many soda companies will install complete systems for their customers to promote the sales of their products. These will quite naturally be systems which dispense their pre-mixed soda.

Companies that sell beverage dispensing systems generally carry post-mix systems. Beer lines may be incorporated into the dispensing units. Variations are almost unlimited. The pros and cons relating to possible increased profits from post-mix opposed to pre-mixed systems should be investigated and considered. Ask the supplier to show you a system in use and talk with the operator.

BEVERAGE SYSTEM COMPONENTS

Below are listed some of the many available components of beverage systems. Starting with the dispensing valves and working back through the systems. First, all style valves are available for either pre-mix.

INDIVIDUAL VALVES — Push-back style, with product labels available electric or manual operation and with quick disconnect mount.

HAND HELD VALVES — Grouped valves with product hose for bar or other high traffic areas. Push button selection available with up to 7 product lines. Electric or hydraulic action. Electric units may have illuminated push buttons.

VALVE STANDS — Many styles available - single or multiple valve towers - mounting plates for under or over bar, expandable to 7 valves. Single tower unit with multiple product push-button valves and many others.

COOLING UNITS — Plates for ice cooling average 10" x 15" for 1, 2, 3 or 4 product lines and 17" x 19" for 2, 3, 4, 5 or 6 product lines. Others available.

REFRIGERATED COOLING UNITS — Often the cooling unit is an integral part of the dispensing unit in counter top models. These are usually display style models with 4 or 5 product valves. Typical capacity 1/4 HP - 271 drinks per hr.; 1/3 HP - 675 drinks per hr.. Recovery 2 to 3 drinks per minute.

REMOTE COOLING UNITS — These must be properly sized according to the number of products to be accommodated. The number of dispensing stations to be served. The distance between the cooler and the farthest dispensing station and the total volume of soda to be dispensed. Some typical sizes are shown below. Capacties based on 75⁰ ambient, water and soda temperatures using 6 oz. drinks as basis.

Compressor	Drinks Per Hr.	Plus Soda Water
1/4 HP	120	1½ Gallons
1/2 HP	240	3 Gallons
1 HP	360	3 Gallons
2½ HP	900	6 Gallons

(Typical only - many others available)

CARBONATOR: Typical unit 1/4 HP approx. 6½" x 17" x 13" high. Capacity 100 gallons per hour.

SYRUP TANKS: Typical - 5 Gal. (640 oz.) tank 8½" dia. x 25" high. 3 Gal. (384 oz.) tank 8½" dia. x 16¾" high.

CO_2 CYLINDERS: 20 lb. capacity, 8¼" dia. x 26" high w/valve. 50 lb. capacity, 9" dia. x 54¼" high w/valve.

WATER FILTER CYLINDERS: 4" dia. x 15" high, 60 GPH flow rate. 22½" high unit has 100 GPH flow rate. Units may be duplexed. Units remove musty tastes and odors and chlorine residuals particles to 1/25,000.

HIGH PRODUCTION CUP FILLER

A 6'-0" or a 10'-0" semi-automatic soda cup filler is available for high volume installations such as stadiums. The units have semi-automatic icers which at the pull of a lever drops from 1 oz. to 6 oz. ice into 24 cups at one time. The tray of cups is then moved under dispensing heads with foot-pedal control to fill 4 or 8 cups simultaneously. The units are available with carbonators for use with postmix. Standard are 8'-0" product lines and CO_2 lines. The units employ 17" x 19" cold plates for cooling. A 3'-0" ice storage bin is optional. Automatic cup drop and cappers are available from cup suppliers.

6'-0" units have 1-4 valve tower, 2 carbonators for post-mix and 3 cold plates.

10'-0" units have 2-4 valve towers, 4 carbonators and 5 cold plates. The units require 115 V power, water and drains.

Chapter Eight

KITCHEN TOOLS
AND
DINING
SUPPLIES

Listed in this chapter are nearly all of the common kitchen, serving and dining area tools and supplies rated by capacities and/or dimensions. If you are unable to find what you are looking for, please refer to the index. It may be in another chapter.

This chapter is an excellent guide for those who wish to become more familiar with the many sizes of various tools which are available. Steam table pans, bun pans, trays, etc. are listed by dimension and capacities.

The chapter provides a simplified check list for anyone equipping a new kitchen or seeking to replace smaller items.

Should you find an item with which you are unfamiliar use F.E.F. Personal Assistance Service.

GUIDE FOR UTENSIL SELECTION
IN KITCHEN TO FEED 100 PEOPLE

Bake Shop

Items	Quan.
Egg Beater	1
Measuring Spoons	1 set
Oven/Freezer Mit	2 pr.
Pastry Brushes, flat & round	4
Rolling Pin	1
Whip, Piano 10", 12", 16", 18"	4
Whip, French 14"	1
Cake Covers/Stands	2
Display Cases	1
Pie Markers	1
Bread Pans	12
Cake/Sheet Pans, assorted sizes	6-12
Jello Molds, individual or large	36/3
Muffin Tins, 24 cup	6
Pie Tins	12
Dredges	2
Funnels, several sizes	3
Measures 1, 2, 4 qt	3

Scoops 24, 32, 48 oz	3
Pastry Bags	6
Pastry Tips	6
Bakers Scraper	2
Food Storage Boxes	6
Ingredient Bins	3
Utility/Dish Pans	2
Mixing Bowls, assorted sizes	12
Scale, portion control	1
Scale, bakery	1

Utensils

Storage Containers	12 ea.
Insulated coffee tank, 3.5 gal.	1
Multipurpose rubber matting (26" x 50')	1 roll
Safe-t-mats	3-6 ea.
Ice Cream Scoops various sizes	6
Juice Dispenser	1-2
Juice Extractor	1

(Continued)

GUIDE FOR UTENSIL SELECTION
IN KITCHEN TO FEED 100 PEOPLE (Cont.)

Coffee Making
  Equipment.................. 1-2
Coffee Decanters........... 6-12
Silver Compartment
  Storage Boxes................ 3
Sauce Pans 1½, 2¾
  3¾, 5½, 7, 10 qts.............. 6
Sauce Pots 14, 26 qts........... 2
Stock Pots 3, 6,
  10 gal. or larger.............. 3
Double Boilers 8, 12 qts........ 2
Bake Pans
  various sizes................. 6
Roast Pans
  various sizes................. 2
China Caps 9''................. 1
Colander...................... 1
Strainer 6'', 8'', 10'', 12''......... 4
Hot Food Service
  Pan 200 series -
  full, 1/2, 1/3, 1/4, 1/6.......... 24
Covers for Pans assorted...... 12
Skimmers 4½'', 6''............ 2
Fry Pans 8'', 10'', 12'', 14''....... 6
Butter Spreaders............... 1
Egg Poacher................... 1
Steak Weight.................. 1
Thermometers:
  Deep Fat.................... 1
  Oven........................ 1
  Pocket...................... 1
  Roast....................... 1
Basting Spoon, (solid,
  perforated, slotted)........... 6
Ladles, 1-24 oz. assorted....... 6
Paddles 30-48''................ 1
Tongs 6, 9, 12''................ 6
Turner........................ 2
Can Opener, #1 or #2.......... 1
Cheese Cutter................. 1
Egg Slicer..................... 2
Food Mill..................... 1
Tomato Tamer................. 1
Baker's Scrapers.............. 1

Boning Knives................. 2
Cleaver....................... 1
Paring Knives................. 6
Pot Forks..................... 2
Slicers, assorted sizes........ 4-6
Spatulas...................... 2
Box Grater.................... 1
Broiler Scraper................ 1
Carton Opener................ 1
Lobster Crackers.............. 24
Parers & Corers............... 6
Poultry Shears................ 6
Clam/Oyster Knives........... 3
Sharpening Stones............ 1
Storage Containers
  2-22 qts................. 10-12
Chopping Bowls............... 1
Cutting Boards................ 2
Dish Cloths................... 24
Towels, linen................. 36
S/S Pails.................... 1-2
Liquid Grill Cleaner............ 1 gal.
S/S cleaner................... 1 case
Aluminum Foil
  (several sizes)............... 3 units
Grill Bricks.................. 12
Neoprene Gloves.............. 6 pr.
Plastic Aprons................ 6
Plastic Bags for garbage....... 1 unit
Scouring Pads/Sponges....... 12
Floor Squeegee................ 1
Mops/heads................... 6
Brooms....................... 2
Mop Wringer/Pail.............. 1
Pick-up Brush/Pan............. 1
Vacuum Cleaner............... 1
Storage Container,
  flour, sugar, etc.............. 3
Waste Receptacles
  (various sizes)............. 6-12
Glass Washing Brush.......... 1
Oven Brush/Scraper........... 2
Urn Brush.................... 1

250

STANDARD 18" x 26" PAN CAPACITIES

Item	Portions Per Pan
Juice Glasses, 5 oz.	84
Water Glasses, 10 oz.	40
Plates, 7-3/8"	8
Salad Bowl, 5½"-6"	11
Creamers - Individual	126
Paper Creamers	135
Milk Containers ½ pt., 2-7/8" square	40
Bowls, 5"	15
Sherbet Dishes	40

TYPICAL TRAY CAPACITIES

	14" x 18"	12" x 20"	10" x 16"
Juice Glasses	35	35	28
Water Glasses	20	20	12
Plates, 7-3/8"	4	3	2
Bowls, 5"	5	5	2
Creamers, 1 oz.	48	45	32

THERMAL CONDUCTIVITY OF FOOD SERVICE EQUIPMENT METALS

Material	Shown as % of 1.000
Copper	.941
Alum. Sheet	.460
Alum. Cast	.320
Carbon Steel	.124
Cast Iron	.112
Stainless Steel	.0036

ALUMINUM UTENSILS

STANDARD SIZE BAKE PANS

	8 Oz. Servings
9-3/4" x 13-3/4" x 2-1/4"	17
10-7/8" x 16" x 2-1/4"	21
11-7/8" x 17-3/4" x 2-1/4"	32
12-1/2" x 18-1/2" x 2"	27
13-1/2" x 22-7/8" x 2"	40
12-5/8" x 23" x 2-1/4"	48
14" x 24" x 3-1/2"	54
10-7/8" x 19-3/4" x 2-1/4"	3 Quarts
10-7/8" x 19-3/4" x 3-1/2"	7 Quarts

Bun Pans

17-3/4" x 25-3/4" x 1"	Full Size
17-3/4" x 12-7/8" x 1"	1/2 Size
17-3/4" x 25-3/4" x 2-1/4"	Deep

CUP CAKE OR MUFFIN PAN SIZES

12 Cup	10-3/4'' x 14-1/8'' x 1-3/8'' Deep
24 Cup	20-3/4'' x 14-1/8'' x 1-3/8'' Deep

BRAZIERS

Top Diam.	Depth	Qts.	8 Oz. Servings
14''	5-5/8''	15	49
16''	5-3/8''	18	59
18''	5-1/2''	24	78
20''	5-1/4''	28	94

ROUND LAYER CAKE PANS

Depths: 1'', 1½'', 2'', 3''.
Diameters: 5'', 6'', 7'', 8'', 9'', 10'', 11'' 12'', 13'', 14'', 15'', 16'', 17'', 18'', 20'', 22''. Any depth x any diameter.

SPRING CAKE FORMS
(With or without tubes)

7'' x 3''	10'' x 3''
8'' x 3''	12'' x 3''
9'' x 3''	

COLLANDERS

Quarts	Top Diameter	Quarts	Top Diameter
9	12-7/8''	16	16-1/2''
11	15-1/4''	18	16-1/2''
13	15-1/4''	24	16-1/2''

CHINESE PERFORATED PANS

COLLANDERS

Top Diameter	Depth	Top Diameter	Depth
11-1/2''	4-3/4''	11-1/2''	4-3/4''
12-1/2''	5''	12-1/2''	5''
15-1/4''	5-1/2''	15-1/2''	5-1/2''
16;1/2''	6''	16-1/2''	6''

UTILITY COLLANDERS · CHINESE PERFORATED

Diameter	Depth
8-1/4''	3-1/4''
9-3/8''	3-1/2''
10''	4''

FOOD CONTAINERS · CHINESE PERFORATED

Diameter	Depth
13-1/2''	9-1/4''
14''	11-1/4''
15-1/2''	13-1/4''
17-1/4''	14-1/4''
20-1/2''	17''

CHINA CAPS

Top Diam.	Quarts
7-7/8''	2-3/4
9''	4-1/2
10''	5-1/2

DISH PANS · SIDE HANDLES

Quarts	Top Diameter	Depth
21	17-7/8''	6-1/2''
27	19-5/8''	6-7/8''
40	21-1/2''	7''

DOUBLE BOILERS · FLAT BOTTOM

INSIDE PAN			OUTSIDE PAN		
Diam.	Deep	Quarts	Diam.	Deep	Quarts
9''	8''	8-1/2''	9''	8-5/8''	9''
9-3/4''	9-1/8''	11''	10''	9''	12''
11-7/8''	9-3/4''	17-1/2''	12''	10-1/2''	20''

FRY PANS

Top Diameter	Depth
7''	1-1/2''
8''	1-7/8''
10''	2''
12''	2-1/4''
14''	2-1/2''

ALUMINUM ITEMS CONTINUED

PIE PANS

Outside Top Diam.	Depth of Slant	Outside Top Diam.	Depth of Slant
8''	1-1/16''	11''	1-1/2''
8''	1-5/8''	11-3/4''	1-1/2''
9''	1-1/2''	12''	1-1/2''
10''	1-1/8''	13''	1-3/4''
10-1/2''	1-5/8''	16''	2''
10-3/4''	1-1/2''		

STANDARD PIE MARKERS AND CUTTERS

Available 6, 7, 8, 9, 10, 12 marks or cuts to the pie.
Pie marker diameters: 9" or 10".
Pie knives 10-1/2" overall, blade sizes 2-1/4" x 4-1/2" or 2-1/2" x 5".

TYPICAL ROAST PAN SIZES

Sizes	Quarts
10-7/8" x 19-3/4" x 3-1/2"	7
11-1/8" x 20" x 6-1/2"	15
19-3/4" x 21-3/4" x 3-1/2"	15
20-1/8" x 22-1/8" x 6-1/2"	32

	8 Oz. Servings
16" x 20" x 4-1/2"	80
18" x 24" x 4-1/2"	112
17-3/8" x 20-7/8" x 7"	172

Full Size Roast Pans
17-3/4" x 25-3/4" x 2-1/4"
17-3/4" x 25-3/4" x 3-1/2"

FRY PANS

Standard top diameters: 7", 8", 10", 12", 14", 16".

SAUCE PANS (Singlehandle)

Top Diam.	Depth	Quarts	8 Oz. Servings
6"	5-1/4"	1-1/2	5
7-3/4"	6-1/2"	2-3/4	9
8-3/4"	7-1/8"	3-3/4	12
9-1/8"	7-1/2"	4-1/2	14
9-7/8"	7-5/8"	5-1/2	17
10-5/8"	8-5/8"	7	22
11-1/4"	9-3/4"	8-1/2	27
11-3/4"	10-1/4"	10	35

SAUCE POTS (Dual Handles)

Top Diam.	Depth	Quarts	8 Oz. Servings
8-3/4"	6"	6	20
10"	6-3/8"	8-1/2	28
11"	7-1/2"	12	41
12"	7-1/2"	14	48
13"	8-7/8"	20	71
14"	9-7/8"	26	94
16"	10"	34	122
18"	10"	44	158
20"	11"	60	210

STOCK POTS

Top Diam.	Depth	Quarts	8 Oz. Servings
9"	8-5/8"	9	30
10"	9"	12	43
10"	11"	15	55
11"	12-1/4"	20	72
12"	13"	25	92
13"	14-3/8"	32	118
14"	15-1/4"	40	150
16"	17-1/2"	60	210
18"	18-1/4"	80	268
20"	18-1/2"	100	335

SAUTE PANS

Top Diam.	Depth	Quarts
6"	2-1/8"	1
8"	2-3/8"	2
10"	2-3/8"	3
12"	2-5/8"	5
14"	2-7/8"	7½

ALUMINUM UTILITY PANS

Qt. Capacity	Top Diam.	Depth
1½	8½"	2½"
2	9¼"	2¾"
3	11"	3½"
4	11½"	3¾"
5	12½"	4"
6	13"	4¼"
10	15"	5"

ALUMINUM SCOOPS (Hand)

Bowl Sizes	Capacity
4-3/4" x 2-3/8"	5 oz.
6-1/4" x 3-1/8"	12 oz.
8" x 4"	24 oz.
9" x 4-3/4"	38 oz.
10-1/2" x 5-1/2"	57 oz.
12" x 6-1/4"	84 oz.

ALUMINUM FOILS

Gauge	Width	Ft. Per Roll	Weight Per Roll
.0007	12"	1000	10 lb.
.0010	18"	500	10 lb.
.0010	18"	1000	22 lb.
.0007	18"	1000	15¼ lb.
.0015	18"	500	16½ lb.
.0015	18"	1500	47¼ lb.
.0001	24"	1000	29 lb.
.0007	15"	1000	13 lb.

BLUE STEEL PANS

BAKE SHEETS - 1" deep

12" x 18"	16" x 22"	19" x 26"	18" x 22"
14" x 18"	16" x 24"	20" x 22"	18" x 24"
14" x 20"	18" x 20"	20" x 24"	18" x 26"
16" x 20"			

ROAST PANS - 3½" deep

11" x 17"	14" x 20"	16" x 24"	19" x 26"
12" x 15"	15" x 18"	17" x 26"	20" x 20"
12" x 17"	15" x 20"	18" x 18"	20" x 22"
12" x 18"	15" x 22"	18" x 20"	20" x 24"
13" x 19"	16" x 16"	18" x 22"	21" x 26"
13" x 22"	16" x 18"	18" x 24"	22" x 22"
14" x 14"	16" x 20"	18" x 26"	22" x 24"
14" x 16"	16" x 22"	19" x 22"	24" x 24"
14" x 18"			

BREAD PANS

TOP DIMENSIONS SIZES

8" x 4"	10" x 4¾"
8½" x 4½"	10" x 5"
9" x 4½"	10½" x 4½"
9-7/8" x 4¼"	12¼" x 4½"
10" x 4-3/8"	12¼" x 4¾"

All available 4", 4½" or 5" deep.

BUN AND ROLL PANS

12" x 18"	8" x 16"
14" x 20"	8" x 18"
14" x 22"	8" x 20"
16" x 24"	10" x 20"
8" x 12"	9" x 26"
8" x 14"	

All 1" deep.

STEEL RANGE TOP DEEP FRYERS

Quarts	Top Diam.
4	9"
5	10"
8	12"
14	14"
24	16"

CAST IRON PRODUCTS

FISH PAN - 12" x 20" x 3" deep.

DUTCH OVENS

Capacity	Top Diam.	Depth
5 Qts.	10"	3-7/8"
6 Qts.	11"	4-1/4"
9 Qts.	12-7/8"	4-3/4"

CHICKEN FRYER

Top Diameter 10" — Depth 3" with cast strainer

BREAD STICK PANS

Capacity	Size
6 Sticks	7¼" x 7¼"
11 Sticks	13¼" x 7¼"
22 Half Size Sticks	13¼" x 7¼"

ROUND GRIDDLES - 9¼" or 11" Diameter

RECTANGULAR GRIDDLES

17" x 9-3/8"
20-3/4" x 9-1/8"
24-7/8" x 13-7/8"

SQUARE SKILLETS

9-1/2" x 9-1/2"
11-1/4" x 11-1/4"

ROUND SKILLETS

Standard top diameters: 6-1/2", 7", 8", 9-1/8", 9-7/8", 10-1/2", 11-3/8", 11-3/4", 13-3/8", 15-1/2" and 20". The 20" diameter skillet has 2 side handles, the rest only one.

STAINLESS STEEL ITEMS

The following charts describe by dimension and capacities a number of stainless steel pans which are often described as steam table pans, especially those adaptable to standard 12" x 20" openings. These pans are more appropriately called multi-purpose pans. They have many uses in either hot or cold units as well as in holding and transporting foods. The variances in dimensions and capacities by manufacturer is negligible.

STANDARD 12" x 20" MODEL PAN SIZES
(Overall of Flanges)

Full Size..................................12-3/4" x 20-3/4"
Half Size (short).........................12-3/4" x 10-3/8"
Half Size (long)..........................20-3/4" x 6-3/8"
Two Thirds Size.........................13-3/4" x 12-3/4"
Third Size................................12-3/4" x 6-7/8"
Quarter Size.............................10-3/8" x 6-3/8"
Sixth Size.................................6-7/8" x 6-1/4"
Ninth Size.................................6-3/4" x 4-1/4"

HELPFUL HINTS

When two half size pans are required in one 12" x 20" opening of a serving unit, using the long pans reduces spillage of one item into the other while ladeling the foods to a plate.

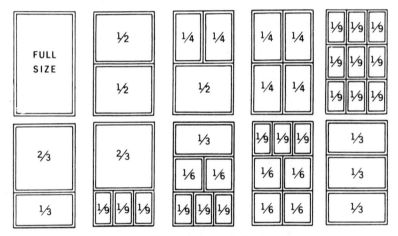

1/2 long pan not shown.

COMMON MULTI-PURPOSE PAN CAPACITIES

FULL SIZE

Depth	Quarts	4 Oz. Portions
2½"	9	72
4"	15	120
6"	22	176
8"	31½	252

HALF SIZE

2½"	4	32
4"	7	56
6"	10	80
8"	15	120

QUARTER SIZE

2½"	1-5/8	13
4"	3	24
6"	4¾	38

TWO THIRDS SIZE

Depth	Quarts	4 Oz. Portions
2½"	6	48
4"	10	80
6"	14¼	114

THIRD SIZE

2½"	2-5/8	21
4"	4½	36
6"	6½	52

(Continued)

258

COMMON MULTI-PURPOSE PAN CAPACITIES (Cont.)

SIXTH SIZE

Depth	Quarts	4 Oz. Portions
2½"	1¼	10
4"	2	16
6"	3	24

NINTH SIZE

2½"	5/8	N.A.
4"	1¼	N.A.

For steam cooking, steam heating or holding of rolls or vegetables in hot food units many of the above pans are available with perforated bottoms and sides. Perforated false bottoms are also available. For use in microwave ovens, serving, holding and freezing Lexan pans are manufactured in all sizes.

ROUND MULTI-PURPOSE POTS
(Shouldered)

Using adapter plates for standard 12" x 20" openings, these pots fit into the round holes. The shoulders prevent the pots from extending too deeply into the well. The depth of the pots under the shoulder is 6". The adapter plates are available with various hole sizes and arrangements.

Fits Opening	Overall Depth	Qt. Capacity
5"	7-7/8"	2-3/8
6-1/2"	8-1/4"	4-1/8
8-1/2"	8-1/4"	7-1/8
10-1/2"	8-1/4"	11

ROUND BAIN MARIE POTS

Similar to those listed above but with straight sides. Available in the following sizes.

Body Diam.	Depth	Qt. Capacity
4-1/8"	5-3/4"	1-1/4
4-7/8"	6-3/4"	2
6-1/8"	7-1/4"	3-1/2
6-1/2"	7-5/8"	4-1/4
7-1/4"	8-5/8"	6
8"	9-3/4"	8-1/4
9"	10-3/8"	12

COVERS FOR MULTI-PURPOSE PANS

Flat, recessed handle covers, with or without ladle handle slots are available for all round pots.

Covers for the 12" x 20" pans are available — flat recessed for stacking, flat with ladle slots and recessed handle, flat solid with recessed handle, flat hinged, hinged dome, solid dome or Lucite high curved dome.

The hinged and dome covers are usually made for only the full and half size pans. All other covers are usually available for all sizes of pans.

PLEXIGLAS DOME COVERS

Available 12" x 20" x 4, 12" x 20" x 4 and 18" x 26" x 4 with handles.

ROUND DOMED DISPLAY COVERS
(For Cakes, Dougnuts, etc.)

6" x 3" high	14" x 5" high
8" x 3½" high	16" x 5" high
10" x 4" high	18" x 6" high
12" x 5" high	21" x 6" high

PUNCH BOWLS

Available in plastic or glass, assorted sizes. Average sizes 1½, 3, 4, or 5 gallon capacity.

WIRE WARE

COMPARTMENT SILVER BASKETS

Compartments	Size	Plus Handles
8	6" x 13½" x 5½" high	6½"
8	6" x 13" x 5½" high	6½"
12	9½" x 13" x 5½" high	3"
16	12½" x 13" x 5½" high	3"

UTILITY BASKETS

10" x 14" x 3"	16" x 22" x 5"
12" x 16" x 3"	16" x 26" x 5"
12" x 20" x 3½"	18" x 24" x 5"
14" x 20" x 4"	

WIRE MESH SKIMMERS

Bowl Diameter	Length
5"	18"
6"	18"
7"	20"
8"	22"
9"	24"
10"	26"

WIRE IMMERSION BASKETS
(For Silver Soaking)

9" x 10"	12" x 14"	12" x 16"
10" x 12"	10" x 14"	14" x 16"
12" x 12"	14" x 14"	16" x 16"

All 8" Deep.

WIRE SKEWERS · ROUND OR OVAL WIRE
(Thickness 1/8" or 1/16")

Common lengths: 7½", 8½", 10½", 12½", 15½", 16¾", 22".

MENU AND CARD HOLDERS

Standard heights: 1½", 2", 3", 3½", 4½", 6", 10" or 12".

EGG OR VEGETABLE BASKETS · BAIL HANDLE

Diameter	Height
6"	5½"
8"	6½"
10"	7½"
12"	9"

CAKE COOLER OR STOCK POT BOTTOMS

6", 7", 8", 9", 10", 12" or 14" diameter.

DOUGHNUT BASKETS

10" x 14" x 2", 12" x 18" x 2", 14" x 18" x 2", 16" x 26" x 2", or
18" x 26" x 2".

MESH ICING GRATE - 1½" LEGS

9" x 14"	16" x 22"
11" x 17"	16" x 24"
12" x 18"	16½" x 26"
13" x 16½"	18" x 25"
14" x 20"	18" x 16"

GLASS DRAINERS - 2" SIDES

12½" x 16¼"	10" x 24"
11¾" x 15"	12" x 24"
14" x 19"	12" x 30"
15" x 21"	12" x 36"

All 2" Deep.

WIRE WELDED BROILERS - HAND HELD
(Lobster - Chicken)

Rib Length	Width	Overall Length
8"	10"	16"
10"	12"	20"
12"	14"	24"
14"	16"	28"
16"	18"	32"
18"	20"	36"

COMMON SIZE STRAINERS

Wood Handle Length	Bowl Diameter
5½"	4"
6"	6¼"
6½"	8"
9"	10"
10"	12"

WOODEN WARE

COMMON WOOD CUTTING BOARDS - 1¾" Thick

12" x 18"	16" x 22"
12" x 24"	18" x 24"
15" x 20"	18" x 30"
18" x 20"	

COMMON WOOD ROLLING PINS - Overall 23" to 29" - plus handles.

12" x 3½"	13" x 3"
14" x 3½"	15" x 3"
16" x 3½"	18" x 3"
18" x 3½"	

COMMON PASTRY BOARDS - ¾" THICK

12" x 16"	18" x 30"
14" x 20"	20" x 28"
16" x 22"	23" x 31"
18" x 24"	

WOOD ITEMS

CHOPPING BOWLS
   Common top diameters: 9", 11", 13", 16", 18", 20".

MAPLE SERVING BOWLS
   Common top diameters: 8", 9", 10", 11", 12", 13", 14", 16", 18" or 20".

MIXING SPOONS
   Common lengths: 9", 10", 12", 14", 16", 18" or 20".

PADDLES
   Common lengths: 18", 20", 24", 30", 36", 42", 48", 54" or 60". Blade size: 3" x 6" or 3" x 7".

WOOD FRAMED SIEVES (S/S/ Wire Mesh)
   Diameters: 10", 12", 14", 16" or 18".

CLOTH ITEMS

OVEN MITTS
   Common sizes: 13", 15", 17".

POT HOLDERS
   Common sizes: 7" square, 8" square.

DISH TOWELS
   Common sizes: 14" x 26" and 20" x 30".

DISH CLOTHS - BAR CLOTHS
   Common sizes: 13" x 13", 18" x 18" and 19" x 18".

TERRY CLOTH TOWELS

- 12" x 12" Wash Cloths
- 16" x 26" Hand Towels
- 18" x 36" Hand/Face Towels
- 20" x 40" Bath Towels
- 22" x 44" or 22" x 48" King Size Bath Towel

MISCELLANEOUS ITEMS

APRONS - TYPICAL SIZES
- Half Aprons, 24" long
- Waist Aprons, 34" wide x 36" long
- Men's Bib Apron, 34" wide x 40" long
- Women's Bib Apron, 34" wide x 36" long
- Bib Apron general use, 28" x 45" long

EGG WEDGER: Cuts 6 equal sections

CABBAGE SLAW CUTTERS - Hand operated
- 1 Knife, 6" x 16" bed, wood
- 2 Knives, 9" x 25" bed, wood
- 3 Knives, 9" x 25" bed, wood

GRATERS: Stainless steel - hand operated
Standard heights: 6", 7", 8", 9" or 10".

CONTINUOUS FEED JUICERS

For extracting juice from carrots, celery, cabbage, ginger root, etc. Product is fed into top of unit, pulp is discharged from chute at one side, juice flows from lower spout on other side. Pitchers available with units.

Approx. production: Carrot or celery - 1 qt. per minute
Cabbage juice - 1/2 qt. per minute
Available models: 3/4, 1 or 1-1/2 HP - 115 or 230 Volts.

ELECTRIC CITRUS JUICER

Round, cone style, spout empties into glass, counter model. Cord and plug counter top model, 115 V, ¼ Hp.

CITRUS SECTIONIZER

Commercial style. Jars or bowls may be placed under knives to catch sections. Hand operated. Interchangeable blades permit cutting of 4, 6 or 8 wedges or 6 slices 5/16" thick. Unit is dishwasher safe. Lever handle action. Measures 15½" high x 15¼" wide x 13-1/8" deep.

WHIPPED CREAM MACHINE

Produces 40 gals. per hr. Yields 2½ to 1 for cream, 4 to 1 for topping, 18" wide x 17" deep x 13½" high.

TABLE TOP WHIPPED CREAM DISPENSER

Totally portable and only 8" square the unit will maintain super dense whipped cream dispensing capability for full day with only one 32° icing. Unit operates on new interlock or air energy system. Units can dispense flavored whipped cream, whipped mousse, whipped yogurt and sour cream or other specialties.

Many sizes, hose connections and propellent tanks available.

264

TENDERIZERS (Hand Held)

Head sizes cast aluminum: 2" x 2-3/8" x 2-3/8", 3" x 3" x 3½".

BELLS

CALL BELLS
Common diameters: 2¼", 2½", 2¾", 3", 3¼" or 4-3/8".

BELLS - Brass Hand Style
Common diameters: 2-5/8", 3-3/8", 4", 5" or 6".

BOX HOLDER
(Fast Food, Clam Shell Box Holder)

3 compartments for 5" boxes. Size of dispenser: 15¾" x 9½" x 9½" high.

BAG HOLDER - FRENCH FRIES

Typically holds 24 bags per rack, 15" wide x 18" deep x 2½" high. French fry box dispenser normally holds 50 boxes per sleeve.

BUS BOXES - PLASTIC

Average sizes: 15½" x 21" x 5" or 6" deep, 13" x 22" x 6" and 17" x 22" x 6". (Some manufactured 12" deep.)

BUTTER DISPENSERS

Rated by the pound. Average patties 60 to 90 per lb. Average unit holds 180 to 270 patties. Available are 115 V plug-in units refrigerated by "Heat Transfer" system or non-refrigerated units cooled by "Freezer Cartridges."

BUTTER CUTTERS

Available to cut 60, 72 or 90 pats per lb.

CREAM DISPENSERS

Standard non-refrigerated style, 2 qt. and 6 qt.

SPECIALTY CUTTERS (Hand Operated)

EGG SLICER: 10 blades, 9 slices and 2 ends (typical)

LETTUCE CUTTER:
Shreds to 3/8" or 3/4" cuts, whole head in one second, 2nd time through makes finer cut.

ONION CUTTER:
3/16", 1/4", 3/8", 1/2" slices, also used for fruit, cukes or potatoes.

TOMATO CUTTER:
3/16" cuts 15 blades
1/4" cuts 11 blades
3/8" cuts 8 blades

WEDGE CUTTER:
6, 12, 12 cut wedges - fruit, steak fry potatoes or salad bar tomatoes.

STORAGE CONTAINERS
(Food and Liquid Polyethylene with snap on covers)

Diameter	High	Quarts
6¾"	4¼"	2
6¾"	7"	3½
8"	8¼"	6
8"	10¾"	8
10"	12"	12
12¼"	13½"	20
12¼"	15½"	24

As Above with No-Drip Faucets for Hot or Cold Liquids

10"	12"	12
12¼"	13½"	20
12¼"	15½"	24

HELPFUL HINTS

A 48" shelf holding three 18 qt. round containers will hold five 18 qt. square containers.

90 qt. Square
54 qt. Round
36 more quarts per 48" shelf

CAN OPENERS

The old reliable, mount it on the edge of the table, whack it down into the can and grind the handle around till the lid pops up is available in two sizes: Heavy duty and twice as heavy. Old reliable opens anything from sardine to gallon cans. There are available magnetic lid holders and a special cleaning tool.

You probably knew all that. You probably know how to change the blade too. But, what you may not know is how to change the gear. It's easy — remove the blade and wedge a screwdriver between the gear and the frame, turn the handle counter-clockwise and the gear will come out. No need to throw "Old Reliable" out, just buy him a new gear.

There is another model of "Old Reliable" available with a rotating knife and gear assembly. The handle turns on a more vertical axis and requires less strength to operate - less tiring for female operators.

LEVER HANDLE CROWN PUNCH CAN OPENERS

Recommended where large numbers of cans of one size are to be opened at one time. Unit will open up to 700 cans per hour. One pull of the handle punches out entire lid. Interchangeable knives, ring guards as base plates permit opening of various cans.

AIR PRESSURE OPERATED CROWN PUNCH OPENERS

Where there is need for opening up to 900 cans of one size at a time with a minimum of effort. Heavy duty models with the same versatility as the lever handle opener are available which operate on air pressure at from 60 to 100 PSI. No electrical connection required. Most institutions which may require this kind of production will have air pressure systems. If not, the units will operate on a 1 HP compressor.

CAN OPENING SYSTEMS

One-operator systems are available that wash cans, spot defective cans, open cans, remove the lids and dump the contents at rates up to 2,400 cans per hour. Use F.E.F. Personal Assistance Service for more information.

ELECTRIC CAN OPENERS

These units are available as bench models or hand held openers. The average production rate is up to 700 #10 cans per hour. Sizes, styles and features vary considerably by manufacturer. Some have built-in knife sharpeners.

CAN VACUUM CHECKING UNIT

To avoid possible food poisoning and to eliminate the unnecessary discarding of suspicious cans, a simple hand held unit with a gauge hooks over the edge of any can. When pressed down it punctures the lid and measures the vacuum. The meter reads from 0 to 30 Hg. Hg. is the standard for measuring vacuums as 1" of mercury rise. Average cans have from 1 to 6 Hg.

ELECTRIC KNIFE SHARPENER

Where the need for sharpening knives is heavy, a separate knife sharpener is recommended. They are designed to keep the knife blade at the proper 12° angle with spring loaded knife glides. Various table top models available.

SHARPENING STONES - FINE AND COARSE OR DUAL

6" x 2" x 1"   8" x 2" x 1"
7" x 2" x 1"   11½" x 2½" x 1"
Available with oil reservoir holders.

HAND CRANK ROTARY SHARPENERS

Units have aluminum-oxide honing wheels. Large model has 5" wheel. Smaller models available. Units are for wall mounting and have built-in oil reservoir.

FRENCH FRY CUTTERS - HAND OPERATED

9/32"   3/8"   7/16"

GUEST CHECK HOLDERS

STYLE:
Slide: Ball bearings hold check in place, 12", 18", 24", 30", 36" or 48" long.

(Continued)

Spring Clip Style: One hand operation

Length	Clips
2 ft.	8
3 ft.	12
4 ft.	16

Wheels: Wheel rotates, ball or spring clip mounts, ceiling, wall, counter or portable.

Wheel Diam.	Clips
14"	12
18"	16
23"	20

ELECTRIC HARD CHEESE GRATERS

These machines are designed especially for grating hard cheeses as romano and parmesan. They are bench type units and vary in horsepower, voltages and style by manufacturer. Three typical units are listed below. Light, medium and heavy duty.

Motor Size	Capacity Per Hour
1/16 HP	35 lbs. granulated grind
1/4 HP	75 lbs. granulated grind
1/2 HP	150 lbs. granulated grind

COMPOSITION CUTTING BOARDS
(Hard Rubber, Lexan or Polyethylene - Common Sizes)

Thickness: 1/2", 3/4", 1"

12" x 18"	18" x 30"
12" x 24"	18" x 36"
15" x 20"	48" x 96"
18" x 24"	Or Custom Cut
15" x 36"	

CONDIMENT DISPENSERS

Electric, 115 V, portion control adjustable. Hold 1 gallon containers — mustard, ketchup, salad dressing, 8½" wide x 15¼" deep, 16" high.

EGG RINGS

Keep eggs round on griddle. Available in 3-1/8" or 3-7/8" diameters

FAT MELTERS

Average 115V, 1200 W, 12" x 12" element.

FUNNELS

Capacity	Top Diam.
2 oz.	2½"
4 oz.	3½"
8 oz.	4¼"
16 oz.	5-1/8"
32 oz.	6¼"
64 oz.	8"

GRIDDLE STONES

Long	High	Wide
6"	4"	4"
9"	4"	4"
4½"	2"	3"

Grill Screens 4½ x 5½.

LOBSTER TAIL SPLITTER

Resembles an office paper cutter. Lobster tail is placed in concave holder. Blade has bumper stop to prevent cutting all the way through tail. Suction cups hold unit to table top. Average production one case thawed lobster in 10 minutes.

OYSTER OPENER

Heavy cast base plate has suction cups to hold unit to table top. Top of plate is grooved surface to hold oyster. As lever handle is pulled downward, wedge shaped tooth on arm forces oyster open. Rubber bumper stops swing of handle.

MEASURING CUPS

Top Diam.	Deep	Capacity
2-5/8"	2-1/2"	1/2 pint
3-1/4"	3-1/2"	1/2 qt.
3-7/8"	5"	1 qt.
4-7/8"	6-1/4"	2 qt.
6"	8-1/4"	4 qt.

FOOD PUMPS

Normally fit following containers:
- Gallon jar 4¼" mouth
- Gallon jar 4-11/16" mouth
- Gallon jar snap lid
- #3½ insert 1 qt. S/Steel
- #5½ insert 2 qt., S/S container
- #10 Can
- #10 Transfer can S/Steel
- #6½ insert 4-1/8 qt. S/Steel
- #8½ insert 7 qt. S/Steel
- #10½ insert 11 qt. S/Steel

PUMPS - PLASTIC OR STAINLESS STEEL
(Soda Fountain Style)

Geared for heavy syrup as chocolate. Direct pump for lighter items. Pumps adjustable from ½ oz. to 1½ oz. per pump.

ICING DISPENSER GUN

Capacity: 42 oz.

PLASTIC ICE MOLDS

Common Types Available:
- Shrimp Boats
- Owls
- Horn of Plenty
- Fish
- Swan
- Horse Head
- Christmas Tree
- Cat
- Dolphin

Small: High approx. 6"-9"; base 4" x 6" to 5" x 9"

LARGER SIZES:
- Mermaids
- Dolphins
- Harmony of Love
- Swan
- Fish
- Horn of Plenty
- Shrimp Boats

Heights from 15" to 24"; bases from 9" x 13" to 11" x 24".

COMMON BLADE SIZES OF CUTLERY KNIVES

Boning Knives........................5", 6", narrow, wide, curved
Bread Knives........................9, 10"
Butcher Knives......................8", 10", 12"
Cleavers ....6", 7", 8"
Cooks Knives........................8", 10", 12"
Fruit Knives ....3¼", 4½"
Paring Knives ....3¼", 3½", 4"
Saws................................18", 24", 27", 30"
Slicers, Ham or Beef................9", 10", 12", 14"
Steels..............................10", 121", 14"
Utility Slicers.....................5", 6", 8", 9"
Forks, overall......................10", 12", 14", 20"

KNIFE RACKS
(Typical Wall or Table Mount)

Removable and cleanable, normally hold 8 knives or 6 knives and 2 steels (each)

ICE CREAM OR FOOD DISHERS
(Thumb operated spring style)

Size	Bowl Diam.	Patties Per lb.	Ice Cream Scoops/Gal.	Fluid Oz.	No. of Tablespoons
6	3"	3	16	4.66	10-2/3
8	2¾	3½	22	3.64	8
10	2-5/8"	4	24	3.19	6²/3
12	2½"	5	26	2.78	5⅓
16	2¼"	6-8	35	2.07	4
20	2-1/8"		42	1.77	3½
24	2"		51	1.49	2²/3
30	1¾"		60	1.03	2-1/5

MINI DISHERS
(Full grip squeeze style · Use right or left hand)

Size	Bowl Diam.	Oz.
12	2¼"	3½
16	2-5/8"	3
20	2½"	2½
24	2¼"	1¾
30	2"	1½
40	1-7/8"	1¼
50	1-7/8"	1-1/8
60	1-5/8"	7/8
70	1½"	5/8
80	1-3/8"	9/16
90	1-3/8"	31/64
100	1-1/8"	3/8

LADLES

Bowl Size By Ounce	Top Diam.	Handle Length
½	1¾"	6"
¾	1¾"	10"
1	1¾"	10"
2	2-3/8"	10"
3	3¼"	12-7/8"
4	3-3/8"	12-3/8"
6	3½"	12-3/8"
8	4"	12-7/8"
12	4-3/8"	12-3/8"
24	6"	18"
72	8¼"	18"

TYPICAL CAPACITIES

Ladle Size	Part of Cup	No. to Qt.
1 oz.	1/8	32
2 oz.	1/4	16
2-2/3 oz.	1/3	12
4 oz.	1/2	8
6 oz.	3/4	5⅓
8 oz.	1	4

NAPKIN DISPENSER

Average size 3½" x 7" long, holds approximately 150 napkins.

PAILS · STAINLESS STEEL · BAIL HANDLE

Top Diam.	Deep	Quarts
12"	10"	12½
12"	10-1/8"	14¾"
14-7/8"	11-7/8"	23

PASTRY TUBE SIZES
(Plain)

Number	Small End Diam.	Teeth in Star
1	3/16"	6
2	1/4"	6
3	5/16"	6
4	3½ 8"	6
5	7/16"	7
6	1/2"	7
7	9/16"	8
8	5/8"	9
9	11/16"	10

CANVAS PASTRY BAGS

Bag No.	Size	Bag No.	Size
0	10'' x 7''	5	17'' x 11''
1	11'' x 7½''	6	18½'' x 12''
2	12'' x 9''	7	20½'' x 13''
3	14'' x 9½''	8	22'' x 14½''
4	15½'' x 10''	9	23'' x 14½''

Sizes vary by manufacturer. Nylon bags available.

BAKING SHELLS

Common size: 4'', 4½'', 5'', 5½''

BAKERS SCALES

Capacity	Rating	Scoops
8 lbs.	1 lb. x ¼ oz.	11¾'' x 21''
16 lbs.	1 lb. x ¼ oz.	10'' x 18½''

HAND HELD PASTRY CUTTERS

DOUGHNUTS: 2'', 2½'', 3-3/8'' diameter

BISCUIT - Scalloped: 2'', 2-3/8'', 2¾'' diameter

BISCUIT - Plain: 1½'', 2'', 2-3/8'', 2¾'' diameter

FLOWER NAILS

NR	Top Diam.	NR	Top Diam.
1	13/16''	6	1-1/2''
2	1-1/8''	7	1-5/8''
3	1-3/8''	8	1-13/16''
4	1-5/16''	9	1-5/16''
5	1-5/8''		

PASTRY BRUSHES

Size	Bristle Length	Size	Bristle Length
1'' Flat	1-7/8''	3'' Flat	2-1/8''
1½'' Flat	2''	8'' Round	2''
2'' Flat	2-1/8''	10'' Round	2''
2½'' Flat	2-1/8''	12'' Round	2½''

LATTICE TOP PIE CUTTERS
(Plain or Fluted)

Small: 4-5/8" dia., 14 wheels, 5/16 centers; Large: 6-5/8" dia., 11 wheels, 5½⁸" centers

HAND HELD MUFFIN BATTER DISPENSER

Hopper capacity, 10 lbs. diameter; height, 14". Plunger style portion control adjustable from 1½ oz. to 3½ oz.

ROLLER DOCKER

For pie shell or pizza dough perforating to avoid bubbling. Hand held roller has stainless steel nails protruding from it. Sizes vary by manufacturer. A very handy tool.

PIZZA PANS (Deep)

¾" deep. Standard top diameters: 6", 7", 8", 9", 10", 11", 12", 13", 14", 15", 16", 17", 18".

PIZZA PANS (Standard)

Top diameters: 7½", 9", 11", 13", 15", 17", 19", 21".

TOMATO STRAINERS - ALUMINUM

Top Diameter	Depth
8"	2¾"
9"	2¾"
10"	2¾"
11"	3¼"

PEELS RECTANGULAR WOOD

Length	Width	Overall
24"	14"	32"
24"	16"	32"
24"	18"	32"
35½"	18"	43½"

PEELS ALUMINUM ROUNDED

Length	Width	Overall
14"	12"	26½"
14"	12"	36"
14"	12"	52"

DOUGH PANS (Stackable)

Diameter	Depth
7¼"	2"
8"	2¼"
9"	2¼"

PIZZA CUTTERS

Typical cutter sizes: 2", 2¼", 2-5/8", 4" Dia.

DOUGH BOXES · WOOD

24" x 24" x 3"	16" x 32" x 3"
16" x 18" x 3"	18" x 26" x 3"
16" x 24" x 3"	

PEELS ROUNDED WOOD

Length	Width	Overall
14"	12"	22"
14"	12"	35½"
14"	12"	42"
14"	14"	23½"
14"	14"	36"
14"	14"	42"
18"	18"	32"

PICKS AND STEAK MARKERS

PICKS
  Sword style: 3" long
  Arrow style: 3½" long
  Frill picks: 3" and 4" long

STEAK MARKERS
  Various styles: paddle, bull

COLOR CODE:		
Rare	....	Red
Med. Rare	....	Pink
Medium	....	Yellow
Med. Well	....	Blue or Brown
Well	....	Black

SERVING SPOONS · COMMON SIZES

11", 13", 15", 17", 21" overall length, plain, slotted or perforated.

WHIPS

8", 10", 12", 14", 16", 18" overall length. French - stiff wires. Balloon (piano wire) flexible.

PADDLES - STAINLESS STEEL, NYLON OR ALUMINUM

Common lengths: 24", 30", 36", 42", 48", 54" or 60" long. Blade sizes: 4½" x 8" or 4¾" x 9¼".

ROUND SALAD BOWLS

Diameter	Capacity	Diameter	Capacity
5"	10 oz.	12"	4 qts.
6"	12-14 oz.	15"	8 qts.
8"	40 oz.	18"	16 qts.
10"	2 qts.	23"	36 qts.

FOOD BY THE OUNCE SCALE

For on-premises food consumption a new concept is being widely accepted. Items such as salads, fruits, desserts, buffet items, etc. are plated to the customer's desires, then weighed and charged for by the ounce at the cashier's station.

A new L.E.D. digital scale for this purpose measures 16" x 16" x 6½" high. Single touch control shows product weight in ounces, price per ounce and total price. Scale automatically allows tare weight of plate or container once programmed. Total of 15 separate programs may be retained. 6 month battery back-up system for program memory retention. Capacity 160.00 x .05 ounce, price to $9.99. 110 V standard plug-in unit.

PORTION CONTROL SCALES
(Resetable dials)

COMMON MARKINGS	COMBINATION
32 oz. x 1/4 oz.	34 oz. x 1000 gram
5 lbs. x 1 oz.	5 lbs. x 2200 gram
25 lbs. x 1 oz.	11 lbs. x 5 kilogram
500 gram x 2 gram	25 lbs. x 11 kilogram
1000 gram x 2 gram	

OVER & UNDER PORTION SCALES
(For same weight type products)

32 oz x 1/4 oz.

16 oz. x 1/4 oz.

8 oz. x 1/8 oz.

PORTION SCALES · TYPICAL DIAL READINGS

16 oz. by ¼ oz.
1 lb. by ¼ oz.
2 lbs. by ¼ oz.
5 lbs. by ¼ oz or 1 oz.
10 lb. by 1 oz.
25 lb. by ¼ oz.
25 lb. by 1 oz.

GRAMS

500 grams x 1 gram
500 grams x 2 grams
1000 grams x 2 grams

HANGING SCALES
(Fish, Vegetable, Butchers Style)

10 lbs. x 1 oz.
20 lbs. x 1 oz.

COMBINATION PORTION SCALES

1000 grams or 34 oz.
2200 grams or 5 lbs.
5 kilograms or 11 lbs.
11 kilograms or 25 lbs.

STAINLESS & ALUMINUM SIZZLE PLATTERS

10-1/2" x 7-1/8"   14" x 9-1/2"
11-1/4" x 7-5/8"   17" x 12"
12-1/2" x 8-1/2"

WOOD UNDERLINERS

12" x 8-1/4"   17" x 10-1/4"
12-3/4" x 9"   21" x 13"
14" x 9-1/2"

OVAL WOOD SERVING PLATTERS
(With drain grooves and well)

6-1/2" x 10"   10-1/2" x 16"
8-1/2" x 12"   11-1/2" x 18"
9-1/2" x 14"   12-1/2" x 20"
9-1/2" x 16"

SPATULAS AND TURNERS

Sandwich spreader: 3½" - 4½" blade
Frosting spatula: 1½" wide, 6½" blade
Spatulas - flexible or stiff:

BLADE SIZE	
Long	Wide
6"	¾"
8"	1¼"
10"	1½"
12"	1¾"
14"	2"

Turner - perforated: 8" x 3"
Turner - hamburger: 4" x 3", 5" x 4", 8" x 3"
Dough cutter/scrapers: 6" blade
Pan and griddle scrapers: 3" or 4" blade
Jar and bowl scrapers (all plastic): overall lengths 9½", 13½", 16½"

STIRRERS - STAINLESS STEEL

Typical disc diameter: 8", lengths: 36", 48", 60"

STEAK WEIGHTS

Standard sizes: 1 lb. or 2 lb.

PLASTIC SQUEEZE DISPENSERS

8 or 12 oz., red, yellow, clear.

TONGS - STAINLESS STEEL

Standard lengths: 6", 9", 12", 18", spring or tension.

TEA KETTLES

Standard capacities: 2½ qt., 4 qt. or 6 qt.

PLASTIC STRAWS

UNWRAPPED

Item	No. to Box	Boxes Per Ctn.
5¼" Milk	500	50
7¾" Jumbo	250	10
7¾" Jumbo	250	50
7¾" Super Jumbo	200	50
8½" Regular	500	50

WRAPPED

5¾" Milk	500	24
7¾" Regular	500	24
7¾" Jumbo	500	10
7¾" Jumbo	500	24
8½" Super Jumbo	500	24
10¼" Jumbo	500	24

STRAW SIZE GUIDE

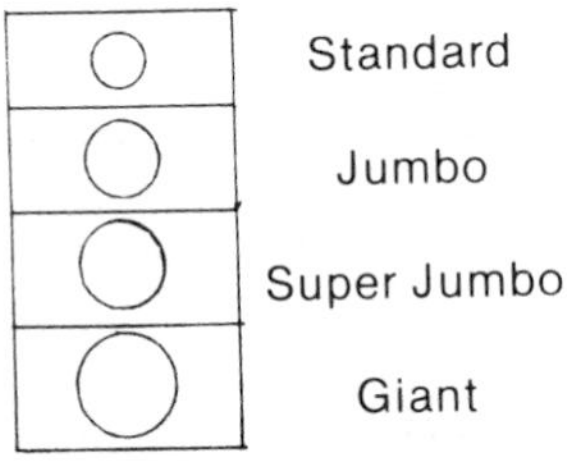

Standard

Jumbo

Super Jumbo

Giant

STRAW DISPENSERS

BULK STRAW DISPENSER: Normal capacity 300 straws

WRAPPED STRAW DISPENSER: Normal capacity 400 straws
   Average size 9" wide x 8½" deep x 10" high.

SUGAR POURERS

Normally 12 oz.

SYRUP PITCHERS

8, 12, 14, 16, 24, 32 oz.

PANCAKE SYRUP WARMER

These units hold the syrup at a perfect 125° serving temperature. Faucets allow serving personnel to control portions. Units are 115 Volt, plug-in available in 2 sizes.
   1 Gallon - 8" dia. plus faucet, 13" high, 53 watts; 2 Gallon - 9" dia. plus faucet, 17" high, 116 watts.

STANDARD THERMOMETER RATINGS

Common Name	Range F.
Deep Fat	50° - 550°
Microwave	0° - 200°
Roast Meat	105° - 185°
Candy	100° - 400°
Oven	100° - 650°
Freezer	-40° - 80°
Ref./Freezer	-35° - 75°

POCKET TEST THERMOMETERS

-40° to 120°F.
50° to 550°F.
-40° to 50°F.
25° to 125°F.
-40° to 125°F.
-40° to 160°F.
-40° to 110°F.

THERMOCOUPLE NEEDLE PROBE - HAND HELD

70° to 370°F.
-20° to 280°F.

For steaks, roasts, chops, poultry, fish, potatoes, lobsters, salads, frozen foods, soups and gravies. Probe 20'' long.

THERMOMETERS

	Range F.
Confections	60° to 360°
	100° to 320°
Deep Fat	60° to 450°
	100° to 400°
Combination Candy, Jelly, Deep Fat	200° to 400°
Water	20° to 220°
Roasting	140° to 190°
	140° to 200°
Oven Baking	150° to 650°
	200° to 500°
Ham Boiling	0° to 270°
Refrigerator/Freezer	35° to 75°
	-40° to 60°
	-40° to 70°

COMMON TRAY SIZES

Cafeteria		Round
5" x 7"	14" x 18"	11"
8" x 10"	15" x 20"	12"
10" x 14"	16" x 22"	14"
12" x 16"	16½" x 22½"	16"
		18"

COMMON OVAL TRAYS

19-1/8" x 23-7/8"
20-3/4" x 25-1/2"
22" x 26-7/8"

TRAPEZOID TRAYS

11" x 21"   14" x 22"
14" x 18"   14½" x 19½"

Many available compartmented.

WAX PAPER DISPENSER

For 12" x 12" papers, measures 12¼" x 12¼" x 2¾".

VINYL WRAP (ROLLS)

MEAT: 12" x 2 or 3,000 ft. lengths
15" x 2 or 3,000 ft. lengths
18" x 2 or 3,000 ft. lengths

PRODUCE: 15" x 5,000 ft.
17" x 5,000 ft.

FREEZER: 15" x 3,000 ft.
18" x 3,000 ft.

ALL PURPOSE: 12" x 2,000 ft.
18" x 2,000 ft.

SEALING PLATES: Base 6" x 9", 500 watts.

PERFORATED ROLLS VINYL POUCHES
(Tear off style)

Size	Roll	Size	Roll
6" x 8"	1000	16" x 20"	400
6" x 12"	1000	18" x 28"	300
8" x 12"	1000	20" x 28"	200
10" x 22"	700	22" x 34"	300
10" x 30"	500	16" x 26"	300
14" x 24"	400		

HEAT-SHRINK WRAPPING UNIT

Portable unit measures 12" x 12" with 7" high pedestal. Standard 115 Volt - 1546 Watt - 13.6 Amp. cord & plug with switch and indicator light. Pre-heat time 3 minutes. Product is placed on pedestal and covered with special film. Heat shrinks film in around plate or product forming an air tight seal. Ideal for pizza and deli platters take out.

Chapter Nine

WAREWASHING
AND
SANITATION

In this chapter we examine production figures of dish, glass, silver and pot washing machinery. Also covered are the allied hot water tanks, hot water boosters and conveyor systems.

Dishtables and complimenting equipment for total warewashing are also discussed. Some equipment such as dish storage trucks will be found elsewhere in F.E.F. Many variables exist in warewashing, primarily space allocation, water condition and the detergent system used.

Local Public Health Departments should be consulted for approval of new installations, as the regulations tend to vary in different localities. Production figures will vary by manufacturer.

WATER

The following facts and charts are intended to show the reader some typical sizes and needs of both primary and boosted water needs in commercial food operations. As we have stated many times, every operation is different and, the intent is to pass a few thoughts and not size your particular needs.

WATER FACTS

1) 1 gallon of water = 8.33 pounds
2) 1 gallon of water = 231 cubic inches
3) 1 cubic foot of water = 62.5 pounds
4) 1 BTU = The quantity of heat to raise the temperature of one pound of water 1°F. between 32°F. and 212°F.
5) One KW hour = 3412 BTU's

TYPICAL HOT WATER USE GUIDE

Type Food Service	Total Water Per Person Per Day	Total Water Per Person Meal Peak
Luncheonette or Drive-In	1.5 Gal.	1.1 Gal.
Full Meal Service Cafeteria or Restaurant	2.0 Gal.	1.5 Gal.
School Lunch	1.4 - 1.6 Gal.	1.0 - 1.2 Gal.
Full Course Restaurant	2.4 Gal.	1.7 Gal.

TYPICAL HOT WATER CONSUMPTION DURING TIME EQUIPMENT IS IN USE

Equipment	Gal. Per Hr.
Vegetable Sink	45
1 Compartment Sink	30
2 Compartment Sink	60
3 Compartment Sink	90
Manual Pre-rinse Hose	45
Scraper - Trough Type	180
Pre-scraper on Dishwasher	360
(If fresh water is used)	

Recirculating scrappers on dishwashing machines use overflow water from the wash tank.

Bar Sinks	30
Lavatory Sinks	5
Mop-Slop Sink	20

The above chart is based on 100% capacity of units.

TYPICAL 180° HOT WATER RINSE FOR WAREWASHING MACHINES (100% Efficiency)

Type Machine	Maximum Gal. Per Hr.
Silver Washer	45
Pot/Pan Washer	75
Undercounter Dishwasher	30
16 x 16 Rack Dishwasher	69
18 x 18 Rack Dishwasher	87
20 x 20 Rack Dishwasher	104
1 Tank Conveyor Dishwasher	416
2 Tank Conveyor Dishwasher	347

SOME SIZES OF COMMERCIAL ELECTRIC PRIMARY WATER HEATERS

Tank Capacity Gals.	Tank Diameter	Tank Height
5	16"	20"
10	18"	26"
15	20"	27"
20	20"	27"
30	20"	35"
40	20"	45"
50	20"	54"
65	24"	50"
80	26"	50"
100	26"	59"
120	28"	63"

TYPICAL PRIMARY WATER HEATERS

		Recovery of Water Gallons Per Hour		
K.W.	BTU'S	60°	80°	100°
12	41,000	82	62	49
15	51,000	103	77	62
18	61,000	123	92	74
24	82,000	164	123	99
27	92,000	185	138	111
30	102,000	205	154	123
36	123,000	246	185	148
40	138,000	277	208	166
45	153,000	306	231	185
54	185,000	369	277	222

Capacities of tank from 50 to 110 gallons. Diameters: 24" to 30", height: 58" to 72".

MANUAL DISHWASHING

When dishwashing is done by hand in your kitchen sink a few aids are available. They include immersion baskets and sink sanitizer heaters. Typical sizes follow:

HAND WASHING IMMERSION BASKETS - DISH BASKETS

TYPICAL SIZES - PLUS HANDLES

8" x 10" x 8"	10" x 14" x 8"
10" x 10" x 8"	14" x 14" x 8"
9" x 12" x 8"	14" x 16" x 8"
12" x 12" x 8"	

ROUND SILVERWARE IMMERSION BASKETS

10" x 8", 12" x 8", 14" x 10" plus handles.

SINK SANITIZING HEATERS
(Raising 140° Water to 180°)

Sink Size	Typical KW
15" x 15"	3
16" x 16"	4-5
18" x 18"	4-5
20" x 20"	6
24" x 24"	6
30" x 30"	9

Built into sink from below.

Also available is a portable sink sanitizer that rests in bottom of sink well. A control for heat is provided at about eye level.

RULE OF THUMB
ELECTRIC BOOSTERS FOR DISHWASHERS

GPH + 10 = KW (40° Rise)

Need 100 Gal. Per Hr. divided by ten (10) = 10 KW or 35,000 BTU's

DISHWASHER MACHINES

The first step up in warewashing machines from a compartment sink is an immersion style dishwasher. In immersion dishwashing the operator manually lifts baskets from pre-rinse area to wash tank and then on to final rinse compartment. This manual style machine is found in smaller kitchens and in those church halls and service clubs that have occasional suppers.

TYPICAL IMMERSION STYLE DISHWASHERS

TYPICAL SIZE: 65" long, 23" deep, 31" high.

TYPES:
   2 deep compartments plus stack area
   2 deep compartments plus pre-rinse area
   3 deep compartments plus small soil compartment

These machines are available with gas or electric heat. The built-in pump circulates 400 gallons of wash water over dishes and the rinse water is held at 180° by thermostat. These pump units may be installed in existing sinks for dish or pot washing. The rating in dishes is 2,000 per hour, working as fast as you can. Racks are available for silver, glasses, trays and dishes.

DISHWASHERS

While dish machines are sized by production capability per hour, the selection of proper warewashing equipment must be carefully analyzed because the variations and possibilities are staggering. These variables include space available, type of service, energy considerations, water conditions, local codes, detergent systems, handling systems, and of course budget among others. The authors after many discussions, have tried to reduce this chapter to plain interesting facts and realize that your ultimate choice will be properly laid out, engineered and installed. Our facts will aid your choice.

GUIDE TO DISHWASHER SELECTION

Meals Per Hour	Style Dishwasher
Up to 50	Counter or Undercounter
50 to 250	Single Tank Door Style
250 to 400	Single Tank Conveyor
400 to 750	Single Tank Conveyor with Pre-wash
750 to 1500	Double Tank Conveyor with Pre-wash
1500 Plus	Flight Type Conveyor

GUIDE TO DISHWASHING AREA
(Probable square feet required)

Meals Per Hr.	Sq. Ft. Needed
200	100
400	200 to 300
800	400 to 500
1200	600 to 700
1600	800 to 900

DISHWASHERS - TYPICAL SIZES

Style Dishwasher	Typical Size
Under Counter - Rack Style	24" x 24" x 36" High
Single Tank - Rack Style	24" x 24" x 58" High
Single Tank Rack Conveyor	44" x 27" x 58" High
Two Tank Rack Conveyor	64" x 27" x 58" High
Rackless - Belt or Flight Style Conveyors	From approximately 9½' to 26'

(One, two, three tank style)

Before we move on to the production rates for these dishwashers a few notes of interest on each style.

UNDER COUNTER DISHWASHERS: These units are available with 2 rack styles, either the standard 19¾" square rack or a fixed style rack that rides on roller wheels. The 19¾" rack style allows the operator to build up racks in advance of washing.

The 19¾" square rack is easily removed after each cycle. The roller bearing style rack is normally loaded and unloaded with the rack remaining in the machine. Styles available include built-in boosters, chlorine styles that require no booster and those that wash and rinse with the same temperature of water. These small machines may also be incorporated into mini dish table set ups that will provide pre-rinsing, scrapping and rack storage in one

287

housing. The 36" high machine is available without top to go under standard counters.

HELPFUL HINTS

Consider raising these machines 18" off floor to work at counter level. Production will increase and back problems decrease.

An expert once formulated the "Basic Law of Dishwashing": there are only two possibilities — either the dish rack moves through a set spray pattern or the spray pattern moves over the dish rack. Motion of either type is essential to cover all of the surfaces of the dishware completely. With this thought in mind, you have the whole concept mastered!

To do an efficient, economical dishwashing job, you have to remember five fundamental cost controls:

1. Optimum utilization of labor of sanitation personnel;
2. Detergent control through adequate prescrapping and prewashing facilities;
3. Machine Running Time control by timing full loads rather than fractional loads;
4. Wetting agent (rinse dry) control;
5. Reduction of Breakage.

The following dishmachines are those requiring wash water and boosted water of normal accepted degrees, energy style machines will follow.

Dishwashing, whether manual or mechanical, can be defined as nothing more than some hot water, detergent, and a lot of motion. In mechanical dishwashing, the three essential ingredients are (1) hot water at NSF approved tsemperatures, (2) detergent, and (3) sufficient gallon-per-minute recirculated flow pattern.

To provide the hot water for a commercial dishwasher, there's a choice of electric, gas or steam.

In electric machines the units are immersed in the water tank, offering the same direct-heat advantages as in electric fryers. These units (up to four in some tanks) are usually 5 kw each.

Heat Levels

Sanitation standards call for specific temperature levels for each of the four processes handled by commercial dish machines:

1. Pre-Rinse Water: 120-130 F. (Removes food soil before dishes enter the wash tank);
2. Wash Water: 150-160 F., maintained by the heat source in the tank. (In this process, the detergent is removed and the dishes heated for final drying);

4. Final Rinse Water: 180-190 F., supplied by booster heater. (To sanitize dishware, kill bacteria).

DOOR TYPE DISHWASHERS

Door type machines can handle 810-1350 dishes per hour, and are designed for operations serving 50-100 people per meal. They have an automatically timed wash cycle of 45 seconds, 3 seconds dwell and 12 rinse, and are equipped with revolving spray arms both for wash and rinse, above and below the dishes. The doors slide upward for loading. The wash water is pumped through double manifold lines leading to the revolving spray arms. A double pipe is used because the wash and rinse water have different temperatures and additives. Water pressure from the pump makes the wash arms revolve. Final rinse water flows from the booster heater to the rinse arms, and into the wash tank causing an automatic water change every 10 cycles. Available for straight run or corner operation.

RACK CONVEYOR DISHWASHERS

Rack conveyor machines move racked dishes by either chain or pawl. Pawl action, like a piston, uses a single rod to pull the racks through. These units come in one-tank models for medium-sized operations (150 per meal), and two-tank for high volume operations (often where space restricts the use of a big belt-conveyor machine). Rack conveyors can handle 4500-5625 dishes per hour. One-tank units prove more efficient when ordered with an integral pre-wash unit (optional). After pre-wash, the dish rack is conveyed through a spray pattern directed from upper and lower stationary spary arms at a prescribed gpm flow rate. When the rack has passed through the wash spray, it moves on to activate the fresh-water final rinse. The final rinse water (from the booster) flows into the wash tank and is recirculated in the wash water, in these models, final rinse only operates when the rack is directly underneath.

Two-tank rack conveyors introduce a power rinse along with the wash and final rinse cycles; the extra tank handles the power rinse. A pre-wash unit, as an integral part of the machine, may be built in at the factory.

PREWASH UNITS FOR CONVEYOR DISHWASHERS
ARE AVAILABLE

The function of these (optional) factory-installed units is to remove the maximum amount of food soil from dishware before it enters the wash tank of conveyor dishwashers, thus increasing ma-

289

chine efficiency and economy. In this process, a controlled flow of 130 F. water is sprayed from upper and lower stationary spray arms.

There are two types. One is a fresh water pre-wash, utilizing the 145 F. outside water line. This has to be mixed with cold water to reduce temperature to the prescribed 130 F.

The other type is a re-circulating pre-wash. This type pumps used water from the wash tank, which contains detergent. In this manner it utilizes the detergent more effectively, thereby reducing the operational costs.

Popular options to conveyor machines beside the pre-wash options described, are condensers for exhaust, side load devices, and blower dryers. Naturally as some of these options are added, the dimensions of the machines will increase; i.e. some pre-wash units add 22" or 36" to the length of the machine.

FLIGHT TYPE DISHWASHERS

Rackless conveyors are also referred to as Belt Conveyors and Flight-Type machines. The name rackless may be misleading, for silverware, glasses and cups may be racked before loading; other dishware may be placed directly on the belt. These are the big volume machines (6750 to 20,000 dishes per hour) for operations catering to more than 1000 people per meal. They should be specified for operations with growth potential, as capacity can be increased by adjusting belt speed. Belt conveyors have a special advantage for cafeteria-type operations with heavy tray traffic. The trays can be placed directly on the belt and fed through the machine.

These machines come in single, two, three or four (specially built) tank models. Single tank models are preferred for schools where the food is plain and the variety fairly limited.

To "size" a belt-conveyor is to determine the dish capacity, belt speed and additional footage needed. NSF uses the following formula:

$$C = \frac{120VW}{D}$$

C = Maximum dish capacity per hour
W = Conveyor width in inches
V = Conveyor speed in feet/minute
D = Distance between pegs (2" in GE machines).

(70% or rated capacity is frequently used as "Normal" sizing)

Belt speed can be varied from 5' to 12' per minute. Belts come in 22½" and 28½" widths. For bigger volume, a 28½" belt should be specified. Use the same formula to figure capacity. Where business growth is anticipated, it's wiser to use the wider belt at slower speeds, which can be increased later to meet higher capacities.

FLIGHT TYPE CONVEYOR DISHWASHER DISH CAPACITY

22½" Wide Belt	No. of Dishes Per Min.	No. of Dishes Per Hour
5 ft. per min.	130	6,780
8 ft. per min. (max. for single-tank unit)	180	10,800
12 ft. per min. (max. for 3-tank unit)	270	16,200
28½" Wide Belt		
5 ft. per min.	143	8,580
8 ft. per min. (max. for single-tank unit)	228	13,680
12 ft. per min. (max. for 3-tank unit)	342	20,520

Two final notes on conveyor and flight machines. By the addition of loading and unloading areas of different configurations, conveyor style machines may form any of the following shapes depending on space available — basic oval, square and rectangular, triangle. When joined together, they make for a continuous run operation, taking soiled dishes away from the operators and returning the finished clean results to the same area. NOTE: Be very careful to check all sizes of trays, serving pieces, and any other odd shaped piece to assure proper clearance in any dishwasher to avoid eventual problems. Some have encountered this unfortunate occurrence with larger than normal hospital tray services. Planning heights for your service may include raising clearance 3" or so, which is easily accomplished at the factory.

OPTIONS

Before we move on to more production figures and other styles of machinery, here are a few more options or in some cases, standard controls available.

- Thermostatically-controlled motor cutoff stops pump motors when temperature falls below proper level.
- Automatic timed fill control minds filling of hot water into wash tank on door machines.
- Electric door lock secures door machines against interruption during timed wash cycles.

291

- Door safety switch protects user from scalding water.
- Final rinse arrester controls final rinse water and rinse dry additives.
- Electric (or steam) thermostat maintains water temperature and protects heating elements.
- Magnet A-C Starter prevents uncontrolled start-up after any power interruption.
- Water (or steam) pressure-regulating valve and gauge maintains rinse water (steam) pressure at optimum levels.
- Steam and hot water mixing valve provides 180 F. rinse water for roll tops or door machines.
- Ventilating end hood expels excess steam from dish room.
- Blower accelerates dish drying on belt conveyors.

TRAY STACKERS

Where dishwashing lay-outs incorporate tray conveyor systems and the incoming trays are to be broken-down on the conveyor, it can be advantageous to incorporate a tray stacker at the end of the belt conveyor. After the dishes, flatware and paper items are removed as the tray progresses to the end of the conveyor, the soiled tray is automatically deposited onto a self-leveling tray cart which when full may be rolled to the dishwashing machine. A second truck would be placed at the end of the conveyor at that time. Guide clips hold the trucks in place.

The stacker units are available as gravity-feed models or motor driven. The powered unit is designed to accelerate tray discharge.

The stacker units are fitted with two limit switch controls. One closes the circuit to the conveyor drive when the self-leveling truck is in position and opens the circuit when the truck is removed. The second switch stops the conveyor when the truck is loaded to full capacity.

TYPICAL DISHWASHER HOURLY PRODUCTION

		Per Hour	
Machine Style	Racks Hr.	Glasses	Dishes
Undercounter			
3½ min. cycle	15	675	375
4½ min. cycle	12	540	300
16 x 16 Rack Style	38	1140	570
20 x 20 Rack Style	51	2295	1275
44" Conveyor	194	8775	4850

Flight type dishwasher production previously given.

NOTE: On above chart the 16 x 16 rack assumes 15 dishes per rack or 30 glasses. The 20 x 20 rack and 44" conveyor machines

292

assume 25 dishes per rack or 45 glasses per rack. For rack sizes, see charts a bit further along.

DISHWASHER WATER REQUIREMENTS

Type Machine	Wash			Final Rinse @ 20 PSI (Flow Pressure)		
	Vol. Water	Min. Expo.	Min. Temp.	Min. Vol. Water	Min. Expo.	Min. Temp.
Single Tank Stationary Rack 16 x 16	60 gal.	40 sec.	150ºF.	1.15 gal.	10 sec.	180ºF.
18 x 18	75 gal.	40 sec.	150ºF.	1.44 gal.	10 sec.	180ºF.
20 x 20	92 gal.	40 sec.	150ºF.	1.73 gal.	10 sec.	180ºF.
Single Tank Stationary Rack Chemical Sanitizing	Total 80 gallons includes sanitizing rinse DISCHARGE TO WASTE		120ºF.	Total 80 gallons includes wash vol.		120ºF., 50 ppm Cl₂ or other accepted sanitizing solution
Single Tank* Conveyor 20 inch width	3 gal./ lin. inch. conveyor	15 sec.	160ºF.	6.94 gal. per min. 7'/min.	Max. conv. speed conveyor	180ºF. 6" spread 5" above
Multiple Tank* Conveyor 20 inch width	1.65 gal./ lin. inch conveyor	7 sec.	150ºF.	4.62 gal. per min.	15'/ min. max. convey. speed	180ºF. 3" spread 5" above conveyor

TYPICAL EXHAUST REQUIREMENTS FOR CONVEYOR AND FLIGHT DISHWASHERS

Machine Style	Cubic Feet of Air Per Min.	
	Entrance	Discharge
44" Conveyor	200	400
64" Conveyor	200	400
Flight Style	500	500 to 1,000

Use the above guide when a blower dryer is not used. This option will change requirements of exhausted air. Normal duct sizes for dishmachines is 4" x 16".

BOOSTERS

A few typical production charts and a wiring guide follow. The booster heater is used to raise the available hot water to the accepted rinsing degree of 180º for warewashing.

293

BTU'S REQUIRED FOR RAISING 130° WATER 50° to 180°

Machine Style	Gallons Per Hour	BTU'S Required
Undercounter	35-40	60,995
16 x 16 Rack Style	69	106,743
18 x 18 Rack Style	87	134,589
20 x 20 Rack Style	104	160,888
44" Conveyor	416	643,552

See the manufacturer's literature for sizes not listed.

ELECTRIC BOOSTER HEATERS

K.W. required to raise incoming water temperatures.

WATER TEMPERATURE RECOVERY TABLE IN GPH

	DEGREE FAHRENHEIT RISE						
	30°	40°	50°	60°	70°	80°	90°
4 kw	55	41	33	27	23	21	18
5 kw	68	51	41	34	29	26	23
6 kw	82	62	49	41	35	31	27
7 kw	96	72	57	48	41	36	32
9 kw	123	92	74	62	53	46	41
10.5 kw	144	108	86	72	62	54	48
12 kw	164	123	99	82	70	62	55
13.5 kw	185	138	111	92	79	69	62
15 kw	205	154	123	103	88	77	68
18 kw	246	185	148	123	105	92	82
24 kw	328	246	197	164	141	123	109
27 kw	369	277	223	185	153	138	123
30 kw	410	308	246	205	176	154	137
36 kw	490	369	296	246	211	185	164
39 kw	533	400	320	267	229	200	178
40.5 kw	554	415	332	277	237	208	185
45 kw	615	462	369	306	264	231	205
54 kw	738	554	444	369	317	277	246
58.5 kw	800	600	480	400	343	300	267
67.5 kw	931	698	558	465	396	349	310

Booster styles and options are varied. Make sure your booster is matched to the dishwasher and has all necessary pressure and temperature controls included.

STEAM BOOSTERS

No attempt is made to size steam boosters. To do this, ask your representative to assist you. They are available in many sizes to match your machines requirements, but must be sized on the site because of the many steam pressure and consumption variables. We do have information available. Use F.E.F. Personal Assistance Service.

ELECTRIC BOOSTER WIRING GUIDE

KW	Volts	Phase	Breaker or Fuse	Copper Wire Size	Conduit Size
6	208	1	40	8	½ "
6	208	3	30	10	½ "
6	240	1	30	10	½ "
6	240	3	30	10	½ "
9	208	1	60	4	1"
9	208	3	50	6	1"
9	240	1	50	6	¾ "
9	240	3	40	8	¾ "
12	208	1	90	2	1"
12	208	3	40	8	¾ "
12	240	1	70	4	1"
12	240	3	40	8	¾ "
18	208	1	125	1	1 ¼ "
18	208	3	70	4	1"
18	240	1	100	3	1"
18	240	3	60	4	1"
24	208	1	150	1/0	1 ¼ "
24	208	3	90	2	1 ¼ "
24	240	1	125	1	1 ¼ "
24	240	3	90	2	1 ¼ "
36	208	1	225	4/0	1 ½ "
36	208	3	125	1	1 ¼ "
36	240	1	200	3/0	1 ½ "
36	240	3	125	1	1 ¼ "
45	208	1	300	350 mcm	2 ½ "
45	208	3	175	2/0	1 ½ "
45	240	1	250	250 mcm	2"
45	240	3	150	1/0	1 ¼ "

GALLONS OF WATER IN 100 FOOT OF PIPE

Pipe Type	Gal. of Water
¾ " Copper	2.5
1" Copper	4.3
¾ " Steel	2.8
1" Steel	4.5

295

LOW TEMPERATURE DISHWASHERS
(Rack Style · Upright Machines)

NOTE: Energy saver dishwashers using chemical sanitizers for rinse action may not be suitable for silver, pewter and some types of plastic ware. Water softeners are recommended and more drying table space will be required.

TYPICAL PRODUCTION
(Racks Per Hour)

Maching Length	Racks Per Hr.
25" - 1 Rack Style	60
44" - 2 Rack Style	120
54" Rack Conveyor	180

The cycle on these machines is from 90 to 120 seconds and the water temperature from 120° to 140°. This will vary by manufacturer. The single rack machine will clean 800 to 1,000 dishes per hour.

EFFECT OF DISHMACHINE CURTAINS ON ENERGY CONSUMPTION

Tests were performed on single and two tank commercial type dish-machines to determine the effect of the curtains on the electrical power consumption of the wash and power rinse tank heaters.

Assuming a rack loading of one per minute, the hourly energy savings with the use of plastic curtains is 6.84 kWhr/hr. With 16 hours of dishwasher operation per day for 365 days per year, the daily and annual savings are 100 kWhr/day and 40,000 kWhr/year respectively. In computing savings, care must be taken to include the fuel adjustment charge, surcharges, and sales taxes in the overall charge/kWhr of electricity.

YEARLY COST OF OPERATION, SINGLE TANK COMMERCIAL DISHWASHING MACHINE, USING **CONVENTIONAL SPLASH CURTAINS**, OF THE 15 KW ELECTRIC WASH TANK HEATER.

Local Electric Rate/KWH	Yearly Cost of Operation
3¢	$2,365.00
4¢	3,153.60
5¢	3,942.00
6¢	4,730.40
7¢	5,578.80
8¢	6,307.20

THE SAME SINGLE TANK MACHINE, USING **ENERGY SAVING CURTAINS:**

3¢	$1,708.20
4¢	2,277.60
5¢	2,847.00
6¢	3,416.40
7¢	3,985.80
8¢	4,555.20

TYPICAL COMBINATIONS OF DISHWASHER CURTAINS

SINGLE TANK CONVEYOR
  Using 2 long curtains
  Using 2 long, 1 short
  Using 3 long
  Above with prewash, add 1 long curtain

TWO TANK CONVEYOR
  Using 3 long, 1 short
  Above with prewash, add 1 long curtain

SINGLE TANK FT. MODELS
  Using 2 long, 1 short
  Above with prewash, add 1 long curtain

STANDARD WIDTH TWO TANK FT. MODELS WITH PREWASH
  Using 4 long, 1 short

EXTRA WIDE TWO TANK FT. MODELS WITH PREWASH
  Using 4 long, 1 short

DISHMACHINE RACK FACTS

Typical sizes: 16" x 16", 18" x 18", 20" x 20", ½ size: 10" x 20".

TYPICAL CAPACITIES

Style	Holds
20" x 20" Plate rack	16 to 18, 9" plates
20" x 20" Tray rack	8 trays per rack
20" x 20" Dome plate cover rack	5 covers per rack
Cup Racks	16, 18, 20 or 25 cups per rack, shape will determine
Silver Racks	100 pieces of silver fanned flat per rack

(Continued)

TYPICAL CAPACITIES (Cont.)

Glass Racks

Number Compartments	Typical Heights of Glass Racks
16 - 4 x 4 Rows	4", 5½", 7",
25 - 5 x 5 Rows	8", 9-7/8" and
36 - 6 x 6 Rows	11-5/16"
49 - 7 x 7 Rows	

SELECTING DISHWASHER GLASS RACKS

To determine the number of compartments needed, place an inverted glass on diagram below. Looking down on the glass, select either 49, 36, 25 or 16 compartment size, making sure that the greatest diameter of the glass is no larger than the appropriate square. (Note: When measuring cups or mugs, be sure to allow for extension of handles.)

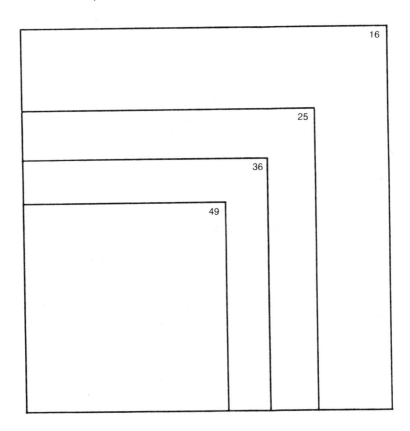

Then measure the overall height of the glass. The rack compartments must be deeper than the height of the glass, not only to allow for stacking, but also to reduce breakage from glasses hitting each other during the washing process.

Racks vary by manufacturer. Some have add-on risers to increase compartment depths, others are of one-piece construction.

TYPICAL RACKS REQUIRED FOR SYSTEMS

Total rack systems provide for washing, delivering, holding and serving from the same rack. Typical rack requirements follow.

CAFETERIAS, FULL SERVICE REST. OR BANQUETS

Number of Seats	100	200	300
5 oz. Juice glass	144	252	350
36 Rack	4	7	10
10 oz. Water glass	300	500	700
25 Rack	12	20	28
12 oz. Ice Tea	200	300	400
25 Rack	8	12	16
10 oz. Goblet	300	500	700
25 Rack	12	20	28
5½ oz. Sherbet	150	250	350
36 Rack	4-5	8	10
5½ oz. Stem	150	250	350
25 Rack	6	10	14
Cups	300	500	700
20 Rack	15	25	35

The above guide shows total glasses required by number of seats plus number of racks recommended.

DISHTABLE FACTS

Our illustrations of typical dishwashing tables shows all the components that make for a total system. Pick the parts that apply to your needs and we have 3 areas of interest left — disposals, conveyors and detergent systems.

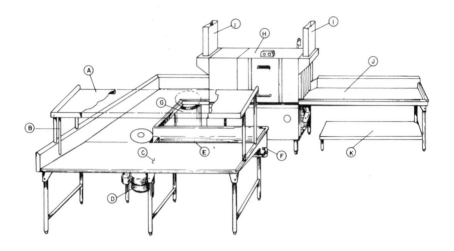

TYPICAL DISHWASHING LAYOUT

A—Rack shelf pitched to waitress' side of soiled dish table
B—Bleeder tube
C—Soiled dish table. Note pitch to trough
D—Garbage disposer. Alternative would be pre-rinse sink
E—Trough to disposer with silver saver stop
F—Water inlet to trough inter-connected with disposer
G—Hot water booster - location optional
H—Dishwashing machine
I—Vent ducts
J—Clean dish table. Suggested minimum length to accommodate 3 dish racks
K—Removable rack storage shelf provides for easy cleaning

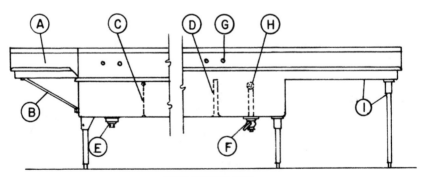

SINK OPTION KEY

A—Removable Drainboard - available in various styles and sizes. As shown with high backsplash to match sink or low splashes with hemmed edges.
B—Bracing - varies by manufacturer. Drainboards over 36" long should have legs.
C—Single thickness sink divider - welded in place with small radius in corners. Usually capped with split tube.
D—Double Wall Sink Dividers - welded in place with full coved corners.

(Continued)

300

(Cont.)

E—Crumb Cup Waste

F—Lever Handle Waste - various sizes and styles available.

G—Faucet Holes - a good point to remember. Some sinks will have provisions for only one faucet for three compartments. Faucets may be centered over each compartment or over each divider. Fast flow faucets are advantageous for large sinks.

H—Connected Overflow - obvious advantages.

I—Integral Drainboard - raises front edge of sink unit 3" as shown. Backsplash may extend to enclose end splash as shown or stop at vertical rise leaving rolled edge to extend beyond backsplash. Drainboards over 36" in length should have supporting legs. Crossbracing on legs is optional. Shelving may be installed under drainboards. Conical or corner gusset are available as shown on each end of the sinks pictured. Adjustable flanged feet are available for bolting to floor. It is advisable to order flanged feet without holes for drilling at installation.

SINK AND DISHTABLE OPTIONS

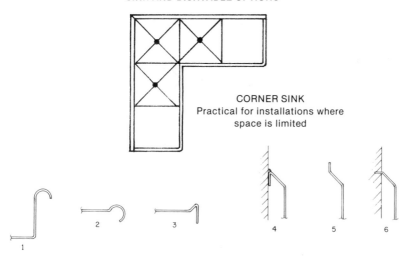

CORNER SINK
Practical for installations where
space is limited

1—Standard Rolled Edge - usually ¾" in diameter x 3" high - normally used for ends and work side of dishtables and sink drainboards

2—Raised Rolled Edge

3—Inverted "V" Edge - either fig. 2 or 3 are used for work tables where water spillage is heavy or frequent wash-down is required. When applied to the clean dish table of a single tank machine these edges provide an auxiliary work table during periods when dishes are not being washed

4—Sink or Dishtable Backsplash - turned back 2" on 45° then down approx. ¾". Sinks and dishtables should be installed at least 3" off from walls. Where necessary the units may sometimes be mounted against the wall and sealed with silicone caulking as shown. Other approved methods are available.

5—Backsplash turned back 2" on 45° and then up. Detail used by some manufacturers.

6—Backsplash kerfed into wall. For high quality installations against masonry or tile walls such as in hospitals, etc. Requires considerable coordination of construction and installation.

HELPFUL HINTS

If Soil or Clean Table Clear Measurement Is	You Will Accommodate This Number of 20 x 20 Racks
3'0''	1
4'0''	2
5'0''	3
6'0''	3
7'0''	4
8'0''	4
9'0''	5
10'0''	6

GARBAGE DISPOSALS

The following chart shows recommended garbage disposer sizes by horsepower, meals served, and the location of disposer.

	HORSEPOWER			
Persons Per Meal	At Dish Table	Veg. Prep.	Salad Prep.	Pot Sink
Up to 100	3/4	1/2	1/3	1/3
100-150	1	3/4	1/2	1/2
150-175	1-1/4	1	3/4	1/2
175-200	1-1/2	1-1/2	3/4	3/4
200-300	2	1-1/2	3/4	3/4
300-750	3	1-1/2	3/4	3/4
750-1500	5	3	1-1/2	1-1/2
1500-2500	5	3	1-1/2	1-1/2

A trough system is available to feed disposers. Using a channel of any length, water floats the garbage to the disposal. This water is recirculated at 70 gallons per minute tempered to 100° and the addition of fresh water to clarify. Other styles discharge water to drain without recirculation.

NOTE: When codes do not permit disposals, a scrapper can be used. This system flushes and reduces by 50% food wastes to a removable stainless steel basket.

WASTE PULPERS

These units may also be built into dishmachine layouts or used free standing.

TYPICAL PRODUCTION
REDUCING SOLID WASTE UP TO 85%

	HORSEPOWER		
Operation	**5 HP**	**7½ HP**	**20 HP**
Food Service	700	900	2000
Documents	300	500	1200
General Waste	500	700	1600

(Pounds Per Hour)

CONVEYORS FOR TRAY AND DISH RETURN

BRAINSTORMING
- Speed fixed or variable
- Floor support or wall mount
- Fixed or portable
- Washers for belt
- Start-stop switches - automatic or manual
- Skirting standard or extra
- Energy saving features for belt washing, water and detergents

FACTS · CONVEYORS

Width Track Clearance	Accommodates
16½"	14 x 18 - 15 x 20 Trays
18"	16 x 22 Trays
24"	20 x 20 Racks

Typical speeds: fixed 40' per minute, variable from 5' to 40' per minute.

CONVEYOR MOTOR SIZES

Shape Conveyor	Distance to			
	25'	**50'**	**75'**	**100'**
Straight	1/4 HP	1/2 HP	3/4 HP	1 HP
U or 2 Turns	1/2 HP	3/4 HP	1 HP	1-1/2 HP
	20'	**40'**	**65'**	**75'**
L Shape	1/4 HP	1/2 HP	3/4 HP	1 HP

DETERGENT SYSTEMS

Complete detergent systems are available nationwide. Early on when you are purchasing a new warewasher, consult your representative for details on the systems. They will need power for wash and rinse equipment (all 5 V electrical outlet, 5' above the floor. Behind the machine is suggested.), and space to store the products. Newer systems available are energy oriented and working with your supplier will give you maximum service on your machine. Many a routine check by detergent service people has saved factory service calls by correcting minor problems early.

CONVEYOR GLASS WASHERS

Typical size: 25" long x 25" deep x 39" high.

Glass Size	Glasses Per Hr.
2" diam.	1500
2½"-2¾" diam.	1250
3" diam.	1000
3½" diam.	700
4" diam.	500
4½" diam.	350
5" diam.	250

Recirculating wash tank 6 gal. capacity, rinse 3 gal. per minute, cold water with sanitizer. Conveyor travels at 1 revolution per 3 min.
Wash tank 300 W at 220V, motor 1½ HP. This unit can be used under bar and will reduce breakage, inventory and save valuable walking time.

Typical size conveyor glass washer, 6' long, 25" deep, 39" high.

Glass Size	Glasses Per Hr.
2" diam.	4000
2½-2¾" diam.	2500
3" diam.	2000
3½" diam.	1500
4" diam.	1000
4½" diam.	750
5" diam.	500

Recirculating wash tank 8.5 gal. capacity, rinse 3.5 gal. per min., cold water with sanitizer. Conveyor travels 14" per minute. Wash tank 4500 W at 220 V, motor ½ HP.

POT WASHERS

Style	HP	Recirculating Wash Tank Cap.
Front Load	5	20 gallon
Pass Thru	7½	30 gallon
Pass Thru	10	58 gallon

Style	Space Required
Front Load	31" wide, 41" deep, 75" high
Pass Thru	33" wide, 36" deep, 77" high
Pass Thru	65¼" wide, 38" deep, 77" high

Style	Capacity in Pans
Front Load	10 - 18" x 26" pans — 8 - 12" x 20" pans
Pass Thru - Single	10 - 18" x 26" pans — 8 - 12" x 20" pans
Pass Thru - Double	20 - 18" x 26" pans — 16 - 12" x 20" pans

Pot washers require venting and booster for the rinse water. The racks per hour vary by manufacturer.

OTHER STYLE POT WASHERS

PORTABLE POT SCRUBBER
This 115 volt unit is available wall mounted or on a rolling dolly. Unit is hand held and features quick change brushes for pots and pans, baked on carbon or utility brush for grills and ranges. Unit has built in electrical protection and an optional foot control assembly is available.

SINK STYLE POT WASHER
These units may be mounted into an existing or new sink. A one hole cutout is sufficient to accommodate the pot washer. The unit plugs into 115 volt outlets and is rated at 650 W. A 1/3 horsepower motor recirculates 500 gallons of water per minute over the soil compartment and will speed up the removal of heavy soil.

POT WASHER SINK
Like the style washer above, also available is a complete pot washing sink. Twin 400 gallon a minute pumps drive a total of 800 gallons a minute of hot sudsy water to clean even dry baked soil from the pots. The unit features 2 - 4" wide soil troughs and the main compartment is 40" x 26" x 18" high. Overall unit is 64" x 32".

VIBRATING STYLE SILVER BURNISHERS

Open top style, this top load burnisher vibrates your silver or hollow ware pieces to restore their original lustre. These units are portable style, with drain hoses and available in capacities of from 100 to 800 pieces of flatware per load. Burnishing balls vibrating over and around the silver return its natural finish.

TYPICAL VIBRATING BURNISHERS

H	W	L	TYPE	MOTOR	LBS. OF BURNISHING BALLS	CAPACITY
31	15½	18½	PORTABLE	⅓ H.P. 110/60/1 OR 220/60/3	75#	100 PIECES FLATWARE / 10" DIA. HOLLOWARE
31	16½	21	PORTABLE	⅓ H.P. 110/60/1 OR 220/60/3	150#	200 PCS. FLATWARE / 12" DIA. HOLLOWARE

(Continued)

TYPICAL VIBRATING BURNISHERS (Cont.)

H	W	L	TYPE	MOTOR	LBS. OF BURNISHING BALLS	CAPACITY
36	18½	25½	PORTABLE OR STATIONARY	⅓ H.P. 110/60/1 OR 220/60/3	300#	400 PCS. FLATWARE 16" DIA. HOLLOWARE
36	18½	29½	PORTABLE OR STATIONARY	½ H.P. 110/220/1 OR 220/440/3	450#	600 PCS. FLATWARE 20" DIA. HOLLOWARE
36	21½	33½	PORTABLE OR STATIONARY	½ H.P. 110/220/1 OR 220/440/3	600#	800 PCS. FLATWARE 24" DIA. HOLLOWARE

OPTIONS—TIMER & DIVIDER—ALL MODELS

DRUM STYLE SILVER BURNISHERS
FOR FLATWARE AND HOLLOWARE

TYPICAL SIZES AND CAPACITIES:

24" long, 16" wide, 31¾" high for seating capacity to 200 and inventory up to 1000 pieces of flatware, 1/3 HP, 115V motor.

34" long, 20" wide, 31¾" high for seating capacity to 400, and inventory up to 2000 pieces of flatware, 1/3 HP, 115V motor.

38" long, 26" wide, 41" high for seating capacity to 800 and inventory up to 4000 pieces of flatware and holloware to 10" diameter, 1/2 HP motor 115V.

51" long, 34" wide, 44" high for holloware only to 18" in diameter, 1 HP, 208/220V, 3 phase motor.

SUGGESTIONS FOR SILVER CARE

A. Regular burnishing definitely improves the appearance of silver-ware — and you receive as a bonus — longer lasting ware.
B. Burnishing does not remove silver. Actually it
1. Prevents the loss of tiny flakes of pure silver
2. Rolls smooth the many tiny scratches silver gets in use.
3. Polishes the silverware to a gleaming finish.
4. Cleans away deposit of impurities from hot water.
5. Preserves the surface hardness and wearing qualities with which the silver left the factory, and greatly extends the service life of silver.
6. Usually it is good practice to burnish silverware at least twice a month (depending on the rapidity with which it tarnishes).

7. Never burnish tarnished silver as it seals the discoloration into the tiny scratches.
8. Use the best soap compounds and burnishing balls.
9. Follow the manufactuere'operation instructions very carefully for maximum results.

AUTOMATIC SILVER SORTER

Length 8'-6", width 28", height 36", 115 volt operation.

This sorter with vibrating action will separate and deposit in storage boxes 5000 pieces of silverware in one hour. The 4 pieces such as knives, forks, spoons and soup spoons (or whatever your particular needs) will arrive in a holding box with handles facing the same direction. The silverware is loaded into a hopper from a 20 x 20 silver wash basket or 8 compartment silver carriers.

SILVERWARE WASHER - DRYERS

The washer and drier was made to do one job exclusively . . . to wash and dry silver and stainlessware . . . not dishes, not glasses. All food stains, grease, film and tarnish are absolutely removed from each piece of silver with each washing. There is never any "slippery feel" to stainlessware, as is the case when washed in a dishwasher.

The washer removes all film because it constantly rolls the tableware, so that every surface and crevice is exposed to cross-jets of water and actual scrubbing action. Shingling of one piece from another is impossible.

Only after thorough, positive cleaning does it sanitize and dry silverware to spotless brilliance in 200° F. forced air. The entire cycle is timed and automatic. There is no possibility of drying bacteria laden film back on the silver.

Two popular sizes of silver washer-dryers are rated as follows: 200 pieces per load, 3,000 pieces an hour or 300 pieces per load, 4,500 pieces per hour. These units are available with removable or non-removable drums. They require water inlet, drain and 180° rinse water.

SMALL TRAY SANITIZER

Size: 8½" x 24" x 23" high, designed for fast food trays. Portable, does not need a water hook up or drain during operation.

Tray sanitizer was developed to fill the need of fast-food chain operations for a unit that can effectively sanitize the small serving trays commonly used there. Sanitizes trays up to 14" long x 11" wide x 1 " deep.

The tray sanitizer sanitizes trays in a vertical position. The tray sanitizer, however, sprays a chemical sanitizing solution of 50 to 80 parts per million chlorine at room temperature over the complete body of the tray. The sanitizing solution recirculates to be sprayed again and again at a rate of approximately two gallons per minute. The vertical position of the tray allows most of the sanitizing solution to drain back into the tank with little carry-out. This allows quicker drying with less sanitizing solution used overall for greater savings.

The specially designed chain conveyor with coated "V" cradles can handle a variety of tray sizes. In the rare case of a tray jam-up, the conveyor automatically stops to prevent damage to trays and machine. Capacity is rated at 950 12" x 16" trays per hour and 1,000 10½" x 14" trays per hour.

GARBAGE CAN WASHERS

A can washer-sanitizer should be installed in a location providing space around it for easy cleaning and ample work area. Storage racks for the cans should be provided to keep them off the floor and permit proper drying.

One manufacturer produces can washer-sanitizers in two sizes. One with a 25" diameter bowl and one 30" in diameter. Either model is available with entirely corrosion resistant materials or less expensive epoxy enamel coated components. Installation requires bolting the tripod base to the floor and supplying ¾" hot and cold water lines and 1½" waste.

The units are designed for cleaning and sanitizing refuse and garbage cans, waste receptacles, food and beverage containers, tubs, drums, barrels and any other round, square or oblong container with an overall top diameter or diagonal dimension not exceeding the units bowl size and having an open end or center opening of at least 4".

In operation the receptacle to be cleaned is placed on the unit in an inverted position.

Foot pedals, with automatic safety locks, control the flow of hot and or cold water to the jet-spray rotary nozzle which cleans and sanitizes the can.

Optional accessories are a rotary table which permits easy rotation of heavy containers for exterior cleaning while cleaning and sanitizing the interiors. For cleaning the exterior of the cans a scrub brush attachment with a 5 foot, high pressure hose and hand valve is available. Another option, also with a 5 foot hose and hand valve is designed to clean faucets and tubes.

Chapter Ten

CHINA
GLASSWARE
SILVER

The variety of patterns and styles in service pieces is infinite. However, the use of the charts in this chapter will give both the purchaser and seller a common ground to compute and budget requirements for new or existing operations.

Cross reference this chapter with others containing complementing information. EXAMPLE: Other table top serving pieces in Chapter 12 or glass rack capacities in Chapter 9.

As mentioned many times F.E.F. Service includes responding to your particular needs or problems. (See statement in front of book.)

HELPFUL HINTS

To reduce dinnerware breakage it is recommended that you have two or three times your base needs cycling in use. This assures an ample supply at points of use during peak periods. "Haste makes waste" — rushing china and glassware through wash cycles is bound to increase breakage.

Next, examine your washing and distribution system. Be sure your dish tables are adequate and efficient. Use mobile dish, glass and cup dollies or elevators to return items to their place of use. Hand carrying trays of glasses and stacks of dishes can be hazardous to their health.

CHINA

In today's marketplace nearly all items of dinnerware are available in china, glass, ceramic glass and plastic ware plus, disposables. Let your distributor salesman help you choose the most practical items for your needs.

HELPFUL HINTS

Lexan pans are available for use in microwave ovens. The advantage of their use is that the bottoms are convex in shape and provide more even cooking. Perforated drainers are available to match the pans. They are useful for defrosting when it is desirable to separate the excess moisture.

SUGGESTED MINIMUM QUANTITIES FOR SPECIFIC OPERATIONS
ITEMS PER SEAT OR BED

ITEM	Fine Dining	Family Dining	Theme Dining	Cafeteria	Banquet	Institutional
Dinner Plataes	2½	3	3	2	1¼	2
Salad/Dessert Plates	2½	3	3	3	2	—
Bread & Butter Plates	2½	3	3	4	2	3
Cups	2½	3	3	2	1¼	1½
Saucers/underliners	2½	3½	3½	2½	1¼	1½
Fruits	2½	3	3	5	2½	3
Grapefruit/Cereal	2	3	2	2½	—	1½

ESTIMATED MINIMUM DINNERWARE REQUIREMENTS BASED ON 100 SEATS

Item	Restaurants	Cafeteria	Church/Club
Cups	15 Dz.	12 Dz.	12-15 Dz.
Saucers	15 Dz.	12 Dz.	12-15 Dz.
Plates 5½"	12 Dz.	15 Dz.	12-15 Dz.
Plates 6½-7"	12 Dz.	15 Dz.	12-15 Dz.
Plates 9-10½"	12 Dz.	12 Dz.	12-15 Dz.
Bowls	6 Dz.	6 Dz.	12-15 Dz.
Fruit/Monkey	15 Dz.	12 Dz.	12-15 Dz.

SCHOOLS · HOSPITALS · NURSING HOMES

The menu and method of serving will greatly influence the dinner-ware requirements for institutions. The general rule of thumb is 3 times the number served will give the maximum use per dollar spent.

TYPICAL AVAILABLE SIZES & PACK PER CARTON

Item	Overall Size	Carton Pack
Plates	5½"	3 Doz.
"	6½"	3 Doz.
"	7¼"	3 Dz.
"	8¼"	1½ Dz.
"	9"	1½ Dz.
"	9-5/8"	1½ Dz.
"	9¾"	1½ Dz.
"	10¼"	1 Dz.

(Cont.)

TYPICAL AVAILABLE SIZES & PACK PER CARTON

Item	Overall Size	Carton Pack
Plates	10½"	1 Dz.
Platters	7¼"	2 Dz.
"	8½"	2 Dz.
"	9-5/8"	1 Dz.
"	10½"	1 Dz.
"	11¼"	1 Dz.
"	12½"	1 Dz.
"	13-3/8"	1 Dz.
Cups	6½ to 7 Oz.	3 Dz.
Bowls	9, 12 & 14 Oz.	3 Dz.
Fruits/Monkeys	4¾ to 5½"	3 Dz.

GLASSWARE

TYPICAL GLASS INVENTORY FOR SELECTED COMMERCIAL OPERATIONS

Coffee Shop	100 seats	200 seats	300 seats
5-oz Juice glasses	24 doz.		
10-oz. Water glasses	36 doz.		
12-oz. Iced-tea glasses	24 doz.		
Dining room			
5-oz. Juice glasses	12 doz.	24 doz.	30 doz.
12-oz. Iced-tea glasses	12 doz.	24 doz.	24 doz.
10-oz. Water goblets	24 doz.	30 doz.	42 doz.
5½-oz. Sherbet glasses	12 doz.	18 doz.	30 doz.
4-oz. Fruit-cocktail glasses	12 doz.	18 doz.	30 doz.
4½-oz. Parfait glasses	12 doz.	18 doz.	30 doz.
Banquet			
5-oz Juice glasses	12 doz.	24 doz.	36 doz.
12-oz. Iced-tea glasses	12 doz.	24 doz.	24 doz.
10-oz. Water goblets	18 doz.	24 doz.	36 doz.
5½-oz. Low sherbet glasses	12 doz.	18 doz.	30 doz.
4½-oz. Fruit-cocktail glasses	12 doz.	24 doz.	30 doz.
5½-oz. Champagne glasses	12 doz.	24 doz.	30 doz.
4½-oz. Parfait glasses	12 doz.	18 doz.	30 doz.

Standard fountain service	25 seats	50 seats	75 seats	100 seats
5-oz. Juice glasses	6 doz.	6 doz.	12 doz.	12 doz.
6-7/8-oz. Beverage glasses	6 doz.	6 doz.	12 doz.	12 doz.
10-oz. Water glasses	6 doz.	6 doz.	12 doz.	12 doz.
10-oz. Malted-milk glasses	6 doz.	6 doz.	12 doz.	12 doz.
12-oz. Soda glasses	6 doz.	6 doz.	12 doz.	12 doz.

TYPICAL BAR GLASSWARE REQUIREMENTS
Dozens needed per 100 seats

Item	Capacity	Bar/Lounge	Restaurant Table Service	Cater
Beer		12 dz.		
Champagne	4½ - 6 oz.	3 dz.	3 dz.	12 dz.
Cocktail	3 - 5 oz.	9 dz.	6 dz.	12 dz.
High Ball	7 - 11 oz.	12 dz.	9 dz.	12 dz.
Wines	6½ - 9 oz.	6 dz.	9 dz.	9 dz.
Sours	5 - 6 oz.	3 dz.	3 dz.	—
Rocks	4 - 7 oz.	9 dz.	6 dz.	9 - 12 dz.
Cordials	¾ - 1½ oz.	3 dz.	3 dz.	—
Collins	9 - 12 oz.	3 dz.	3 dz.	—
Brandy	2 - 20 oz.	3 dz.	3 dz.	—

For other bar serving items see Chapter 11. For rack selection see Chapter 9.

BAR SERVICE GLASSWARE — TYPICAL RUSH PERIOD — 75 PEOPLE

Item	Size Oz.	For	Amount Needed
Whiskey	1 - 2 oz.	Shots	3 Dozen
High Balls	7 - 10 oz.	Mixed Drinks	12 Dozen
Beer - Beverage	7 - 12 oz.	Beer - Soda	12 Dozen
Old Fashion	4 - 7 oz.	On the Rocks	6 Dozen
Cocktail	4½ - 5½ oz.	Martini - Manhattan	4 Dozen
Sour	5 oz.	Sours	3 Dozen
Wines & Champs	4 - 8 oz.	Brandy, Wines, Daiquiri	3 Dozen

SILVERWARE

Common pieces available in stainless steel or silver plate:

Teaspoons
Dessert - Place - Utility Spoon
  (Called Oval Soup)
Bouillon Spoons
Tablespoons
Place/Utility Fork
Dinner Fork

Salad Fork
Iced Tea Spoon
Oyster Fork
Butter Knife
Knife, 1 Pc. Plain
Knife, 1 Pc. Serrated
Gravy Ladle

For Ware Washing Machines, see Chapter 9.

ESTIMATING YOUR STAINLESS STEEL OR SILVERWARE NEEDS

GENERAL "RULE OF THUMB" METHOD

Item	Amount In Service Times Seats	Reserve Times Seats
Knives	2-3	2
Dinner Forks	4	4
Teaspoons	1½-2	2
Soup Spoons	1½	1½
Salad Forks	½	½
Ice Drink Spoons	½	½

MAXIMUM AMOUNT FLATWARE FOR SPECIFIC OPERATIONS

Item	Hotel Formal Service	Restaurant or Coffee Shop
Teaspoons	5	4
Dessert/Soup Spoons	2	2
Tablespoons	¼	¼
Ice Drink Spoons	¾	¾
Ad. Coffee Spoons	2	¼
Bouillon Spoons	2	2
Dinner Forks	3	3
Salad/Dessert Forks	1	1
Oyster Cocktail Forks	½	½
Knives	2	2

(Figures represent requirements per seat)

313

TABLEWARE COST AND AMORTIZATION WORK SHEET
Example shown below —

This work sheet provides a simple method of establishing cost of original installation, replacement cost and cost per meal.

PLACE SETTING CONSISTS OF: 2 Teaspoons, 2 Forks, 1 Soup Spoon, 1/3 Iced Teas, 1/3 Oyster Forks, 1 Knife.

FIGURE COST PER PLACE SETTING With 1 Pc. Knife $7.82

1. Number of seats	200
2. Number of place settings (1.5 x number of seats)	300
3. Number of place settings x cost per place setting	2346.00
4. Cost for 1 years replacement @ 25% ORIG. INSTALL. COST	586.50
5. **Total numbers 3 & 4** to get total 1st year cost	2932.50
Less Trade In or Tax Allowance	$
6. Average number of meals served daily	800
7. Number of annual business days	360
8. Number of meals served per year **(Multiply No. 6 x No. 7)**	288000
9. **Divide dollar total (No. 5) by yearly meals served (No. 8)** to get cost per meal served for **1st** year	.0102¢
10. Cost for 1 years replacement @ 25% original installation cost — (Same as No. 4)	586.50
11. Number of meals served per year — (Same as No. 8)	288000
12. **Divide dollar total (No. 10) by number of meals served (No. 11)** to get cost per meal served for **2nd** year	.0020¢

FINER GLASS SERVING PIECES

HOLLOW STEM CHAMPAGNES
5, 5½, 6, 7, 8 oz.

HOLLOW STEM BEER GOBLETS
10, 12, 13½, 14, 16, 54, 160 oz.

COCKTAIL DECANTERS

Full	To Shoulder
18 oz.	12 oz.
12 oz.	9 oz.
9 oz.	7 oz.
6 oz.	4 oz.
2½ oz.	1½ oz.
2½ oz.	1 oz.

ICE TUBS
48 oz., 52 oz., 54 oz., 60 oz.

SALAD BOWLS

Diameter	Height
13"	4"
10"	3-3/8"
9"	3-3/16"

MUSHROOM COVERS

Diameter	Height
3-3/16"	3-7/8"
4-1/2"	4-1/2"
4-1/2"	4-7/8"
6"	4-3/4"
6-5/8"	6-1/4"

MARTINI SERVERS WITH STIRRERS
14, 18, 30, 42, 60 oz.

ICE LIP WATER JUGS
3½, 7, 10, 16, 19, 32, 42, 48, 64, 80, 120 oz.

PUNCH BOWLS
190, 210, 225, 260, 300, 340 oz.

BUD VASE HEIGHTS
6", 7", 8", 10".

FOOTED VASES
8", 10", 12", 14".

DOMES - Display with or without bases
Diameters 4", 5", 6" — Heights 5", 6", 8", 10", 12"

GLASS PLATTERS

Round: 6, 8, 10, 12, 14, 16, 19" diameters.
Square: 8" x 8", 10" x 10", 12" x 12", 14" x 14", 16" x 16"
Oval Platters: 14" x 19"
Rectangular: 8" x 14", 10" x 16"

We have listed a few of the more common and asked for glass pieces for fine dining. Complete glass service catalogs show infinite variety of available styles. A few of these pieces in use can work wonders with specialty food items.

OVEN PROOF CHINA
(Popular Cook and Serve Dishes)

BAKERS OVAL - NO HANDLES

Capacity	Length	Width	Height
9 oz.	6"	4-1/4"	1-1/2"
11 oz.	6"	4-1/4"	1-7/8"
14 oz.	7"	5"	1-7/8"
20 oz.	7-3/4"	5-1/2"	1-7/8"

WELSH RAREBITS - OVAL
(Lug Handles on Ends)

4-1/2 oz.	6-7/8" x 3-1/2" x 1" high
6 oz.	8" x 4" x 1-1/8" high
8 oz.	8-1/4" x 4-1/4" x 1-1/8" high
12 oz.	8-1/8" x 4-7/8" x 1-3/8" high
15 oz.	10-1/4" x 5-1/2" x 1-1/2" high

SHIRRED EGG - FRENCH
(Round - Lug Handles on End)

	Diameter
5 oz.	4-3/4" x 3/4" high
7 oz.	5-1/4" x 7/8" high
8 oz.	5-7/8" x 1" high
12 oz.	6-1/2" x 1-1/8" high
14 oz.	7" x 1-1/4" high

CUSTARDS

Capacity	Diameter	Height
2½ oz.	2-1/2"	2-1/4"
4 oz.	2-7/8"	2-3/8"
5 oz.	3-1/8"	2-3/8"
6 oz.	3-3/8"	2-5/8"
9 oz.	3-3/8"	2-7/8"

AU GRATIN DISH
(Thicker than Shirred Egg)

Capacity	Diameter	Height
4½ oz.	4-1/2"	1-1/8"
7 oz.	5-1/8"	1"
7 oz.	5-1/2"	1-1/4"
10 oz.	6-1/4"	1-1/4"

Hundreds of sizes, patterns and colors are available in cook and serve dishes. We have listed only a few of the more popular sizes.

SOME POPULAR GLASS SIZES BY OUNCES

STEMMED
- Brandy: 2, 5½, 9, 11½, 17, 22, 32 oz.
- Cordials: ¾, 1, 1½ oz.
- Champagnes: 3½, 4½, 5½ oz.
- Beer: 7, 8, 10, 12, 14 oz.
- Cocktail: 3½, 4½ oz.
- Sours: 4½, 4¾, 5 oz.
- Wine: 2 oz. Sherry, 3 oz. Sherry, 4 oz. Rhine, 4 oz. Claret, 6½, 8½, 10½ Regular

WINES - SPECIALTY: Shapes and sizes too numerous to mention, up to 32 oz. per glass.

ROCKS GLASSES: 5½, 7 oz.

GOBLET: 6, 7, 8, 9, 10½, 12 oz.

WHISKIES — Some popular sizes:
- 3 oz. Plain: 2, 1½, 1¼, 1¾ oz.
- 2 oz. Lined at: ¾, 7/8, 1, 1¼, 1½ oz.
- 1½ oz. Lined at: ½, 5/8, ¾, 7/8, 1 oz.
- 1¼ oz. Lined at: ½, 5/8, ¾, 7/8 oz.
- 1 oz. Lined at: ½, 5/8 oz.

F.E.F. HUMOR

We feel certain that you will find the information in this little book helpful and quite complete, but as a story we were unable to make the plot very spellbinding. To compensate for this we felt that a few industry related true stories from our past might relieve the boredom.

Most of the tales we will tell were not quite so funny at the time they happened but as time passed we were even able to laugh at them ourselves. You will find them throughout the book.

The first one that comes to mind dates back to the "good-old-days" when ice cream parlors had genuine marble counters. Our installation crew was unloading one of the slabs for the die of the counter. An 6'-0" long x 42" high slab of solid marble is very heavy, so our foreman rounded up six fellows to help get it off the truck onto a dolly to roll it into the store. Like plate glass, marble must be handled in an "on edge" position.

The six men lifted the slab from the truck and placed it on edge on the dolly. Then one of the men figured he had completed the task he had been asked to assist in doing, so he turned and walked away. There was no harm in his doing that, except for the fact that the other five men did exactly the same thing at the same time.

All the king's horses and all the king's men could never put that slab of marble together again.

Chapter Eleven

MAINTENANCE

A fast look at some of the more common items used in clean-up and housekeeping for commercial food operations.

From hand dryers and bug killers thru to wash room accessories, common sizes and production figures are listed.

Common brushes, aerosols and chemical check lists are provided for your guidance. While we probably missed a few items, the chapter should be a good basic guide to an often neglected area.

Keep our Personal Assistance Program in mind.

BOTTLE BUSTER

Width 22½", depth 30", height 59½", 1/3 HP motor 115V.

This chute style buster breaks heavy bottles, jugs, beer throw aways, and liquor bottles. Breakage drops to metal basket that holds 60 fifth or quart bottles.

CAN CRUSHER

Width 26", depth 27", height 64", 1 HP motor, 115 or 220 volt.

This unit will crush bottles or cans interchangeably. Reduces up to ten times original bulk of cans and bottles at rate of 50 #10 cans or bottles per minute. GI style can is included.

BUG KILLERS

These units can be very effective at receiving doors or in any area where flying insects may present a problem. They plug into any standard 115 volt outlet. The bugs are attracted by built-in fluorescent lights and killed. Some models may be wall mounted, but they are more effective when ceiling hung where both sides are exposed. Dead bug catchers may be mounted on each side. The effective radiuses shown in the chart below are greatly increased after dark.

INSECT KILLERS			
Width	**Depth**	**Height**	**Effective Radius**
26"	7¼"	16½"	15 to 20 feet
25"	7¼"	29"	30 to 40 feet
49"	7¼"	21"	50 to 75 feet

(Typical sizes - others available)

ELECTRIC HAND AND HAIR DRYERS

Some useful information pertaining to typical hair and hand dryers is listed below. Figures and dimensions were taken from one popular manufacturers literature. Others vary only slightly. They are available either surface mounted or recessed models.

Surface mounted units are 11-3/8" x 9-5/8" x 6-3/8"

Recessed models are 13-1/8" x 13-7/8" x 3-1/2"

Discharge air approximately 150 cubic feet per minute.

MODELS AVAILABLE

	HAND DRYERS		
Time Cycle	Electrical Characteristics		
30 Seconds	115 V.	20 Amp.	2300 Watts
40 Seconds	115 V.	20 Amp.	2300 Watts
40 Seconds	115 V.	15 Amp.	1725 Watts
30 Seconds	208 V.	11 Amp.	2300 Watts
30 Seconds	230 V.	10 Amp.	2300 Watts
30 Seconds	230 V.	10 Amp.	2300 Watts
	HAIR DRYERS		
Time Cycle	Electrical Characteristics		
3 Minutes	115 V.	20 Amp.	2300 Watts
3 Minutes	115 V.	15 Amp.	1725 Watts
3 Minutes	208 V.	11 Amp.	2300 Watts
3 Minutes	230 V.	10 Amp.	2300 Watts
3 Minutes	230 V.	10 Amp.	2300 Watts

Suggested number of hand dryers by number of washbowls are for 1 or 2 bowls, 1 dryer — for 3 or 4 bowls, 2 dryers — for 5 or 6 bowls, 3 dryers. These figures are computed for maximum use periods.

RECOMMENDED MOUNTING HEIGHTS
TO BOTTOM OF HAND DRIER

LOCATION	Surface Mount	Recessed
Men's Room	46"	43"
Women's Room	44"	40"
Children 4-7	32"	28"
Children 7-10	36"	32"
Children 10-13	40"	36"
Children 13-16	44"	40"
Handicapped	38"	35"

RECOMMENDED MOUNTING HEIGHTS TO BOTTOM
OF HAIR DRYER

LOCATION	Surface Mount	Recessed
Men's Dressing Room	68"	67"
Women's Dressing Room	59"	58"
Children 4-7	41"	40"
Children 7-10	48"	47"
Children 10-13	54"	53"
Children 13-17	59"	58"

Elaborate studies have been made comparing paper towels to electric hand dryer costs. The manufacturer states that the statistics used in calculating the savings are available from them upon request. The figures shown below represent the average.

COST ANALYSIS

COST OF ONE CASE of medium quality paper towels......... $15.00
(approximate)

NOTE: Case contains 3,750 towels good for 1500 drys.

COST OF 1500 DRYS with hand dryers (figuring
electricity at an average rate of 5¢ per kwh)............... $ 1.44

NET SAVINGS... $13.56

FLOOR MACHINES
(Buffer Brush Style)

SPECIFICATIONS BY BRUSH DIAMETER						
Brush Diameter	12"	13"	15"	17"	20"	23"
Brush Speed (RPM)	175	175	175	175	175	140
Motor Horsepower	1/3	1/3	3/4	3/4	1	1
Cable Length (ft.)	25	25	50	50	50	50
Cable Wire Size	16-3	16-3	14-3	14-3	14-3	14-3

CHOOSING THE RIGHT SIZE FOR THE JOB:

12" brush for from   300 to 1500 square feet
13" brush for from 1000 to 3000 square feet
15" brush for from 3000 to 8000 square feet
17" brush for from 8000 to 12000 square feet
20" brush for from 12000 to 20000 square feet
23" brush for from 20000 up square feet

FLOOR MAINTENANCE TIME COMPARISON

Sq. Ft. Floor Sq. Ft. Floor	Mop & Pail	Wet Vac. Mach. Plus Wax Buffer	Combination Vac. & Buff Machine
1000	100 min.	60 min.	10 min.
1500	150 min.	99 min.	15 min.
2000	200 min.	132 min.	20 min.
3000	300 min.	195 min.	30 min.
5000	500 min.	330 min.	50 min.

Figures based on 1 man operation each column. Consumed times shown are representative averages only. Very few people work at exactly the same speed.

COMBINATION STEAM CLEANER AND WATER PRESSURE WASHER

All electric, mobile changes from steam cleaner to pressure washer at turn of a valve. Voltage either 230V - 3 phase - 60 amp. or 460 V, 3 phase - 30 amp. 19.5 K.W. Cord, plug and receptacle with machine. Motor 1 HP. Water requirements 4 GPM at 40-60 PSI. Standard 25' cleaning hose. Operator can start and stop machine at cleaning gun. Solution tank 5 gal. capacity.

CAPACITY
Steam cleaner 32 GPH @ 150 PSI - 325°F.
Pressure washer 100 GPH @ 600 PSI - 100°F. temperature rise.

STEAM CLEANER PORTABLE

Size: 36" long x 21" wide, 28" high.

Power Rating . . . . 10 KW
Boiler H.P. 1
Steam Capacity lb./hr. . . . . 34.5 lbs.
BTU at 100% Rating. 33,500
Amps - 220V - 1 Ph. 46
Pressure . . . . 5 to 90 PSIG adjustable

Water supply - standard garden hose.

322

MOPPING EQUIPMENT

TYPICAL MOP HEAD SIZES BY OUNCES:
8, 12, 16, 24, 32 or 40 oz.

TYPICAL MOP BUCKETS:
Oval — 16, 18, 26 or 35 quarts.
Round - 16, 20, 28, 35 or 40 quarts.

TYPICAL WRINGERS:

Cubic Inch Hopper	Mop Size
102	8 - 16 oz.
197	16 - 24 oz.
226	16 - 24 oz.
265	24 - 36 oz.
375 to 415	24 - 40 oz.

MOP BASINS - CAST
(Typical Sizes)

Length	Width	Depth
24"	24"	6 - 12"
32"	32"	6 - 12"
36"	36"	6 - 12"
36"	24"	6 - 12"

ACCESSORIES:
Mop bumper, service faucet, mop hanger, hose and hose bracket.

NOTE: Many Health Departments are requiring either mop basins or sinks and new planning should include provisions for this item.

FACTORS TO CONSIDER FOR IN HOUSE LAUNDRY AND DRYER

1) Value of space to be used
2) Purchase price of equipment
3) Installation cost
4) Labor cost or will existing staff handle
5) Cost of fabric inventory
6) Detergent and utility cost

VERSUS

1) Linen service company
2) Vinyl table covers
3) Disposable table covers

Plus wiping cloths, aprons, hats and uniforms.

ON PREMISE WASHERS
(Smaller Operations, Others to 300 Lb. Hr.)

SIZES

Lbs. Per Cycle	Motor Size	Width	Depth	Height
35	1½ HP	45"	44"	61"
50	1½ HP	45"	49"	61"

CAPACITY PER CYCLE

Item	35 Lb.	50 Lb.
Tablecloths 54 x 54	37	54
Napkins 20 x 20	200	295
Bib Aprons	80	120
Tea Aprons	175	250
Waiter Jacket	25	35
Dress - Uniform	38	55
Uniform Shirts	74	105
Uniform Pants	29	42
Rags - Cleaning	75	110
Mop Heads	23	33
Entrance Mats	25	35

Options: Detergent injection, water recovery systems, programmable console.

LAUNDRY DRYERS
(Commercial)

Typical Size	Rating
Length - 39"	50 Lb. Per Load
Depth - 47"	½ HP Motor
Height - 76"	95,000 BTU of Gas

LAUNDRY TRUCKS - TYPICAL CAPACITIES

OPEN STYLE - LIDS OPTIONAL

Bushes	Gallons	Load Limits
6	48	300
8	64	300
10	80	400
12	96	400
14	112	500
16	128	500
18	144	600
20	160	600

WASTE COMPACTORS

Some typical models are listed, others are available. As always specifications vary by manufacturer. The compaction ratio of waste matter varies from an average of 10 to 1 up to 15 to 1, depending on the nature of the waste material. Compacted material is disposable in bales, bags or boxes. All of the machines listed in Fig. 12-5 are mounted on locking casters for mobility and easy housekeeping.

OPTIONS TO BE CONSIDERED:
1. Ultra violet light mounted within compactor destroys bacteria, virus, mold spores and odors.
2. Reusable heavy duty container into which the waste is compacted then may be removed, emptied and reused.
3. Lift style hand truck. Compacted waste may be slid directly onto the platform of the hand truck, rolled to dumpster, lifted to a height of 45 inches and emptied.
4. Platform truck holds 4 boxes of compacted waste for easy transport.
5. Bag dispenser mounts on top of units for convenient storage of bags in rolls.
6. Automatic disposal chute permits continuous use - buzzer sounds when box is full.
7. Cafeteria type chute with pre-set timer control eliminates attendant.

TYPICAL SPECIFICATIONS

Height	Width	Depth	HP	Voltage	Commpaction Force	Time Cycle	Compacted Cube Size
59½"	21"	22"	½	110/220	9,000 lbs.	10 sec.	16"x15"x16"
70"	24.6"	25"	½	110/220	14,000 lbs.	18-22 sec	16"x20"x18"
76"	28"	30½"	½	110/220	14,500 lbs.	18-22 sec	18"x24"x23"
79"	40"	30½"	1	220-1 phase	28,500 lbs.	20-25 sec	35"x24"x17"

WASTE GENERATION TABLE

Type of Establishment

	Lbs. Waste
Cafeterias	1/2 to 3/4 meal served
Clubs	2 lbs. meal served
Department Stores	1/25 lbs. sq. ft. of floor space
Hospitals	7-10 lbs./bed
Hotels (First Class)	2 lbs./guest rm. plus 2 lbs./meal served
Hotels (Medium Class)	1-1/2 lbs./guest room plus 1-1/2 lbs. meal served
Institutions	3 lbs./person
Restaurants (First Class)	1-1/2 lbs./meal served
Schools	8 lbs./classroom plus 2/3 lb./pupil, if cafeteria
Residential	5 lbs./home plus 1 lb./bedroom
Nursing Rest Homes	3 lbs./person daily

Type of Waste

Type	Lbs./Cu. Ft.
0 Trash, paper, cardboard wood boxes, sweepings	8-10
1 Rubbish, same as Type O except up to 20% food waste is included	8-10
2 Refuse, 50-50 rubbish and garbage	15-20
3 Garbage, animal and vegetable food wastes	30-35
4 Compact solid waste, office files, documents, EDP cards, etc.	35-50

Type of Waste for Average Hospital

Paper (Everything from Cardboard cartons to mail)	64%
Food Service	16%
Glass	7%
Plastics	5%
Metal	2%
Other Wastes	6%

SELECTED SURFACE MOUNTED WASHROOM ACCESSORIES

Item	Capacity	Size		
		Wide	High	Deep
Liquid Soap Disp.	40 oz.	4½"	8-1/8"	5-1/8" to button
Soap Leaf Disp.	1000 leafs	5¼"	11½"	2½"
Towel Disp.	400	12½"	7¼"	6-1/8"
Waste Receptacle	7 gal.	14"	18"	6"
Feminine Napkin Disp'r.	50	11-7/8"	25-7/8"	6½"
Feminine Napkin Disposal	—	8"	11"	4"
Toilet Tissue Disp.	1330 single folds	5"	8½"	3"
Ash Tray	3½ gal.	11"	23½"	5¼"
Paper Cup Disp.	150 - 3 oz.	3¼"	14½"	3¼"

Above list is guide only and not to be considered as complete. We have listed these items because in planning they are often neglected.

WASHROOM MIRRORS
(Stainless Steel Frames · Shelves Available)

STANDARD SIZES

Wide		High	Wide		High	Wide		High
12"	x	18"	18"	x	30"	24"	x	36"
14"	x	20"	20"	x	26"	24"	x	48"
16"	x	22"	20"	x	60"	24"	x	60"
16"	x	24"	24"	x	24"	48"	x	30"
18"	x	24"	24"	x	30"	72"	x	24"

TRASH CONTAINERS
(Common Sizes · Round)

Gallons	Size
10	17½" x 15½" diam.
20	22½" x 19½" diam
32	27-3/8" x 22" diam.
44	31½" x 24" diam.
50	35¼" x 22" diam.

FAST FOOD STYLE with Swing Door Domes.

65 gal.   43½" high, 28½" x 28½"

TORPEDO STYLE with Round Domes

15 gal.   37" x 15" diam.
21 gal.   41½" x 18" diam.

NOTE: Magnetic silver savers are available for many sizes of trash containers.

326

COMMON WASTE BASKETS

Height · Width · Depth	Capacity
9" x 10" x 7"	8 qt.
12" x 11" x 8"	13 qt.
15" x 14" x 10"	28 qt.
20" x 15" x 11"	41 qt.
18" x 16" diam.	44 qt.
29" x 20" x 10"	18 gal.
26" x 16" x 16"	25 gal.
31" x 16½" x 16½"	32 gal.

GARBAGE BAG SIZES

12 x 8 x 22	7 gal.	23 x 17 x 48	40-45 gal.
15 x 9 x 24	7½-10 gal.	22 x 14 x 40	55 gal.
15 x 9 x 33	12-16 gal.	22 x 14 x 60	55 gal.
16 x 14 x 37	20-30 gal.	13 x 4 x 18	Step on can
18 x 8 x 43	30 gal.	22 x 22 x 47	6 bushel
23 x 10 x 40	33 gal.		

SAFETY TREADS

Abrasive, self-adhesive rolls, available 1", 2" or 4" widths in rolls of 60, 120 or 240 feet. For tile floors, stairs, ramps, etc. Adhesive tiles 5-5/16" x 5-5/16" are also available.

ENTRANCE MATS · CARPET STYLE

Typical sizes: 3' x 4', 3' x 6', 4' x 8', 3' x 5', 4' x 6'. Rolls normally 36" - 48" wide by 20' - 60' long.

DUST MOPS AND SQUEEGIES

DRY DUST MOPS
Typical 13" wide. Lengths: 27", 29", 35", 59", 71", 83". Many variations in sizes by manufacturer.

FLOOR SQUEEGIES
18", 24", 30", 36" wide.

WINDOW SQUEEGIES
7½", 12", 15", 18" wide.

PUSH BROOMS
Common brush sizes: 10", 12", 14", 16", 18", 24", 30", 36".

WAX APPLICATORS
Typical size wool pads: 6 x 10, 6 x 12, 6 x 14, 6 x 16, 6 x 18.

327

FOOD SERVICE BRUSHES CHECKLIST

☐ Pot Brushes
☐ Wood Block Brush
☐ Kettle Brush
☐ Kettle Drain Brush
☐ Glass Washer Brush
☐ Bottle Brush
☐ Oven Brush/Scrapper
☐ Vegetable Washing Brush

☐ Grill Oil Brush
☐ Pastry Brushes
☐ Coffee Urn Brush
☐ Coffee Bowl Brush
☐ Urn Gauge Glass Brush
☐ Bakers Table Brush
☐ Waffle Iron Brush

AVAILABLE AEROSOL CANS

- Air Sanitizers
- Ant and Roach Killers
- Fly/Mosquito Killer
- Glass Cleaners
- Furniture Polish

- Stainless Steel Cleaner
- Stainless Steel Polish
- Oven and Grill Cleaner
- All Purpose Cleaner

TABLETS

Sanitizing tablets for pot and bar sinks.

FOOD SERVICE CHEMICALS

COMMON LIQUIDS
Normal packs - 6/1 gallon jugs, 5 gal. pails, 30 or 55 gallon drums.
- Liquid detergent - hand dishwashing, pot washing
- Bar glass detergent
- Electric glass washer detergent
- Scented disinfectant
- Liquid hand soap
- Stainless steel cleaner
- Grill and oven fat fry cleaner
- Spray degreaser
- Ammoniated cleaner
- Lime scale remover
- All purpose (tile & walls) cleaner
- Rinse - dishwashing

POWDERS

- Pre-soak (for flatware)
- Glass washing

- Dishwashing
- Hand washing

Chapter Twelve

BAR
COUNTER AND
DINING ROOM

Illustrations showing typical bar and counter details of construction are in this chapter along with many facts and charts dealing with cost control and descriptions of the latest in liquor and beer dispensing systems. Design brainstorming sections are also included.

The dining room section covers waitress call systems, table and booth space allocation, portable dance floors and much more.

TYPICAL CAPACITIES OF BACK BAR COOLERS

Length	Barrels Total	6 Packs 12 oz. Cans	6 Pack Bottles NR	6 Pack Returnable
92" with comp.	4	208	165	106
79" remote	4	208	165	106
69" with comp.	3	161	130	90
59" with comp.	2	134	110	72
72" end comp.	3	142	118	76
59" remote	3	142	118	76

DEEP WELL BOTTLE COOLERS

Length	Comp. Size	Corded Bottles 6½ oz.	12 oz.	12 oz. Cans Corded
50"	1/3	24	17½	23
65"	1/3	34	25½	34
80"	1/2	44	32	45
95"	1/2	54	39	55

DRAFT BEER FACTS

1/2 Barrel Beer = 1,984 fluid ounces
165.33 - 12 oz. bottles
6.89 cases 12 oz. bottles

DRAUGHT BEER · GLASSES PER 1/2 BARREL

TYPE GLASS		FOAM	
Hour Glass	1" Head	¾" Head	½" Head
10 oz.	264	248	233
11 oz.	235	220	205
12 oz.	220	204	189
13 oz.	198	184	173
Mug Stein			
10 oz.	248	233	223
12 oz.	203	189	176
14 oz.	169	158	153
16 oz.	149	140	134
Heavy Goblet			
9 oz.	378	331	294
10 oz.	330	296	264
12 oz.	248	220	204
14 oz.	209	194	172
Sham Pilsner Glass			
8 oz.	343	325	283
9 oz.	292	279	260
10 oz.	265	245	223
12 oz.	221	204	186
Tulip Goblet			
8 oz.	305	292	275
10 oz.	248	230	207
11 oz.	227	209	185
12 oz.	210	191	167
Footed Pilsners			
8 oz.	325	292	280
9 oz.	282	259	245
10 oz.	250	233	215
Shell Glasses			
7 oz.	360	336	315
8 oz.	315	292	275
9 oz.	270	255	243
10 oz.	245	236	220

Pitchers	1" Head	1½" Head
54 oz.	47	50
60 oz.	39	42
64 oz.	35	38

SELECTED BAR MIXES - DRY POWDER

Type	Size Oz.	Pack	Yield
Lemon	24	12	1 Gallon
Pina Colada	8	12	1 Quart
Bloody Mary	10	12	1 Quart
Orange Screwdriver	11	12	1 Quart

TYPICAL LIQUID MIX PACKS

Lemon Mix . . . . Gallons
Pina Colada . . . . Quarts
Grenadine . . . . 8, 16, 24, 32 oz. and Gallons
Sugar Syrup . . . . 32 oz. - 1 Gallon

BAR DRAIN OVERFLOW PIPES
(Standard Sizes)

Drain Size	Tube Length	Drain Size	Tube Length
1/2"	4-1/2"	1-1/2"	8"
1"	7-1/2"	1-1/2"	10"
1-1/2"	7"	1-1/2"	12"
1-1/2"	7-1/2"	2"	12"

STANDARD BAR FAUCETS

Mounting: flat or deck, wall mount.
Centers: 1¾", 2", 3½", 4", 8"
Spout lengths: 6", 8", 10", 12"

BEVERAGE DISPLAY MERCHANDISER

This unit features round rotating shelves with a full view glass hinged door. The fully refrigerated interior will hold 24 to 30 cases of soda or beer.
Typical size: 34½" x 34½" x 84" high, 115 volt operation.

GLASS FROSTERS

Circulating 10 to 25 below, arctic air glass frosters bring glasses to frosting in a few minutes. These units feature automatic timed defrost.

(Continued)

(Continued)

TYPICAL SIZES

Length	Depth	Height	Capacity
24"	26½"	38"	Frosts up to 300 assorted glasses per hour — top
46"	26-7/8"	38"	2 compartments frost and holds up to 216 - 10 oz. mugs or 400 - 8 oz. shell glasses - closed top

Also available are conveyor style glass frosters that frost to 600 mugs per hour and will store 120 - 8 oz. mugs at the same time.

TYPICAL BAR SINK SIZES ASSUMING SINK IN CENTER (Adjust drainboard size if sink are to one side)

Length	No. of Sinks	Drainboard Each Side
3'	1	12"
4'	1	18"
4'	2	12"
5'	2	18"
5'	3	12"
6'	3	18"
6'	4	12"
7'	2	30"
7'	3	24"
7'	4	18"
8'	2	36"
8'	3	30"
8'	4	24"
9'	4	30"
10'	4	36"

Depths available: 18", 21", 24", front to back of unit.

UNDER BAR SINK AND COCKTAIL UNIT OPTIONS

STAINLESS STEEL FILLER SECTIONS:

To fill in space between underbar workboard units at either inside or outside corners. Provide additional shelf space. Available angled to fit 15°, 30°, 45°, 60°, 75° or 90° corners.

OTHER AVAILABLE OPTIONS:

- Bottle opener/catcher
- Waste chutes for liquids
- Cold plates (built-in)
- Blendor stands
- Towel rings
- Continuous waste assemblies for drains
- Lexan domes to cover ice in cocktail units
- Speed rails in front of sink drainboards to accommodate bottles 2', 3', 4', 5' and 6' long, approximately 3 bottles to the foot.

BAR SERVICE CHECKLIST
(Small Wares)

	Bar & Lounges	Restaurants
Blendor	2	1
Ice Scoop	2	1
Cocktail Shakers	6	3
Jiggers	2	2
Pourers	6 dz.	4 dz.
Cutting Board	2	1
Towel Holders	3	1
Julep Strainer	1	1
Wire Bar Strainer	2	1
Fruit Knife	2	1
Fruit Peeler	2	1
Mixing Spoons	4	2
Muddler	2	1
Sugar Caddy	2	1
Bar Fruit Caddy	2	1
Cork Removers	3	2
Speed Racks	3	1
Stirrers	10m	10m
Ice Buckets	2	4
Water Pitchers	3	3
Beer Pitchers	3	6

Assumes 100 people served and the bar at restaurant is service type or minimum amount stools.

BAR MIXERS · BLENDORS

Typical container sizes: 24, 32, 40, 44 oz.

Container available in glass, lexan or stainless steel.

Motor choices: single speed, two speed, five speed, seven speed. Ratings up to 1/2 HP available. Timed from 1 to 60 seconds. RPM's from 3,500 to 18,000. Also available for kitchen use 1/2 and 1 gallon styles. Blades available for cocktail use, or liquifier.

BAR BEVERAGE DISPENSERS, SODA
(Remote or self contained under bar)

TYPICAL PRODUCTION

Rating	Comp. HP	Drinks Per Minute	Drinks Per Hour
Small Volume	1/6	4-6 oz.	75
Medium Volume	1/4	4-6 oz.	325
High Volume	1/3	4-6 oz.	575
Heavy Volume	1	15-6 oz.	1550

333

Compressor recovery rates will vary. Guide suggests selection to be made on hourly recovery closest to your peak serving period, and considering how many stations and how far a run will be made with beverage lines will determine final selection.

For typical syrup tank size for above post mix systems and related information, see Chapter 7, Holding, Serving and Transporting.

BEER PORTION CHECK UNIT

This remarkably small solid state unit is mounted directly on top of the beer dispensing faucet. The identifying tap knob is removed, the metering device is screwed in place, then the tap knob is screwed into the top of the unit. The unit is then easily calibrated to the existing rate of flow without changing pressure or temperature. No part of the unit comes into contact with the product.

Programmed to compute the rate of flow at a given faucet, this information is converted from a time flow to an ounce count by the minicomputer within the unit. The ounce or glass count is shown by continuous accurate L.E.D. readout. Comparison of the readings with cash register tapes provides accurate check against losses and pilferage. Ideal for parties and banquets to eliminate disputes over quantities served.

Unit operates on a 6 volt AC/DC converter. An optional back-up power cable which would attach to a 6 V lantern battery is available.

SUMMARY OF FEATURES:
Profit control, easy installation, solid state dependability, tamper alarm, L.E.D. readout, complete accounting forms, can also meter wines, house drinks or any beverage dispensed through a faucet.

Other systems using faucet control available.

COMPUTER BARS

Programmed system can control 72 different brands, cocktails, highballs and soda. Distribution to a maximum of four separate stations. Drinks mixed and portioned to your requirements. Remote storage rack holds 112 fifths, quarts or 1/2 gallons.

MAIN COMPONENTS

1) Under bar main station houses wines and mixes, dispensing tower, ice storage bin, programmable keyboard for calling up drinks and cash register.
2) Guest check printer, optional accessory
3) Accounting printer for management functions as product breakdown totals, and inventory control is also an optional accessory.

GRAVITY LIQUOR DISPENSERS

Tamper-proof neck lock attachments fit on the liquor bottles. Inverted, the bottles are inserted into dispenser/counter units with a simple tool and key. Many styles of dispenser units are available.

Units adjust to pour from ½ to 2 oz. portions. Options include: hand held hose type dispensers - racks to hold gangs of same brand liquor - wall mounts - over or under bar mounts or lazy-susan racks. Interfacing with cash register and interconnection with beer system may be accomplished.

INDIVIDUAL ELECTRONIC LIQUOR BOTTLE CONTROL SYSTEM

This system employs price coded pourers which are inserted into and.sealed to any and all bottles. A control box, 15" x 13" x 7", may be mounted under bar top. An activator ring is connected to the control unit by a ten foot pig-tail cord resembling a telephone cord. To pour drinks, the bartender slips the bottle up through the activator ring and pours with the usual pouring motion.

The control unit instantly and accurately dispenses and records the price of each drink. Portions adjustable in ¼ oz. increments up to 6 oz. Unit has locking "Happy Hour" switch.

WINE DISPENSING

No matter what your needs are there is a wine dispensing system available to fulfill them. With a word of caution to check your local laws governing bulk wine dispensing and a suggestion that you contact your equipment supplier.

Many decorative units involving the wine barrel theme are available as refrigerated free standing, mobile or back-bar units.

Gallon bottles may be poured into the above units or they may use 3 gallon, nitrogen powered, pressure cans resembling soda syrup cans or "Bag-in-Box" containers from the wineries. (Check local laws.)

MOBILE WINE DISPENSER

One typical unit measures 36" long, 30" deep and 60" high. Electronic dispenser rated at 3 oz. per second, holds 3 three gallon nitrogen powered wine tanks and is factory set to dispense 4 oz. glass, 17 oz. (½ liter) or 34 oz. (liters). Temperature adjusts from 45° to 60°. Lockable control panel contains on/off switch, non-resetable counters for each pour size and adjustable solid state portion control for each wine.

Superstructure holds stem wine glasses and has an attractive back lighted wine sign. Unit has simlulated wood grain finish. Work tap is stainless steel, casters 5" poly tired.

BAR CONTROL DAILY RECEIPT CALCULATOR

Number of Drinks	.75	.80	.85	.90	.95	1.00	1.10	1.25	1.50	1.75	2.00
1	.75	.80	.85	.90	.95	1.00	1.10	1.25	1.50	1.75	2.00
2	1.50	1.60	1.70	1.80	1.90	2.00	2.20	2.50	3.00	3.50	4.00
3	2.25	2.40	2.55	2.70	2.85	3.00	3.30	3.75	4.50	5.25	6.00
4	3.00	3.20	3.40	3.60	3.80	4.00	4.40	5.00	6.00	7.00	8.00
5	3.75	4.00	4.25	4.50	4.75	5.00	5.50	6.25	7.50	8.75	10.00
6	4.50	4.80	5.10	5.40	5.70	6.00	6.60	7.50	9.00	10.50	12.00
7	5.25	5.60	5.95	6.30	6.65	7.00	7.70	8.75	10.50	12.25	14.00
8	6.00	6.40	6.80	7.20	7.60	8.00	8.80	10.00	12.00	14.00	16.00
9	6.75	7.20	7.65	8.10	8.55	9.00	9.90	11.25	13.50	15.75	18.00
10	7.50	8.00	8.50	9.00	9.50	10.00	11.00	12.50	15.00	17.50	20.00
11	8.25	8.80	9.35	9.90	10.45	11.00	12.10	13.75	16.50	19.25	22.00
12	9.00	9.60	10.20	10.80	11.40	12.00	13.20	15.00	18.00	21.00	24.00
13	9.75	10.40	11.05	11.70	12.35	13.00	14.30	16.25	19.50	22.75	26.00
14	10.50	11.20	11.90	12.60	13.30	14.00	15.40	17.50	21.00	24.50	28.00
15	11.25	12.00	12.75	13.50	14.25	15.00	16.50	18.75	22.50	26.25	30.00
16	12.00	12.80	13.60	14.40	15.20	16.00	17.60	20.00	24.00	28.00	32.00
17	12.75	13.60	14.45	15.30	16.15	17.00	18.70	21.25	25.50	29.75	34.00
18	13.50	14.40	15.30	16.20	17.10	18.00	19.80	22.50	27.00	31.50	36.00
19	14.25	15.20	16.15	17.10	18.05	19.00	20.90	23.75	28.50	33.25	38.00
20	15.00	16.00	17.00	18.00	19.00	20.00	22.00	25.00	30.00	35.00	40.00
21	15.75	16.80	17.85	18.90	19.95	21.00	23.10	26.25	31.50	36.75	42.00
22	16.50	17.60	18.70	19.80	20.90	22.00	24.20	27.50	33.00	38.50	44.00
23	17.25	18.40	19.55	20.70	21.85	23.00	25.30	28.75	34.50	40.25	46.00
24	18.00	19.20	20.40	21.60	22.80	24.00	26.40	30.00	36.00	42.00	48.00
25	18.75	20.00	21.25	22.50	23.75	25.00	27.50	31.25	37.50	43.75	50.00
26	19.50	20.80	22.10	23.40	24.70	26.00	28.60	32.50	39.00	45.50	52.00
27	20.25	21.60	22.95	24.30	25.65	27.00	29.70	33.75	40.50	47.25	54.00
28	21.00	22.40	23.80	25.20	26.60	28.00	30.80	35.00	42.00	49.00	56.00
29	21.75	23.20	24.65	26.10	27.55	29.00	31.90	36.25	43.50	50.75	58.00
30	22.50	24.00	25.50	27.00	28.50	30.00	33.00	37.50	45.00	52.50	60.00
31	23.25	24.80	26.35	27.90	29.45	31.00	34.10	38.75	46.50	54.25	62.00
32	24.00	25.60	27.20	28.80	30.40	32.00	35.20	40.00	48.00	56.00	64.00
33	24.75	26.40	28.05	29.70	31.35	33.00	36.30	41.25	49.50	57.75	66.00
34	25.50	27.20	28.90	30.60	32.30	34.00	37.40	42.50	51.00	59.50	68.00
35	26.25	28.00	29.75	31.50	33.25	35.00	38.50	43.75	52.50	61.25	70.00
36	27.00	28.80	30.60	32.40	34.20	36.00	39.60	45.00	54.00	63.00	72.00
37	27.75	29.60	31.45	33.30	35.15	37.00	40.70	46.25	55.50	64.75	74.00
38	28.50	30.40	32.30	34.20	36.10	38.00	41.80	47.50	57.00	66.50	76.00
39	29.25	31.20	33.15	35.10	37.05	39.00	42.90	48.75	58.50	68.25	78.00
40	30.00	32.00	34.00	36.00	38.00	40.00	44.00	50.00	60.00	70.00	80.00
41	30.75	32.80	34.85	36.90	38.95	41.00	45.10	51.25	61.50	71.75	82.00
42	31.50	33.60	35.70	37.80	39.90	42.00	46.20	52.50	63.00	73.50	84.00
43	32.25	34.40	36.55	38.70	40.85	43.00	47.30	53.75	64.50	75.25	86.00
44	33.00	35.20	37.40	39.60	41.80	44.00	48.40	55.00	66.00	77.00	88.00
45	33.75	36.00	38.25	40.50	42.75	45.00	49.50	56.25	67.50	78.75	90.00
46	34.50	36.80	39.10	41.40	43.70	46.00	50.60	57.50	69.00	80.50	92.00
47	35.25	37.60	39.95	42.30	44.65	47.00	51.70	58.75	70.50	82.25	94.00
48	36.00	38.40	40.80	43.20	45.60	48.00	52.80	60.00	72.00	84.00	96.00
49	36.75	39.20	41.65	44.10	46.55	49.00	53.90	61.25	73.50	85.75	98.00
50	37.50	40.00	42.50	45.00	47.50	50.00	55.00	62.50	75.00	87.50	100.00

336

SOME CHARTS ON LIQUOR LOSSES

SHOTS PER BOTTLE BASED ON ONE (1) U.S. QUART
2 oz. - 16 shots • 1½ oz. - 21 shots • 1¼ oz. - 25 shots
1-1/8 oz. - 28 shots • 1 oz. - 32 shots • 7/8 oz. - 36 shots
¾ oz. - 42 shots • 5/8 oz. - 51 shots

DOLLARS AND U.S. QUART BOTTLES PER MONTH LOST TO BAR BY WASTAGE AND OVERPOURING (BASED ON 1 U.S. OUNCE SHOT)

Oz. per bottle wasted or overpoured	No. of cases bought per mo. at average wholesale cost of $72.00 per case					
	10 cases	20 cases	30 cases	40 cases	50 cases	60 cases
2 oz. per bottle	$45.00 or 7½ bottles	$90.00 or 15 bottles	$135.00 or 22½ bottles	$180.00 or 30 bottles	$225.00 or 37½ bottles	$270.00 or 45 bottles
4 oz. per bottle	$90.00 or 15 bottles	$180.00 or 30 bottles	$270.00 or 45 bottles	$360.00 or 60 bottles	$450.00 or 75 bottles	$540.00 or 90 bottles
6 oz. per bottle	$135.00 or 22½ bottles	$270.00 or 45 bottles	$405.00 or 67½ bottles	$540.00 or 90 bottles	$675.00 or 112½ btls.	$810.00 or 135 btls.

REVENUE LOST BY WASTAGE AND OVER-POURING BASED ON RETAIL PRICE PER OUNCE

Price Per Oz.	Oz. Per Btl. Wasted	10 Cases Per Month	20 Cases Per Month	30 Cases Per Month	40 Cases Per Month	50 Cases Per Month
$ .75	1 oz.	$ 90.00	$180.00	$ 270.00	$ 360.00	$ 450.00
	2 oz.	180.00	360.00	585.00	720.00	900.00
	3 oz.	270.00	540.00	810.00	1,080.00	1,350.00
$ .80	1 oz.	96.00	192.00	288.00	384.00	480.00
	2 oz.	192.00	384.00	624.00	768.00	960.00
	3 oz.	288.00	576.00	864.00	1,440.00	1,530.00
$ .85	1 oz.	102.00	204.00	306.00	408.00	510.00
	2 oz.	204.00	408.00	663.00	816.00	1,020.00
	3 oz.	306.00	612.00	918.00	1,224.00	1,467.00
$ .90	1 oz.	108.00	216.00	324.00	432.00	540.00
	2 oz.	216.00	432.00	702.00	864.00	1,080.00
	3 oz.	324.00	648.00	972.00	1,296.00	1,620.00
$ .95	1 oz.	114.00	228.00	342.00	456.00	570.00
	2 oz.	228.00	468.00	741.00	912.00	1,140.00
	3 oz.	342.00	684.00	1,026.00	1,368.00	1,710.00
$1.00	1 oz.	120.00	240.00	360.00	480.00	600.00
	2 oz.	240.00	480.00	780.00	960.00	1,200.00
	3 oz.	360.00	720.00	1,080.00	1,440.00	1,800.00
$1.05	1 oz.	126.00	252.00	378.00	504.00	630.00
	2 oz.	252.00	504.00	819.00	1,008.00	1,260.00
	3 oz.	378.00	756.00	1,134.00	1,512.00	1,890.00
$1.10	1 oz.	132.00	264.00	396.00	528.00	660.00
	2 oz.	264.00	528.00	858.00	1,056.00	1,320.00
	3 oz.	396.00	792.00	1,188.00	1,584.00	1,980.00
$1.20	1 oz.	144.00	288.00	432.00	576.00	720.00
	2 oz.	288.00	576.00	936.00	1,152.00	1,440.00
	3 oz.	432.00	864.00	1,296.00	1,728.00	2,160.00
$1.25	1 oz.	150.00	290.00	450.00	600.00	750.00
	2 oz.	300.00	600.00	975.00	1,200.00	1,500.00
	3 oz.	450.00	900.00	1,350.00	1,800.00	2,250.00

PROCEEDS FROM BOTTLE OF LIQUOR
(Shown for 750 ML - 1 Liter and 1.75 Liter)

750 ML (25.4 oz.) 4/5 QUART (25 oz.)
PRICE PER DRINK

Size	No. Drinks	.75	.90	1.00	1.35	1.50	1.90	2.00	2.25
5/8oz	40.6	30.45	36.54	40.60	54.81	60.90	77.14	81.20	91.35
3/4oz	33.8	25.35	30.42	33.80	45.63	50.70	64.22	67.60	76.05
7/8oz	29.0	21.75	26.10	29.00	39.15	43.50	55.10	58.00	65.25
1 oz	25.4	19.05	22.86	25.40	34.29	38.10	48.26	50.80	57.15
1-1/8oz	22.5	16.87	20.25	22.50	30.37	33.75	42.75	45.00	50.62
1-1/4oz	20.3	15.22	18.27	20.30	27.40	30.45	38.57	40.60	45.67
1-3/8oz	18.4	13.80	16.56	18.40	24.84	27.60	34.96	36.80	41.40
1-1/2oz	16.9	12.67	15.21	16.90	22.81	25.35	32.11	33.80	38.02
1-5/8oz	15.6	11.70	14.04	15.60	21.06	23.40	29.64	31.20	35.10
1-3/4oz	14.5	10.87	13.05	14.50	19.57	21.75	27.55	29.00	32.62
1-7/8oz	13.5	10.12	12.15	13.15	18.22	20.25	25.65	27.00	30.37
2 oz	12.7	9.52	11.43	12.70	17.14	19.05	24.13	25.40	28.57

LITER (33.8 oz.) . . . REPLACES QUART (32 oz.)

Glass Size	No. Drinks	.75	.90	1.00	1.35	1.50	1.90	2.00	2.25
5/8oz	54.0	40.50	48.60	54.00	72.90	81.00	102.60	108.00	121.50
3/4oz	45.0	33.75	40.50	45.00	60.75	67.50	85.50	90.00	101.25
7/8oz	38.6	28.95	34.74	38.60	52.11	57.90	73.34	77.20	86.85
1 oz	33.8	25.35	30.42	33.80	45.63	50.70	64.22	67.60	76.05
1-1/8oz	30.0	22.50	27.00	30.00	40.50	45.00	57.00	60.00	67.50
1-1/4oz	27.0	20.25	24.30	27.00	36.45	40.50	51.30	54.00	60.75
1-3/8oz	24.5	18.37	22.05	24.50	33.07	36.75	46.55	49.00	55.12
1-1/2oz	22.5	16.87	20.25	22.50	30.37	33.75	42.75	45.00	50.62
1-5/8oz	20.8	15.60	18.72	20.80	28.08	31.20	39.52	41.60	46.80
1-3/4oz	19.3	14.47	17.39	19.30	26.05	28.95	36.67	38.60	43.42
1-7/8oz	18.0	13.50	16.20	18.00	24.30	27.00	34.20	36.00	40.50
2 oz	16.9	12.67	15.21	16.90	22.81	25.35	32.11	33.80	38.02

1.75 LITER (59.2 oz.) . . . REPLACES 1/2 GALLON (64 oz.)

Glass Size	No. Drinks	.75	.90	1.00	1.35	1.50	1.90	2.00	2.25
5/8oz	94.7	71.02	85.23	94.70	127.84	142.05	179.93	189.40	213.07
3/4oz	78.9	59.17	71.01	78.90	106.51	118.35	149.91	157.80	177.52
7/8oz	67.6	50.70	60.84	67.60	91.26	101.40	128.44	135.20	152.10
1 oz	59.2	44.40	53.28	59.20	79.92	88.80	112.48	118.40	133.20
1-1/8oz	52.6	39.45	47.34	52.60	71.01	78.90	99.94	105.20	118.35
1-1/4oz	47.3	35.47	42.57	47.30	63.85	70.95	89.87	94.60	106.42
1-3/8oz	43.0	32.25	38.70	43.00	58.05	64.50	81.70	86.00	96.75
1-1/2oz	39.4	29.55	35.46	39.40	53.19	59.10	74.86	78.80	88.65
1-5/8oz	36.4	27.30	32.76	36.40	49.14	54.60	69.16	72.80	81.90
1-3/4oz	33.8	25.35	30.42	33.80	45.63	50.70	64.22	67.60	76.05
1-7/8oz	31.5	23.62	28.35	31.50	42.52	47.25	59.85	63.00	70.87
2 oz	29.6	22.20	26.64	29.60	39.96	44.40	56.24	59.20	66.60

WINE PROFIT
(Based on cost of $18.00 per case, 4 gal. Bulk Wine)

Size	Cost	Selling Price	Profit Per Glass	Profit Per Gallon
4 oz. serving	$.14	$ .60	$ .46	$15.18
(6 oz. glass)		.75	.61	20.13
		.90	.76	25.08
		$1.00	.86	28.38
5 oz. serving	.17	.75	.58	15.66
(7-8 oz. glass)		.90	.73	19.71
		1.00	.83	22.41
		1.25	1.08	29.16
6 oz. serving	.20	.75	.55	12.10
(7-9 oz. glass)		.90	.70	15.40
		1.00	.80	17.60
		$1.10	.90	19.80
		1.25	1.05	23.10

WIRE SHELVES - WINE STORAGE

Contoured shelves to accept wine bottles are available in standard sizes as follows. Bottles lay down and are tilted.

Shelf Sizes

Length	Width	Bottles Per Shelf
36"	15"	8
42"	15"	10
48"	15"	12

Above shelves are available in these standard heights.

Height	Shelves	
63"	12	Times bottes from
73"	14	above for total
88"	17	capacity

Typical 4' long x 63" high would hold 144 bottles.

COMPRESSED AIR PROPELLENT SYSTEM

For use with beer, wine or soda systems. The air used in these systems is filtered to remove 99.99% of all contaminates, then compressed and held in tanks at 60 lbs. pressure.

For use with beer systems a control box, 10" high x 10" deep x 19" wide adds additional filtration and mixes 12% CO_2 to air. Controlled pressure and low CO_2 content eliminates over-foaming and reduces CO_2 costs up to 70%. The same system may be used with soda or wine systems.

An optional system to propel soda or wine uses only the air as a propellent. CO_2 consumption is reduced to only that which is needed for the carbonator (approx. 30%). As a wine propellent the high cost of nitrogen is eliminated.

A third system for low volume consists of an air pump with filtering attachment and a 50 PSI max. tank.

LIQUOR POURERS

Ounce Pour Size	Yield Per Qt.
5/8	51 pours
3/4	42 pours
7/8	36 pours
1	32 pours
1-1/8	28 pours
1-1/4	25 pours
1-1/2	21 pours
2	16 pours

AVERAGE LIQUOR BOTTLE SIZES:
1 Quart - 3¼" x 11½" high
½ Gallon - 5" x 12¼" high
1 Gallon - 6½" x 13" high

RECEPTION DRINK* ESTIMATOR

	DRINKS PER GUEST					DRINKS PER BOTTLE			RECEPTION SERVICE ESTIMATOR			
No. of Guests	1/2 Hour	One Hour	1-1/2 Hours	Two Hours		Bottle Size	Drink Size	No. of Drinks	No. of Guests	No. of Bar-tenders	No. of Waiters W/Food	No. of Waiters W/O Food
25-55	2	3½-4	4-4½	4½-5		4/5 Qt.	1 oz.	25	25-100	1	2	1
60-104	2	3½-4	4	4½-5		4/5 Qt.	1¼ oz.	20	105-205	2	3	2
105-225	2	3	4	4½-5		4/5 Qt.	1½ oz.	17	215-325	3	3	2
230-300	1½-2	2½-3	3	3½-4		Quart	1 oz.	31	350-475	4	4	3
315-& Up	1½-2	2½-3	3	3½-4		Quart	1¼ oz.	25				
						Quart	1½ oz.	21				

*Based on male attendance — Easy access to bars
With 50% female attendance — Average 2½-3 per hour.   With 100% female attendance — Average 2-2½ per hour.

BEER DISPENSING SYSTEMS

Take out the carbonator in any soda system and you have a beer dispensing system.

Basically a beer system provides a means of supplying beer at the ideal serving temperature of 40°F to the beer tap. The simplest possible means of accomplishing this is to place the keg in a tub of ice, pump air into the keg and draw the beer. We've all seen these hook-ups at picnics.

In the process of evolution through the ice-box age, before the refrigerator, the kegs were stored in the cellar. Pressure was supplied by an air compressor that pumped damp musty air into the kegs to force the beer through lines which were coiled in the ice compartment of the dispensing unit of the bar above. The ice man made daily deliveries of ice which he chopped from slabs which had been cut from the lake during the winter. The bartender dutifully pounded the ice down against the cooling coils with the end of a baseball bat as it melted away from the coils and ran down the drain.

The advent of mechanical refrigeration greatly simplified the process. Today the simplest form of beer dispensing is called "Direct Draw". This is to place the keg in a refrigerated unit and tap the beer directly through the wall or top of the unit. Air compressors, with filters added are still used to provide propellent force but are often replaced by CO_2 tanks.

Direct draw units are available in many sizes ranging from a unit 27" square with a self contained refrigeration unit, a small CO_2 cylinder and a plastic bottle for holding spillage from the beer tap. They may be ordered as mobile units for banquet service, etc.

The next step up is to under bar or back bar units sized to hold 2, 3 or 4 kegs. These refrigerated units are available with air compressors or for use with remote CO_2 tanks. Many styles of dispensing heads are available and may include soda heads.

The remaining style of direct draw application is, of course, to use a walk-in cooler to house the kegs. Walk-in coolers are available specifically for this purpose. One wall of the cooler is constructed to actually form the back bar itself.

Remoting the dispensing heads from the refrigerated keg storage unit necessitates some means of holding the beer in the connecting lines at approximately 40°F. The pioneering attempts to accomplish this required that the walk-in cooler be located directly below the dispensing unit with an air shaft from the cooler run directly up to the beer taps. Cold air was forced through the shaft by fans. Some installations of this style still exist.

Many refinements of the system are now available. The beer lines from the cooler to the taps are run in insulated tubes. Some systems run the refrigeration lines inside the tubes with the beer lines. Others use recirculating ice water in the tubes with the beer lines. A reservoir at the dispensing head keeps the taps cold. The ice water is generated by the same unit that cools the storage unit. Larger walk-ins will require separate cooling systems.

The options to the systems include multiple draft stations and incorporation of soda systems and the many methods of computer or other cost control systems.

BAR CONSTRUCTION

At this point, even though it is not the purpose of this book to become involved with design, equipment layout or decor, the authors feel a strong responsibility to make some suggestions for your consideration if you are planning to install a bar. Naturally, we would like you to feel free to ignore them if you wish.

Regarding the first point we would like you to consider, think of 3 or 4 people approaching a long conference table to discuss any topic. They would very unlikely sit down in a straight line at one side of the table. They would gather around one end so they could see each other and the persons on either end would have no need to stick their necks out and shout to the other. Design as many friendly corners into a bar as possible.

Many times an owner will state that he wants his new bar to run straight down along a certain wall. What he really said was, "I want 30 of my best customers to sit all evening and stare at a wall."

Another point to consider in connection with the long straight bar is that the money is made only where the stools are. Properly planned long bars do not need back bars of equal length and the cost of the back bar can easily exceed that of the front.

To solve both problems, run one end leg of the bar out approximately 13 feet from the wall, form a friendly corner, run the bar parallel to the wall approximately 7 feet, form another friendly corner and run the back bar toward the wall to the point where it meets the section of bar which comes out from the wall at the other end of the back bar and turns at the standard 7 foot distance from the wall to run parallel to it. You now have a bar with three friendly corners, a much more interesting appearance and a shorter back bar.

Two suggestions for back bars are to plan the overall layout so that a walk-in cooler may be located behind the back bar wall for direct draw of beer from the cooler. The other is to have a pass window at one end of the back bar to a waitress service station for the dining room. Both may be incorporated into one plan.

When planning large island type bars, consider the slow periods when only one bartender is on duty and will need roller skates to run around the island. Divide the island into sections leaving walk-through space.

If your preference is to serpentine, round ends or curved bars, weigh carefully the esthetic value against the much higher construction costs and remember the underbar sinks and coolers. To place a long bottle box or draft beer unit under a curved bar, not having an exceptionally large radius, could make it impossible for the bartender to reach far enough to be able to serve a customer sitting in front of the under bar unit.

If the authenticity of your decor absolutely demands it, spend a lot of money on your front bar. Otherwise forget it. Remember, you really hope it's so crowded at your bar that no one will ever see it. What color were the fronts of the last two bars you sat at? Inexpensive paneling or applying carpet to the bar front are usually quite satisfactory.

Rough sawn lumber or masonry brick fronts provide an attractive rustic appearance and can be particularly pleasing if you enjoy spending half of your profits buying panty hose and gowns for your female patrons and new suits for the males who destroyed them on the rough surfaces.

A word to the "Do-it-yourselfers" — all that is required to support a bar top is a ¾" plywood panel. The step on the front, the corners and the top itself when secured in place will make it all very sturdy. Building a 2" x 4" stud wall, finished on both sides is an unnecessary waste. Typical bar construction details are illustrated later in this chapter.

Now, the biggie — the conventional 42" high "stand-up" bar VS the 30" high "sit down" bar. For what it's worth, one of the co-authors of this book hates "sit down" bars with a vengeance. That's mainly because he is 6'-2" tall. When the bar is crowded it is the wives who get the seats and he is left standing behind them looking like a telephone pole, wondering what the conversation down there is all about. He can't join in the conversation for any prolonged period without permanent back damage. There is no place to set his drink unless there happens to be a flat headed bald person in front of him and communication with the bartenders, who look like a bunch of midgets in a pit, is nigh on to impossible. If he is lucky enough to get a seat, his knees won't fit because if they put enough overhang on the front of the bar the midgets in the pit couldn't reach it.

It has been the author's experience that the only people who like "sit down" bars are short people. Their preference for the low bar is based on the fact that when they sit on a stool their tootsies dangle in midair. The author has some suggestions as to what they should do with their little tootsies but the only printable solution to their problem would be to have the type of bar stools that have wrap-around foot rests.

If you still feel that the added expense of either building the floor of the entire cocktail lounge up 12" or digging a foot deep pit behind the bar is well worth it. Just forget about the added difficulty involved in trying to get hand trucks for restocking or mobile glass ware carts into the hole and go ahead and build it, really, it's OK.

BAR PLAN WITH THREE CORNERS

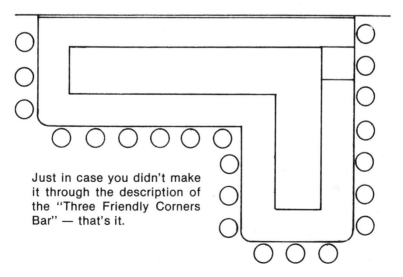

Just in case you didn't make it through the description of the "Three Friendly Corners Bar" — that's it.

SOME TYPICAL BAR CONSTRUCTION DETAILS

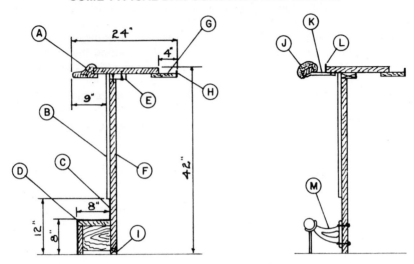

STANDARD BAR DETAILS

A—Arm rest - typical wood shape shown - many styles available including formica finishes

B—Decorative finish - wood panel, tongue and groove board, carpet, upholstery, ceramic tile, you name it, they have it.

C—Kick plate - linoleum, formica, etc.

D—Foot rest - linoleum, slate, hard wood, etc.

E—Cleat - for securing top to die, varies by manufacturer

F—Bar Die - usually ¾" plywood

G—Liquor gutter - usually constructed as shown. May be formed in one piece mahogany bar top.

H—Water stop - ¼" thick black formica or wood. Cut down for cleaning at ends.

I—Shoe - To prevent moisture from separating laminations of the plywood die, a solid wood base strip or metal channel shoe is desirable.

J—Extended arm rest - wood, formica or upholstery. Many styles available.

K—Extension bar - brass or black iron

L—Water stop - same as 'I'

M—Brass foot rest - rail usually 2" dia. swing-away support to floor optional. Check thickness of brass rail your supplier proposes. They are rather expensive.

COMPLETE UNDERBAR ICE CREAM DRINK UNIT

Size: 16½" wide x 26" deep x 30" high. Unit houses a 3 gallon ice cream compartment, a dipper well and a two speed blender with ·automatic shut-off. A feature is a 100 drink library of flip-index cards which attach to top of unit. Unit is 115V plug-in. Requires water and drain. Features stainless steel exterior.

LUNCH COUNTER BRAINSTORMING

THE OPTIONS:

- Sinks
- Adjustable Shelves
- Water Stations
- Ice Bins
- Refuse Bins
- Drop in soup warmers
- Electric distribution systems
- Counter on legs or pylons
- Dispensers for cups & plates
  (China or disposable)
- Cup and glass rack holders
- Built-in cantelever stools
- Package rails
- Footrail or steps
- Ice chests
- 115 Volt outlets
- Drop in burners
- Drop in coffee warmers
- Adjustable shelves
- Silver bins
- Take-out area
- Cash register

LUNCH COUNTER DETAILS

One important rule for counters, or any dining seating is that the height of the seat, stool or chair should be 12" less than the height of the counter or table top. Pedestal or other fixed mount stools should have a dimension of 18½" from the face of the counter to the center of the stool seat.

Average heights of counters are 42", 36" or 30". 42" or 36" counters may have package rails under the front overhang. The step or foot rest of a 42" high counter should be approximately 9" high x 9" wide. The overhang on the front top of 42" high counters should be a minimum of 9". The lower the counter and stool are, the further out the patron's knees extend, therefore the counter overhang must be increased. A 36" high counter should have 10" to 11" overhang with a 7" or 8" high foot rest or step. A 30" high counter requires no step and should have a minimum 12" overhang.

Cantilevered stools, anchored in and extending out from the step may be used with 36" or 42" high counters.

Stools without backs are normally mounted on 24" centers. Stools having backs should be mounted on 26" or 27" centers depending on thickness of backs. The stools should revolve without hitting each other.

COAT WARDROBE FACTS

COAT TREES
Average base diameters: 13", 14", 15", 17"
Average heights: 66", 68", 72" from floor

COAT HANGERS:
Average 17" length

COAT RACKS:

Available with and without hat racks. Capacities 4 to 5 coats per foot.

Coat rack averages:

Average width: 12", 15", 18"

Average lengths: 3', 3½', 4', 5' or 6'

Average height: 66", 68", 72"

Available mobile, stationary and collapsible for out of season storage. Above units available for wall mounting, without bases.

UMBRELLA STANDS

Average height: 18". Capacity of umbrellas: 6, 10, 12 18 or 24. Styles available include aluminum, wood and plated metals.

TRAY STANDS

Tray stands: average length, 24"; average width, 18"; average height, 30".

NAPKINS · TYPICAL SIZES

17" x 17" Regular

20" x 20" Popular

22" x 22" Formal

PAPER NAPKIN DISPENSERS

Napkin Size	Approx. Capacity Dispenser
3½" x 4½"	125
3½" x 7"	135

PEDESTRAIN CONTROL

Portable posts or fixed bases are available. Rails are available in metal chain style, velour rope and various vinyls.

Average post heights: 38" to 40".

Average height to hook rings: 31" to 36".

Average length rails: chain or rope 2', 3', 4', 5'*, 6', 7', 8'

Average post diameter: 2"

Average post distance: 5' to 8' apart

BANQUET TABLES · COMMON SIZES

30'' x 60''	36'' x 72''
30'' x 72''	36'' x 96''
30'' x 96''	

60'' Round — Seating 10
72'' Round — Seating 12

Table storage trucks: Flat bed hold approximately 10 - 72'' or 96'' tables. Round table truck holds 10 tables upright.

FOLDING CHAIR TRUCKS

Length

6'	Upright	32 chairs
8'	Upright	42 chairs
10'	Upright	53 chairs
8'	Flat	42 chairs
10'	Flat	53 chains

Two tier high truck = 84 chairs upright

MULTIPLE SEATING UNITS

We have all seen these units in fast-food installations. The chairs and table are all supported by a single metal frame.

They are available in many, many combinations and arrangements as follows:

- Single units - 2, 4 or 6 seats with table
- Designed for at wall or island seating
- With stool style or chair seats
- With swivel or stationary seats
- With return swivels
- Two seats each side of table or one at all 4 sides
- Round or square tables for 4 side seating
- Frame styles vary - usually one leg under each seat supports entire unit

Designed as mobile units or secured to floor. Colors, table sizes and finishes unlimited. Chair selection equal to normal chairs. Larger institutional units available.

SALAD BAR
CHECKLIST OF COMPONENTS

Salad bars are available in infinite combinations of materials and options, every conceivable size and shape. Look over the list of possibilities for ideas.

1) Mobile or permanent
2) Free standing portable or drop in style
3) Refrigerated by ice or compressor - depth of ice pan? Frost top?
4) Pans - bowls or combinations
5) Tray rail needed
6) Plate storage
7) Sneeze guard attached - hanging
8) Lights needed
9) Drain to pan or evaporator
10) Soup wells
11) Space for bread cutting
12) Plate levelers
13) Refrigerated truck for plates
14) Carving board needed
15) Hot hors d'ouevers or dessert truck to be used?

SCHOOL DINING AREA GUIDE

	Rectangular Folding Tables with Attached Benches		Rectangular Folding Tables with Attached Stools		Rectangular Tables with Stacking Chairs		Square or Round 48″ Tables with Stacking Chairs [1]	
	Approx. Sq. Ft. Per Student	Number of Students Per Table	Approx. Sq. Ft. Per Student	Number of Students Per Table	Approx Sq. Ft. Per Student	Number of Students Per Table	Approx. Sq. Ft. Per Student	Number of Students Per Table
Elem K–6	8–10	16	8–10	16	10–12	12	11–14	4–6
Jr. High 7–8	9–11	14	9–11	14	11–14	12	11–14	4–6
Sr. High 9–12	11	12	11	12	11–14	12	11–14	4–6

[1] Trapezoidal-shaped trays should be used with round tables and square tables.

CONSIDERATION WHEN DETERMINING SPACE REQUIREMENTS

Using number square feet per student as a basis for determining room size should be used cautiously. It should be used only for budget or planning. If room is intended for multipurpose use, the other uses may dictate the size and shape of area.

The square footage for dining area depends upon such variables as (a) configuration of dining space, (b) obstructions within such as support columns, piping, etc., (c) aisle (space) between tables and walls, (d) age and size of students.

DINING ROOM EQUIPMENT

1. **Considerations in Selecting Dining Room Equipment:**
   Prior to the selection, certain considerations must be made to ensure that the type of equipment purchased adequately meets the needs of the school.

   a. Intended Use of Room: If the dining room is going to be used for other purposes, the equipment that is chosen must be compatible with those purposes.
   b. Age of Students: The age of students determines the height of the furniture and the space required per student.

	Height of Tables	Height of Chairs	Linear Space Per Person
Elementary	25" to 27"	13½" to 17"	18" to 24"
Junior High	27" to 30"	15" to 17"	20" to 24"
High School	29" to 30"	17" to 18"	20" to 24"

   c. State and Local Codes: The size of the dining room and equipment must comply with State and local codes.
   d. Available Space: Certain types of equipment occupy less space and allow more seating per square foot.
   e. Types of Trays: Trapezoidal trays should be used with round, curved, small square tables, and odd shaped tables.
   f. Cost of Labor: The cost of labor must be considered for cleaning the dining room. Mobile furniture should be considered if labor costs are high.
   g. Aesthetic Appearance: The appearance of a dining room can be enhanced if tables and seating are in a variety of shapes, sizes, patterns, and colors. Within budget limitations, this should be considered to avoid the institutional atmosphere created by the use of similar tables.

DINING ROOM EMERGENCY LIGHTS

Typical styles plug in 115 volt come on in case of power failure and have 5 to 7 year battery life. Other styles can be remoted to desired areas.

Size	Illuminated Area Covered
12¾" wide x 4" deep x 14" high	3,750 sq. ft.
12¾" wide x 4" deep x 14" high	7,500 sq. ft.
15½" wide x 6¾" deep x 17½" high	10,000 sq. ft.

Normally will provide light for 3-4 hours and recharge to 100% in 12 hours.

PORTABLE WOODEN DANCE FLOORS

Available in 3' x 3' or 3' x 6' panels. Charts show number of panels and total running feet of edging required to form various sized dance floors.

USING 3' x 6' PANELS

Floor Size	Panels	Edging	Floor Size	Panels	Edging
6' x 9'	3	30'	12' x 18'	12	60'
9' x 12'	6	42'	12' x 21'	14	66'
9' x 18'	9	54'	12' x 24'	16	72'
12' x 12'	8	48'	15' x 18'	15	66'
12' x 15'	10	54'	15' x 24'	20	78'

USING 3' x 3' PANELS

Floor Size	Panels	Edging	Floor Size	Panels	Edging
6' x 9'	6	30'	12' x 18'	24	60'
9' x 9'	9	36'	21' x 21'	28	66'
9' x 12'	12	42'	12' x 24'	32	72'
9' x 15'	15	48'	15' x 15'	25	60'
9' x 18'	18	54'	15' x 18'	30	66'
12' x 12'	16	48'	15' x 21'	35	72'
12' x 15'	20	54'	15' x 24'	40	78'

ROLL-UP DANCE FLOORS

Available in wood or vinyl. Standard sizes:

12' wide x 18', 21' or 24' long
15' wide x 15', 18', 21' or 24' long

SELECTING A WAITRESS CALL SYSTEM
WITH DINING ROOM LIGHTS

A) Determine number of switches - 1 for each waitress, plus 1 for management.
B) Pick out dining room locations for display lights
  1. Wall or ceiling mount?
  2. Color of panel and lights?
  3. Will chime be needed?
  4. Single or double face panel?
  5. Horizontal or vertical display?
C) Select kitchen location for control panel. Will chef and waitress use same panel or will waitress use separate switch-off panel?
D) Measure for cable length between kitchen boards if used - then add length from kitchen to dining room panels, allowing for up, down and over for total cable needs.

CHECK LIST DINING ROOM SERVICE

For all food operations, this chart may be used as a guide to formulate amounts of serving pieces needed and type of service.

- Ash Trays
- Bud Vases
- Condiment Holders
- Sugar and Creamers
- Napkin Holders
- Candle Lamps
- Bread and Cracker Service
- Salt and Peppers
- Tea Pots
- Water Pitchers
- Plate Covers
- Trays
- Tray Stands
- Baby Chairs
- Chafing Dishes
- Serving Trucks
- Bussing Trucks
- Table Numbers

- Coffee Servers
- Oil-Vinegar Cruets
- Bread Boards
- Relish Dishes
- Wine Coolers
- Table Top Range
- Table Coffee Warmers
- Cheese Tray
- Tip Trays
- Pastry Carts
- Wine Carts
- Salad Carts
- Wine Baskets
- Pepper Mills
- Mustard Jars
- Service Plates
- Wine Decanters
- Reserved Signs

TABLE TOP SERVICE ITEMS
FOR 300 SEAT RESTAURANT

Seating Capacity: 300 (20 2-seat tables; 50 4-seat tables and booths; 50-seat counter)

Quantity	Description	Application to Operation
18	Coffee Server – 54 oz.	Counter and table service
24	Water Pitcher – 54 oz.	Counter and table service
110	Envelope sugar w/ divider	1 for each three seats at counter – table service
20	Oil and vinegar sets	Table and counter
24	Replacement bottles for above	Replacement use
50	Coffee service – 32 oz.	Table serv. 3 or 4 people
25	Coffee service – 18 Oz.	Table serv. 1 or 2 people
50	Cream Pitcher – 8 oz.	Table service – 3 or 4
84	Cream Pitcher – 5 oz.	Table for 2, counter – syrup
25	Tea Pot – 11 oz.	Table and counter
80	Bread Tray – 10½	Table service
48	Mustard Pot	Corned beef
140	Round Au Gratin	Welsh rarebit
8	Spare glass for mustard	Replacement use
100	Ftd. Supreme, complete	General use
90	Short cake Dish w/drain	Butter service table
48	Short Cake Dish	Short cake or spec. dessert
120	Ice Cream Stand	Ice Cream
50	Relish Dish – 4 comp.	Table service, relish, jam

SERVICE STATIONS FOR DINING ROOM AREA

TYPICAL SIZES AVAILABLE

Wide		Deep
24"	x	19" or 24"
31"	x	19" or 24"
48"	x	19" or 24"

STANDARD OPTIONS:

- Glass shelf above
- Side menu holders
- Coved silver bins
- Water station
- Sinks
- Ice Station
- Bread drawers

- Butter pans
- Coffee warmers
- Adjustable undershelf
- Open base
- Hinged or sliding doors
- Locks for doors
- Rack glides

Finishes available in either formicas or wood. Modular construction allows banking units together.

MENU BOARDS

Some typical sizes of menu boards and suggested amount of numbers and letters required.

Size Board	Total Letters & Numbers
15" x 20" to 18" x 24"	250
22" x 32" to 27" x 39"	600
32" x 44" to 36" x 60"	900
36" x 72" to 48" x 96"	1200

(Unlimited varieties available.)

COMMON HEIGHTS OF LETTERS

1/4", 3/8", 1/2", 3/4", 1", 1-1/2", 2", 3".
Many type faces available.

STANDARD DINING TABLE SIZES IN INCHES

18 x 18	30 x 30	36 x 36
24 x 24	30 x 36	36 x 48
24 x 30	30 x 42	36 x 60
24 x 36	30 x 48	36 x 72
24 x 42	30 x 60	36 x 96
24 x 48	30 x 72	42 x 42
24 x 60	30 x 96	42 x 48
24 x 72		

SIZING GUIDE FOR TABLE CLOTHS

	Table Size	Tablecloth Size
	24'' x 24''	42'' x 42''
	30'' x 30''	42'' x 42''
	36'' x 36''	52'' x 52''
Up to	40'' x 58''	52'' x 70''
	40'' x 78''	52'' x 90''
	40'' x 96''	52'' x 108''
	40'' x 108''	52'' x 120''
Round	40'' rd.	52'' rd.
	48'' rd.	60'' rd.
	54'' rd.	60'' rd.
	60'' rd.	72'' rd.

The above chart shows standard sizes of tables and table cloths. Preferred dimensions of tablecloth drops are 12'' for square tables, 6'' for round tables. This may not always be possible unless custom tablecloths are used.

SUGGESTED INVENTORY IF OWNER OWNED

Napkins: 12-15 per chair
Tablecloths: 5-7 per table

ROUND TABLES

Top Diameter	Seats No. of Guests
18''	2
24''	2
30''	4
36''	4
42''	5
48''	5
51''	6
54''	7
60''	8

SOME TABLE FACTS

Table tops are available in unlimited styles and finishes and with many types of edges. That is common knowledge. One item that is too often overlooked is use of drop-leaf tables. These can convert square tables to either rounds or oblongs in seconds for flexibility in seating plans. When not in use the drop leaves fold completely up under the table top.

SOME STANDARD SQUARE TO ROUND SIZES

30" square, seats 2 - Opened to 42" round, seats 5
34" square, seats 4 - Opened to 48" round, seats 5
36" square, seats 4 - Opened to 51" round, seats 6
42" square, seats 4 - Opened to 60" round, seats 8

SQUARE TO OBLONG SIZES

24" x 27" seats 2 - Opened to 24" x 43", seats 4
30" x 30" seats 2 - Opened to 30" x 48", seats 6
36" x 36" seats 4 - Opened to 36" x 54", seats 6

Table bases and columns are also available in many styles to match any decor. All that can be said here is be sure the base is adequate to support the table. Order carpet glides for on carpet installations and for hard floor installations a wobble stopping glide is available. They do not level the table but by the action of silicone "bouncing" putty they adjust to uneven floors and re-adjust if the table is moved.

HELPFUL HINTS

Square corner tables are usually less expensive than rounded corners BUT they can be very troublesome if installed with booths. They will gouge thighs and rip skirts. Rounded corners should always be put on the outside edge of booth tables.

SNAP-ON TOPS

Normally table tops and bases are delivered in separate pieces. Usually the supplier will assemble them at the site and fasten the base to the top with screws.

One manufacturer offers a patented snap together table assembly along with a full line of tables and bases.

Various cantilever supports for wall mounting booth tables are available. We offer one word of caution when planning for any wall mounted equipment. Make certain there is something in the wall at the proper height to support it. Particularly with metal stud walls it can be a serious problem.

DINING ROOM OR LOUNGE DECOR

The following decor items, miniatures or full scale models, plaques and paintings are usually readily available from a full service equipment dealer. If you are unable to locate them use F.E.F. Personal Assistance Service.

354

NAUTICAL THEME

- Anchors
- Lobster traps
- Harpoon-whalers
- Manilla rope
- Spanish cork
- Portholes
- Glass floats
- Fish nets
- Anchor lights
- Buoys
- Men of the sea plaques
- Ships models
- Ships wheels
- Block and tackle
- Nautical telescopes
- Ships flags
- Divers helmets
- Life preservers
- Wicker covered rum bottles
- Engine room artifacts
- Oars
- Harpoons
- Crows nest
- Wire fish baskets

EARLY AMERICAN THEME

- Copper pots and pans
- Colonial shovel
- Dueling pistols
- Indian figures
- Barrel stool
- Barrel tables
- Fife and drums
- Boots
- Spittoon
- Powder horn
- Gun racks
- Colonial clamps
- Williamsburg plaques
- Early American notices
- Saloon signs
- Cafe doors
- Railroad plates
- Advertising mirrors
- Beer and soda mirrors
- Wagon wheels
- Whiskey barrels
- Covered wagon lamps
- Old West clocks
- Yoke wall fixtures

WESTERN THEME

- Steer hide
- Steer skull
- Indian blankets
- Pot belly stove
- Oak barrels
- Bridle rack
- Boots
- Horseshoes
- Oxen yoke
- Covered wagon plaques
- Horse collar mirror
- Early tools
- Western street scenes
- Wanted signs
- Wanted bulletin boards
- Cigar Store Indians

MEXICAN THEME

- Metal light fixtures
- Bull fight scenes
- Matadors
- Street scenes
- Aztec clocks
- Street musicians
- Spanish ladies
- Conquistadors
- Violin
- Guitar
- Trumpet
- Wrought iron
- Pancho
- Donkeys

MEDIEVAL THEME

- Wall mount lantern
- Spanish helmet
- Normandy shield
- Battle axes
- Crossed swords
- Edwardian plaques
- Coat of Arms
- Medieval armor
- Mace
- Crossbow
- Breast plates
- Gauntlets
- Old world maps
- King Arthur plaques
- St. George and the dragon
- Roman soldiers

DINING ROOM TABLE SERVICE CARTS
(Furniture Style)

Facts on the possibilities:
- Table top drop in butane burners
- Drop in salad bowl and condiment pans
- Drop down shelves
- Bar sink - fruit wells - bottle storage
- Shelves above
- Wine glass racks above
- Bus boxes under shelves
- Hidden waste basket
- Sliding doors below
- Self closing silver drawers
- Brass guard rails around
- Oval pastry shelves
- Mirror trays
- Push handles
- Drop in ice bins
- Carving boards
- Full size ice pan
- Dome covers

Carts are available in wood, formica and various metals.

STEPS FOR SELECTION OF TABLE SKIRTING

- How many tables to be skirted.
- What is table height.
- To determine clip size, measure thickness of the table or stage.

STANDARD TABLE SIZES AND SKIRT REQUIREMENTS

ROUND TABLE		48" DIA. 13 ft.	60" DIA. 16 ft.	66" DIA. 17½ ft.	72" DIA. 19 ft.
HEAD TABLE	6" RETURNS ON OPEN SIDE	30x72 12 ft.	30x96 14 ft.	36x72 13 ft.	36x96 15 ft.
BUFFET TABLE	SKIRTED 4 SIDES	30x72 17½ ft.	30x96 21½ ft.	36x72 18½ ft.	36x96 22½ ft.

If your table tops are non-standard, measure the perimeters to determine the "horizontal width" needed, then add approximately 3 inches to allow for clip clearance.

DINING MENUS CHECK LIST FOR SELECTION

- Single, double or triple fold
- Size per page - overall menu size
- Color of cover and page
- Style of print
- Menu material
- Breakfast menu inserts
- Tassel cords
- Menu clips
- Round corners for longer wear
- If vinyl, do you want wax coating?
- Printed or blank inserts
- Washable
- Art work or photographs

FLOOR PLAN GUIDE

All suggestions given are approximate and minimum. It should be pointed out that no rule of square feet per person can be exact, because too many variables exist. Seating capacities can only be determined by a final layout, but the approximate capacity of a room can be determined by this rough guide:

Banquet or institutional seating . . . . 10-12 sq. ft. per person
Cafeteria or lunchroom seating . . . . 12-14 sq. ft. per person
Fine dining . . . . 14-16 sq. ft. per person

SUGGESTED TABLE SIZES:

	Banquet Institutional	Lunchroom Cafeteria	Fine Dining
2 persons	24"x 24"	24"x 30"	24/30"x30/36"
4 persons	30"x 30"*	30"x 30"*	36"x 36" or 42"x 42"
4 persons	24"x 42"*	24/30"x 48"*	30"x 48"
6 persons	30"x 72"	30"x 72"	52" diameter
8 persons	30"x 96" to 60" diam.	30"x 96"	60/72" diameter
10 persons	72" diameter	30"x 120"	96" diameter

In self service cafeterias, tables should be of adequate size to accommodate the trays.

SUGGESTED MINIMUM AISLE DIMENSIONS:

	Customer Access Aisles	Service Aisles	Main Aisles
Institutional Banquet	18"	24/30"	48"
Lunchroom cafeteria	18"	30"	48"
Fine dining	18"	36"	54"

Allow 18" from edge of table to back of chair in use. For diagonally spaced tables allow 9" more between corners of tables than needed for the type of aisle needed (e.g. for 30" service aisle, allow 39".)

As rough rules of thumb, remember that tables laid out diagonally will increase seating capacity, and a smaller quantity of tables with greater seating per table increases seating capacity but reduces flexibility.

TYPICAL SEATING LAYOUTS

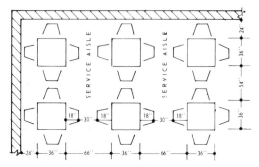

SQUARE SPACING

DIAGONAL SPACING

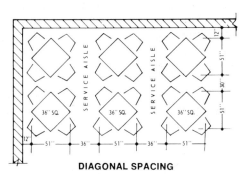

FOUR-SEATERS

SCHOOL DINING AREAS
APPROXIMATE SPACE ALLOCATIONS
(Three shift lunch periods)

No. of Students	Seats	Sq. Ft. Per Person	Total Sq. Ft.
950	320	9	2,880
1350	450	10	4,500
2000	650	10	6,500

BOOTH SIZES

The average booth in lunch rooms, sandwich shops and cocktail lounges will have a table 24" wide x 42" long. The overall dimension of the booth will be 5'-6". A 27" wide table would increase the overall dimension to 5'-9" — 30" tables bring it to 6'-0". Molded plywood or plastic booths without upholstered backs may sometimes be set on 5'-0" centers. Tables should be 30" high, chair or booth seats are 18" above the floor or 12" below the table top.

Give careful consideration to the size table you select. Standard booths may also be 48" wide. Booths in full service restaurants should be designed to accommodate 30" x 48" tables. A 27" x 42" table may be fine for you.

SEATING PLAN SUGGESTIONS

It may almost be considered a universal fact that anything round or curved costs more to construct. This brings us back to the battle of the budget vs. the esthetics. You may prefer the appearance of round tables to square ones. Let's think about this — tables are usually made from plywood or particle board covered with plastic laminate. To make a 36" diameter table the factory must cut 4 corners off of a sheet that could have produced a 36" square table. Guess who pays for the extra labor and the corners that went into the trash bin. The 36" square table would have had 1296 square inches of surface, the round one only has 1018. That means 278 square inches, or a little table 27" long x 10½" wide, which you paid for, went into the trash bin.

Add to that, the fact that 4 people sitting at either a 36" round or 36" square table take up exactly the same amount of floor space. You can't butt round tables together to accommodate large parties either.

Regarding circular or corner booths or settees, the general rule of thumb is that you pay twice for the corners. Check the cost difference before you decide which style you want. If you like booths erence before you decide which style you want. If you like booths and also want the flexibility of seating provided by a long wall settee a good idea is to have the seat of the booth in the corner run straight down the other wall to form the settee or wall bench.

Using only tables and chairs will provide maximum flexibility in seating. Try to always size your tables so that one side of a deuce table will match one side of the 4 passenger tables.

It is a psychological fact that two persons entering a near empty dining room will nearly always sit at seats against the wall or a room divider. Line your 2 passenger tables up there.

When considering six passenger booths keep in mind the fact that they are difficult to get into and out of, particularly if the person on the inside finds it necessary to venture to the plumbing department. They are also quite difficult to serve. Which brings to mind a true story you may enjoy.

Some of the fellows from the office went to lunch at a place where attractive, young, short skirted waitresses were employed. They were seated directly across from a six passenger wall booth occupied by a group of men not known to any of our group. At a point when our group was nearly finished eating, the waitress came down the aisle with a cup of soup for one of the fellows seated on the inside of the other booth. The waitress reached over the extra long table to place the soup before the gentleman who ordered it. She then politely turned to our group and inquired if there was anything else any of them would like. Our chief engineer, Don Francis, answered for the group, stating that there wasn't but they would be more than glad to buy that fellow another cup of soup.

ELECTRONIC TABLE MANAGEMENT

One available system provides complete control over all tables including those not visible from the hostess' station, such as balconies or remote dining rooms. A master control panel with a duplication of your complete seating plan is located at the Maitre D' or Hostess station. Each dining area has a remote panel with a duplication of the seating in that area for use by waitresses or bus boys.

The system provides "light-fast" communication between hostess and service stations. The status of every table is known at all times. Soft lights indicate tables in use. Distinctive signals give advance notice of "tables coming up" so that new parties can be readied for seating. Another signal tells the hostess when she can seat the table with complete confidence that it is correctly re-set and waiting.

On command the system delivers a constantly updated flow of information on table turns and covers counts. It gauges hostess seating efficiency and waitress productivity. Since data accumulates in memories until cleared, the manager can easily chart restaurant activities by lunch or dinner, by day, week or month. More accurate forecasting of business activity related to food purchases and size of staff required becomes available, and provable. This data may be considered confidential and is therefore protected by a key activated switch issued only to authorized personnel.

Since the unit incorporates a microprocessor, it is a flexible and expandable management system. It now delivers the following functions:

DIGITAL READOUT: Time of Day Clock accurately reads hours and minutes. In management mode it converts to digital presentation of the information requested.

Control buttons on the main console panel are capable of accomplishing the following:

READ: Puts the computer into read modes.

TABLES: Reads out the number of times each table has been turned at lunch and dinner. Counts accumulate till cleared.

TOTAL: Reads total table turns for entire restaurant, separately for lunch and dinner.

LUNCH - DINNER: Triggers the computer to read back the information requested for that meal only.

RESET: Instantly returns the unit from management mode to operational mode.

DINER TIMER: Starts automatically each time hostess "occupies" a table. Times are set to any desired length for lunch and dinner. Visual signal advises staff of overtime. Lengths of time and procedures are determined by restaurant's management.

MANAGER CALL: Activated from all stations. Hostess or manager can determine which area of restaurant requires personal attention.

DELTA: Clears memories of data stored during operations. Individual table memories and accumulated totals are cleared separately.

EMERGENCY POWER: An internal battery provides take-over power during electrical outages of 3 to 4 hours. Information stored in memory is retained.

COVERS: Reads out actual number of guests that have been seated at each table, separately for lunch and dinner.

AUTO: Instructs the unit to read back, automatically, in sequence, the times each table has turned at lunch and at dinner. Completes the auto cycle by reading total turns for the restaurant. Also reads, covers, in sequence by table, for lunch and dinner. Completes cycle with total covers.

DINER TIMER: Enables manager to set Timer by size of party with times for each table adjustable up to four hours. Timer is started automatically each time a party is seated.

INDIVIDUAL: Allows quick access to individual table turn and cover count information, not in sequence.

DIGITAL READOUT: Time of Day Clock converts to read "time remaining" on any individual table so waiting times can be quoted with greater reliability.

OPTIONAL FEATURE

INTERCOM: Provides voice communication between all stations. Enables hostess to request special table settings without requiring her to leave station.

A much less complicated system is available from the same manufacturer. The system consists of a wall hung or recess mounted control panel with the restaurant seating plan duplicated on it. Remote controls contain only coded switch/lights when a table is readied. The waitress or bus boy turns that table's switch/light on. The corresponding table lights at the hostess station as customers are escorted to the table the light is switched off.

Another system employing L.E.D. (light emitting diodes) is also now available.

HELPFUL HINTS

Automatic swivel return seats are desirable for fixed stool installations at lunch counters. Stools with backs present a very disarranged appearance and hamper easy access.

Chapter Thirteen

FOOD
SERVICE
HARDWARE

This is a short but informative chapter. It contains descriptive information on many items which at one time or another most of us have spent many hours looking for.

Some items listed are sneeze guards, door kick plates, drive-in pass windows, dumb waiters and typical first aid kits. Check the index. The item for which you are searching may be in another chapter.

STAINLESS STEEL FACTS

Common gauges used in fabricated stainless steel food service equipment:

Item	Recommended Gauge Stainless Steel
Bain Marie	14
Hoods	20
Drainboards	12 - 14 - 16
Sinks	12 - 14 - 16
Steam Tables	14 - 16
Counters	14 - 16
Urn Stand	14
Wall Backings	20 - 22
Trucks	16 - 18
Truck Body Enclosures	20
Doors	18 - 20
Bases	18
Shelving	16 - 18
Side Panels	16 - 18 - 20
Legs	10 - 12 1-5/8'' O.D. or 2'' x 2'' x 1/8'' 1-1/2'' x 1-1/2'' x 1/8''

NOTE: 12 gauge stainless steel is exceptionally heavy and usually specified only for institutional items.

STAINLESS STEEL THICKNESS

Gauge	Thickness	Decimal
12	7/64''	0.1046''
14	5/64''	0.0747''
16	1/16''	0.0598''
18	3/64''	0.0478''
20	1/32''	0.0359''
24	1/40''	0.0239''

363

TEMPERATURE METERS

A portable temperature reading system for all food operations. All equipment probes are housed in portable case. Overall size of the case is 8¾" x 7¼" x 4". No power required. Unit is self-powered with thermocouple system. Readings range from -20° to 730°F. 3' probe cord provided. The probes are for meat, air, liquids, ovens and surface. The face of the system provides a temperature check list and easy to read temperature dial.

DIGITAL TEMPERATURE METER

A hand held digital temperature meter is available that provides readings in red light emitting diodes. The unit is operated by 9 volt battery and is 5-3/16" x 3" x 13/16". It comes with a standard 8" probel. 4" probe and extension cables are available. Used for checking temperatures of fryers, kettles, drinks, refrigeration, or cooked foods as roasts, vegetables or desserts.

F.E.F. NOTE: New systems of the temperature reading and monitoring are available with range of several hundred feet. Operator monitors from a central location.

SMALL CORNER GUARDS

Standard size lexan or stainless steel corner guards for walls.

Size		Length
3/4" x 3/4"	x	4' high
1-1/8" x 1-1/8"	x	4' high
2-1/2" x 2-1/2"	x	4' high

CARD HOLDERS FOR HOSPITAL AND BANQUET TRUCKS

Overall Size	Card Size
2" x 1"	1-5/8" x 3/4"
2-1/2" x 1-1/4"	2" x 1"
3-3/8" x 1-3/4"	2-7/8" x 1-3/8"

Holders may be glued or screwed to face of trucks.

PILASTERS, STAINLESS STEEL
(Adjustable Shelf Supports)

Standard lengths: 4', 5', 6', 12'
Shelf adjustments: 1/2" or 1"
Two styles available: Permanent screwed style or thumb screw removable. An excellent use of these easy to clean pilasters is found under counters in coffee shops or in waitress service stands.

STAINLESS STEEL EDGES FOR GLASS

Stock lengths 6 and 12 feet. Available 'U' shaped channels or tapered inward to provide clamp fit on glass eliminating need for tape or adhesive.

Tapered styles are 7/16" wide with 7/32" opening tapering to 9/32" for 1/8" thick glass — and 7/16" wide with 3/16" opening tapering to 17/64" for 1/4" plate glass.

Straight 'U' styles, as follows:

Opening		Width
1/4"	x	5/16"
9/32"	x	7/16"
3/8"	x	3/4"
13/32"	x	5/16"

PLUMBING FIXTURES - MISCELLANEOUS

Standard overflow tubes (bar sink style) available — plastic, brass, chrome.

Drain Size	Pipe Length
1/2"	4-1/2"
1"	7-1/2"
1-1/2"	1", 8", 10", 12"
2"	12"

STANDARD DRAIN PLUG ASSEMBLIES

Overall Thread Size	Flange Diam.	Depths
1/2"	1-1/8"	2"
1"	2"	1-1/2"
1"	2"	3-1/4"
1"	2"	4"
1-1/4"	3"	3"
1-1/2"	3"	1-1/2"
1-1/2"	3"	3"
2"	3-1/2"	2"

FAST FLO FAUCETS FOR POT SINKS

Inlet Pressure	GPM Hot or Cold Open	GPM Both Open
20	17 GPM	31 GPM
30	21 GPM	39 GPM
40	25 GPM	47 GPM
50	29 GPM	55 GPM

LEVER HANDLE WASTES

These are available in many styles and sizes, most fit 3" or 3½" sink openings — larger available. Most are designed for sink overflow assembly connection — available without connection. The units may have either twist or lever action handles. Units designed for 1½" or 2" waste connections.

TAIL PIECE ASSEMBLIES

Thread Size	Length
1"	2"
1¼"	4"
1½"	4"
2"	4"

FIRE EXTINGUISHERS - TYPICAL OSHA WALL TYPE

Powder Capacity Lbs.	Ht. Inches	Diameter
2¾	14½	3"
6	17¼	4"
10	16½	6"

The above dry chemical units are rated for ABC fires. Classes A, B, C capability as follows:

A. Wood, paper cloth
B. Flammable grease, fats, gas, paint
C. Electrical, motors, switches and appliances

OSHA APPROVED FIRST AID KITS

Kits available to handle 10, 25, 50, 75, 100 people.

STANDARD PACK 50 PEOPLE:
- 100 - ¾" adhesive bandages
- 10 - Sterile pads, small
- 10 - Sterile pads, medium
- 20 - Sterile pads, large
- Gauze bandage 1", 2", 4" - 3½ yds. each
- 5 yards first aid tape
- 10 - Cleansing wipes
- 10 - Ammonia inhalants
- 2 - Triangular bandages
- 4 - Non-adhering dressings
- 1 - 3 oz. first aid spray
- 4 - Eye solutions
- 1 - Tourniquet
- 1 - 2" elastic bandage
- 1 - Rescue blanket
- 6 - Combined dressings 5" x 9"
- 1 - Sicssors, 1 tweezers
- Guide book
- 10 - Antiseptic swabs
- 2 - Surgical pads 5" x 9"

FIRE BLANKET

Blanket size: 62" x 84", red metal box measures 16½" wide, 13½" high, 5½" deep. Glass inspection opening. For wall mounting where required.

SELF ADHERING REFRIGERATION GASKETS - SPONGE RUBBER
(Neoprene Cover)

Wide	Thick	Standard Length
1/2"	5/32"	50'
3/4"	5/32"	50'
1"	5/32"	50'
1/2"	5/16"	50'
3/4"	5/16"	50'
1"	5/16"	50'
7/8"	3/8"	30'
1-1/4"	3/8"	30'
3"	1/2"	30'
4"	1/2"	30'

KICK PLATES

Up to 4" high - mop plate
Up to 16" high - kick plate
Over 16" high - Armor plate
Normally 2" narrower than door.

STANDARD SIZES:
Height in inches: 4, 6, 8, 10, 12, 16, 20, 24, 30, 34, 36, 38, 40, 42, 44, 46, 48
Width in inches: 24, 26, 28, 30, 32, 34, 36, 38, 40, 42, 44, 46, 48

STANDARD SIZE: Door push plates, wrought or cast metals and plastics.

2-5/8" x 16"	7-1/2" x 15"
3-1/2" x 15"	7" x 15"
4" x 16"	8" x 16"
6" x 12"	10" x 20"

STAINLESS STEEL HINGES CONTINUOUS

Width	Length	Gauge	S/S Pin Diameter
7/8"	72"	.042	.091
1-1/16"'	72"	.035	.085
1-1/6"	72"	.042	.091
1-1/2"	72"	.035	.085
1-1/2"	72"	.042	.091
1-1/2"	72"	.062	.120
2"	72"	.042	.091
2"	60"	.052	.120
2"	72"	.062	.187
2-1/2"	72"	.062	.187

Commonly referred to as "piano hinges", they are used for hinging such items as doors for trucks, shelf covers and display covers.

Also available in bright steel or brass, plain for spot welding or with holes for riveting or bolting.

STANDARD STAINLESS STEEL LEGS FOR COUNTER EQUIPMENT
(Heavy duty equipment with mounting plates or threaded studs)

Length	Shape	Plus Adjustment of
1-1/8"	Taper	3/8"
2-1/2"	Taper	1"
4"	Taper	1-1/2"
4-9/16"	Taper	1"
4-11/16"	Taper	1"
4-7/8"	Taper	1"
6"	Straight	1-3/4" - 2" - 3"
6"	Taper	1-3/4" - 2" - 3"
9-3/8"	Taper	1"
9-1/2"	Taper	1"
9-11/16"	Taper	1"
11-1/2"	Straight - Taper	1"
11-5/8"	Straight - Taper	1"
11-13/16"	Straight - Taper	1"

Available zinc plate, stainless steel or aluminum. Feet of stainless steel, white metal or plastic.

LIGHT SHIELDS
(For 1½" Diameter Fluorescent Tubes)

Lamp Size	Shield Size
15"	13"
18"	16"
24"	22"
28"	26"
33"	31"
36"	34"
42"	40"
48"	44"
48"	46"
60"	56"
64"	62"
72"	68"
84"	82"
96"	92"

RECOMMENDED MOUNTING HEIGHT FOR ACCESS BY HANDICAPPED PERSONS IN WHEELCHAIRS

Item	Size	Height
Towel Dispenser, Roll	13" long x 1¾" base	3'-4" to mount holes
Sanitary Napkin Disp.	12" W, 28" H, 7½" D	4'-11" to top of unit
Paper Cup Disp.	3-1/8" x 3-1/8" x 14" H	4'-6" to top of unit
Hand Dryer	10" L x 8" H x 7" D	3'-6" to top of unit
Hair Dryer	10" L x 8" H x 7" D	3'-6" to top of unit
Water Fountains		31" to 35" to bubbler

NEED HELP WITH

- Door handles
- Door Hinges
- Door Locks
- Door Closers
- Foot Pedals
- Door Pulls
- Door Knobs
- Shelf Clips
- Brackets
- Gaskets
- Burner Parts
- Thermostats
- Faucets
- Valves
- Casters
- Wheels
- Filters

We may have in our library some helpful information to assist you Send a self-addressed stamped envelope with sketch or written details.

SNEEZE GUARDS - GUIDE TO SELECTION

1) Sketch showing overall area to be covered
2) Allow at least 3" from edge of table all sides
3) Suspended guards - what is height from top of table to ceiling?
4) What is desired - food clearance from table top to bottom of sneeze guard?
5) Type of mounting needed - brackets, chain, portable?
6) Will the sneeze guard be moved or permanently attached?
7) Contour of the sneeze guard - flat, rolled, any lights in the plans?
8) Average height of customers mouth from floor will be 4'-6" to 5' for adults - adjust in schools for children
9) Will guard be hung flat, angled or have a pastry shelf?

369

CEILING LOUVERS · FOR VENT FANS

Hole Size	Fan Size
27 x 28	24"
31 x 34	30"
32 x 43	36"
34 x 34	30"
36 x 40	36"
36 x 43	36"
39 x 40	36"
36 x 52	42"
39 x 49	42"
42 x 46	42"
36 x 67	48"

Frame adds two inches to overall size.

DRIVE IN WINDOW ASSEMBLIES

We have available information from 6 manufacturers of these pass thru assemblies. Some typical facts follow. Send for more information if needed.

STYLE · NON ELECTRIC

FACTS
- Wall opening: 20½" wide, 15½" high
- Wall thickness: Up to 12"
- Body overall size: 20-1/8" wide, 15" high, 25" front to back. Flange on sides and bottom closes opening
- 46" from road surface to TOP of drawer unit
- Face extension: 2" beyond wall
- Drawer travel: 23" total beyond wall face
- Door swing: 12" beyond face

ACCESSORIES:
Audio system, vision windows, bullet resistive windows, cash drawers, pavement bell ringing hoses.

OPERATIONAL FEATURES:
Inside, a plexiglass cover restricts air flow in or out as the drawer is extended to the customer. Outside, double doors are over lapped and weather sealed, saving energy and eliminating pest problems. Lockable at night. this unit requires no electrical power, manually operated push/pull handle on the counter side. Front edge of the transporter tray is rubber cushion bumper to eliminate accidental contact.

Many other styles available including overhead track systems to serve multiple lanes of autos at the same time.

DUMB WAITERS

The storage or usable area of a dumb waiter is referred to as car size. The following chart will show a few representative sizes.

DIMENSIONS AND CAPACITIES AND CAR SIZES

Capacity	Width	Depth	Inside Height
200 lbs.	24"	24"	36"
300 lbs.	30"	30"	36"
500 lbs.	36"	36"	48"

Entrance doors to dumb waiter cars come slide down, slide up, bi-parting and swing style. Some of the features of dumb waiters include mechanical reversing to eliminate over travel of the cars, overload protection, arrival lights, door open bells, car gate instead of door, and door interlocks.

An under counter unit is available where upper landing will be under a counter, back bar or cabinet.

The complete specifications for dumb waiters will normally be furnished by a food service consultant or architect.

Check with your health department, insurance agency and fire inspector for all regulations affecting installation in your area.

FOOD SERVICE DOORS

Specialized doors for food service applications are one of the bugaboos that many operators have contended with for years. Others have researched or found at various trade shows that there is an answer. One manufacturer and perhaps more, have available at a reasonable cost doors for our indusrry. Available in aluminlum, or solid core metal clad and gasketed doors, these doors are available in stock sizes.

ONE DOOR OPENING: Widths - 24, 28, 30, 32, 36, 40, 42, 44"
TWO DOOR OPENING: 48, 56, 60, 64, 72, 80, 84, 88"
Heights 80" and 84".

These swing easy doors feature the following safety and convenience specifications: no springs, effortless opening, time delay positive closing, quiet operation, ease of cleaning and surface mounted hardware.

Available in decorator colors, with vision windows and many options, these doors deserve your consideration. Need more info — use F.E.F. Personal Assistance Service.

LOCKERS

Wide	Deep	High
12''	12''	60''
12''	15''	60''
15''	18''	60''
18''	21''	60''
12''	12''	72''
12''	15''	72''
15''	18''	72''
18''	21''	72''

Available singly or ganged. Flat or slant tops, solid fronts or vented. Many other styles available. Stacked two to six high and in gangs.

INDIRECT WASTES

It has been the experience of the authors that many people in the industry are confused as to exactly what an indirect waste is and where they are required.

In its simplest form, an indirect waste provides an open air space in a vertical drain line which makes it impossible for sewage to back up into the unit being drained. The most common use of indirect wastes are at ice cube machines where the drains from both the ice making unit and the storage bin will be run to a point where they drip into a floor drain.

As to where they are required, local codes from your health department and building inspector will dictate where they must be used. In general, any appliance or receptacle, having a fixed drain, and which may contain any food item must have an indirect waste.

An iced salad bar may of course drip into a pail but if it is permanently connected to a sewer line, it must employ an indirect waste.

We cannot overstress the importance of giving very careful consideration to drainage requirements in planning for either new or revised installations. Hot or cold water lines, electric and gas supply lines may be run up over doorways or snaked around under counters or bars but water in drain lines will not flow uphill.

Since so many buildings are being constructed on grade with solid concrete slab floors, both the salesman and purchaser must always give careful consideration to any drainage requirements of equipment to be installed. This is particularly true where a new item is to be added to an existing installation. The cost of tearing up and replacing a finished floor to provide an indirect waste for a small undercounter ice machine could easily exceed the price of the unit.

Floor drains are most commonly used where indirect wastes are required but there are many alternatives. The line from the equipment may simply drain into a larger funnel shaped drain with the required vertical air space between them. Drain troughs or floor sinks may be employed or the floor itself may be recessed or curbed and pitched to a floor drain where batteries of steam cooking equipment is to be installed. Recessed floors or drain troughs are preferred over curbing.

Installations having basements beneath may use the simple method of running all indirect waste lines to a single sink installed for this purpose in the basement.

Two final suggestions in closing this chapter:

1. When planning new installations the walk-in cooler and freezer and the ice machine may often be so arranged that one floor drain will provide the indirect waste for all three units.

2. Since cocktail units, ice machines and ice storage bins all require indirect wastes and during peak periods some under bar sink units may be used for ice storage, it is suggested that all cocktail bar equipment drains be indirectly connected. It makes the health department happy and is easily accomplished if there is a basement below. The sinks could cause an overflow problem if on grade.

FEF FUN FACTS

Typical Speed of Peripheral edge of Garbage Disposer Rotors in Miles Per Hour

½ HP . . . . 26 to 32 MPH
1 HP . . . . 26 to 37 MPH
1½ HP . . . . 34 to 43 MPH
2 HP . . . . 38 to 43 MPH
3 HP . . . . 38 to 43 MPH
5 HP . . . . 48 to 58 MPH
7½ HP . . . . 54 to 58 MPH

— NOTES —

Chapter Fourteen

ENERGY

Yes, we know, you're thinking you've heard all about the energy starved eighties many times before. But, be patient and read on, you may not be aware of all of the new items available for conserving energy. Remember when you cut down on the use of energy in your kitchen, you build up bucks in your cash register.

Described in this chapter are many cost savers, some mentioned for the first time ever in a book on food service equipment.

Discussed are systems that utilize normally wasted heat from refrigeration and air conditioning compressors to produce hot water, systems that divert waste water from dishwashers to supply garbage disposal units, and in-line water conditioners that can save your coffee equipment. Read on — that's just a few.

New energy saving devices are being developed every day. They will be included in future editions of F.E.F. as they become available.

Also energy savers are the tempered make-up air systems discussed in Chapter 6, Ventilation.

ACCOUNTING NOTE

Many of the equipment pieces described in this chapter will qualify for various tax credits and depreciation. Credits will be capital investment and/or energy credit. Your payback on these energy control systems and equipment should be considered on a basis of cost plus allowable credits and depreciation. The higher initial costs often have a payback of a few short months.

TIPS ON ENERGY MANAGEMENT AND COST SAVINGS

Cooking Equipment
1. Preheat only equipment to be used . . . just before using.
2. Reduce temperature or turn equipment off during slack periods.
3. Cook full loads on every cooking cycle . . . when possible.
4. Use the correct size equipment for all operations.
5. Avoid slow loading and unloading of ovens and opening doors unnecessarily.
6. Keep equipment clean for efficient operation.

Hot Food Holding and Transporting
1. Preheat equipment before loading.
2. Always use at full capacity . . . when possible.
3. Clean thoroughly, daily.

Refrigeration Equipment
1. Keep doors tightly closed and avoid frequent or prolonged opening.
2. Place foods in refrigerator or freezer immediately upon arrival from supplier.
3. Keep evaporator coils free of excessive frost.
4. Keep condenser coils free of dust, lint or obstructions.

Warewashing Equipment
1. Always operate equipment at full capacity . . . when possible.
2. Flush after heavy meal periods — clean thoroughly, daily.

Water Heating
1. Repair leaking faucets as soon as possible.
2. Reduce temperature where possible.
3. Insulate hot water pipes.

Ventilating System
1. Use only the number of fans necessary at all times to provide adequate ventilation.
2. Turn fans off upon completion of cooking processes.
3. Operate two-speed fans on the lower speed . . . when possible.
4. Keep filters and extractors clean.

TIPS FOR THE USE OF WALK-IN BOXES THAT HELP CONSERVE ELECTRICITY

Electricity is expensive and it will never become less costly. You can help conserve electricity and control your costs by adopting the following practices in the use of your walk-ins.

USE PROPER OPERATING TEMPERATURES
Many users set thermostats lower than necessary, causing a waste of electricity. If in doubt about the proper temperature, contact your supplier.

ORGANIZE STORED PRODUCTS FOR FEWEST DOOR OPENINGS
Infrequent, short openings mnimize cold air loss. Don't prop doors open.

KEEP COOLING COILS CLEAR OF STORED PRODUCT

TURN OFF INSIDE LIGHTS WHEN THE WALK-IN IS UNOCCUPIED
Lights consume electricity and generate heat.

ELIMINATE UNNECESSARY PACKAGING MATERIAL
These materials retard product cooling and increase electricity use.

LEAVE AIR SPACE BETWEEN STORED PRODUCTS
Use additional slotted metal shelves to permit air to circulate freely over and around products.

COOL HOT FOODS TO ROOM TEMPERATURE BEFORE PLACING THEM INTO THE WALK-IN
Most foods can be cooled to room temperature before being placed in the cooler or freezer. If in doubt, check with local health officials.

USE PROPER DEFROST CYCLES IN FREEZERS
Two defrost cycles are all that is required for normal use. If excessive frost forms on the coils, call your serviceman.

KEEP COMPRESSORS CLEAN
Dirt, leaves, paper and other matter on the compressor increases electricity use. Vacuum the compressor regularly.

MAKE CERTAIN COMPRESSORS GET ADEQUATE AIR
Cartons, building walls, air discharges from other compressors, in fact anything that restricts airflow, increases electricity use and cost.

The tips listed above apply generally to all refrigeration units and refer only to the use of the unit itself. Listed further on in this chapter are energy saving systems and devices that incorporate the units themselves.

ENERGY SAVING COOKING EQUIPMENT

FLUID GRIDDLE:
Using fewer kilowatts, this new process is like reverse refrigeration. Built in elements transfer 100% of the energy to a sealed evaporator. Heated fluid vaporizes and condenses under the griddle. Surface air flows back to evaporator to repeat the cycle. Units have solid state controls.

COMING SOON — MAGNETIC INDUCTION RANGES:
The first units to become available will be griddles and saute ranges.
In operation the power supply (208 or 220V) is converted to direct current. The magnetic field is pulsed at the rate of 25,000 times per second. When a ferrous metal pan is placed on the unit the mag-

netic field acts directly on the pan.

Programmable, infinite touch controls will assure exact heat. Manufacturers predict 20% reduction in cooking time and 25% energy savings.

Units expected to become available this year (1980).

ENVIRONMENT CONTROLLED REFRIGERATION SYSTEMS

Refrigeration compressors and condensers installed without consideration of surrounding temperature will perform poorly in cold weather and work extremely hard during summer months. This shortens compressor life, increases power costs and can necessitate oversizing of units.

Opening dates can be delayed and labor cost increased due to delivery delays or loss of parts, i.e. controls, defrost time clocks, site glasses, driers, etc. which are not factory installed on equipment when shipped.

Undercounter compressors in cafeterias, lunch counters take up valuable space, usually cannot breathe and interrupt service when they need repair.

All of the above problems can be solved by the use of remote environmentally controlled compressor housing. These units, available to house one or all of your compressors from ¼ HP to 40 HP. Size ranges from approximately 1'-9" to 20'-4".

They are custom designed to operate in any climate. Roof or outdoor pad mounting optional.

The units provide environmentally controlled ambient temperature for the compressors. Side or top discharge of air optional. All accessories are factory installed. Pre-wired control panel supplied with main disconnect switch for one-point electrical connection. Pre-piped refrigeration lines and accessories brought to one area of unit.

These and other similar units should be investigated, particularly when planning a new establishment.

Use F.E.F. Personal Assistance Service for further information.

HEAT RECOVERY FROM ICE MACHINES

This system utilizes heat generated by ice machine compressors to supplement primary hot water supply. It may be used with either air or water cooled ice machine compressors.

The unit is comprised of an 80 gallon insulated water tank and regulating devices. Hot gas from the ice maker is routed past the ice maker's own condenser and is piped directly to the unit. Incoming water from the main is also routed directly to the unit before going to the water heater. Double walled heat exchange coils preheat the incoming water prior to entering the water heater.

In addition to supplementing the hot water supply the unit acts as as a remote water cooled condenser for the ice machine. The ice maker's standard condenser is pressure controlled to remain inactive as long as the heat exchanger is able to maintain a preset maximum head pressure in the ice maker.

Ideally suited to the high volume ice and hot water users. Charts on potential savings available.

ENERGY SAVING UNITS RELATED TO HOT WATER PRODUCTION

1. PRIMARY WATER HEATERS:
   A new style hot water tank has a built-in device that suspends sediment deposits and in turn reduces costs of water heated by eliminating chemical build up in the tank. Test results available.
2. HOT WATER RECOVERY FROM DISHWASHER:
   This unit fits under dishtables and recovers 75^0 to 90^0 hot water from dishwasher. Overflow is routed to a heat exchanger located before hot water tank. A single tank dishwasher could consume over 100,000 gallons of hot water a year = to 100 million BTU's. Certainly a good source for reducing hot water costs.
3. HOT WATER PRODUCTION FROM COMPRESSORS:
   Using your refrigeration compressors lines to surround a hot water tank you may raise water to over a 100^0 production. Determined by size and running time of your compressors.

POSSIBLE CAPABILITIES

Refrigeration Load	Gallons Per Hour
2 Ton (24,000 BTU Hr.)	30 - 140°F. Water
3 Ton (36,000 BTU Hr.)	60 - 140°F. Water
4 Ton (48,000 BTU Hr.)	90 - 140°F. Water

Available for air cooled and water cooled installations. Many options available. Details F.E.F. Personal Assistance Service.

PROGRAMMABLE TEMPERATURE CONTROL SYSTEMS

Typical functions of temperature control systems include:
1. Heat reduction at end of the day
2. Maintains minimum desired temperatures to avoid freezing and condensation
3. Activate heating system in the morning at the desired time and control temperature sequence
4. Activate timed ventilation if needed
5. Advance pre-heating interval during closed times to compensate for heat loss

6. Down heat cycle for days closed
7. Early shutdown for selected days
Payback savings are listed as 20% to 30%. Indoor and outdoor probes and sensors provide key to exacting control.

TEMPERATURE MONITORING SYSTEMS

These systems are available in 8 - 16 - 24 temperature channels. The probes can be placed up to 2000' away with no accuracy loss. This unit can monitor in water, air or refrigeration areas. From $-58°$ to $+300°F$. they may be interfaced to printers for exact cost analysis. Management, from one location can monitor, halls, hot water, walkins, etc. enabling the operator to react to any responses necessary at once. Scanning can be selective or automatic. Readings are shown by light emitting diodes. Energy control afforded by this system could provide substantial dollar savings.

WATER CONSUMPTION REDUCING SYSTEM
(Dishwasher overflow to disposer)

Waste water from dishwasher overflow is diverted to scrappers or disposers, reducing fresh water consumption by at least one third. Maximum savings are attained by intermittent disposal use.

Disposal conservation kit assuming 480 gallons of water per hour will reduce consumption to about 300 gallons. The breakdown using this kit would be as follows.

1. 1 gallon fresh water per minute to cone hopper - 60 gallons per hour.
2. 8 gallons per minute to disposal grind chamber - intermittent = 160 gallons per hour.
3. 1.3 gallons per minute from pre-rinse assembly - 78 gallons of water an hour.
Total: 298 gallons per hour.

DOOR CONDENSATE CONTROL FOR
WALK-IN REFRIGERATORS - FREEZERS

A new control designed to control heat at entrance doors and frames. A manual control allows settings for proper conditions and not one temperature as was previously done, and not often needed.

SETTINGS:
1. Winter and low room humidity
2. Freezer - low humidity - cooler normal or high humidity
3. Freezer - normal or high humidity $-10°$ to $-20°$
4. Freezer temperatures from $-20°$ to $-40°$

WATER CONDITIONING FILTERS

The results of lime and scale build up in coffee makers, ice machines, dishwashers, water heaters can lead to frequent service calls and very inefficient operation of the equipment.

The following chart shows the percent of total efficiency drop as scale builds up in a water heater.

Thickness of Scale in Inches	Loss of Efficiency	Gas Wasted Per 1000 Cu. Ft.
1/64 or .01562	4½	40 cu. ft.
1/32 or .03124	7½	70 cu. ft.
1/16 or .06248	11½	110 cu. ft.
1/8 or .125	27½	270 cu. ft.
3/16 or .1875	27½	380 cu. ft.
1/4 or .25	28½	480 cu. ft.
3/8 or .375	48½	480 cu. ft.
1/2 or .5	60½	600 cu. ft.
5/8 or .625	74½	740 cu. ft.
3/4 or .75	90½	900 cu. ft.

To extend the life of your equipment and to cut energy cost, in-line filters which hold impurities in suspension are available. Some typical sizes are shown below.

Diam.	Length	Inlet-Outlet	Capacity
1¼"	5¼"	¼" Compression	3 GPH
1¼"	6"	¼" Compression	6 GPH
1¼"	10½"	¼" Compression	15 GPH
1¼"	12¼"	3/8" Compression	60 GPH
1½"	13¼"	½" N.P.T.	3 GPM
1¾"	13½"	¾" N.P.T.	6 GPM
2¼"	14½"	1" N.P.T.	12 GPM

Your supplier will size the proper unit for your needs.

WATER HARDNESS FACTS

Grains per gallon	Part per million	Description
Less than 1.0	Less than 17.1	Soft
1 to 3.5	17.1 to 60	Slightly hard
3.5 to 7.0	60 to 120	Moderately hard
7.0 to 10.5	120 to 180	Hard
10.5 and over	180 and over	Very hard

ABOVE GROUND PROPANE GAS CYLINDER SIZES

Capacity	Height Overall	Diameter
100 lbs. or 24 gal.	48¾"	14½"
150 lbs. or 35 gal.	48¼"	18½"
300 lbs. or 70 gal.	62½"	24"
420 lbs. or 100 gal.	55½"	29"

381

The larger tanks, that always look like little submarines out in back of the buildings, are usually of 500 or 1000 gallon water capacity. The 500 gal. tank is 4'-0'' in dia. x 10'-0'' in length. The 1000 gal. tank is 4'-0'' in dia. x 18'-0'' in length. Larger tanks are available.

Propane gas is highly inflammable and the installation of tanks is governed by the National Fire Protection Association.

The smaller tanks, less than 125 gal. capacity have strict regulations as to location distances from door or window openings, corners of the building, etc. The larger tanks, above ground or buried must be installed in accordance with regulations governing distances from buildings and property lines, depths if buried, pitch of ground, etc.

Consult your insurance carrier.

STANDBY POWER SUPPLY

An emergency power source for low wattage cash registers, security systems and electronic scales. Unit is 12'' w. x 10'' D. x 13'' H. A completely self contained back up power source, upon loss of commercial power, this unit provides stand by power at once. Approximate output drop is from 500 watts to 100 watts in six hours. Maintenance free battery is kept charged under normal circumstances by 120 volt source.

POTENTIAL SAVINGS USING AIR CLEANERS

ASHRAE, American Society of Heating, Refrigeration and Air Conditioning Engineers, have established codes for ventilation in public buildings. The following chart shows air changes per hour required for various establishments.

| | AIR CHANGES PER HOUR | |
Type of Operation	Mild Smoke Level	Severe Smoke Level
Office	3	8
Store	3	8
Meeting Hall	5	10
Restaurant	8	11
Cafeteria	13	15
Bar and Lounge	15	20

Another ASHRAE chart shows make-up air CFM requirements and allowances if properly sized air cleaners are used.

Occupancy (No. of Persons)	Make Up Air Required	Allowed Reduction with Air Cleaner
20	1,000	680
40	2,000	1,360
60	3,000	2,040
100	5,000	3,400
200	10,000	6,800

The following chart was calculated with figures based upon costs of $1.60 per 1000 cubic feet of gas and $.035 per KWHR for electricity. They assume a 200 hour per month operation with a 20° to 70°F. rise for heating and a 95° to 75°F. drop for cooling:

Air Exhausted (cfm)	Heating Cost/Month	Cooling Cost/Month
500	$11.54	$15.08
1000	23.07	30.15
1500	34.60	45.23
2000	46.13	60.31
2500	57.67	75.38

These are the extra costs you pay to heat or cool replacement air. And often replacement air available from outside is no cleaner than the air exhausted. An Air Cleanser used for the same number of hours would cost as little as $3.64 per month, and you can be sure the air is clean.

For example, imagine a night club that contains 160 people. ASHRAE recommended fresh air and ventilation requirements are 20 cfm per person or 3200 cfm total (160 people x 20 cfm). With the installation of a properly sized Air Cleanser system, the fresh air requirement can be reduced to 7.5 cfm per person or 1200 cfm total (160 people x 7.5 cfm). This is a reduction of 2000 cfm, and from the table, translates in to a $46.13 per month savings on heating and a $60.31 reduction in cooling costs.

Naturally, the amount of savings incurred by the use of the Air Cleanser is dependent upon the conditions and practices at a given establishment and those shown in the example are for a particular situation. However, the above example does indicate the general order of heating and cooling savings with the use of an Air Cleanser.

To try to provide specifications for all of the many good air cleaners on the market would be an exercise in futility. They are available in many sizes and styles with capacities 8,000 to 60,000 or more C.F.M.'s.

Air cleaners are available as wall mount, ceiling hung and free standing units. Others are designed to be built into ventilation duct work.

TYPICAL CEILING FAN FACTS

Energy may be saved by either circulating warm ceiling air downward in winter, or moving chilled air in the summer. Both are possible with properly sized and located fans.

TYPICAL CEILING MOUNT FAN SPECIFICATIONS

Fan Blade Sweep	56″
Number of Blades	3
Floor Area Affected	2025 sq. ft.
Watt Consumption at Full Speed	150
Volts	120V, 60Hz
RPM at Full/Bottom Speed	285/102
Amps	.084
CFM at Full Speed	16,800
Maximum Air Velocity	660 ft./min.
Maximum Efficiency Ceiling Height	40′
Recommended Distance, Ceiling to Bottom of Fan	4′
Minimum Distance, Ceiling to Bottom of Fan	12″
Maximum Distance, Ceiling to Bottom of Fan	15′
Maximum Distance from Floor to Fan	37′
Minimum Distance from Floor to Fan	9′
Number of Speeds	Variable
Shipping Weight	23 lbs.
Color	White
Air Movement	1 Million cu. ft./hour

DISHWASHER ENERGY CONTROL

This unique system essentially automates the dishmachine, booster water heater and exhaust fan; allowing them to operate only when a rack is actually in the machine. In addition, an integral demand control is included to lower peak electrical demand.

This system can save between $1000 and $2500 per year in energy costs, with a payback on investment of under six months in some cases.

Your actual payback on this system will be determined by the amount of reduced time your hot water booster and tank heat will be operating. A typical sequence of operation of this system follows.

DISHWASHER ENERGY CONTROL
SEQUENCE OF OPERATION

AUTOMATIC OPERATION

OPERATION	FUNCTION	lites
Before Rack Enters Machine	Dishtable Start Switch—OFF Pump & Motors—OFF Tank Heat—ON Detergent Dispenser—OFF Rinse Injector—OFF Final Rinse Solenoid—OFF Booster Water Heater—OFF Exhaust Fan—OFF	Dishwasher—OFF Tank Heat—ON Booster—OFF Fan—OFF

DISHWASHER ENERGY CONTROL
SEQUENCE OF OPERATION

AUTOMATIC OPERATION (Cont.)

Rack Enters Machine	Dishtable Start Switch—ON Pump & Conveyor Motors—ON Tank Heat—OFF Detergent Dispenser—ON Rinse Injector—OFF Final Rinse Solenoid—OFF Booster Water Heater—ON Exhaust Fan—ON	Dishwasher—ON Tank Heat—OFF Booster—ON Fan—ON
Rack Exits Machine	Dishtable Start Switch—OFF Pump & Motors—ON Tank Heat—OFF Detergent Dispenser—ON Rinse Injector—ON Final Rinse Solenoid—ON Booster Water Heater—ON Exhaust Fan—ON	Dishwasher—ON Tank Heat—OFF Booster—ON Fan—ON
After Rack Exits Machine	Distable Start Switch—OFF Pump & Motors—OFF Tank Heat—ON Detergent Dispenser—OFF Rinse Injector—OFF Final Rinse Solenoid—OFF Booster Water Heater—OFF Exhaust Fan—ON DELAY	Dishwasher—OFF Tank Heat—ON Booster—OFF Fan—ON
Rack Back-Up Into Machine	Dishtable Start Switch—OFF Pump & Conveyor Motors—OFF Tank Heat—ON Detergent Dispenser—OFF Rinse Injector—OFF Final Rinse Solenoid—OFF Booster Water Heater—OFF Exhaust Fan—ON Clean Dishtable Limit Switch—ON	Dishwasher—OFF Tank Heat—ON Booster—OFF Fan—ON

MANUAL OPERATION

Bypass Switch in "MANUAL" Position	Dishtable Start Switch—BYPASS Pump & Motors—BYPASS Tank Heat—ON Detergent Dispenser—ON Rinse Injector—ON Final Rinse Solenoid—BYPASS Booster Water Heater—ON Exhaust Fan—ON	Dishwasher—ON Tank Heat—ON Booster—ON Fan—ON

POWER DISTRIBUTION SYSTEMS

These systems have numerous features and advantages which should be investigated by anyone planning remodeling or building. They could be extremely advantageous for anyone planning to lease

385

an existing building particularly if the building has a poured concrete slab floor.

In its simplest form the power distribution system can deliver electricity, gas, steam, hot and cold water to any point in the building requiring them. The manufacturers claim considerable savings over conventional wiring and plumbing installations. A most important factor is that the entire system is an integral part of the equipment not a part of the building. In the event of relocation it can be taken out with the rest of the equipment. This factor qualifies it for tax credits discussed at the beginning of this chapter. If energy saving control systems (also available) are incorporated they will qualify for energy credits.

Before entering into descriptions of how the system works let us state that all or any part of the system may be employed to fill your specific needs. Many modules are available.

If it is to be used as a total power distribution system all supply lines to be incorporated, water, gas, electric and steam, would be brought to one location and be distributed to all necessary points of use encased in stainless steel raceways. Any lines not requiring metering or central control could be picked up at individual points of origin. Modular design of the raceways permits lengthening or shortening of the chain. Corner units permit running up over doorways around pilasters, anywhere. Electric outlets with point of use breakers may be mounted in the raceways and provide flexibility to add or change equipment of varying voltage and amperage.

The raceways or, power chain, systems have many options and advantages — all amperages up to 100 amps for voltages from 100V to 600 single or three phase. All control wiring is easily connected or disconnected permitting addition of fire - fuel shut-off, ground fault protection, etc. Plumbing and gas quick-disconnects may be employed. Steam assemblies include internal insulation. Overhead systems may accommodate any combination of utilities and lighting, signal and communication wiring and customized controls. They may be run along counter top and around corners in back-splash fashion and house telephone and communications wiring, digital clocks, timers, laboratory fixtures, plumbing and electrical fixtures. Other options or combinations thereof available.

Modular, point-of-distribution units to which the power chains or raceways may be connected are as follows:

POWER POLES — For mobile cafeteria and buffet units, point of sale display, telephone, etc.

Unit stretches from floor to ceiling - provides power anywhere ceiling box is installed.

TRAY SLIDE UNIT — Top provides tray slide for cafeteria counters. Recessed front panels may be stainless steel or formica to match counter. Power raceway under tray slide provides any and all utilities required for entire cafeteria counter.

UTILITY STATION — Houses digital LED timer for VCM or mixer, integral sink, water meter and kettle fill hose. Optional booster heater for 190° water.

DISHWASHER ENERGY UNIT — Incorporates pre-rinse hose, disposer controls, detergent dispenser and rinse injector along with all power and water requirements.

MAIN COOKING BATTERY UNIT — Power distribution raceway houses all power requirements, disconnects and any items required for the range battery. This raceway is supported by floor to ceiling pylons as required. Suitable for wall or island installation. End pylon may house all necessary controls, power, water and drain line for automatic wash-down exhaust hoods. Air make-up controls may be incorporated. Steam energy control unit is available. This unit eliminates condensate build-up and necessity to "blow-down" every morning. Savings on wasted steam may be substantial. 7 day, 24 hour timer included.

STEAM CONTROL CENTER — Contains all necessary valves and traps, steam purging system, large capacity kettle filler, electronic digital water meter with automatic shut-off when gallons set on dial is reached. Electronic steam control insures perfect cooking, cantilever supports kettle providing ease in cleaning.

VERTICAL CUTTER MIXER CONTROL — Provides point-of-service disconnect, ground fault protection, internal magnetic overload protection for motor, two minute adjustable LED timer for exact cutting/mixing and more.

The possibilities and combinations in which the components of this system may be used are endless.

DEMAND CHARGE

Now there's a nasty sounding heading and it means exactly what it says. Your friendly neighborhood utility company may be charging you $250.00 a month or more for electric ower you never used and they demand that you pay it. Here's how they manage that:

Demand Charge — A relatively large consumer of energy will probably have two charges on the electric bill — one charge for energy used and one charge for demand. The energy charge is based on the number of kilowatt-hours of electrical energy consumed during the billing period.

The demand charge is based on the costs to the utility of maintaining sufficient generating capacity to properly supply the large, short-term energy demand put on the utility lines by the customers. The two are not interrelated.

The demand charge, which is separately identified on the electric bill, is based on the maximum kilowatt demand imposed on the utility lines during a short interval, generally a fifteen minute period, during the billing period. The maximum demand is measured by a demand meter and the bill is based on the maximum demand, KW, times the demand charge, $/KW, for the billing period. For example, if a peak usage for a given billing period was 50 KW and if the demand charge is $5 per kilowatt, the demand charge for that period will be $250, even if this peak has been reached for one fifteen minute period during the month.

Demand charges may constitute a large percentage of the total electric utility bills. A serious energy management program needs to focus on demand as well as energy use because significant savings can be realized by lowering the peak demand.

The kilowatt-hour demand meter may be separate from or be a component of the kilowatt-hour meter. Due to the many variations in demand meters and methods of reading each, the utility company should be consulted for instructions in reading specific demand meters.

ENERGY MANAGEMENT SYSTEMS

As stated in the front of this book, all equipment from all manufacturers cannot possibly be listed. The manufacturer of the items for power distribution systems also supply the energy control systems described in this segment of the book. Similar systems are available from other sources.

The energy control system may be installed independently or be incorporated into the power distribution system.

In brief form, the energy management system establishes your lowest possible demand load and maintains it.

The system is best suited for operations with utility bills of $500 to $5000 a month, reportedly saves between 30 and 50 percent demand kilowatt; up to 10 to 20 percent kilowatt hour usage for cubic foot of gas. Payback on investment varies between 12 and 36 months for the system.

In operation the system controls all on-and-off equipment. In a restaurant this includes heating, ventilating, cooling and air make-up, as well as equipment loads. It controls energy usage by controlling hours of operation of all equipment in half-hour increments. Hours of operation are controlled by use of a matrix board and peg-type programming diodes. There are 20 to 100 control points, which can accommodate up to 200 circuits.

It controls peak demand by load management. Major load centers are automatically turned off and on, in rotation, to maintain a level load demand. Equipment sheds from five seconds to three minutes on a rotating basis. The key has been to be able to adjust the system to the equipment. Convection ovens and griddles can be shed without affecting production, but fryers can be shed for only a few seconds at a time.

The console is usually mounted in the manager's office and continually reads the demand. Once the demand is set, it is all automatic and does not need any adjustment. Once installed, management can vary demand levels, priorities and hours of operation to determine minimum energy usage and maximum personnel efficiency. The system is equipped with a manual override that can be used to change programming with no effect on the demand setting.

Use F.E.F. Personal Assistance Service for further information.

DISCONNECTS · TYPICAL GAS HOSE FACTS

(NPT — National Pipe Thread)

NPT	Natural Gas BTU Hr.	Standard Lengths
1/2"	95,000	36", 48", 60", 72"
3/4"	255,000	36", 48", 60", 72"
1"	435,000	36", 48", 60", 72"
1-1/4"	875,000	36", 48", 60", 72"

Available in carbon steel, brass, bronze and stainless steel.

Water and steam hose assemblies available in the following sizes: 1/4", 3/8", 1/2", 3/4", 1", 1-1/4". Lengths available from 3' in increments of 12" to desired length. Available stainless steel and heavy duty plastics.

STRIP CURTAINS FOR RECEIVING AND WALK-IN REFRIGERATOR DOORS

These double hung, overlapping, see thru, plastic strip doors, are designed for use at receiving and walk-in refrigerator doors.

The annual dollar loss associated with the operation of freezers and coolers can be substantially prevented through the use of plastic strip doors which will reduce cold loss by 60-80%. Based upon the above annual dollar loss figures, approximate savings per year through the use of the strip door will be as follows:

Temperature	Annual Dollar Savings (60% Loss Prevention)	Annual Dollar Savings (80% Loss Prevention)
33°F	$1,208.00	$1,584.00
0°F	$2,064.00	$2,752.00
-10°F	$2,658.00	$3,544.00

Depending upon circumstances, the cost of a plastic strip door ranges from $300-$500, installed. It is obvious from these figures that, in all cases, the payback time of initial investment costs could be less than six (6) months and could be considerably less.

While good housekeeping habits can reduce cold air loss from coolers and freezers, loss will inevitably occur. The installation of plastic strip doors cuts these losses significantly, not only for coolers and freezers, but for wherever cold air and hot air meet during periods of human activity. For example, another such application for these effective conservation tools is the store (or warehouse) loading dock during winter months. Here, of course, the subject is not to prevent the loss of cold air, but of heated air as well.

The critical factor in the performance of strip doors is the mounting of the plastic strips. Consequently, professional help with the application, if necessary, will insure maximum effectiveness and hence maximize savings.

It is obvious that there are merits to using plastic strip doors. Considering the quick payback, compared to maintenance and installation of the doors, it is easy to conclude that these doors are a simple and effective way to save energy dollars and thereby enhance profitability.

IMPORTANT ADVICE BEFORE ORDERING AND USING ELECTRICAL EQUIPMENT

Wires too small will result in improper heating, frequent blowing of fuses, and possible fire hazards.

If you use a 230V device connected to a 115V circuit it will produce only 25 per cent of its rated output.

If you use 230V equipment on 208V lines, you'll lose approximately 20 per cent efficiency, and slow down pre-heat time as well as recovery of temperature.

If you use 208V equipment on 230V lines, you'll boost the wattage by approximately 25 per cent. This overloaded condition will reduce the life of the heating elements. When in doubt, always consult your electric utility specialist and/or electrical contractor before installing new equipment.

Here's a final tip: Always secure a recommendation from your utility specialist for the method of metering to obtain best possible electric rates.

WIRING CAPACITY TABLE

MAXIMUM KW LOAD PER CIRCUIT*				AMPERES CAPACITY			
Single Phase or DC		Three Phase Balanced		Fuse	Switch	Circuit Breaker	Size Type RHW or THW Wire (Awg.)
120V	240V	208V	240V				
2.0	2.8	4.2	4.9	15	30	15	12**
When	3.8	5.7	6.6	20	30	20	12
Appliance	5.7	8.5	9.9	30	30	30	10
Rating	7.6	11.5	13.3	40	60	40	8
Is More	9.6	14.3	16.6	50	60	50	6
Than	11.5	17.2	19.9	60	60	60	6
2.0 KW	13.4	20.1	23.2	70	100	70	4
220-240	15.3	23.0	26.6	80	100	80	4
Volt	17.2	25.9	29.9	90	100	90	2
Equipment	19.2	28.7	33.2	100	100	100	2
Should	21.1	31.6	36.5	110	200	110	2
Be	24.0	35.9	41.5	125	200	125	1
Recommended	28.8	43.1	49.8	150	200	150	0

*KW load is based on 80% of circuit capacity. **For commercial work, wire size should not be smaller than No. 12 Awg. For runs longer than 50 feet, use next larger size wire.

AMPERE FORMULAS

$$\frac{W}{V} = A$$

Formula for determining Amperes for Single Phase Power Supply:
Watts divided by volts = Amperes:
Example: 200 W ÷ 120 Volts = 1.66 Amperes

Formula for determining Amperes for Three Phase Power Supply:

$$\frac{W}{1.73 \times V} = A$$ $$\frac{Watts}{1.73 \times Volts} = Amperes$$ Example: $\frac{8000}{1.73 \times 230} = 20.1$ Amperes

U.S. VOLTAGE / PHASE COMBINATIONS

1. 110-120 Volts - Single Phase :
A two-wire system consisting of one hot and one neutral wire. The voltage between hot and neutral is 125 volts maximum.

2. 220-240 Volts - Single Phase :
A two-wire system consisting of two hot wires. The voltage between the two hot wires is 250 Volts maximum.

3. 110-120/220-240 Volts - Single Phase :
(Edison System) A three-wire system consisting of two hot and one neutral wire. The voltage between either hot and neutral is 125 volts maximum and the voltage between the two hot wires is 250 volts maximum.

4. 110-120/208 Volts - Three Phase :
A four-wire system consisting of three hot and one neutral wire. Used for three phase power circuits and single phase light and power branch circuits. The voltage between any single hot wire and neutral is 125 Volts maximum. Voltage between any two hot wires is 208 volt single phase. Voltage between three hot wires is 208 volt three phase.

5. 220-240 Volts - Three Phase :
A three-wire Delta Connected system consisting of three hot wires. The voltage between any two hot wires is 250 Volts maximum.

6. 440-480 Volts - Three Phase :
A three-wire Delta Connected system consisting of three hot wires. The voltage between any two hot wires is 480 Volts maximum.

7. 110-120/220-240 Volts - Three Phase :
A four wire Delta Connected system with Center Tap consisting of three hot wires and one neutral wire. The voltage between either hot line adjacent to the center tap and neutral is 125 Volts maximum. The voltage between any two hot wires is 250 Volts maximum.

8. 440-480/277 Volts - Three Phase :
A four-wire system consisting of three hot wires and one neutral wire. Used for 480 Volt three phase power circuits and 277 Volt single phase lighting circuits. The voltage between any hot wire and neutral wire is 277 volts maximum. The voltage between any two hot wires is 480 Volts single phase and between three hot wires is 480 Volts three phase maximum.

GROUND CONNECTIONS TO ANY OF THE ABOVE SYSTEMS ARE REQUIRED BY CODES.

STANDARD PLUGS AND RECEPTACLES

An industry wide standard has been in effect for a number of years to standardize the configuration of electrical plugs and receptacles. These are shown below.

VOLTAGE	STD. CORD SIZES	WATTAGE	SINGLE PHASE NON-LOCKING RECEPTACLE	SINGLE PHASE NON-LOCKING PLUG	SINGLE PHASE LOCKING RECEPTACLE	SINGLE PHASE LOCKING PLUG
110-120 VOLTS 15 AMPS	18/3 16/3 14/3	USED WITH UNITS OF 1500W OR LESS	5-15R	5-15P	L5-15R	L5-15P
110-120 VOLTS 20 AMPS	12/3	USED WITH UNITS OF 1500-2000 WATTS	5-20R	5-20P	L5-20R	L5-20P
110-120 VOLTS 30 AMPS	10/3	USED WITH UNITS OF 2000-3000 WATTS	5-30R	5-30P	L5-30R	L5-30P
110-120 VOLTS 50 AMPS	6/3	USED WITH UNITS OF 3000-5000 WATTS	5-50R	5-50P		
208, 220-240 VOLTS 15 AMPS	18/3 16/3 14/3	USED WITH UNITS OF 3000W OR LESS	6-15R	6-15P	L6-15R	L6-15P
208, 220-240 VOLTS 20 AMPS	12/3	USED WITH UNITS OF 3000-4000 WATTS	6-20R	6-20P	L6-20R	L6-20P
208, 220-240 VOLTS 30 AMPS	10/3	USED WITH UNITS OF 4000-6000 WATTS	6-30R	6-30P	L6-30R	L6-30P
208, 220-240 VOLTS 50 AMPS	6/3	USED WITH UNITS OF 6000-10,000 WATTS	6-50R	6-50P		

Approximate diameter of power supply cords
Two wire conductors with ground wire. Diameters shown in inches.

CORD SIZES:
.330 diam. — 18/3
.430 diam. — 16/3
.560 diam. — 14/3
.630 diam. — 12/3
.690 diam. — 10/3
1.010 diam. — 6/3

ENERGY UNIT MEASURE BTU CONVERSION CHART

Convert energy usage to Btu's (British Thermal Unit) to eliminate differences in unit measurement for types of fuel.

Electricity: kilowatt hours (kwh) x 3413
Natural gas: cubic feet x 1000

Kerosene: gallons x 134,000
Butane: gallons x 103,300

Propane: gallons x 91,600
Steam: pounds x 1000
Coal: pounds x 13,000
Wood: pounds x 8,800

#2 oil: gallons x 138,200
#4 oil: gallons x 144,000
#5 oil: gallons x 150,000
#6 oil: gallons x 152,000

Convert to million Btu's by dividing figures by 1,000,000 OR to therms by dividing figures by 100,000.

ELECTRICAL POWER REQUIREMENT CHART

The following tables are included to aid you in determining the power requirement for your equipment. By locating the proper voltage and wattage on the chart, the current consumption of the equipment can be determined. The current consumption shown in the chart is in Amperes.

WATTS	500	1000	1500	2000	2500	3000	3500	4000	4500	5000
VOLTS	Values shown in chart are Amperes.									
110-120 Single Phase	4.2	8.3	12.5	16.7	20.8					
208 Single Phase	2.4	4.8	7.2	9.6	12.0	14.4	16.8	19.2	21.6	24.0
220-240 Single Phase	2.1	4.2	6.3	8.3	10.4	12.5	14.6	16.7	18.8	20.8
208 3-Phase	1.4	2.8	4.2	5.6	6.9	8.3	9.7	11.1	12.5	13.9
220-240 3-Phase	1.2	2.4	3.6	4.8	6.0	7.2	8.4	9.6	10.8	12.0
440-480 3-Phase	.6	1.2	1.8	2.4	3.0	3.6	4.2	4.8	5.4	6.0

WATTS	5500	6000	6500	7000	7500	8000	8500	9000	9500	10000
VOLTS	Values shown in chart are Amperes.									
110-120 Single Phase										
208 Single Phase	26.4	28.8	31.3	33.7	36.1	38.5	40.9	43.3	45.7	48.1
220-240 Single Phase	22.9	25.0	27.1	29.2	31.3	33.3	35.4	37.5	39.6	41.7
208 3-Phase	15.3	16.7	18.1	19.5	20.8	22.2	23.6	25.0	26.4	27.8
220-240 3-Phase	13.2	14.5	15.7	16.9	18.1	19.3	20.5	21.7	22.9	24.1
440-480 3-Phase	6.6	7.2	7.8	8.4	9.0	9.6	10.2	10.8	11.4	12.0

BOTTLE GAS - HOW IT IS SOLD

Sale Unit		BTU's
Cubic Foot	=	2,520
Decitherm	=	10,000
Pound	=	21,000
Gallon	=	91,584
Therm	=	100,000

UNIT COMPARISON

Electric		Natural Gas		Bottle Gas
.739 kw	=	2.4 cu. ft.	=	1 cu. ft.
2.931 kw	=	9.52 cu. ft.	=	1 Decitherm
6.331 kw	=	20.57 cu. ft.	=	1 Pound
26.842 kw	=	87.22 cu. ft.	=	1 Gallon
29.308 kw	=	95.23 cu. ft.	=	1 Therm

ENERGY CONVERSION TABLE

BTU
   Amount of heat necessary to raise one lb. of water $1^{0}F$ = 1 BTU.
GAS
   One cu. ft. natural = 1050 BTU
   One cu. ft. l.p. = 2500 BTU
   One cu. ft. natural gas will heat 58,333 cu. ft. air $1^{0}F$ @ 100% efficiency.

ELECTRICITY
One kw/hr. electricity = 3412 BTU
One kw/hr. will heat 189,555 cu. ft. of air 1°F @ 100% efficiency.

STEAM (at sea level)

At 0 lbs. = 212°F	At 10 lbs. = 240°F	
At 5 lbs. = 227°F	At 15 lbs. = 250°F	

Steam contains 970 BTU per lb. at 212°F = heat of condensation.
One boiler horsepower = approx. 10 kw or 34,000 BTU

TYPICAL BOILER HORSEPOWER AND STEAM FLOW FOR KITCHEN EQUIPMENT

Item	B.H.P.	Steam Flow
Steam Jacketed Kettle (per 10 gals.)	3/8	12
Steam Table (per sq. ft.)	1/20	1.8
High Pressure Steamer @ 15 psi (1 comp)	1/2	17
Low Pressure Steamer @ psi (2 comp)	2	50
Coffee Urn (per 10 gals.)	1/10	3.5

GAS BURNERS · RATINGS BY SIZE
(Round Style)

Diameter Burner Top	BTU/Hr.	Recommended for No. Gals.
3"	5,000	1 - 3 gals.
4"	7,000	3 - 4 gals.
2¾"	8,000	3 - 5 gals.
4"	12,000	5 - 8 gals.
5"	20,000	8 - 16 gals.
7"	30,000	8 - 40 gals.

TYPICAL THERMOSTAT KITS · ELECTRIC

Temperature Range	Capillary Length	Bulb Size
60-250°F	60"	3/8" x 4-1/2"
60-250°F	60"	1/4" x 9-1/2"
100-450°F	60"	3/16" x 13"
200-400°F	60"	3/8" x 5-3/4"
200-400°F	60"	5/16" x 7-1/2"
100-500°F	60"	3/16" x 13"
300-700°F	60"	3/16" x 12-1/4"

THERMOSTAT KNOBS

Temperature Range	Markings on Knob
1 - 10	100-550°
Hold 1, 2, 3	200-400°
60° - 250°	200-550°
100° - 450°	300-700°

AMPS CHART
(Sample Guide by Meals Served)

Meals Per Week	Approximate Amps Needed
Under 2,000	400 amps
2,000 plus	600 amps
10,000 plus	800 amps
20,000 plus	1200 amps

Quite naturally amps depend on equipment used, but the authors have found this is a fair average for users of both gas and electric in kitchen area.

PIPE CAPACITIES - CUBIC FT. GAS PER HOUR

CAPACITY OF PIPES

Capacity of pipes in Cubic Feet of Gas Per Hour

Length of Pipe in Feet	3/4"	1"	1 1/4"	1 1/2"	2"	3"	4"
10	212	425	725	1170	2360	6250	12800
20	150	300	510	810	1700	4500	9300
30	122	252	425	670	1400	3750	7500
40	105	218	370	580	1200	3200	6400
50	95	195	330	520	1080	2850	5800
75	77	160	270	420	865	2300	4800
100	66	134	232	365	740	2000	4200
150	55	110	190	300	620	1680	3500

For EACH elbow or tee bend add

1"	2 feet	2"	5 feet
1 1/4"	2.6 feet	3"	9 feet
1 1/2"	3.5 feet	4"	14 feet

METER CAPACITIES

Meter Capacities, Cu. Ft. Hr. (Continuous Service)

Meter	Cap. Cu. Ft. an Hr.
5A	100
5B	150
10A	275
20A	600
30A	700
60A	1200
150	2200

ANNUAL ENERGY COSTS AT VARIOUS EFFICIENCY LEVELS — ICE CUBE MACHINES

KWH REQUIRED PER 100 LBS. ICE	COST PER 100 LBS. BASED ON 5¢ PER KWH		COST PER 100 LBS. BASED ON 7¢ PER KWH	
	PER DAY	PER YEAR	PER DAY	PER YEAR
6	30.0¢	109.50	42.0¢	153.30
6.5	32.5¢	118.63	45.5¢	166.08
7	35.0¢	127.75	49.0¢	178.85
7.5	37.5¢	136.88	52.5¢	191.63
8	40.0¢	146.00	56.0¢	204.40
8.5	42.5¢	155.13	59.5¢	217.18
9	45.0¢	164.25	63.0¢	229.95
9.5	47.5¢	173.38	66.5¢	242.73
10	50.0¢	182.50	70.0¢	255.50
10.5	52.5¢	191.63	73.5¢	268.28
11	55.0¢	200.75	77.0¢	281.05
11.5	57.5¢	209.88	80.5¢	293.83
12	60.0¢	219.00	84.0¢	306.60
12.5	62.5¢	228.13	87.5¢	319.38
13	65.0¢	237.25	91.0¢	332.15

FLOODING OR WATER SENSING ALARMS

These self-contained, battery powered units, less than 6" in diameter x 1¼" high produce intermittent alarms which can be heard through average floors and walls. Sensors are adjustable to activate at from 1/64" to 1/8" water depth. Accessories for system installations include: low voltage power consoles for installations where batteries are undesirable; consoles with indicator lights, test switches and sound alarms for multiple sensor installations and power-failure units for automatic switching to battery power. All console units measure 8½" wide x 9½" deep x 2½" high. They stack neatly or wall-mount frames are available. All units are easily integrated into existing security systems.

Chapter Fifteen

MISCELLANEOUS
ITEMS
AND FACTS

It's been great taking you step by step and fact by fact through the commercial food operations. Now that the end is near, let us know if we goofed anywhere or how we can improve on future editions.

If you have a "Helpful Hint" you would like to share, it will be more than welcome. We tried to make the book interesting, helpful and worthwhile and we sincerely hope you enjoyed it.

Before you leave, read on, there may be some items in this chapter which are new to you. Chapter 15 is comprised of miscellaneous items that simply didn't fit into any specific category. This chapter and others will be expanded as newer items become available through the eighties.

Thank you

Carl and Jim

FRUIT PRESSES · WINE · CIDER

Tub Diam.	Height	Tub Holds Lbs. Crushed Fruit
9	11	60
10	15	145
12	18	250
16	22	500
18	24	800

Add for stand and press height.

CHARRED WOOD BARRELS AND KEGS

1/5 gal.	Novelty Item
1 gal.	4 bands
2 gal.	4 bands
3 gal.	4 bands
5 gal.	6 bands
10 gal.	6 bands
15 gal.	6 bands
20 gal.	6 bands
30 gal.	6 bands

YOU CAN PREVENT DEATH FROM CHOKING ON FOOD

It is estimated that, nationwide, approximately 4,000 persons die each year from choking on food. Death from choking, usually on food, ranks as the sixth most common cause of accidental death in the United States. Often occurring in a licensed food service establishment, the mishap is so frequently mistaken for a heart attack that it has become known as a "cafe coronary." Pathologist Roger K. Haugen is the Fort Lauderdale physician who first correctly identified the real cause of the "cafe coronary" as food obstruction rather than a heart attack. Dr. Haugen believes an informed bystander can determine the difference by asking the victim, "can you speak?" If the victim has swallowed food and cannot jkspeak, it is safe to assume he is choking. A simple lifesaving technique developed by Dr. Henry Heimlich, Director of Surgery, Cincinnati Jewish Hospital, could significantly reduce the number of deaths due to choking. The procedure is termed the "Heimlich Maneuver" and is described as follows:

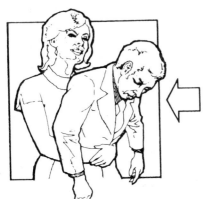

Standing behind the victim, place your arms around the victim's waist, slightly above the belt line and below the rib cage. Allow his head, arms and upper torso to hang forward.

Grasping one wrist with the other hand, press into the victim's abdomen rapidly and forcefully, repeating several times. This "reverse bearhug" pushes the diaphragm upward, compressing air in the lungs, and results in the object being expelled from the breathing passage.

If the victim is lying on the floor, face and kneel astride him. Place one of your hands on top of the other and with the heel of your bottom hand, press in on the victim's abdomen with strong upward thrusts.

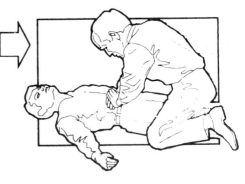

If you're alone and start to choke on food, wrap your arms tightly around your abdomen, bend over at the waist, and push in on your abdomen with the same upward movements described above.

RODENT MACHINES

115 Volt, emits timed ultrasonic vibrations at high frequency that rodents cannot tolerate.
1) Light duty - protects 2500 sq. ft. area.
2) Medium duty - protects 5000 sq. ft. area in 2 directions
3) Heavy duty - central power supply with four remote sound systems for areas to 20,000 square feet

VENDING MACHINES
(Sizes vary by manufacturer)

Some typical sizes and capacities:

Style	Wide	Deep	High	Capacity
Canned Soda	33"	25"	68"	250 - 12 oz. cans
Snacks	38"	28"	68"	350 Snacks
Cigarettes	36"	22"	68"	620 Packs
Coffee/Chocolate	32"	22"	68"	350 Cups
Sandwich	32"	28"	68"	5 Selections, 69 capacity plus storage for 75

NOTE: Power requirements for heat and refrigeration vary by manufacturer. Options also vary. We have more information. If you need it please use F.E.F. Personal Assistance Service.

REFRIGERATED GARBAGE STORAGE

In any establishment where food waste is excessive, consideration should be given to refrigerated garbage storage rooms. These also are usually most conveniently located adjacent to receiving areas. Whether pre-fab or built-in the walk-in cooler to be used for storage of garbage should quite naturally be so constructed that it may easily and regularly be cleaned.

Since it is not designed for the storage of food items a floor drain is permissible within the unit. A quarry tile floor with a coved base and pitched to a central floor drain would be ideal.

Where feasible the unit should be located outside of the building to one side of the receiving dock. Two doors might be considered. One for direct access from the preparation or kitchen area. The second door on the outside of the cooler for garbage removal.

TYPICAL REVIEW CARD · FAMILY STYLE RESTAURANT

Location _____

WE VALUE YOUR OPINION

We would appreciate a moment of your time in completing this card. Your satisfaction is important to us. Please fill in this card and drop in comment box at register. Thank you.

Date _____ Time _____ A.M. P.M. Waitress _____

	Excellent	Good	Below Average
1. QUALITY OF FOOD	[ ]	[ ]	[ ]
2. QUALITY OF SERVICE	[ ]	[ ]	[ ]
3. CLEANLINESS OF DINING AREA	[ ]	[ ]	[ ]
4. CLEANLINESS OF REST ROOMS	[ ]	[ ]	[ ]
5. CLEANLINESS OF EMPLOYEES	[ ]	[ ]	[ ]
6. COFFEE	[ ]	[ ]	[ ]

7. How did you hear about us? _____

8. COMMENTS: _____

_____

Name _____ Address _____

(OPTIONAL)

HOTEL DINING AREAS AND TURNOVER FACTORS

Type of Service	Sq. Feet Dining Area Per Seat	PATRONS PER SEAT		
		Per Hr.	2 Hrs.	3 Hrs.
Cafeteria	16-18	2-3	5-6	8-9
Counter	18-20	3-4	6-7	9-10
Banquet	9-10	—	—	—
Table Service				
Deluxe	15-18	1-1¼	2-2½	3-4
Popular	10-14	1-2	2-3	4-5

Based on average industry figures, turnover assumes maximum square feet per person and average service.

KITCHEN PLANNING CONSIDERATIONS

1) Work Areas - compact
2) Step saving
3) Proper working heights
4) Adequate storage areas
5) Garbage disposal/storage areas
6) Hot water adequate
7) Ventilation conforms to codes
8) Sanitary ease of cleaning materials
9) Labor saving preparation equipment
10) Energy saving cooking equipment
11) Lighting adequate

400

PLANNING CHECKLIST — LEST WE FORGET!

- ☐ Voltage
- ☐ Phase
- ☐ Amps
- ☐ L.P. Gas
- ☐ Natural Gas
- ☐ Low Beams
- ☐ Columns
- ☐ Pipes
- ☐ Radiators
- ☐ Floor drains
- ☐ Meter location
- ☐ Panel boxes
- ☐ Lockers
- ☐ Phones
- ☐ Vending machines
- ☐ Hand sinks
- ☐ Cash location
- ☐ Computer Fryer
- ☐ Hot water supply
- ☐ Gallons per minute
- ☐ Building access
- ☐ Max. width entry
- ☐ Height
- ☐ Length
- ☐ Hood
- ☐ Fire system
- ☐ Make up air
- ☐ Air cleaners
- ☐ Air conditioners
- ☐ Hand-Hair dryers
- ☐ Music system
- ☐ Coat rooms
- ☐ Rest rooms
- ☐ Energy management
- ☐ Power systems
- ☐ Security system
- ☐ Health insurance and fire regulations that may apply.

SAFETY FIRST CHECKLIST FOR ANY FOOD OPERATION

RECEIVING AREA

Are floors in safe condition? (Are they free from broken tile and defective floor boards? Are they covered with non-skid material?)

Is there a proper rack for holding garbage containers? Are garbage containers on dollies or other wheel units to eliminate lifting by employees?

Are adequate tools available for opening crates, barrels, cartons, etc. (hammer, wire cutter, cardboard carton openers and pliers?

WALK-IN COOLERS AND FREEZERS

Are floors in these units in good condition and covered with slip-proof material? Are they mopped at least once a week? If floor boards are used, are they in safe condition (free from broken slats and worn areas which could cause tripping)? Are portable storage racks and stationary racks in safe condition (free from broken or bent shelves and set on solid legs? Are blower fans properly guarded?

Is there a bypass device on the door to permit exit if an employee is locked in?

Is adequate aisle space provided?

Are employees properly instructed on placement of hands for movement of portable racks to avoid hand injuries?

Are shelves adequately spaced to prevent pinched hands?
Is the refrigerant in the refrigerator non-toxic?

FOOD PREPARATION AREA
Are electrical switches located so that they can be reached readily in the event of an emergency?
Are the switches located so that employees do not have to lean on or against metal equipment when reaching for them?
Do cutters and choppers have effective guards?
Is adequate storage space for blades and attachments provided?
Are slicers located away from areas in which there is considerable traffic? (Are they securely mounted, guarded and electrically grounded?)

DESSERT INFLUENCE CHART BY RANK
(What sells desserts best)

1) Dessert cart
2) Display case
3) Menu photos
4) Menu description
5) Dessert menu
6) Days special
7) Employee suggestions
8) Table cards
9) Menu clip ons
10) Restaurant advertising
11) Wall poster displays
12) Chalk board advertising

COMMON FOOD OPERATION SIGNS
(Usually available from your supplier)

- Cafeteria
- Cashier
- Checkroom
- Dining room
- Entrance
- Exit
- For members only
- Ladies
- Gentlemen
- House phone
- Kitchen
- No smoking
- Pay bills here
- Private
- Pull
- Push
- Receiving
- Ring bell
- Telephone
- Use side door
- Walk in
- Washroom
- Delivery
- Deliver all goods in rear
- Lobby
- Office
- Please be seated
- Public phone

402

FASTEST GROWING EQUIPMENT ITEMS
(Our guess for the mid 1980's)

1. Quartz cheese melters
2. Microwave ovens
3. Convection ovens - cook and hold
4. Broilers
5. Computer fry systems
6. Energy management systems
7. Climate control systems
8. Convection steamers
9. Food processors
10. Automatic bar systems
11. Energy saver disposals and hot water systems
12. Conveyor toasters
13. Soup - salad bars
14. Ice makers
15. Slicing machines
16. Low temp. dishwashers
17. Automatic coffee systems

FOOT CANDLES LIGHT MEASUREMENT

DEFINED: The intensity of light at a distance of 1 foot from a candle.

FOOD SERVICE OPERATIONS STANDARD FOOT CANDLES

Area	Recommended Foot Candles
Cashier	50
Fast Food Restaurant	75-100
Food Displays	50 plus
Cleaning	25
Storeroom	25
Dishwashing	75
Preparation	75
Cooking	75
Family Restaurant	30-35
Intimate Restaurant	15-20

EGG PRICES PER POUND

	PER DOZEN		
Price Per Lb. 16 oz.	Medium 21 oz.	Large 24 oz.	X-Large 27 oz.
40¢	.52½	.60	.73
50¢	.65½	.75	.84
60¢	.79	.90	1.01
70¢	.92	1.05	1.18
80¢	1.05	1.20	1.35

EXAMPLE: Large eggs at 90¢ a dozen = 60¢ per pound. Medium eggs at 92¢ per dozen = 70¢ per pound.

COOKING FISH BY THE INCH
(Temperature of Oven 450°)

Size Thickness	Condition	Time
1/4"	Frozen	5 min.
1/4"	Thawed	2½ min.
1/2"	Frozen	10 min.
1/2"	Thawed	5 min.
1"	Frozen	20 min.
1"	Thawed	10 min.

TELEPHONE BOOTHS

Two booths closed allow 18 sq. ft. Two booths open allow 8 sq. ft.

DO YOU NEED ANY OF THESE BOOKS?

- Menu planners
- Finance
- Security
- Interiors
- Promotion
- Purchasing
- Food production
- Fast Food
- Menu design
- Accounting
- Management
- Bar control
- Buffet
- Catering
- Energy
- School lunch
- College feeding
- Hospital feeding

OR — information regarding any of the following items relating to the food service industry: tapes, films, short courses, lists of schools, resume preparing assistance of employment agencies.

Send us a letter stating your interests along with a stamped self addressed envelope. We will promptly send the information you need.

NATIONAL SANITATION FOUNDATION
PURPOSE AND ORGANIZATION

NSF — the National Sanitation Foundation — is a nonofficial and noncommercial agency. It is incorporated under the laws of Michigan as a not-for-profit organization devoted to research, education and the development of standards for health related products and services. It seeks to solve problems involving man and his environment. It wishes to promote man's health and enrich the quality of life through conserving and improving that environment. Its fundamental principle of operation is to serve as a neutral medium in which business and industry, official regulatory agencies, and the public come together to deal with problems involving products, equipment, procedures and services.

The NSF seal on a product is widely recognized as a sign that the equipment complies with public health requirements. NSF operates its own testing laboratory in Ann Arbor. This laboratory conducts research. It tests and evaluates equipment, products and services for compliance with NSF standards and criteria; and grants and controls the use of the NSF seal.

A brochure is available discussing the standards and listing program of NSF. It describes the way in which distinguished leaders from business, industry, public health and related professions give generously of their time and talent in helping achieve NSF objectives. The brochure, "In Quest of Environmental Quality," is available without charge on request.

LATE ARRIVAL

A new tool for the man that loves spaghetti and thought he had everything — Read on —

Invention stops spaghetti mess

Are you tired of getting tomato sauce stains on your clothes while trying to twist spaghetti around the fork?

Janos Zapomel, a hardware store owner in Basel, Switz., has the answer.

Janos has invented a spaghetti wrapper that prevents any sauce from spattering onto the tablecloth or clothing. The winder is a circular device that attaches to the end of the dish. The eater pushes a forkload of spaghetti into the device and winds a special collar.

When the fork is removed, it contains a neatly wrapped, non-dripping supply of spaghetti.

WE NEEDED — WE PURCHASED

We Needed	We Purchased
15 lbs. beef browned 7 min. for taco production	20 qt. self contained table top kettle electric
Gravy 15-20 minutes	40 quart table top kettle electric
20 quarts German chocolate icing ½ hour	40 quart table top kettle electric
80 gallons clam-shrimp chowder per week	20 quart table top kettle electric

(Continued)

35 to 50 gallons of soup re-heated daily OR 20 quarts every 20 minutes from refrigerated	2 - 20 quart table top kettles electric
10 lbs. spaghetti al dente in 8 min., 60 pieces frozen ravioli in 22 min., 10 lbs. shells in 11 min.	40 qt. table top kettle, electric
400 4 oz. portions chocolate pudding from scratch - 15 min.	40 gal. self contained kettle gas
Boil 144 bagels same time	40 gal. self contained kettle gas
6 to 12 gal. cream pie filling in 30 min.	40 gal. self contained kettle gas
30-35 lbs. of boiled beef and and gravy - 2 hrs.	20 gal. self contained kettle gas
40 gal. stew - 2½ hrs., or 40 gal. chop suey - 2½ hrs. or 20 lbs. pasta - 20 min. 40 gal. water to boil - 10-15 min.	40 gal. self contained kettle electric
40 servings 4 oz ea. rice pudding 25 min.	Tilting 10 qt. kettles electric

SAFES, BURIED AND FREE STANDING

Style	Wide	Deep	High	Floor Load Per Sq. Ft.	Cubic Inch Capacity
Floor	15"	15"	17"	122 lbs.	3825
Floor	18½"	15"	20"	124 lbs.	5500
Floor	18½"	15"	31"	159 lbs.	8500

BURIED: 8-5/8" diameter, 16¼" deep, 653 cubic inch capacity, 9" square anchor steel plate on bottom. Also available as double chamber.

VAULT STYLE DEPOSITORY: Size 6 x 6 x 11½" high. Features anchor expansion bolts for cement installation. Available solid top or slotted to receive cash and checks. Baffled top to prevent fishing items back thru slot, excellent for night shifts.

SECURITY

Features of a complete food operation system, with central security control. The control stations monitor building via telephone lines.

AREAS OF CONTROL

1) Safe protection
2) Window and door protection
3) High risk areas that are restricted from employee or customer entry
4) Hostage protection - activated switches from inside walk in coolers or freezers, or dry storage areas
5) Fire protection detection from detector and sprinkler systems
6) Closed circuit television monitor capability
7) Hold up protection at point of service, activated by button, foot rail or pedal by operator. Silent Isignal alerts central security. In moments help is on the way.

BURGLAR ALARM

This computerized alarm system electronically separates normal everyday sounds such as voices, and telephones from breaking glass, door forcing, prying metal and related noises. When a break in sound is detected, the unit will turn on lights, radios, sirens in and outside or whatever else is interfaced to the activator. These units also feature battery back up in case of power outages and a 30 second time entry and exit delay to enable the operator to activate or deactivate the system.

CLOSED CIRCUIT TV FOR SECURITY

BASIC SMALL SYSTEM:
Size: TV monitor 13" wide, 9" deep, 8" high, picture 9" diagonal. Camera 2½" wide, 5½" deep, 5" high. Interphone speaker 3" wide, 1½" deep, 4½" high. Cable lengths from 25' to 200'.

Lens available - fixed focus, wide angle or telephoto. 1, 2 or 3 cameras available with basic system. Basic system consists of a camera, camera table, camera stand, interphone and TV. The camera has automatic light compensation. Camera power is lthru the TV and requires no special connections. Phone is connected thru the camera and amplified thru the TV monitor. Excellent security system for many cash control areas, delivery areas and hard to monitor sections of restaurants, game rooms and convenient food stores.

WORD JUMBLE

GLIRL _____	ERFEZRE _____
RRFEY _____	OHDO _____
GNREA _____	OERCIAVWM _____
NVOE _____	FECOFE _____
ROEBRIL _____	NDBELRO _____
ESROTAT _____	TKLSIEL _____
RIEXM _____	ANF _____
KSIN _____	OKOC _____
SRMETAE _____	RKSEMIM _____
RWMREA _____	FETUFB _____
GRNEYE _____	VLIESR _____
SAGLS _____	RVEISGN _____
HCIAR _____	RAOTSEG _____
TFILRE _____	CNILGSI _____
ZTRQAU _____	ROBOTSE _____

DOFO NMEQTUPIE TCASF

ABBREVIATIONS COMMON TO THE FOOD SERVICE INDUSTRY

AGA..... American Gas Association
ASME ... American Society of Mechanical Engineers
BTU ..... British Thermal Unit
NEMA ... National Electrical Manufacturers Association
NFPA ... National Fire Protection Association
NSF..... National Sanitation Foundation
UL ...... Underwriters Laboratory
KW...... Kilowatt
AMP..... Ampere
FEF ..... Food Equipment Facts
FEF-PAS Personal Assistance Service

QUOTATIONS

HELPFUL HINTS

A few key points to cover or have covered in a quotation - food service equipment.

1) Job reference
2) F.O.B. _____
3) Weight
4) Estimated freight or prepaid
5) Delivery common carrier or delivered, erected, leveled and set in place - connected - demonstrated
6) Price each - Total price
7) Terms
8) Order is subject to acceptance within (how many) days
9) Final connections to be made by whom?
10) Approximate length of delivery time

FOOD SERVICE EQUIPMENT BIDS AND SPECIFICATIONS

We may do another book in the future on this most important subject. A few of the reminders listed below will be very basic, but worthy of mention. To go to the depths of this subject is actually a trip into the legal field, which points to its very complicated nature.

PARTS TO A BID

1) Instruction to Bidders
2) Bid Form
3) Bidders Certificate
4) Resolution for Corporate Bidders
5) Non Collusion Statement
6) Non Collusive Bidding Certification
7) Actual specifics of equipment to be bid

BID FORM

TYPICAL TEXT
We the undersigned, propose and agree to furnish to _____ one or all items upon which we have bid, for the prices indicated herein.

The proposal is subject to all the terms of the specifications as listed herein and we hereby agree to enter into a written contract to furnish such items or item as may be awarded to us and to furnish such security as these specifications require.

The undersigned bidder certifies to having read these specifications and offers to furnish the articles specified in exact accordance with the specifications and at the prices stated.

Signed: Name and Title, Name of Company and Address

SAMPLE EQUIPMENT RECORD CARD 3" x 5"

EQUIPMENT RECORD

Equipment Item.......................... Inventory No..........
Trade Name.................. Manufacturer...................
Model No. .... Serial No. .... Motor No. ....
Capacity.................... Attachments.....................
....
....
Operation: ☐ Electric ☐ Gas ☐ Steam ☐ Hand
Utility Consumption/Hr. of Operation..............................
Purchased from............... ☐ Used ☐ Used Cost $...........
Purchase date......Guarantee Period.......Free Service Period.......

(Front of Card)

EQUIPMENT RECORD

Date	Repairs and Parts	Cost
....
....
....
....
....
....
....
....
....
....
....

(Back of card)

CASH MANAGEMENT AND INVENTORY CONTROL

Features of a total system, sample capabilities showing remote accessories from a restaurant computer.

1) The restaurant computer can control up to 16 remote components. Some are listed below. Changes and updates are easily programmable.
2) The register, activated by user's badge, can handle to 350 entries, spells out menu item and can be interfaced to other

areas, can print customer receipt tape.

3) Guest check printer spells out menu items and computes taxes and totals from register described. May also be used for employee time cards.

4) Inventory management - The beginning inventory is entered in computer, as the product is used it is reflected as a deduction. Even fractions can be entered, as .10 of a pound of mushrooms. The data is costed, approximate waste can also be entered. The operator calls up reports as needed to reflect actual inventory and costs as needed.

5) Labor applications - Thru the register all time keeping functions can be performed, including production by employee. Round the clock capability for 3 shifts, closing 1 day out and opening the next work day.

6) Positive cash control - Tracks checks and servers each cashier, cash and sales reports. actual menu items sold, controlled by the hour, shift. Day to day reports available that assist in employee scheduling and food preparation.

7) Kitchen display - Shows cumulative totals for most ordered items, routes order to specific area as salad, dessert areas. Can be used separately or with printer described below. Totals of displayed items appear in LED numbers. May be interfaced to specific departments.

8) Kitchen printer - Prints from dining room entries to point of preparation. When more than one printer is used routing is done directly to proper station in kitchen.

Management systems of course, vary by type of food operation and by manufacturer. Typical reports that are available from some of the systems follow. The specific system for your operation must of course, come from a professional representative. And we only try to point out some of the functions available.

CASH MANAGEMENT AND INVENTORY CONTROL COMPUTERS
(As previously discussed)
TYPICAL REPORTING FUNCTIONS

Report No.

1	Revenue Report, daily and accumulated control totals
2	Item Usage, quantity sold of all menu items
3	Computed Usage, reports raw products used
4	24 Hour Report, reports revenue, labor and transaction count for each hour
5	Item Revenue Report, reports revenue received from each menu item
6	Price and Class Report, lists classification (product group) and selling price
7	Recipe Report, lists the quantity of raw products associated with menu items
8	Tax Table, reflects current tax bracket ranges stored in memory
9	Item Cost Report, reflects current cost of each menu item stored in memory
10	Variance Quantity Report, lists overages and shortages of inventory items
11	Opening Inventory Report, represents opening inventory status
12	Raw Product Waste Report, lists quantities of raw products subtracted from inventory
13	Closing Inventory Report, represents closing inventory status

14   Merchandise Usage Report, reflects use of inventory items, balances with sales and completed product waste

15   Variance Dollar Report, lists overages and shortages of inventory in dollars

16   Revenue Factor Report, reflects dollar value of each raw product stored in memory

17   Store and forward report provides up to 25 numeric entries for tele-communications. Management data may be stored such as deposits, miscellaneous paid outs, etc. Print-out may be accomplished even if tele-communications is not used.

19   Cost of Goods Sold, lists the cost of goods sold for each menu item

20   Discount A Report, list and quantity of menu items sold under this discount

21   Discount B Report, list and quantity of menu items sold under this discount

22   Discount C Report, list and quantity of menu items sold under this discount

23   Coupon Sales Report, reflects the number of times that coupon was used and the dollar value subtracted from sales

24   Class Total Summary - reports item revenue in each of the classes (product group)

25   Timekeeping in-out Report, lists each employee clock-in and clock-out entry during the day

26   Daily Timekeeping Hours Report, lists in employee order, total time recorded for that day

27   Period Timekeeping Hours Report, lists in employee order, total time recorded for the period

28   Item Dollar Percentage Report, reports dollar percent of each item sold against total

29   Station Totals Report, reports revenue, customer count and discounts for each station

30   Associated Percentage Report, reports percentage of each item sold against a given product class

31   Scanner Item Sequence Table, identifies each item on menu with corresponding keyboard location as stored in memory

32   Waitress Assignment Report, lists all active and inactive waitress assignments.

33   Total Waitress Summary Report, lists in active waitress order, the cash revenue, the quantity of selected item sold, the number and average check amounts.

34   Individual Waitress Summary Report, is the same as Report 33, except it is for a single selected waitress

35   Monthly Quantity Sold Report, is an accumulation of Report 2

36   Daily Inventory Report, reflects all activity associated with each raw product

37   Monthly Inventory Report, accumulates totals of Report 36

38   Shelf Status Report, represents the expected inventory of each raw product before inventory is entered

KEYBOARD FEATURES

- 88 item keys, 10 numeric keys, 14 control keys

- Removable lens keycaps for each description change

- 18 column receipt/report printer

- Full front and rear display

- Error indicators

- Cash drawer control; up to two per master and remote

- System interlocks for added control

SPECIFICATIONS

- Power: 117 volt AC ± 10%, 60 Hz
  Back up battery support

- Environment: 40°F to 104°F. 5% to 95% relative humidity

- Dimensions: 13" W x 22" L x 14½"

- Weight: 51 pounds

SCANNER REMOTE FEATURES

- Mark Sense Reader   Optically reads marks.
- Validator   Marks form after processing to prevent re-run.
- Digital Display   Provides four digit display, left and right for each of two cash drawers.
- Function Indicators   Unit busy alert and error alert lights.
- Cash Drawer Control   Each remote controls up to two cash drawers.
- Dimensions   Remote 22" Deep x 13" Wide x 9½" High, External display 7" Deep x 3" Wide x 5" High
- Weight   39 pounds
- Form Size   4¼" Wide, up to 14" Long

CASH MACHINE · POINT OF SALE ACCOUNTING

Combining cash register functions and time clock, the new style terminals feature the following operator benefits.

1. Automatic and accurate summation and calculation of all charges to cover one check.
2. Increased Sales Production.
    - Relieving waitress involvement in pricing and computation of tax.
3. Waitress sales reporting by sales volume, productivity by class of item, tips, adjustments and missing checks.
4. Revenue reporting by cash, credit card and discount.
5. Cash drawer control balancing with cash report.
6. Sales analysis by menu item for external inventory control and menu planning.
7. Banquet Accounting.
8. Reduction in cash shortages
    - Elimination of arithmetic and pricing errors.
    - Positive income and revenue reporting by revenue center.
9. Reduction in labor costs
    - Less employee pressures, easier training and optimum use of skills - reduces turnover.
    - Management reports reduce clerical activity necessary to generate meaningful management information.
10. Timekeeping reporting of accumulated hours by employee carried forward for the desired pay period.
11. Price changes easily made by management personnel in seconds.

COLLEGE FEEDING VALIDATION CONTROL

A new system using computerized cash control.

A computerized plastic card, bearing the student's photo and account number, is inserted by the checker into a card reader at the

413

dining room entrance. The data encoded in the magnetic strip on the back of the card is electronically scanned and sent back to the memory for validation. The memory unit then transmits whether the card is valid or invalid by means of an indicator light and audio signal at the card reader.

The new system speeds service and provides greater convenience. It has many advantages over the old coupon book system. The financial impact to students due to lost or stolen coupon books will almost be eliminated.

On the system, a student needs to pick up a card only once each semester. After every purchase students can see the amount of purchase and their remaining balance right on the computer/monitor. Meal cards are non-transferable. Meals cost money, no matter who eats them. A system which effectively prevents meals being eaten by unauthorized persons assures paying board plan members of getting all of the services for which they pay.

POSSIBLE FAST FOOD RESTAURANT MENU
WITH NO HOOD OR EXHAUST SYSTEM REQUIRED

Using toasters, microwaves, hot food well and sandwich unit.

HOT SOUPS - CHOWDER
1/4 Pound Hot Dog with
  1) Sauerkraut
  2) Chili Sauce
  3) Cheese
  4) Cheese and Bacon
  5) Burgers - pre-cooked - frozen

MELTS
Toasted cheese, cheese and tomato, cheese and bacon, cheese and ham, cheese and tuna

HOT SANDWICHES
Western egg, corned beef, pastrami, ham and cheese, roast beef, turkey and bacon club, tuna and cheese club, ham and cheese club, ham, bacon and cheese club.
All done with no cooking hood or ventilators.

GENERAL EQUIVALENTS

16 tablespoons	=	1 cup
1 cup (standard measure)	=	½ pint (8 fluid ounces)
2 cups	=	1 pint
16 ounces	=	1 pound
3 quarts (dry)	=	1 peck

4 pecks	=	1 bushel
32 ounces	=	1 fluid quart
128 ounces	= 8 pounds =	1 fluid gallon
1 No. 10 can	=	13 cups
1 pound margarine	=	2 cups
1 pound flour	=	4 cups

The number of the scoop determines the number of servings in each quart of a mixture, i.e., with a No. 16 scoop, one quart of mixture will yield 16 servings.

DECIMAL EQUIVALENTS OF FRACTIONS

DECIMAL		FRACTION
.25	=	1/4
.33	=	1/3
.5	=	1/2
.66	=	2/3
.75	=	3/4

The abbreviation beside the fraction tells what unit of measure to use.

Examples

0.25 cup	=	1/4 cup
0.25 lb.	=	1/4 lb. or 4 oz.
0.33 cup	=	1/3 cup
0.5 lb.	=	1/2 lb. or 8 oz.
0.5 gal.	=	1/2 gal. or 2 qt.
0.66 cup	=	2/3 cup
1.66 cup	=	1-2/3 cup
0.75 cup	=	3/4 cup
2.75 lb.	=	2 lb. 12 oz.

GUIDE FOR PORTION SIZES

The average stomach holds approximately 2 lb. - 2½ lb. of food comfortably (including both solid and liquid).

It is more economical to give seconds to the few and far between "hoarders" than to fill garbage pail with food left on plates from a majority of customers.

	2 lb.	2½ lb.
Appetizer	2 oz.	3 oz.
Salad	2 oz.	3 oz.
Soup	6 oz.	7 oz.
Vegetable	2 oz.	3 oz.
Potato	4 oz.	4 oz.
Meat	3 oz.	5 oz.
Bread - Butter	2 oz.	3 oz.
Dessert	4 oz.	5 oz.
Beverage	7 oz.	7 oz.
	32 oz.	40 oz.

If Soup or Appetizer omitted - other portion sizes need not be changed.

One Year Warranty Plan

STANDARD

·————, INCORPORATED, warrants this refrigerated equipment to be free from defects in materials and workmanship for normal use and service.

Our obligations under this warranty shall be limited to repairing or replacing any parts of said refrigerated equipment F.O.B. Factory which prove thus defective within Twelve (12) Months from the date of invoice thereof, and which ————, NCORPORATED, examination discloses to its satisfaction to be thus defective.

This warranty shall not apply to the refrigerated equipment or any part thereof which has been subject to any accident caused in transit, alterations by unauthorized service, negligence, abuse, misuse, or damages by flood, fire or acts of God.

This warranty shall not be deemed to place any liability on ————, INCORPORATED, for any transportation charges, any labor, or costs in the replacement of any part or parts, and this warranty shall be in lieu of any other warranties expressed or implied, and of all other obligations or liabilities on the part of ————, INCORPORATED, excepting only the specific obligation of the four (4) year replacement warranty set forth hereon, and this warranty shall not be assignable, and shall be operative only in favor of the original purchaser to whom this warranty has been delivered.

We shall not be liable under this warranty of four year replacement warranty for any default or delay in performance thereunder caused by any contingency beyond our control including war, governmental restrictions or restraints, strikes, fire, floods or short or reduced supply of raw material.

416

Additional Four Year Warranty

AT ADDITIONAL COST

In addition to the one year warranty on this refrigerated equipment, _____, INCORPORATED, agrees to replace for the original purchaser only, the hermetically sealed motor-compressor, up to and including suction and discharge valves only, said compressor body to be replaced by similar or interchangeable parts in design and capacity, at any time during the four (4) years following the first year warranty period, if it is shown to the satisfaction of _____, INCORPORATED, that the sealed-in system is not operative due to defects in factory workmanship or material as originally supplied and that normal use and reasonable care have been excercised.

This four (4) year replacement warranty does not apply to the cabinet, fan, fan motor, controls, or any part other than the hermetically sealed system. The warranty does not apply to accidents or damage in transit, alterations by unauthorized service, abuse, misuse, or damage by flood, fire, or by acts of God.

This replacement warranty, together with the first year warranty as set forth hereon, is in lieu of all other warranties expressed or implied, and releases _____, INCORPORATED, of all other obligations or liabilities, and this warranty shall not be assignable and shall be operative only in favor of the person or persons who originally purchased and paid for this warranty.

It neither assumes, nor authorizes any person to assume, any obligation other than that covered by this warranty, and applies only within the continental boundaries of the United States of America, its territories and possessions, and Canada.

Written permission is required for the return of any parts or equipment and any such return must be made on the basis of transportation charges prepaid.

EQUIVALENTS

	Equals	
1 teaspoon	=	60 drops
1 pinch (few grains)	=	1/16 teaspoon
3 teaspoons	=	1 tablespoon
16 tablespoons	=	1 cup
1 jigger	=	1-1½ ounce
2 cups	=	1 pint
2 pints	=	1 quart
4 quarts	=	1 gallon
8 quarts	=	1 peck
4 pecks	=	1 bushel
16 ounces (liquid)	=	1 pound or 1 pint (liq.)
8 ounces (liquid)	=	1 cup (liquid)
1 ounce	=	2 tablespoons (approx.)

SCOOP, LADLE AND CAN PORTION GUIDE

Scoop Measures:

Scoop No.	Level Measure	Ounces	Approx. Servings Per Quart
6	⅔ cup	5	—
8	½ cup	4	8
10	⅖ cup	3¼	10
12	⅓ cup	2¾	12
16	¼ cup	2	16
20	3⅕ T.	1½	18-20
24	2⅔ T.	1⅓	24
30	2⅕ T.	1	28-30
40	1⅗ T.	0.8	44-45

Ladle Measures:

Ladle Size	Measure	Ladle Size	Measure
1 oz.	2 T.	12 oz.	1½ c.
2 oz.	¼ c.	16 oz.	2 c. (pt.)
4 oz.	½ c.	24 oz.	3 c.
6 oz.	¾ c.	32 oz.	4 c. (qt.)
8 oz.	1 c.		

Common Can Portions:

Can Size	Cups	Ounces	Fluid Ounces
6 oz.	¾ c.	6 oz.	6 fl. oz.
8 oz.	1 c.	8 oz.	7¾ fl. oz.
No. 1 (picnic)	1¼ c.	10½ oz.	9½ fl. oz.
No. 300	1¾ c.	15½ oz.	13½ fl. oz.
No. 303	2 c.	1 lb.	15 fl. oz.
No. 2	2½ c.	1 lb. 4 oz.	1 pt. 2 fl. oz.
No. 2½	3½ c.	1 lb. 13 oz.	1 pt. 10 fl. oz.
No. 3 cyl.	5¾ c.	2 lb. 14 oz.	1 qt. 14 fl. oz.
No. 10	12 c.	6 lb. 9 oz.	3 qt.

Substituting Smaller Cans:

Can Size	Approx. Number of Smaller Cans Equivalent to a No. 10 Can
No. 303	7 cans
No. 2	5 cans
No. 2½	4 cans
No. 3 cyl.	2 cans

A CUSTOMER . . .
Is the most important person in any business

A CUSTOMER . . .
Is not dependent on us — we are dependent on him

A CUSTOMER . . .
Is not an interruption of our work — he is the purpose of it

A CUSTOMER . . .
Does us a favor when he calls — we are not doing him a favor by serving him

A CUSTOMER . . .
Is a part of our business — not an outsider

A CUSTOMER . . .
Is not a cold statistic — he is a flesh and blood human being with feelings and emotions like our own

A CUSTOMER . . .
Is not someone to argue or match wits with

A CUSTOMER . . .
Is the life-blood of this and every other business

A CUSTOMER . . .
Is a person who brings us his wants — it is our job to fill those wants

A CUSTOMER . . .
Is deserving of the most courteous and attentive treatment we can give him

A CUSTOMER . . .
Is the fellow that makes it possible to pay your salary whether you are a truck driver, plant employee, office employee, salesman or manager.

METRIC CONVERSIONS

CONVERTING U.S. TO METRIC

	Multiply:	by	To Find:
LENGTH	inches	25	millimeters
	inches	2.5	centimeters
	feet	30	centimeters
	yards	0.9	meters
	miles	1.6	kilometers
AREA	square inches	6.5	square centimeters
	square feet	0.09	square meters
	square yards	0.8	square meters
	square miles	2.6	square kilometers
	acres	0.4	square hectometers (hectares)
MASS	ounces	28	grams
	pounds	0.45	kilograms
	short tons	0.9	megagrams (metric tons)
VOLUME	ounces	30	milliliters (cubic centimeters)
	pints	0.47	liters
	quarts	0.95	liters
	gallons	3.8	liters
	cubic inches	16.4	cubic centimeters
	cubic inches	.016	liters

CONVERTING METRIC TO U.S.

Multiply:	by	To Find:
millimeters	0.04	inches
centimeters	0.4	inches
centimeters	.033	feet
meters	1.1	yards
kilometers	0.6	miles
square centimeters	0.16	square inches
square meters	11.1	square feet
square meters	1.2	square yards
square kilometers	0.4	square miles
square hectometers (hectares)	2.5	acres
grams	0.035	ounces
kilograms	2.2	pounds
megagrams (metric tons)	1.1	short tons
milliliters (cubic centimeters)	0.034	ounces
liters	2.1	pints
liters	1.06	quarts
liters	0.26	gallons
cubic centimeters	.06	cubic inches
liters	61	cubic inches

BOILING TEMPERATURE OF WATER AT VARIOUS ALTITUDES

Altitude	Boiling Point	
Sea Level	212.0°F.	100.0°C.
2,000 Ft.	208.4°F.	98.4°C.
5,000 Ft.	203.0°F.	95.0°C.
7,500 Ft.	198.4°F.	92.4°C.

CONVERSION FACTORS

DEGREES	
F.	C.

```
210   100
200    90
190
180    80
170
160    70
150
140    60
130
120    50
110
100    40
 90    30
 80
 70    20
 60
 50    10
 40
 30     0
 20
 10   -10
  0
 10   -20
      -10
```

Length

1 centimeter	0.394 inch
1 inch	2.540 centimeters
1 meter	3.2808 feet
1 foot	0.305 meter
1 meter	1.0936 yards
1 yard	0.9144 meter
1 kilometer	0.62137 mile
1 mile	1.60935 kilometers

Area

1 square centimeter	0.1550 square inch
1 square inch	6.452 square centimeters
1 square meter	10.764 square feet
1 square foot	0.09290 square meter
1 square meter	1.1960 square yards
1 square yard	0.8361 square meter
1 square kilometer	0.3861 square mile
1 square mile	2.590 square kilometers
1 acre (U.S.)	4840 square yards

Volume

1 cubic centimeter	0.0610 cubic inch
1 cubic inch	16.3872 cubic centimeters
1 cubic meter	35.314 cubic feet
1 cubic foot	0.02832 cubic meter
1 cubic meter	1.3079 cubic yards
1 cubic yard	0.7646 cubic meter

Capacity

1 milliliter	0.03382 ounce (U.S. liquid)
1 ounce (U.S. liquid)	29.573 milliliters
1 milliliter	0.2705 dram (U.S. Apothecaries)
1 dram (U.S. Apothecaries) ..	3.6967 milliliters
1 liter	1.05671 quarts (U.S. liquid)
1 quart (U.S. liquid)	0.94633 liter
1 liter	0.26418 gallon (U.S. liquid)
1 gallon (U.S. liquid)	3.78533 liters

WEIGHTS

1 Cubic
Foot = 1728 Cu. Inches
7½ Gallons
62½ Lbs. Water
34 Lbs. Flour
30 Lbs. Frozen Food
24 Lbs. Flaked Ice
55 Lbs. Block Ice
4/5 Bushel

1 Gallon = 231 Cu. Inches
128 Ounces
4 Quarts
8 Pints
16 Cups
8-1/3 Lbs. Water
31½ Gallons - 1 Barrel

1 Bushel = 2150 Cu. Inches
4 Pecks
32 Quarts

COMMON INTERNAL MEAT TEMPERATURES

Beef	Rare	Medium	140º
	Medium	155º	
	Well Done	170º	
Veal		170º	
Lamb	Medium	175º	
	Well Cone	182º	
Pork	Fresh	185º	
	Cured	160º-170º	

TYPICAL MEAL COMPUTATION - 400 PEOPLE

Item	Portions	Total
Vegetable soup	400 x 8 oz	= 25 gallons
Roast lamb	400 x ½ lb	= 200 lb
Baked potatoes	400 x 1	= 400 potatoes (160 lb)
Peas	400 x 8 oz	= 200 cups (1.6 bushels)
Salad	No cooking required	
Apple pie	400 x ⅛	= 50 pies
Ice Cream	No cooking required	
Hot rolls	400 x 2 rolls	= 800 rolls (33 lb)
Milk	400 x 8 oz	= 25 gal or 400 containers

SAMPLE PURCHASING GUIDE - MEAL FOR 100
(By Portion Sizes)

Food	Size of Serving	Order for 100
Bakery Products		
Bread, Pullman Loaf—30 oz.	1 - 2 slices	4 - 8 loaves
Crackers	2 crackers	2 lbs.
Rolls	1 ½ - 2	12 - 17 doz.
Beverages		
Cocoa	1 C.	1 lb.
Coffee	1 C.	2 - 2 ½ lbs.
Coffee, instant	1 C.	2 - 3 small jars
Fruit or tomato juice	½ C.	4 No. 10 cans
Milk	6 oz. glass	5 gal.
Punch	½ C.	3 gal.
Tea	1 C.	5 oz.
Cereals and Cereal Products		
Cereal to be cooked		
Macaroni	6 oz.	12 lbs.
Noodles	6 oz.	8 lbs.
Rice	6 oz.	10 lbs.
Spaghetti	6 oz.	12 lbs.
Dairy Products and Eggs		
Butter	1 - 1 ½ pats	2 - 3 lbs.
Cheese, cottage	⅓ C.	17 lbs.
Cheese, longhorn	1 ½ oz.	9 ½ lbs.
Eggs	1 - 2	8 ⅓ - 16 ⅔ doz.
Ice cream, brick	....	14 - 16 bricks
Ice cream, bulk	No. 12 dipper	4 gal.
Fruit		
Canned fruit		4 No. 10 cans
Fresh fruits		
Apples, for 8″ pie	7 cuts per pie	30 lbs.
Cherries, for 8″ pie	7 cuts per pie	16 - 20 qts.
Strawberries, for shortcake	½ C.	12 - 16 qts.
Frozen fruits		
Apples, cherries for 8″ pie	3 oz.	20 lbs. (8 pkgs.)
Meats		
Beef		
Hamburger patties	3 ½ oz.	28 lbs.
Rib roast	2 oz.	40 - 50 lbs.
Round steak, ½″ thick	3 oz.	30 lbs.
Fish		
Fish, fried	4 ½ oz.	32 - 36 lbs.
Oysters		3 - 4 gal.
Shrimp (cooked)	1 ¼ oz.	14 lbs. raw
Lamb		
Roast leg, 6 lb. each	2 ½ oz.	8 legs

SAMPLE PURCHASING GUIDE - MEAL FOR 100 (Cont.)

Food	Size of Serving	Order for 100
Pork		
Frankfurters 12/1	2 each	16 - 20 lbs.
Ham, to bake	3 oz.	40 lbs.
Pork chops	1 each	
	4/1 or 3/1	25 lbs. - 32 lbs.
Pork loin	3 oz.	32 - 40 lbs.
Sausages, link 16/1	2 each	12 ½ lbs.
Poultry		
Chicken, for dishes using cut-up cooked chicken		40 - 50 lbs. raw
Chicken, fried	¼ - ½ chicken	26 - 50 fryers at 2 ½ - 3 ½ lbs. each
Turkey		
Turkey, dressed	2 ½ oz.	80 lbs.
Salads		
Cabbage, raw for coleslaw	⅓ C.	16 lbs.
Fish or meat salad	½ C.	12 ½ qts.
Fruit salad	⅓ C.	8 ½ qts.
Potato salad	½ C.	12 ½ qts.
Lettuce, head, garnish		8 - 10 heads
Tomatoes, sliced	3 oz.	20 - 25 lbs.
Sauces and Dressing		
Gravy	2 Tbsp.	4 qts.
Salad dressing, thin	1 Tbsp.	2 qts.
Salad dressing, thick	1 ½ - 2 Tbsp.	2 ½ - 4 qts.
Vegetable sauce	2 - 3 Tbsp.	4 - 6 qts.
Sandwiches		
Sandwich fillings	¼ C.	6 qts.
Cold cuts	2 oz.	13 lbs.
Vegetables		
Canned vegetables		4 No. 10 cans
Dried beans	5 - 6 oz. (baked)	12 lbs.
Fresh vegetables		
Beans, green	3 oz.	20 - 24 lbs.
Beets	3 oz.	26 - 28 lbs.
Head lettuce	1/6 head	16 - 20 heads
Potatoes, Irish, baked	6 oz.	40 lbs.
Potatoes, to mash	½ C.	30 lbs.
Potatoes, sweet	4 ½ - 5 oz.	36 - 40 lbs.
Frozen vegetables	2 ¼ - 2 ½ oz.	26 - 34 (10 - 13 oz. pkgs.) or 8 (2 ½ lb. pkgs.)
Miscellaneous		
Carrot, strips, 3"	2 - 3 pieces	4 - 5 lbs.
Celery, strips, 2 ½ " pieces	1 piece	4 bunches
Jelly	2 Tbsp.	6 lbs.
Nuts for tea	1 Tbsp.	3 lbs.
Olives	3 - 4 olives	4 qts.
Pickles	2 small pickles	3 lbs.
Potato chips	¾ - 1 oz.	6 lbs.

MISCELLANEOUS PLASTIC OR PAPER DISPOSABLES

Product	Size	Description	Case Pack
Cold Drink Cups	5 oz.	Flat bottom	2½M
All Waxed Treated	6 oz.	Tall, flat bottom	2.4M
	7 oz.	Tall, flat bottom	2.4M
	8 oz.	Tall, flat bottom	2.4M
	9 oz.	Wide base, flat bottom	2.4M
	10 oz.	Wide base, flat bottom	2.4M
	12 oz.	Wide base, flat bottom	2.4M
	14 oz.	Wide base, flat bottom	2.4M
Jumbo Milk Shake	12 oz. to lid	Wide base, flat bottom	1.0M
& Soda Cups	14/16 oz.	Tall, flat bottom	1.0M
All Waxed Treated	16 oz. to lid	Squat, flat bottom	1.0M
	16 oz. to lid	Tall, flat bottom	1.0M
	20 oz. to lid	Tall, flat bottom	1.0M
	24 oz. to lid	Tall, flat bottom	1.0M
	Liter to brim	Tall, flat bottom double wrap	500
Hot Drink Cups,	6 oz.	Single wrap w/o handle	1M
All Mira-Glaze	8 oz.	Single wrap w/o handle	1M
Polylined	12 oz.	Single wrap w/o handle	1M
	6 oz.	Single wrap with handle	1M
	8 oz.	Single wrap with handle	1M
	6 oz.	w/white insul band	1M
Paper	4 oz. to lid	Squat, treated	2½M
Containers	5 oz. to lid	Semi squat, treated	1M
	8 oz. to lid	Squat, treated	1M
	8 oz. to lid	Soup, moisture and grease proof	1M
	8 oz. to lid	Squat, double wrap, untreated	1M
	8 oz. to lid	Squat, double wrap, treated	1M
	16 oz. to lid	Squat, double wrap, untreated	1M
	16 oz. to lid	Squat, double wrap, treated	500
	32 oz. to lid	Tall, double wrap, untreated	500
	32 oz. to lid	Tall, double wrap, treated	500
	8 oz. to brim	Squat, flush fill polylined	1M
	16 oz. to brim	Tall, flush fill, polylined	1M
	32 oz. to brim	Tall, flush fill, polylined	500
	8 oz. combo.	Squat, flush fill, polylined	250 ea.
	16 oz. combo.	Tall, flush fill, polylined	250 ea.
	32 oz. combo.	Tall, flush fill, polylined	250 ea.
Plastic	8 oz.	Super Squat	500
Heavy Duty Containers	12 oz.	Super Squat	500
	16 oz.	Squat	500
	32 oz.	Tall	500
	8 oz. combo.	Combo Pack	250 ea.
	16 oz. combo.	Combo Pack	250 ea.
	32 oz. combo.	Combo Pack	250 ea.
	Lid	White—fits all	500
	Lid	Clear—fits all	500
Plates	6″	Standard weight	1M
	9″	Standard weight	1M
	7″	Heavy weight	1M
	9″	Heavy weight	1M
Bowls	6″	Polycoated bowl	500
	7″	Polycoated bowl	500
Food	5 oz.	Treated flat bottom	2M
Dishes	5 oz.	Mira glaze, flat bottom	2M
	7 oz.	Mira glaze, flat bottom	2M
Carry Out Cartons	3″ x 9″ x 5″	Carton, polycoated	250
	2⅝″ x 11⅜″ x 6¼″	Family snack carton, polycoated	250
	2¾″ x 7″ x 4¼″	Snack carton, auto bottom, non-polycoated	250
	3½″ x 9″ x 5″	Dinner carton, auto bottom, non-polycoated	250
	3½″ x 8½″ x 5½″	5 lb. barn carton, non-polycoated	250
	6½″ x 9″ x 6″	10 lb. barn carton, non-polycoated	200
	4⅛″ x 3⅝″ x 1¼″	Finger food carton, non-polycoated	1.5M
	1″ x 5″ x 3½″	Pillow pak pie carton, non-polycoated	2M

TYPICAL HEALTH INSPECTION SHEET

DESCRIPTION

- No permit; permit not displayed
- Economic violation; food item misrepresented, no oleo license
  #### PUBLIC HEALTH HAZARDS
- Food present from unknown or unapproved source; adulterataed; contaminated; unfit for human consumption
- Potentially hazardous food held for an improper period of time at an unacceptable temperature
- Unwrapped or potentially hazardous food reserved to consumer
- Toxic items improperly labeled, stored or used
- Persons with diseases transmissible by food not restricted
- Potable water supply not in compliance
- Cross-connection endangering water system
- Sewage not disposed of in an approved and sanitary manner
  #### FOOD PROTECTION
- Food not protected from contamination during storage and transportation
- Food not protected from contamination during preparation; handling excessive; good sanitary techniques not used
- Food not protected from contamination during display and service
- Potentially hazardous food not properly thawed
- Potentially hazardous food not properly refrigerated or heated to the required temperature
- Food not properly labeled and/or identified
- Employees handwashing, hygienic practices, personal cleanliness poor; eating, drinking, smoking in restricted area; lack hair restraint
  #### FOOD EQUIPMENT
- Inadequate; inconvenient hot/cold storage facilities
- Thermometers not present, used, accurate
- Food dispensing utensils not properly handled/stored between usage
- Food contact surfaces not clean and sanitized
- Non-food contact surfaces of equipment and utensils not clean
- Clean equipment and utensils not properly handled or stored
- Single service items not provided where required, not protected in storage or properly dispensed; reused

DESCRIPTION

- Food contact surfaces not cleanable, properly ˉdesigned, constructed, maintained or located
- Non-food contact surfaces not cleanable, properly designed, constructed, located, maintained
- Dishwashing facilities not acceptable, constructed, located, maintained, or installed properly
- Dishwashing procedure not satisfactory, not following manufacturer's instructions
- Sanitization procedure not satisfactory, improper temperature or chemical concentration
- Wiping cloths misused; not sanitary; sponges, scouring pads misused
  #### CONSTRUCTION
- Rooms and equipment not properly vented; creating a nuisance
- Lighting inadequate; fixtures not shielded
- Floors not constructed/maintained, clean
- Walls and ceilings not constructed/maintained or clean
- Light fixtures, vent covers, wall mounted fans, etc. not maintained clean and in good repair
- Toilet facilities not provided, convenient, adequate, clean, good repair, no handwashing signs or toilet tissue
- Handwashing facilities not provided, convenient, adequate, clean, good repair, no hand cleanser, sanitary towels
- Proper plumbing not provided, installed or maintained
  #### OTHER OPERATIONS
- Garbage and refuse handling and storage inadequate; not maintained
- Cleaning facilities not adequate, cleaning operations contaminate food
- Premises not maintained free of litter, unnecessary articles; maintenance equipment not properly stored
- Traffic of unnecessary persons not restricted, living area not separate, dressing facilities inadequate
- Soiled and clean linens not handled properly; laundry operations not separate
- Insects/rodents present; no birds, turtles or other animals
- Insect-proofing/rodent stoppage needed

426

FREIGHT FACTS

Truck rates are set by law.

Truck companies have minimum rates. This may be based on a hundred pounds.

Remote areas may have to pay a service charge from nearest city. If a shipment is refused the first time and a driver returns a second time there may be an additional charge.

Many truck shipments are freight collect. If arrangements are made in advance many firms prepay the freight and add to the customer invoice. Others prepay charges based on a minimum order or minimum weight.

Make sure your freight carrier can find the delivery site. Many times a sign is not in place or your neighboring business does not know your corporate name. Again this can result in double charges.

C.O.D. deliveries are normally subject to a special service charge on top of the freight costs.

On lost or missing freight, contact the shipper and ask for the original company that picked up the merchandise, trace thru by invoice or pro number to your end carrier and alert his dispatcher.

On new construction sites be sure a responsible party is available to receive merchandise and that the proper insurance is in force for your protection.

CONVERSION CHART
(Horsepower to Kilowatts)

If Horsepower is	KW =
3	3.
5	5.
7.5	7.
10	9.5
15	12.5
20	15.5
25	18.0

To determine kilowatts formula:

KW = Kilowatt PF = Power Factor
E = Voltage Or use 0.9
HP = Horsepower

$$1 \text{ Phase} = \frac{E \times I \times PF}{1000} = KW$$

$$3 \text{ Phase} = 1.73 \times \frac{E \times I \times PF}{1000} = KW$$

DIRECTORY OF FOOD SERVICE ASSOCIATIONS AND ORGANIZATIONS

AMERICAN DIETETIC ASSOCIATION
430 N. Michigan Ave., Chicago, Il. 60611

AMERICAN GAS ASSOCIATION
1515 Wilson Blvd., Arlington, VA 22209

AMERICAN HOTEL & MOTEL ASSOC.
888 Seventh Ave., New York, NY 10019

AMERICAN RESTAURANT CHINA COUNCIL, INC.
328 N. Pitt St., Alexandria, VA 22314

AMERICAN SCHOOL FOOD SERVICE ASSOC.
4101 E. Iliff Ave., Denver, CO 80222

ASSOCIATION FOR FOOD SERVICE MANAGEMENT
4902 Tollview Dr, Rolling Meadows, IL 60008

BAKING INDUSTRY SANITATION STANDARDS COMMITTEE
521 5th Ave., New York, NY 10017

CLUB MANAGERS ASSOCIATION
7615 Winterberry Pl., Washington, DC 20034

COMMERCIAL FOOD EQUIPMENT SERVICE AGENCIES
6650 Northwest Hwy., Chicago, IL 60631

COMMERCIAL REFRIGERATOR MANUFACTURERS ASSOCIATION
1730 Pennsylvania Ave., NW, Washington, DC 20006

CULINARY INSTITUTE OF AMERICA
Albany Post Rd., Hyde Park, NY 12538

FOOD EQUIPMENT MANUFACTURERS ASSOCIATION
One IBM Plaza, Chicago, IL 60611

FOOD FACILITIES CONSULTANTS SOCIETY
135 Glenlawn Ave., Sea Cliff, NY 11579

FOOD SERVICE EXECUTIVES ASSOCIATION
508 IBM Bldg., Fort Wayne, IN 46802

FOODSERVICE EQUIPMENT DISTRIBUTORS ASSOCIATION
332 S. Michigan Ave., Chicago, IL 60604

GAS APPLIANCE MANUFACTURERS ASSOCIATION, INC.
1901 N. Ft. Myer Dr., Arlington, VA 22209

HOSPITAL INSTITUTIONAL AND EDUCATIONAL FOOD SERVICE SOCIETY
430 N. Michigan Ave., Chicago, IL 60611

INTERNATIONAL FOODSERVICE MANUFACTURERS ASSOCIATION
United of America Bldg.
1 E. Wacker Dr., Chicago, IL 60601

MARKETING AGENTS FOR FOOD SERVICE INDUSTRY
35 E. Wacker Dr., Chicago, IL 60601

NATIONAL ASSOCIATION OF FOOD EQUIPMENT MANUFACTURERS
111 E. Wacker Dr., Chicago, IL 60601

NATIONAL AUTOMATIC MERCHANDISING ASSOCIATION
7 S. Dearborn St., Chicago, IL 60603

NATIONAL FOOD BROKERS ASSOCIATION
The NFBA Bldg., 1916 M St., NW Washington, DC 20036

NATIONAL FROZEN FOOD ASSOCIATION
1 Chocolate Ave., Hershey, PA 17033

NATIONAL INSTITUTIONAL FOOD DISTRIBUTORS ASSOCIATION, INC.
1755 The Exchange, Suite 330, Atlanta, GA 30339

NATIONAL RESTAURANT ASSOCIATION
311 First St. NW, Washington, DC 20001

NATIONAL SANITATION FOUNDATION
3475 Plymouth Rd., Ann Arbor, MI 48106

PERMANENT WARE INSTITUTE
111 E. Wacker Dr., Chicago, IL 60601

RESTAURANT AND HOTEL RESEARCH LABORATORY
Purdue University, West Lafayette, IN 47907

SOCIETY FOR ADVANCEMENT OF FOOD SERVICE RESEARCH
665 Northwest Hwy., Chicago, IL 60631

428

FOOD SERVICE INDUSTRY PUBLICATIONS

CHEF INSTITUTIONAL
441 Lexington Ave., New York, NY 10017

CLUB MANAGEMENT
408 Olive St., St. Louis, MO 63102

COMMERCIAL KITCHEN AND
DINING ROOM
209 Dunn Ave., Stamford, CT 06905

COOKING FOR PROFIT
1202 So. Park St., Madison, WI 53715

FOOD EQUIPMENT FACTS
9 Glenmore Rd., Troy, NY 12180

FOOD & EQUIPMENT PRODUCT NEWS
347 Madison Ave., New York, NY 10017

FOOD EXECUTIVE
508 IBM Building, Fort Wayne, IN 46805

FOOD MANAGEMENT
757 Third Ave., New York, NY 10017

FOODSERVICE EQUIPMENT SPECIALIST
5 S. Wabash Ave., Chicago, IL 60603

FOOD SERVICE MARKETING
2132 Fordem Ave., Madison, WI 53701

HOSPITALITY PUBLICATIONS
614 Superior Ave. W, Cleveland, OH 44113

HOTEL & MOTEL MANAGEMENT
745 Chicago Ave., Evanston, IL 60202

INFO-EXPEDITERS
P.O. Box 93543, Atlanta GA 30318

INSTITUTIONAL DISTRIBUTION
633 Third Ave., New York, NY 10017

JOURNAL OF AMERICAN DIETETIC
ASSOCIATION
430 No. Michigan Ave., Chicago, IL 60611

LODGING AND FOOD SERVICE NEWS
131 Clarendon St., Boston, MA 02116

METROPOLITAN RESTAURANT NEWS
1225 Broadway, New York, NY 10001

NATION'S RESTAURANT NEWS
2 Park Ave., New York, NY 10016

RESTAURANT BUSINESS
633 Third Ave., New York, NY 10017

RESTAURANTS & INSTITUTIONS
5 So. Wabash Ave., Chicago, IL 60603

SCHOOL FOODSERVICE JOURNAL
4101 East Iliff Ave., Denver, CO 80222

SERVICE WORLD INTERNATIONAL
205 East 42nd St., New York, NY 10017

TRUCK STOP MANAGEMENT
1155 Waukegan Rd., Glenview, IL 60025

VENDING TIMES
211 East 43rd St., New York, NY 10017

INDEX

INDEX

INDEX